Joe Cambria

ALSO BY PAUL SCIMONELLI
AND FROM McFARLAND

*Roy Sievers: "The Sweetest Right Handed Swing"
in 1950s Baseball* (2018)

Joe Cambria

*International Super Scout
of the Washington Senators*

PAUL SCIMONELLI

McFarland & Company, Inc., Publishers
Jefferson, North Carolina

This book has undergone peer review.

LIBRARY OF CONGRESS CATALOGUING-IN-PUBLICATION DATA

Names: Scimonelli, Paul, 1949– author.
Title: Joe Cambria : international super scout of the Washington Senators / Paul Scimonelli.
Description: Jefferson, North Carolina : McFarland & Company, Inc., Publishers, 2023 |
Includes bibliographical references and index.
Identifiers: LCCN 2023004075 | ISBN 9781476681474 (paperback : acid free paper) ∞
ISBN 9781476648415 (ebook)
Subjects: LCSH: Cambria, Joe, 1890–1962. | Baseball scouts—United States—Biography. |
Washington Senators (Baseball team : 1901–1960)—History. | Baseball—United States—History—
20th century. | BISAC: SPORTS & RECREATION / Baseball / History
Classification: LCC GV865.C28 S35 2023 | DDC 796.35709092 [B]—dc23/eng/20230216
LC record available at https://lccn.loc.gov/2023004075

BRITISH LIBRARY CATALOGUING DATA ARE AVAILABLE

ISBN (print) 978-1-4766-8147-4
ISBN (ebook) 978-1-4766-4841-5

Front cover: Baseball scout Joe Cambria
(National Baseball Hall of Fame Library, Cooperstown, N.Y.)

Printed in the United States of America

*McFarland & Company, Inc., Publishers
Box 611, Jefferson, North Carolina 28640
www.mcfarlandpub.com*

Contents

Acknowledgments

I will be forever indebted to the following people. My most humble thanks go to:

Virginia Atwell, for her magnificent compilation of the entire Cambria Genealogy.

Richard Harris, for his help with early Rhode Island minor league baseball.

James P. Quigel, Jr., for his book and personal help with Williamsport baseball history.

Professor César Brioso, for his kindness with phone numbers for Cuban contact information.

Dr. Marysol Quevedo, for her help with the University of Miami's Cuban Heritage collection.

Ozmen Gonzáles, friend and neighbor, for his steady help with Spanish language interpretation and translation.

George Case III, valued friend and son of speedy former major leaguer George Case, Jr., for his help with World War II baseball, Senators history and many pictures.

Roberto González Echevarría, Yale University Sterling Professor of Hispanic and Comparative Literature, for his guidance on Joe Cambria's early life in Cuban baseball.

Rebecca Ross, Esq., for her help with Draft laws research.

Benno Rosenke, for his exemplary work with Cambria's Canadian baseball record.

Joanne Hulbert, for her help and background on Roberto Estalella.

Glenn Scimonelli, brother and video editor extraordinaire, for his help with all of the photos.

Dr. Bernard McKenna, University of Delaware English Professor, for his kindness in sharing research on Joe Cambria's involvement with the Baltimore Black Sox.

J. Kent Ashcraft, friend and guitar wizard, for his magnificent work in content editing my manuscript and putting up with my constant misuse of apostrophes.

John Schnitger, Esq., longtime friend and great pianist, for his legal research help on World War II draft laws.

Dr. Nicholas Sheets, for all his research and translations of many Spanish articles at the University of Miami Cuban Resource Center, undertaken, no less, in the middle of the pandemic.

Kathleen Klebba and the Howard County Library archives staff, for their help with inter-library loans, transfers and finding long-forgotten texts.

Amanda Hughes, chief archivist at the Enoch Pratt Free Library, for her assistance with early twentieth-century Baltimore business records.

Joseph T. Hetrick, owner of Pocol Press, for creating the index.

And as always, to my wife Virginia and my children and grandchildren, who are my constant source of inspiration. Without you, there is no me.

Preface

Not long after my first book was published a few years back, having completed my early promotional efforts, I did what the other baseball authors I know often do—cross fingers in the hope of modest success and begin to think about the next book project.

My first thought was to write about sluggers who never received their due recognition but were legitimate headaches for pitchers in both leagues. Guys like Hank Bauer, Hank Sauer, Joe Adcock, Ted Kluszewski, Rocco Colavito, Dick Allen, Vada Pinson, Boog Powell, and Norm Cash, to name a few.

I passed it by my editor, who said, basically, Nah. I then pitched him a proposal about the Washington Senators I grew up with, those lovable losers of the 1950s. Strike two.

So, he asked, how about a biography of Joe Cambria? I said, Who?

I was in fact vaguely familiar with Cambria. I knew from previous research that he had signed some of the great Cuban players of the 1950s Senators, guys I actually saw play in Griffith Stadium: Camilo Pascual, Pedro Ramos, Julio Becquer, José Valdivielso, and Zoilo Versalles, among others.

Dozens of newspapers, 24 books, endless internet searches, and a dozen interviews later, I was truly amazed by the impact Joe Cambria had on major- and minor-league baseball. Overlooked because he did not swing a hot bat, throw a heavy curve, or broadcast great games, Joe Cambria was without doubt one of the seminal figures in baseball and American history. His contributions to baseball in general, to the Washington Senators in particular, and to racial integration in the United States cannot be overlooked.

Cambria's life story is the essence of the can-do, pull-yourself-up-by-the-bootstraps, American Dream movies of the 1930s and 1940s. Forged in the fires of the great turn-of-the-century Italian migration, Cambria came up from the very modest, lower-class enclaves of South Boston to become a leading force in American minor-league baseball and beyond.

Although he had 10 years of management experience with his laundry business, he had no practical knowledge of the intricacies of baseball management when he started his journey in 1928. He learned as he went along, made dozens of mistakes, engaged in some very questionable decisions, and ran afoul of baseball czar Kenesaw Mountain Landis on more than one occasion, all the while forging the destinies of hundreds of young baseball players with whom he identified. His own baseball career stunted by a serious injury, Joe Cambria's impetus was to give the young, eager baseball "boy" the chance he felt he never got. This kinship he felt strongly. Certainly, he lived vicariously through their young eyes and delighted in their successes.

Through sheer determination, ambition, and unquestionably some dumb luck, Joe

1

Cambria was able to forge a farm system for Clark Griffith when others said it couldn't be done. Through scouting and scores of signings and trades, he was able to keep the cash-strapped Washington Senators competitive for decades. With a bravery that could rival a lion tamer, he mined the island of Cuba for gold nuggets, many of whom went on to have significant and, in some cases, Hall of Fame careers in major-league baseball.

Race, in particular that of dark-skinned players, had been a factor in baseball almost since the game's inception. Playing for Toledo in 1884, Moses Fleetwood Walker, the first African American man to play in an organized baseball game, was subjected to vile taunts and threats throughout his 42-game playing career. Clark Griffith himself tested the racial waters by signing two dark-skinned Cuban ballplayers, Armando Marsans and Rafael Almeida, for the Cincinnati Reds in 1911.

Although Griffith adhered weakly to the gentlemen's agreement to exclude Blacks from baseball held by all of the team owners during the first half of the century, Cambria was able to "pass off" many of his darker-skinned players as white because of their hustling play and happy demeanors. Cambria's early Cuban signees, like Roberto Estalella, Thomas De La Cruz, and Gilberto Torres, all of whom later admitted to having "negro blood," were accepted benignly by the Washington press as being "born of Spanish parents in Havana."

Cambria tried unsuccessfully to convince Griffith that the Negro League players, playing winter ball in Havana, would be of tremendous value to the Senators. Cambria was fond of saying that he could have had "Cool Papa" Bell, Josh Gibson, Satchel Paige, and Minnie Minoso all in their prime. Instead, Griffith believed firmly that the Negro Leagues should organize better and put a better product on the field for all to see. He even went so far as to suggest a three-way World Series between American, National, and Negro League teams. Griffith would finally relent and sign his first black player, Carlos Paula (a Cuban scouted and signed by Cambria) in 1954, a full seven years after Jackie Robinson's debut. It would not be until 1957 when Griffith would sign ex–Dodgers great Joe Black as his first African American player.

The life of a baseball scout is defined by the hundreds: hundreds of miles traveled, hundreds of ball games seen, hundreds of cheap hotels, hundreds of bad meals, and hundreds of kids that got away. If they are lucky, they land that one big fish that turns the baseball world around.

Mickey Mantle, signing with the Yankees in 1948, would make Tom Greenwade a legend, although he signed such other greats as Pee Wee Reese, Gil Hodges, Hank Bauer, and Elston Howard. Cy Slapnicka, scout and general manager for the Cleveland Indians, would earn legend status by signing a young Bob Feller out of high school, as well as Hall of Famer Lou Boudreau, Roger Maris, and Bobby Avila. Howie Haak (like "cake") would earn his gold star by signing Roberto Clemente, Tony Pena, and Gino Cimoli.

Joe Cambria would get lucky and land a couple of "big fish" who would go on to the Hall of Fame; however, the "minnows" he reeled in would go on to impact baseball significantly. Although most well-known for his Cuban signees, Cambria had some great success with American-born players as well.

Mickey Vernon, coaxed off the playing field at Villanova University by Cambria, became a two-time American League batting champion, beating out Ted Williams to do so, as well as becoming the first manager of the expansion Washington Senators in 1961.

Ed Yost, "stolen" by Cambria from the Red Sox, became legendary for getting on base, earning a berth in the top 100 All-Time on-base percentages with a .394 average.

Cambria alerted Chattanooga's Joe Engle to a young Southern boy, Pete Runnels. A 40-foot-high, right field concrete wall in cavernous Griffith Stadium would prove to be Runnels's nemesis during his tenure with Washington; however, after he was sold to Boston, friendly Fenway Park plus the tutoring of Ted Williams helped turn Runnels into a two-time American League batting champion.

Joe Cambria would "borrow" George Case, Jr., from Connie Mack. Case would become the first player in American League history to lead the league in stolen bases for six consecutive years.

Signed by Joe Cambria out of a Senators rookie camp, Alabama farm boy Early Wynn would struggle with the Senators before gaining his Hall of Fame stride with the Cleveland Indians and the Chicago White Sox, where he had his Cy Young Award–winning season in 1959.

The Cuban players Joe Cambria signed would, however, bring him everlasting fame in Washington.

A 39-year-old rookie named Conrado "Connie" Marrero would have a mediocre five-year career for the Senators but a legendary one in Cuba. Known as *El Curveador* (The Curveballer) and *El Premier* (Number One) in Cuba and as "The Cuban Perfecto" and "Connie the Conqueror" in Washington, Marrero became the best reliever for the cellar-dwelling Senators of the early 1950s and later become the third-oldest baseball player in any league at the time of his passing at age 103. Marrero is also enshrined in every Latin baseball Hall of Fame.

Signed as teenagers out of the Cuban amateur leagues, Camilo Pascual and Pedro Ramos would become aces for the Senators and the Minnesota Twins. Zoilo "Zorro" Versalles would become the first Latin American import—actually the first-ever non–USA-born athlete—to capture an MVP Award with the Twins in 1965. Pinar del Río native and Hall of Famer Tony Oliva would become the first Cuban to win Rookie of the Year honors in 1964 and the first Cuban to win back-to-back batting titles.

However, writing this book posed more of a challenge to me, and that challenge lay with Cambria himself. My first book was a biography of my boyhood hero, Roy Sievers, and writing about your boyhood hero is a pleasant task, a labor of love. Sievers had as good a career as he could have, playing for losing teams for over half his baseball life. His numbers would have been better had he not lost so much time in the batter's box due to injuries. But with all great figures in sports, be it Sievers, Babe Ruth, Mickey Mantle, Willie Mays, or countless other boyhood heroes, there is a certain transparency that occurs. Their sports exploits are chronicled in newspapers, magazines, and in some instances in film and television. Their lives are equally scrutinized, and their off-field antics become the stuff of legend. They play, they retire, they become immortalized, and they pass away, leaving us with our memories of their accomplishments.

Writing about Joe Cambria was much more difficult: it carries more academic weight. Other than a brief and unremarkable minor-league career, cut short by serious injury, Cambria had no great baseball accomplishments upon which to fall back. His marriage and relationship with his wife were one of mystery. They had no children, and little is known of his nephews and nieces. His daily life seemed to be completely wrapped up in baseball. He left a very small personal footprint.

Cambria also had more of a complex historical interrelationship. He was dealing with tan-skinned ballplayers during the most tumultuous racial times of the century. His actions were groundbreaking and their effects historic. He did as much to democratize baseball as did Branch Rickey, if not more. He rubbed elbows with presidents and dictators. His daily activities seemed to be concerned only with finding the next "can't miss" prospect. His relationship with Clark Griffith was almost childlike in its loyalty. His relationships with other people? Not so much.

It must also be taken into consideration that, since almost all of Cambria's post-baseball life was spent scouting for the Washington Senators, his biography would become inexorably intertwined in the history of the Senators. It would be impossible to talk about one without the other. So, the team—the players, the managers, and its owner—all become essential characters in this drama.

Shrewd and calculating at times, Cambria had more moxie than brains at others. His dealings in Cuba seemed to echo the ugly side of American colonialism in Latin America. He participated in some shady player deals and oftentimes left his players unprepared for the racial hardships they were to face in a new country. His record-keeping was atrocious. He was at times both giving and parsimonious. Could he have been "mobbed up" in Havana in the fabulous Cuban 1950s? Could he have been a snitch for Batista? The good must be weighed with the bad.

Through it all, Joe Cambria's unabashed love for the game and for "the little guy" was his ultimate driving force. UPI beat writer George Kerksey, quoted in the 1940 *Dayton Journal Herald*, described Cambria as "a swarthy individual who moves in strange, inexplicable ways." Jess Losada, dean of the Cuban baseball writers, derisively called Cambria the "Christopher Columbus of Cuba," raping his beautiful island of its baseball wealth. Part rabid baseball fan, part carnival huckster, and a "Veeck before Veeck," Joe Cambria helped to create a Washington Senators team that would eventually become a championship Minnesota Twins baseball club, all the while changing the lives and destinies of hundreds of young men.

Remaining loyal to Clark Griffith for his entire baseball scouting journey, Joe Cambria's last wish was to be buried in a Senators uniform.

Introduction

The story of Joe Cambria begins, as many immigrant stories do, on a boat. He was a baby when he and his family emigrated to the United States shortly before the turn of the twentieth century. From his humble beginnings in rural Boston, to the ballfields of Canada, to the sugar cane field and grand hotels of Havana, Joe Cambria's life will weave into the tapestry of history, covering the lives of countless young men whose own American dreams were realized through his influence.

From laundry store owner to minor-league baseball magnate to major-league baseball scout, Joe Cambria's life story is both colorful and controversial. A true entrepreneur, Cambria was a "Veeck" before his time. Embroiled in several questionable decisions, he always managed to emerge relatively unscathed, due in no small measure to the assistance he received from his boss and mentor, Clark Griffith, revered owner of the Washington Nationals, to whom he was deeply devoted.

Joe Cambria's signing of young Cuban ballplayers, starting in the mid–1930s, helped to pave the way for the final racial integration of baseball by Jackie Robinson in 1947 and, ultimately, the integration of the Washington Nationals in 1954. Some of his signees went on to have outstanding major-league careers; others did not stick. Some say he helped many young, poor Cuban boys find a path to the American dream. Others say he robbed the Cuban amateur baseball leagues of countless boys who could have made a good living in their native Cuba, only to lose their amateur status by not making it into the American major leagues.

But all those boys called him "Papa Joe," always ready with lunch money, cab fare, or words of encouragement. His connections with the Cuban government sometimes allowed him to extricate players' whole families from the clutches of Fidel Castro's regime.

To others, he was the "Christopher Columbus" of Cuba, mining the island for his own gain, another example of post–War American colonialism.

Clark Griffith swore by him. Others swore at him.

"I believe that everybody was happy with Joe. Joe give a lot of chance to a lot of young kids to send to the U.S., so I believe that nobody say any bad things about Joe Cambria."—Pedro Ramos

"O my goodness, [Joe] was very good. He give me the opportunity. At that time, you know, if Cambria sign somebody, you know some young kid he's doing nothing in Havana, he's got no future. He give you the opportunity to be a baseball player, what else do you want more?"—Camilo Pascual

"I had a very close relation with Joe, in Havana. He was a hell of a guy! He loved Cuba, he wore the white Cuban shirt [guayabera] and a white hat. I appreciate his friendship. He was very, very nice to me. So, I want to give good memories about him and clear up his name. In Cuba, a lot of ballplayer say he ruined their life. That's a big lie. He was helping out everybody and [some] people didn't make the grade and then they blame Joe for that."—Lazaro "Cholly" Naranjo

"He was a very sweet, generous old man. He was always just very jolly and everybody called him Papa Joe, and he accepted that."—Pedro Sierra

"I met Joe Cambria in 1960 through a guy who played for the Senators, his name was Roberto Tapanes. He was the one who saw me first in Los Palacios in Pina del Rio province and he invited Joe Cambria to come see me. Tapanes thought I was a good ballplayer. So, Cambria came out to Los Palacios to watch me play one game and he liked what he saw, and he signed me the same day. He offered me the opportunity to play baseball [in the United States.] No money, just $250 a month. And everyone who knew me thought I was a rich man already because $250 a month was a lot of money in Cuba then. That was about the most money you could make in Class-A ball back then, but no bonus! Joe Cambria was really the Godfather of Cuban baseball players! When I come to spring training my first year, we got a lot of Cuban players there. There was about 10 Cubans at springtime in those days."—Hall of Famer Tony Oliva

"When we first became the Twins, we had [the logo] TC on our caps and it used to be a W. And we went around to stadiums like Detroit, that was strange to them. 'What's the TC for,' they'd ask, and we would say '20 Cubans!' We had Pascual, Ramos, Oliva, Versalles, Carlos Paula, Julio Becquer, and on and on. Minnie Mendoza and Joe Cambria had a lot of influence on those young players like Tony Oliva."—Hall of Famer Jim Kaat

"Joe used to send a banana boat every year at spring training, always about 10 or 15 players. He was known as 'the big cigar' of the Latin ballplayers gettin' signed. He really was the King of the Latin scouts."—Hall of Famer Whitey Herzog

CHAPTER 1

The American Dream

In a scene from the Academy Award–winning film *The Godfather Part II*, a young Vito Andolini from Corleone, Sicily, stares placidly at the towering Statue of Liberty as his rusted old passenger ship glides gently into New York harbor. Around him, scurrying with excitement, are hundreds of fellow wistful dreamers, each seeing their own heavenly idea of America. The scene is poignantly reminiscent of what occurred day after day in New York Harbor between 1880 and 1915 when, during the great *fin de siècle* migration, more than 13 million Italians immigrated to the United States. Predominantly farmers and laborers from the southern regions of Campania, Apulia, Basilicata, Calabria, and Sicily, these migrants were escaping the crushing poverty and high taxes brought about by the *Risorgimento*, or the unification of Italy. Some came only to work, send money home, and eventually return to their homelands. Others came to seek the new life in the great land of opportunity.[1]

Joe Cambria and his family were among those teeming masses, arriving via passenger ship in 1893, when Joe was still a child.

When Giovanni Emilio Cambria married the lovely Santa Palella, daughter of Giuseppe Palella and Giovanna Colloga of Messina, Sicily, in 1877, little did they know of the great changes they would live through. The dutiful Santa would give birth to three strapping young boys: Pasquale Emilio ("Charles") was born first, in 1881 or 1882; Giovanni Edward ("John") followed four or five years later, on April 28, 1886. Carlo Giuseppe ("Joe") Cambria came along as the decade came to a close.

His Sicilian birth records list July 9, 1889, as his birth date; however, on subsequent official documents such as his naturalization papers and his draft cards, Cambria consistently listed his birth date as July 5, 1890. The 1900 Census records have Joseph Cambria listed as a dependent in the household of Emilio Cambria, his age given as 11 years old, which would lend credence to an 1889 birth date. It was commonplace for birthdates to be fudged at the turn of the century for a variety of reasons, predominantly for employment purposes. The possibility also exists that once he started playing semi-pro baseball in his teen years, Joe could have intentionally changed his birthday to appear younger to scouts. He is also listed as 26 years old on his World War I draft registration card.[2]

Messina holds a unique and historic, albeit tragic place in Italian history. Located on the island of Sicily, immediately adjacent to the very tip of the Italian "boot," Messina, with its deep-water port, became a vital link to trade and commerce not only to and from the Italian mainland but also throughout the Mediterranean basin. Since its founding by the Greeks in the 8th century, it was captured or overtaken by innumerable dynasties, Carthaginians, Romans, Goths, Byzantines, Arabs, Normans, and lastly the

French. It has been plagued by plagues, volcanic eruptions, numerous earthquakes, and resultant tsunami. As the last Nazi stronghold in Italy in World War II, it was the site of severe Allied bombings in 1943.[3]

But it would be the *Risorgimento*, or the unification of Italy spearheaded in 1860 by Giuseppe Garibaldi, that brought about the greatest hardship for the young shoemaker and farmer, Giovanni Cambria. For four decades after Victor Emanuel was proclaimed King in 1861, Italy, Sicily in particular, suffered through extreme poverty, disease, high infant mortality, looting, brigandage, high taxes, political unrest and corruption, violent crime and *vendetta* (blood feuds), riots, land robbing, and regional uprisings. The great Italian migration began in the 1880s, and by 1895, more than a quarter of all immigrants came from Sicily.[4]

By 1890, Giovanni Cambria had had enough. He left Messina and established his shoe cobbler business in Boston. He returned to Italy to collect his wife and children, and on June 7, 1893, they left Naples, arriving in New York on July 15. Records indicate that his wife Santa died June 7, 1898, and Giovanni is listed as a widower in the 1900 census.[5]

Those familiar with greater Boston proper will know that the North End was and still is the epicenter of all things Italian. First settled by the Irish and the Jews, the great Italian immigration of the 1880s soon displaced those ethnicities. By 1905, 22,000 of the 27,000 residents of the North End were Italians.

How and why the Cambrias did not settle there is lost to history. The 1900 Federal census records show they lived in Ward 6, which would be South Boston. The 1910 Census shows them in Ward 17, which would be further south in Roxbury, towards Milton, and the 1920 census has them in Ward 2, which would be over the Mystic River in Charlestown. Joe would give his address as Roxbury. Roxbury in the 1900s would still be "inside the Beltway" of Boston but it would not be nearly as crowded as Boston city proper, still city but a little rural as well. Joe and his brothers would grow up and be schooled in the area school systems, become naturalized American citizens here, and enjoy the idyllic life of rural Boston.[6]

Young Joe Cambria was an American now and wanted to assimilate into the fabric of society in any way he could. And what better way to do this than to embrace the truly American "national pastime" of baseball. Kids played baseball, town ball, rounders, "skin the cat," and dozens of stick and ball variants throughout all the towns and cities of nascent New England.

Amateur baseball was played under the Knickerbocker rules beginning in 1846, through the Civil War and into the next decade. Organized baseball was in its infancy. The Cincinnati Red Stockings were the first to openly declare themselves a paid professional team in 1869, with many others following suit. The National League of Professional Baseball Clubs was established in 1876, followed by many attempts by others to start rival leagues. The American League was formed in 1901, out of Ban Johnson's minor Western League of 1893. Cow pastures would give way to wooden covered ball parks and city stadiums, and the game would become gentrified enough to allow women to attend.

A teenaged Joe Cambria read of the exploits of the greats of the Deadball Era like Ty Cobb, Honus Wagner, Walter Johnson, and Cy Young, and dream of being one of them. He played amateur and semi-pro ball throughout the area of Boston: Roxbury, Lowell, Medford, and into Rhode Island. He took to the game and became a standout sandlot star.

Cambria began his baseball journey with a little sandlot team, the Roxbury Reds. He showed great promise and was soon making money playing in nearby Mattapan. Nineteen-year-old Joe's first true professional team was the Newport Trojans of the Independent Rhode Island League in 1909. In his brief online biography of Cambria, Brian McKenna quotes the *Newport Daily News*'s description of the young outfielder as "a short right-hander" who in his pro debut robbed a batter of an extra base hit by making a bare-handed catch, "bringing spectators to their feet."[7]

Joe Cambria returned to Newport for the entire 1910 season. In 1911, he took a sojourn to Canada to play for the Berlin Green Sox. Due to a dispute with the city over a stadium, the Green Sox left town and became the Peterborough White Caps. They were replaced by a new team, the Berlin Busy Bees. Cambria played for the Green Sox and did not make the switch to the White Caps.

The Green Socks, as they were called briefly, had a fluid roster. A week before Opening Day, they released an outfielder named Phinninger, who "wasn't there with the willow," which meant he was a weak batter. A deaf pitcher named Conley had arrived with Cambrey (name misspelled by the *Berlin News Record*) days before Opening Day. Cambria was a replacement for Phinninger. He was said to have "great range and carried a good stick." He was the opening day center fielder. He was 0-for-5 that day but made two catches in the outfield.[8]

On June 16, Joe Cambria made his one and only headline in the *Register*, which stated, "Cambria Heads Batting for Green Sox with .356." According to noted Canadian baseball researcher Benno Rosinke, this was a case of mistaken identity. Someone from the paper must have mixed up his notes and cited Cambria instead of Ray "Scotty" Cameron. Cameron ended the season with a .340 batting average. Joe Cambria hit .243. Cameron became the league MVP and was picked up by the Athletics. Joe Cambria not so much. His stats compiled from box scores of the day read as such:

Games = 92	Hits = 78	Triples = 2
At-Bats = 321	Doubles = 5	Homers = 0
Runs = 45		Batting Average = .243[9]

The 1911 team won the Canadian League championship with a record of 70–40, 11 games ahead of the second-place London Tecumsehs. Cambria returned to the Busy Bees (nee Green Sox) for the 1912 season. Somewhere between spring training and the start of the regular season, he was switched from center field to second base.

Cambria managed to make a few write-ups during the year. The June 16 *Register* said, "Little Joe is making good at second." The June 26 "Caught in the Box Scores" article stated, "Little Joe could easily qualify for a waiter. The second sacker looks the pitcher's offerings over with the scrutiny of a woman on a shopping expedition."

In its July 4 edition, the *Register* noted that "Biddy Burns took Cambria's place at second base and Bramble occupied the left pasture." A day later, the reason for the switch was spelled out: Cambria had sprained his ankle and was on crutches. According to researcher Rosinke, there would be no more mentions of Cambria in the sports pages after that. In several news articles in the 1930s and 1940s, Cambria stated unequivocally that the "sprained ankle" was in fact a broken ankle sustained in a bad slide into third base. Managers at that time did not have a track record of protecting injured players, so it was highly likely that he was released sometime during the summer.[10]

Joe Cambria's baseball career came to an end. His baseball dreams, however, did not.

Cambria returned to Boston sometime in 1912, to recuperate and find work around the Boston, Roxbury and Lowell area. As always, "love springs eternal" and Joe found his in Charlotte "Lottie" Kane, a young Irish lass five years his senior, the daughter of Michael and Margaret Kane of Lowell, Massachusetts. Lottie and Joe were married on a bright and cold, 30-degree January 4, 1916.[11]

Then Uncle Sam came a-knockin'.

On June 5, 1917, 26-year-old Joe Cambria registered for the World War I draft. Asked on the form for a reason for exemption, he wrote "wife sickly." Consequently, it is uncertain if he was actually inducted into a service branch. Suffice it to say, Cambria did the "American" thing and registered; however, a tip from a friend who owned a laundry business in Washington, D.C., would lead him to Baltimore and into a whole new world fraught with possibilities.

CHAPTER 2

The 1920s: Blowing the Bugle

According to a Richard J. Conners article in the December 14, 1933, *Sporting News*, Joe Cambria, while still on crutches from his broken ankle in 1912, went to visit a friend who owned a laundry business in Washington, D.C. His friend gave him a tip about a laundry business in Baltimore that was up for sale. This could be a case of writer's hyperbole, because the veracity of the statement is questionable. It would be six years before Cambria ventured to Charm City, with a war and a marriage intervening in between 1912 and 1918. Exactly how and when Joe and Lottie got to Baltimore is still shrouded in the ages.

But if ever there was a city for a baseball-loving guy to settle into, Baltimore was that place. Just like crabs and Natty Boh beer, Francis Scott Key and the row houses of Hamden, baseball had been part of the warp and woof of Baltimore. Beginning with the Baltimore Excelsior in the late 1850s, baseball has been integral to the life of the city and its people. Baseball was played in the camps of the Union soldiers during the Civil War. Say Baltimore and baseball fans there will begin to recite the litany of their patron saints: Brooks and Frank, Cal and Eddie, Weaver and Palmer, Boog and Belanger. And lest we forget the pioneers: Joe "Kingpin" Kelly, "Wee" Willie Keeler, Hughie "EE-YA" Jennings, Joe "Iron Man" McGinnity, and of course "The Babe."

Every type of baseball existed in the city, from pure sandlot all the way up to John McGraw's Baltimore Orioles in the newly formed American League in 1901. Ball fields were put up and taken down with regularity. Leagues of every kind were formed and disbanded, then reformed. It was baseball on Saturday, church on Sunday.

Joe Cambria was in baseball heaven. But he would have to make a living for himself and his bride.

In 1918, the Cambrias settled into a quaint row house at 2325 Maryland Avenue, a veritable stone's throw from Druid Hill Park. He and Lottie took ownership of the Bugle Coat and Apron Company, located at 224 St. Paul Street. The industrious Mr. Cambria would drive a horse and wagon around the town, delivering and picking up laundry, while the lovely Mrs. Cambria would run the books. Within two years, the company moved and expanded to 112 South Gay Street. In 1923, the company moved again to occupy almost an entire half-square block at the corner of 1501 North Chester and Olive Streets, now called the Bugle Coat, Apron and Towel Supply Company. The Bugle Company, maintaining over 250 employees and a fleet of 30 trucks, would become the largest laundry and linen supply house for hotels, motels, restaurants, boarding houses and nursing homes in the city, providing their customers with clean sheets, pillowcases, tablecloths and napkins as well as waiters' aprons and chefs' coats. They also did residential laundry. The hard-working Joe Cambria would sell his first "American Dream" to Industrial Laundry Corporation for a handsome profit in 1938 in order to begin a new dream.[1] But not without controversy.

All businesses have their share of legal problems, and Joe Cambria's business was no exception. In May of 1922, the business was denied a permit to build a garage on their property by the Baltimore Building and Regulations Committee.[2] In October of the same year, the company was given a permit for a 100-gallon gas tank to be located on their property as part of a deal with the Standard Oil company. People who protested the action were assuaged after Mayor William F. Broening convinced them that gasoline would drive away rats.[3]

In February of 1924, a Mr. James Mullineaux was awarded $15,000 in damages after being struck earlier in the year by a Bugle delivery truck.[4] The company continued to have its share of ups and downs throughout its tenure in the city; a Mrs. Pearl Lubik was awarded $2,000 in a personal injury claim in 1933.[5]

There is an old adage which states, "the burnt child fears the fire." In the case of Joe Cambria, one might instead say, the hurt ball player yearns for the game." Cambria loved baseball. Period. One would be safe to assume that he felt his broken ankle cheated him out of his proverbial shot at the title. He was determined to get back into the game, and turn-of-the-century Baltimore was a hotbed of baseball activity. (The *Baltimore Sun* has articles on baseball being played in the city as far back as 1859.)

Like most towns and cities in the nascent United States, especially on the East Coast, Baltimore had dozens of teams, leagues, and ball fields. In 1924, the Baltimore Baseball Federation (the ruling body of amateur league baseball) reported they would have up to 15 separate baseball leagues, 135 teams and leagues of every iteration: juvenile, sand lot, semi-pro, police and fireman, Sunday schools, Catholic, hotel employees, and of course Industrial leagues.[6] Joe Cambria wanted to be part of that.

Writing for the *Washington Post*, Shirley Povich described Cambria as "an incurable fan and a purveyor of money."[7] This sobriquet would be ever so apt for our Mr. Cambria. He was a hard-working immigrant who saw his laundry business as a means to an end and utilized it as such to start a baseball empire.

If there was a spare acre or two of pastureland in Baltimore City, a ball field was constructed. The minor-league Baltimore Orioles played in several ball parks before coming to roost in the renamed Memorial Stadium in 1954, and then to iconic Oriole Park at Camden Yards in 1992. From the 1880s through the 1940s, dozens of ball fields would spring up throughout Baltimore City, only to be torn down to feed the need of the burgeoning population.

Cambria's first step was to buy an old ball field called The Label Men's Oval. In a 1953 reminiscence article for the *Baltimore Sun*, a Mr. Edward C. Lastner recalled how in 1912, he and several of his fellow co-workers received a $100 gift from their boss, Mr. Henry Doeller, Sr., owner of the Simpson & Doeller label works, to build a ball field. They found a cow pasture east of what is now Belair Road (in the Orangeville section of Baltimore) at the corner of Federal Street and Edison Highway (US Route 1). Mrs. Carrie Snyder owned it, and they rented it from her for $25 a year. He and his friends leveled the field, built a small grandstand, and—beginning in 1912—the Label Men's Athletic Society Baseball Club won the city's amateur championship four out of seven years, tying twice. The team played there until World War I shut everything down in 1918. With most of the men gone, the field was sold that year to Dr. Edward J. Cook, who owned the St. Andrews team.[8]

The ball field was in an ideal spot for two reasons. First, it was in walking distance for most downtown Baltimore residents. (As a point of reference for those who have enjoyed the friendly confines of Oriole Park at Camden Yards, one would walk about a quarter-mile up Calvert Street, turn right on East North Avenue [Route 40] for a good quarter-mile, then a few blocks south of the Baltimore Cemetery to the corner of Edison Highway and Federal Street. It later became a trolley stop for the No. 27 car.)

Second, since the park was technically on the outside of Baltimore City proper, Sunday baseball was allowed.

Cambria bought the ballpark from Dr. Cook sometime in 1924 and renamed it Bugle Field, in honor of his laundry business. He set about to renovate it into one of the finest semi-pro ball fields in the city. The park had a built-in fan base and soon became one of the foremost sports venues in the city. Bugle Field would become home to his first team and home to the Baltimore Black Sox in 1930 and in 1938 to the Baltimore Elite Giants. Between 1928 and 1938, when he sold it to the Gallagher Realty Company, Joe Cambria expanded the grandstands to seat up to 3,900 fans, improved the roads surrounding the field, installed lights for night baseball, and built team clubhouses with running water.[9]

Cambria's first foray into team ownership seems to have occurred in mid–May of 1928, when he took over the Homesteads in the Baltimore Amateur League from manager Bud Stack. Cambria's timing could not have been more propitious. The Homesteads had won the league championship in 1927 and were considered one of the strongest in the league. When he took over the team, he renamed them the Bugle Coat and Apron Company after the laundry business. It was obviously too long a name to print in the minuscule box scores of the day, so they were promptly christened the Bugles and sometimes the Buglers by the local press.[10] With Bugle Coat emblazoned on their jerseys, Joe Cambria had his first baseball dream and a lot of free advertising for the business!

The Bugles' first game was a 10–9 loss to the Foresters, unfortunately. But their bad fortune did not last long. The Bugles played good ball in May, and with their 9–4 win over the Alcazar Athletic Club on June 4, they climbed into second place in the standings.[11]

The Bugles seesawed their way in the standings through June and July, suffering a crushing 15–0 loss to Clifton on July 16.[12] They would bounce back, however, with decisive wins on July 16, 23 and 30.

In August, Cambria abruptly decided to move the team into the Baltimore semi-pro league, playing the likes of Hampden, Georgetown, Alco, and Bethlehem Steel teams. No data exists as to how well they placed in that league; however, the Bugle Coat and Apron baseball team, as well as their manager, Joe Cambria, were off to a very auspicious start.

The Bugles started 1929 full of hope. Cambria decided to play in the Interclub League on Saturdays and the Semi-Pro League on Sundays. Ducky Knoedler, who had pitched brilliantly during the 1928 campaign, was named player-manager for the season.

The Bugles played well in April and May, with decisive wins over Fells Point, Edgewood, Arsenal, and Brighton. However, by June 4, they were mired in a three-way tie for third place in the Interclub League. Looking to shake things up a bit, Joe Cambria hired Bill Callahan, the former manager of the Hampden Club, as the new manager, and Ducky Knoedler went back to his position as ace of the pitching staff.[13]

The shake-up seemed to work. With a doubleheader win against the Baltimore

Athletic Club on June 24, the Bugles began winning consistently, even between the two leagues. The fought their way into the Interleague Championship game with the Bloomingdales on September 8. But alas, hoisting the gonfalon was not to be. Playing on the Bloomingdales' home field with the score tied 3–3 in the bottom of the ninth and a man on third, pitcher Ray Atkinson was brought in to save the game and take it to extra innings. But his first pitch bounced a foot in front of the plate, allowing the runner on third to practically walk in for the winning run.[14]

Revenge, always served cold, would be on the menu a month later, however. In a season-ending special series played in October, the *Baltimore Sun* reported that the Bugles took a doubleheader over the Bloomingdale Club before a crowd of 8,900 at the club's home field.[15]

Sometime during the year, Cambria was appointed Commissioner of the Baltimore Baseball Federation Association, the City's baseball ruling body. Through this, he would be able to get a great look at all that Baltimore sandlot baseball had to offer, which would come in very handy for him in the foreseeable future.

Nineteen twenty-nine was the year for him to flex his entrepreneurial muscle. He kept the Bugles busy from April through October, playing games in the Baltimore Inter-club League and the Semi-Pro League, as well as contests with independent and barn-storming teams.

July 8 saw the Bugles hosting the barnstorming House of David ball club for a special Monday night exhibition game at Bugle Field. The House of David, a benign Adventist cult founded by Benjamin and Mary Pernell in Benton Harbor, Michigan, prohibited all their members from having sex, drinking alcohol, eating meat, and their men from cutting their hair or shaving their beards. Their hirsute appearance was a humorous attraction to the conservative "shaven and shorn" society of Baltimore, not to mention their tremendous baseball skills. The original Benton Harbor team was started in 1915 as a means of physical exercise for the men and as a way to thwart their minds' amorous intentions. They barnstormed with great success starting in the early 1920s. Needing help with the nuances of the game, the team hired several famous major-league players as coaches and to make guest appearances. Notable alumni included Mordecai "Three Finger" Brown, Grover Cleveland Alexander, and the omnipresent Satchel Paige. Babe Ruth was famously photographed in a House of David uniform and fake beard and at one time was offered a contract after his playing days were over; however, the team was advised that the Babe's notorious off-field activities were in direct opposition to their religious tenets, and the offer was rescinded. The team became the "Harlem Globetrotters" of baseball, rarely losing a game.[16]

This night, however, they would have to work for their supper in a close, 10–8 win over the Bugles. The Bugles actually shut out the Davids, 4–0, for the first four innings, but the Davids finally figured out the Bugles' pitchers and quickly turned the score around. The stadium was packed with appreciative fans and Cambria was smart enough to see they were "good gate." They were invited back regularly throughout the 1930s.[17]

Always the showman, Joe Cambria and his Bugles played host to the Bloomer Girls of New York the following weekend. The Girls played respectfully well in spite of the apparent odds, losing by only an 8–3 margin. A Miss Houghton provided one of the more spectacular plays of the day. Her long line drive to deep center field forced the Bugles' Freddy Fitzburger to make a spectacular, over-the-shoulder, bare-handed catch to end a rally.[18]

On August 5, Cambria was able to coax future Hall of Famer Charles "Chief"

Bender out of retirement to pitch the first game of a Monday doubleheader for the Bugles against the North Philadelphia Club. Bender, one of the winningest pitchers for Connie Mack's early Philadelphia Athletics, easily outpaced the North Philly club, 8–2. The Bugles' ace, Joe Atkinson, threw a masterful game to win the nightcap, 14–2.[19]

Cambria was quick to utilize the talents of former major leaguers as a gate attraction, most notably former Washington Senators spitballer Allan Russell, Washington, D.C., sandlot legend and Babe Ruth teammate Walter Beall, and former St. Louis Browns and Cleveland Naps hurler Thomas "Lefty" George. These players, a bit past their prime, still supplied valuable teachings to the young Bugles teams.

September 7 saw the Bugles in an epic battle, splitting a doubleheader with the Cuban Red Sox. The Cubans had a huge fan following, and in anticipation of a full house, Cambria rented out the International League Oriole Park.

Originally formed in 1907 as a Negro League ball club, the Cuban Red Sox was made up of African Americans predominantly and with a couple of Cuban black players. Thus, they were called "Cubans" to gain acceptance with white audiences. By 1929, however, this iteration of the Red Sox featured a predominantly Cuban team with several American-born African American players. Most notable on the team was their ace, a young Luis Eleuterio "Lefty" Tiant, Sr., father of the Boston Red Sox great, Luis Clemente Tiant, a hero of the 1975 World Series. In addition to being skilled players, the Red Sox were showmen:

> The pregame festivities at Oriole Park started out with the Red Sox coming onto the field wearing their navy blue uniforms with red trim and lettering and performing their famous rendition of shadowball, a synchronized pantomime in which they went through their infield and outfield drills without using a baseball. The Cubans engaged in their on-field chatter in Spanish during this dazzling presentation while singing their signature song, "Whoopee." The Havana team was made up of some of the most talented players from Cuba. In addition to their skills on the diamond, they were entertainers in the same vein as the latter-day Harlem Globetrotters basketball team.[20]

The first game featured a 0–0 pitching duel between Cuban Red Sox ace Tiant and the Bugles' ace, Joe Atkinson, for the first two innings. But the Bugles got to Tiant for four runs in the bottom of the third and five runs in the home fifth, and that would be all for "Lefty." The Bugles would score three more runs, Atkinson would give up four runs in the late innings, but the damage had been done. Bugles 12, Cubans 4.

In the nightcap, the Bugles were no match for the Red Sox's two biggest hitters, Tomas "Pipo" de la Noval and Basilio "Home Run" Cueria. The darkness-shortened second game went only seven innings, with the tired Bugles losing, 5–1.[21]

The Bugles proved their mettle by winning at least one game of the twin bill with such a decisive score and against one of the all-time great Cuban players of the century. Luis Tiant, Sr., would go on to be a major force in Latin American and Mexican baseball until 1947 and would be enshrined in the Cuban Baseball Hall of Fame.

The Bugles, emboldened by their great showing against the Cubans, invited the Eastern Colored League champions Baltimore Black Sox to Bugle Field for a September 20 doubleheader. Victory eluded the Bugles, with the Black Sox easily taking both games 6 to 2 and 5 to 4. The Black Sox became frequent visitors to Bugle Field in the 1930s, and Cambria, figuring "if you can't beat 'em, join 'em," bought the team in 1932.[22]

The Bugles Nine played hard and stayed competitive to the end, losing to the Baltimore City Police team and finishing second in the semi-pro league.[23]

From 1928 until he sold it in 1938, the indefatigable Mr. Cambria utilized his Bugle Field to its fullest advantage year-round. Even before the baseball season had finished, he promoted both sandlot and semi-pro football games at the field, as well as renting it out for high school contests. In the spring, he promoted lacrosse and soccer matches. He leased out the park and promoted boxing and wrestling matches throughout the year when the ball team was not using it. And if that was not enough, he would do the same for traveling circuses and Wild West shows. Add to that the revenues engendered from the barnstorming team matches, and Cambria would make a comfortable profit from the use of the ball field.

All to be used in building his empire.

CHAPTER 3

1930–1935:
From the Blue Ridge League
to the NNL

As Red Barber liked to say, Joe Cambria was "sittin' in the catbird seat."

The Baltimore press had taken notice of what Joe Cambria was doing for Baltimore baseball. In a 1930 *Sun* article, sports editor Paul Menton wrote, "When everyone else said sandlot baseball in Baltimore was dead, Joe Cambria said it was not true, organized the Bugle team, built Bugle Field and has offered fine games each Sunday to steadily increasing crowds."[1]

Emboldened by his success with the Bugles ball team and the baseball field itself, Joe Cambria would end his 1920s decade and begin the 1930s by plunging right into the deep end of the pool.

In December of 1929, Cambria took $2,500 ($37,500 in 2020 dollars) of his modest profits from his laundry and baseball interests and bought the Hagerstown Hubs in the Class D Blue Ridge League. In almost every newspaper account of the time, he was referred to as "the Baltimore laundry man" or some such usage. Most of the scribes were duly incredulous that a man with such limited baseball management experience would take on a professional league franchise. Little did they realize that he had been working and managing a major and profitable business in Baltimore for ten years. Safe to say he was not totally bereft of management experience, just a bit naïve about baseball management.

Cambria would confound his detractors further still by owning the team independently of any big-league franchise. The Frederick (MD) Warriors were owned by the Cleveland Indians, and the Hanover (PA) Raiders had a working agreement with the Detroit Tigers. Connie Mack's Athletics owned the Martinsburg (WV) Blue Sox, the Waynesboro (PA) Red Birds were affiliated with the St. Louis Cardinals, and the Yankees were the proud owners of the Chambersburg (PA) Young Yanks.[2] All of these teams could funnel players from within their own organizations and had a plethora of talent with which to do that. They could also support their teams financially.

Joe Cambria, on the other hand, had a deep, abiding faith in the local talent residing in Maryland. He felt strongly about building talent from the ground up and believed that Hagerstown would be that ideal spot for young players from all over the state to try out for professional baseball. Cambria, from the very beginning of his baseball journey, felt strongly about this and may have been the reason for starting the Bugles. In a *Frederick News* article, Cambria said, "I have been lucky in Baltimore, along with plenty of hard work. I get all my fun out of sports, particularly baseball, and I would like to give

17

some of the young chaps a lift that I didn't get. Unless I thought that buying the Hagerstown franchise would be a benefit to the Blue Ridge League and baseball in Baltimore, I wouldn't consider the purchase."[3]

The Blue Ridge League had been in existence since 1915. As one of the founding members, Hagerstown was anxious to get a good team. One small stumbling block in the Hagerstown deal was the question of the stadium. The Hagerstown School Board had already taken an option on the existing Hubs field, and they decided they would exercise their option to build a new school.

However, one bright spot existed. The Hagerstown Field and Athletic Association guaranteed Joe Cambria a stadium, and damned if they did not come through. They mounted a tremendous public fundraising campaign, and the Hagerstown Municipal Stadium was built in the short period of six weeks.

Win-win for Cambria.

The team trained and played at Bugle Field in Baltimore while the stadium kerfuffle was ironed out, and they would play Sunday baseball there. (Maryland Blue Laws prohibited Sunday baseball in Hagerstown, but not in Baltimore County.) Bugle Field had been a hub of baseball activities, drawing 5,000 to 6,000 fans on any given Sunday. The Bugles, along with the Hubs, were sure to draw many, if not more, rabid fans to the friendly confines of Bugle Field.

Cambria was quick to jump into the fray. One of the first things he did was to name John "Poke" Whalen as a secretary, coach, and scout for the team. "Poke" was a local legend, having been a catcher for the Frederick Hustlers of the old Blue Ridge League from 1915 through 1921. He went on to manage in the Eastern Shore League from 1922 to 1928. He became a great scout for the Pirates, Athletics, Orioles, and Indians.[4] Joe Cambria and John Whalen would go about populating the Hubs with the finest young players they could find, then round out the team with a few veterans. "Poke" Whalen would be part of Cambria's entourage for many years.

After Whalen, Cambria named Emil "Pop" Reitz as his Vice President and secretary. "Pop" Reitz played for a year with the York White Roses in 1910 and in Baltimore semi-pro baseball around the city after that. His son, Emil "Lefty" Reitz, played on the Bugles and appeared in three games with the Albany Senators in 1933, a team owned by Cambria. "Lefty" Reitz became the outstanding and much-beloved Athletic Director at Loyola College of Maryland from 1938 through 1973.[5]

The Model Is Started

Cambria was now legitimate. He was the sole owner of a recognized Class-D baseball club, subservient to all rules and regulations concomitant to that agreement. He was now duty bound to pay his players a salary to play for his team. He no longer had the luxury of just inviting a young and promising player to play a little ball for his Bugles; he must now physically find good, talented players, recruit them, and pay them to play for the Hubs.

This would take some doing.

Without any big-league affiliation, Cambria would be responsible for all the expenses of running a franchise: stadium utilities, field upkeep, salaries, printing, advertising, uniforms, equipment, and so much more. His only working income would be through ticket and concessions sales, as well as the sale of promising players. (He probably funneled money from the laundry business when he got short.) Baseball games had just begun being broadcast on radio in 1921. The medium was still in its infancy, and broadcast rights were in their nascent stages. Advertising and brand marketing were virtually non-existent.

Cambria had his work cut out for him. The governing body of the Blue Ridge League, who officially ratified the transfer and sale of the franchise and welcomed him to the league, had reduced the number of games in the season to 100, down from 120. All teams would be limited to 14 players with a player-manager, and salaries were capped at $2,800.[6]

Joe Cambria began his business model that he would adhere to throughout his career:

1. Buy a franchise for as little money as possible.
2. Keep administrative costs low by hiring friends or relations.
3. Pay as little as possible for players and try to get a gate attraction.
4. Sell talent for a profit.
5. Build attendance at the gate.
6. If things go really bad, relocate to a larger city or sell out.

True to their word, Cambria and Whalen wasted little time building the team. In January, they signed four young prospects from the Baltimore amateur leagues, Frank Jordan and James Kerr, both catchers, Dave Chilcoat and Ike Whalen.[7] By March, it was a feeding frenzy. Whalen signed 66 players for the Hubs, with only four holdovers from the previous season.[8]

The ever-gracious Mr. Cambria stated to the good folks of Hagerstown, "I want to congratulate the people of this city on their work. I will try to put a team on the field that will be a credit to the city as well as to the ballpark in which they play."[9]

Cambria then went out and signed the Hubs' 1929 bullpen workhorse, Mike Meola, and third baseman Ed Donaghey, former captain of the Harvard University nine.

Spring training started in March, and after two rigorous weeks of training, Joe Cambria named right fielder Jake Miller as the new player-manager. Miller started his career with the Southern Association Mobile Bears in 1919 and had Class B, A, and AA stints in Wichita Falls, Toronto, Birmingham, Portland, and York up to 1927. He worked his way up to a three-game "cup of coffee" with the Pittsburgh Pirates in 1922. He was a "seasoned veteran" who could bring a wealth of knowledge and experience to the young Hubs.[10]

Cambria did everything he could to increase attendance. In May, he announced that every Friday would be Ladies' Day, with free admission for the fairer sex. In mid–June, he arranged for a bus to pick up and shuttle fans to the park from the town square, free of charge. On June 27, he had a double special: Ladies' Day and Boosters' Day, with a ticket price of 40 cents for any seat in the house. In an attempt to bring in more working folks, Cambria arranged for a 5:30 p.m. twilight game on Monday, June 30. He also graciously agreed to postpone a Hubs game in order to host the American Legion's championship series from August 13 through 15.[11]

But all of this was a precursor to Cambria's biggest promotion, night baseball. Cambria hired the American Floodlighting Company to install 11 light stanchions around the park for the August 12 game. He invited Maryland's Governor Albert Ritchie, local and state officials, and, in what he hoped would be his biggest draws, invited Washington Senators owner Clark Griffith to throw out the first ball. He also asked Griffith to bring along Nick Altrock and Al Schacht, the "Clown Princes of Baseball," to entertain the fans.[12]

Try as they might, though, the Hubs did not do well, and by mid-season manager Jake Miller was replaced by Cambria himself. League champs in 1929, the Hubs placed a mediocre third in 1930, with a 52–64 record.

The one bright spot in the firmament was Ernest Gordon "Babe" Phelps, a young phenom Joe Cambria found in Odenton, MD. Phelps led the league with a .376 batting average and 175 hits.[13] Phelps garnered the "Babe" moniker due to his six-foot two-inch, 235-pound physique and his left-handed batting style, similar to that of the great Bambino.

In need of a catcher, Clark Griffith showed great interest in Phelps, so much so that he asked Cambria to bring him in from the outfield and keep him behind the plate as a catcher for as long as he could. Phelps went on to play for the Senators, Cubs, and the Dodgers and became the first big money maker for Cambria.[14]

All of Cambria's efforts did not go unnoticed by the Hagerstown faithful. Frank Colley, sports editor of the *Hagerstown Daily Mail,* summed up the town's feelings: "Joe Cambria at least deserves a medal for his efforts and work in trying to give Hagerstown a winner. Every day Cambria, after getting his business moving in Baltimore, jumps a car and comes to the Blue Ridge League, out on the coaching lines and scouting here and there…. The boss of the Hubs realizes that his team needs capable hurlers to go through and he is going to get them if possible."[15]

Joe Cambria was putting some miles on the ol' Chevy with the 140-mile round trip between downtown Baltimore and Hagerstown. He still had his lucrative laundry business to run. (He would handle the day-to-day operations, while Charlotte handled the administration.) Plus, his Bugles baseball team was still the talk of the town.

The Buglers easily dispatched the Harrowgate Club of North Philadelphia, both games of a doubleheader on two separate occasions and, in a much-touted event, beat a colored House of David team in a doubleheader in June.[16]

Cambria also invited back the Cuban Red Sox for a series. Led by the pitching of aces Walter Beall and Ducky Knoedler, the Bugles took both games of their doubleheader, 13–2 and 9–8.[17]

Try as they might, though, they could not tame the Baltimore Black Sox. The rivalry had built to such a fever that Cambria made arrangements with owner George Rossiter to play an eight-game series. Interest in the matchups became so intense that Cambria announced that he would put up lights at Bugle Field for the August series, but then he decided not to. Had he done so, he would have had the first team to play under the lights in Baltimore. They lost seven out of eight to the Sox in April, June, July, August, and September.

Through it all, Cambria still came out victorious. By beating Bloomingdale six out of eight times, the Bugles claimed the state semi-pro championship for 1930.[18]

All the aforementioned car miles took their toll on Joe Cambria. On a dark August 2 night, he was involved in a three-car accident in Frederick, 20 miles east of Hagerstown. A car driven by Francis Barnes of Sykesville collided with a vehicle driven by William Rever of Mt. Airy. Mr. Rever's car spun out and hit Joe Cambria's car, which was being driven by Bernie Ciprano. Mr. Barnes unfortunately died of head injuries, while Cambria and all others escaped unscathed.[19]

The First of Many

Mention of the accident is important in light of what transpired earlier in the year. Cambria got into trouble for the first time with Kenesaw Mountain Landis, commissioner of baseball. In a ruling that defies explanation, Cambria was reprimanded by Landis for using an ineligible player on his Bugle team, second baseman Tony Citrano. An article in the *Baltimore Evening Sun* mentioned that the player in question might be playing under an assumed name, possibly Bernie Ciprano. Although the Bugles team was not in organized ball, Cambria, as owner of the Hagerstown club, was, and he had to abide by all minor-league rules concerning players.[20]

Citrano had been under contract with Jack Dunn's International League Baltimore Orioles but jumped ship with no notice to play for the Baltimore Dry Docks back in 1919. He continued to play "under the radar" until 1926, when he asked the commissioner for forgiveness but was evidently denied.[21]

How Citrano thought he could get away with it was counterintuitive at best. The *Evening Sun* published his signing with the Bugles in February of 1930. The Bugles were the hottest team in the Baltimore semi-pro leagues, and the baseball-hungry scribes were wont to cover everything in which Joe Cambria was involved, so word of Citrano was public knowledge.

Some agreement must have been reached because Citrano was reported as a player-coach for the Hubs in 1931 and became the manager of the Youngtown Buckeyes in 1932.[22]

Joe Cambria was nothing if not intrepid. Once the season was over, Cambria let no moss grow under his feet. In September, he sold three players to the Senators: Tommy Thompson, Art Fidler, and John Peregoy. Of the three, Thompson would go on to have a long career in baseball, spending six years with the Boston Braves and Chicago White Sox and 23 seasons in the minors.[23]

Cambria continued his wheeling and dealing throughout the winter, selling off almost the entire team in December. Cambria told the *Hagerstown Daily Sun* that 90 percent of the players would be new to Hagerstown fans, and he hoped that the fans would warm up to the club and help place a winner in the Hub City.[24]

In total, he dealt 14 players to both major- and minor-league clubs. Through these player sales, Cambria was able to show a small but modest profit for the year, unheard-of for a first-year owner in a D league.

Clark Griffith took notice.

Since the winter months were too cold for baseball, our indefatigable Mr. Cambria needed something to do, so he started a basketball team!

Cambria put together a squad, called the Bugle Club, made up the best players from the Baltimore Catholic and the Washington Independent leagues. Even before he had a full team in place, he booked a match with the Major League All-Stars, led by none other than Philadelphia Athletics World Series Champions Mickey Cochrane and Mule Haas, as well as New York Yankees pitcher Roy Sherid.

Their first game was played Saturday, February 7, at the One Hundred and Fourth Regiment Armory to a sellout crowd.[25]

But not without controversy.

Before the games began, Albert Wheltle, president of the Baltimore Basketball League, sounded this warning to Cambria's team:

The Baltimore Basketball League has no quarrel with the newly organized Bugle team, which Joe Cambria is sponsoring. We wish it success. There is room in Baltimore for a professional basketball team, but I think it only fair to warn the players of our league that if any of them are considering playing for the Bugles, whether it be for one game of permanently, they are likely to forfeit their amateur status. Certainly, they will as far as the Baltimore Basketball League is concerned.[26]

Despite being suspended, Cambria's guys from the Catholic Leagues agreed to play the games. Because of his protestations and those of several other club managers, the Catholic Basketball League abolished their newly formed advisory board and installed an independent arbitration board to oversee such rulings. The boys were eventually reinstated.[27]

They went on to win the game with the All-Stars. Joe Cambria also arranged games with the original House of David basketball team, Brooklyn Visitation College, Villanova College, and the Reading Bearcats.[28]

1931

Things did not look good for the Blue Ridge League. Even before the 1930 season finished, two teams, Hanover and Martinsburg, dropped out of the league because their major-league parent clubs dropped their support, leaving the league to finish the season with only four teams. At the winter meetings on February 9, 1931, after sending numerous requests to all of the major-league and AA minor-league teams, President J. Vincent Jamison, Jr., was unable to get financial backing for three of the six teams in the loop; consequently, the league was forced to disband. President Jamison also asked for and received permission for individual owners to seek out franchises in other leagues.[29]

Two days later, the intrepid Mr. Cambria wasted no time in putting in his application to move the Hagerstown club into either the Class-C Mid–Atlantic or the New York-Penn League. Getting promises from both Washington and Baltimore, he settled on the Mid–Atlantic League after being voted into the new 12-team league at a special meeting in Pittsburgh. With Cambria logging hundreds of miles between Baltimore, Hagerstown, and Pittsburgh to secure the franchise, Frank Colley, *Hagerstown Daily Mail* sports editor, lauded Cambria thusly:

> Followers of the national game in this city should certainly lend their wholehearted support to Joe Cambria for his untiring efforts to give organized baseball to them and to keep Hagerstown on the map in sports. All that Cambria asks is the attendance of the fans and he promises to place a team on the field that will be right up among the leaders in the race for the pennant. The Baltimore sportsman has gathered together a likely looking bunch of youngsters and has been promised help from Washington and Baltimore teams. Give the Hubs a hustling bunch of players and fans will come out to the games, and that is just what the owner of the Hagerstown franchise plans to do.[30]

Opening Day, May 7 saw Joe Cambria's new friend, Clark Griffith, throwing out the first ball of the season for the Hubs. The "Old Fox" would be a frequent visitor to the Hubs' new stadium.

One of the biggest stumbling blocks in the road to Joe Cambria's success in Hagerstown was the Maryland blue laws, which prohibited a large variety of activities on Sundays, not the least of which was professional sports. Attendance at sports events of any kind was prohibited by arcane 18th- and 19th-century religious laws, meant to make the Christian Sabbath a day of rest and reflection. Multitudinous blue laws also varied from state to state, county to county, and in some case from town to town, sometimes ignored and sometimes enforced. The laws also prohibited religions that practiced a Saturday sabbath, such as the Jewish and Seventh Day Adventist faiths, from opening their business on Sundays.

In January, Francis A. Michel, Speaker of the Maryland House of Delegates, prepared a bill which was sponsored by delegate Thomas D'Alesandro to liberalize all of the Maryland blue laws, which would include allowing movies on Sundays. As expected, opposition and support were intense in equal measure. Theodore McKeldin, secretary to Baltimore mayor William Frederick Broening, openly stated that Baltimore "remains in a hick town classification" because of the Sunday blue laws and its inability to support a major-league baseball team.[31]

"Jabbering Joe," as he was now labeled by the press, made no secret as to his stand on the matter when he told the *Hagerstown Sun*: "I am optimistic concerning the chance for Sunday baseball in Hagerstown and I will be a very disappointed man if the General Assembly does not take favorable action in the matter. Without Sunday baseball, I don't see how the Hagerstown Club can exist in the Middle Atlantic League."[32]

After much wrangling, the bill to repeal passed the House and Senate in early April and was signed into law by Governor Ritchie on April 17. The first Sunday game was played in June; however, after similar legislation in the Pennsylvania House of Delegates was defeated, opponents from the Lord's Day Alliance, National Federation of Men's Bible Classes, and the Hagerstown Ministers Association were successful in getting a referendum passed which stopped Sunday games after July 1.

Earlier in the year, in March, Cambria proposed the idea of splitting the season between Saturday and Sunday ball in Martinsburg and weekday and night games in Hagerstown; however, after the successful referendum by the religious groups, he felt he had not gotten the support he needed, both from the fans and the city council. Beaten and bemused, Cambria had no alternative. With a 12-team league and a 132-game schedule, he needed Sunday and night baseball to survive. Vacillating between Martinsburg and Parkersburg, West Virginia, he decided to move the team west to Parkersburg on June 28, becoming the Parkers for two weeks, and then farther west and north to Youngstown, Ohio, becoming the Tubers on July 12.

Unable to acquire the services of ex–Pittsburgh Pirate and Blue Ridge League favorite Clyde Barnhart as manager, Cambria took over managing the team for the season. Despite good hitting from his stars, Sam Thomas, Bill Prichard, and Babe Phelps, the Buckeyes finished in ninth place, a dismal 23½ games behind the league champion Charleston Senators. Babe Phelps, though, led the league with a .408 batting average and 178 hits, earning him a two-week "cup of coffee" with the Washington Senators late in the 1931 season.

Back in Baltimore, the Bugles continued to play well. They held their own in the league but did not make it to the championship. Joe Cambria kept them busy playing exhibitions with the Hubs, as well as the House of David, and a unique event, a game against the Hollywood Movie All-Stars girls baseball team. The girls were no slouch, making sensational fielding plays throughout the contest. That the Bugles won, 13–8, was more of a testament to the girls' skills than to the Bugles'. The Baltimore Black Sox, who beat the Bugles every game they played, would soon become a new member of the Cambria army.

Two things occurred at this juncture in 1931: the beginning of Cambria's and Griffith's lifelong relationship and the beginning of a true farm system for the Senators. At the confluence of this juncture sat Commissioner Kenesaw Mountain Landis.

The Great Depression brought with it an overarching austerity that everyone felt, rich and poor alike. Griffith, who grew from humble farming beginnings in Illinois, did not come from money. He did not have the fortunes of a William Wrigley or a Jacob Ruppert. He literally had to sell the ranch he and his brother owned in Montana in order to become the Senators' chief stockholder and manager in 1912. Before Joe Cambria came along, Griffith relied on the baseball savvy of Joe Engle, his one and only scout, for talent acquisition. Engle, a one-time pitcher for Griffith's Senators, did have a knack for finding good talent. He was responsible for finding Bucky Harris, Fred "Firpo" Marberry, Joe Kuhel, Ossie Bluege, Buddy Myer, and "The Boy Wonder," Joe Cronin, all of whom were instrumental in winning pennants for the Senators in 1924, 1925, and 1933. However, by 1929, Branch Rickey of the Cardinals had developed a farm system of nine teams, with hundreds of kids laboring in obscurity for him. By the 1930s, Griffith no longer had the money to buy expensive talent to put on the field.

Frank H. Young, writing for the *Washington Post* in 1932, elucidated the problem with crystal clarity.

1. Griffith just did not have the money to land a "Lefty" Gomez or a Jimmie Foxx. Instead, he tried to buy Danny MacFayden (17-year career, 123–159, 3.98 ERA) from the Red Sox, only to be outbid by the deep pockets of the Yankees. Consequently, he spent wads of cash and players and settled for Dick Coffman (1–6 in 1932) and Alphonse Thomas (8–7 in 1932). These guys would probably be a fourth or fifth starter for today's MLB teams.

2. Joe Engle just did not have the time to "hunt for the ivory" and run an AA ball club at the same time. Joe Cambria had just affiliated with the Senators and was in a C League.

3. By 1932, most of the major-league clubs had secured an affiliation with a AAA or AA club. They, in return, had affiliated with lower-level clubs. Consequently, finding a youngster in a D league did not mean he was unprotected by the parent club. The Senators were wont to look for kids on the sandlots of Idaho, almost.

So, with a bankroll too small to buy near stars and a handicap in properly developing talent two or three years away from the majors, about the only avenues open to the Nats to add strength are via the trade route—and the other fellow also has to think that he is getting the better of the deal, friendships ceasing when it comes to trading among the major league magnates—and through the Chattanooga club, as it is hardly likely that a Youngstown product could make the "big time" in one jump. From the above it appears that the Nats will be up against it in landing spare parts and replacements until, by hook or crook, they can make enough additional minor league affiliations to put them on a par with their rivals, and that's hard to do without a big pocketbook full of money out here and there.[33]

The writing was on the wall, and it read farm system.

Griffith had never been a fan of the farm system and was loath to endorse Branch Rickey's concept that "from quantity comes quality." Griffith and Connie Mack were the last of the starched-collared "dinosaurs" left in baseball, still believing in acquiring players the old-fashioned way: trading around for one or two marquee players or maybe some past their prime, scouting, bird-dogging, and acting on tips and hunches from friends, relations, and self-appointed experts who knew little or nothing. They would "coach up" the young rookies for a few years, then tie a rope around their waists and throw them into the major-league waters to see if they could swim. It had worked for Walter Johnson, why not for others?

But the times they were a-changin'.

Joe Cambria's belated Christmas present came in March, when it was announced that he had signed a working agreement with Clark Griffith and the Washington Senators for rookie talent. Griffith had Joe Engle, owner of the Chattanooga Lookouts, send Cambria a dozen players for tryouts that March. Even better news was that Griffith had finally warmed up to the idea of a farm system.[34]

But now, Griffith was in the catbird seat. His affiliation with Cambria and the Hubs made perfect sense. A working agreement meant Griffith would help out a little bit financially, but not totally. Cambria was a successful independent owner who was responsible for all his own bills.

Without benefit of any contract, they struck an understanding: Cambria would sign players with his own money. Griffith would supply him with young talent. Griffith would have first call on any player Cambria deemed worthy of his notice. If one of them stuck with the parent club, Cambria would receive fair compensation, no questions asked.

In return, Cambria received the sage counsel and mentoring of Griffith, one of the most powerful and respected men in baseball, and some financial assistance, not a lot, through the years of their relationship.

Instead of spending tens of thousands of dollars on a Kiki Cuyler, Mule Haas, or Bill Terry, Griffith could expend a few thousand on promising prospects who, if they did not make it the first year, could still make a living in the high minors while they "seasoned up" and returned to the parent club. If they did do well, their value would only increase over the years.

Their relationship proved especially fortuitous to Joe Cambria. Between 1930 and 1940, Cambria's business operations were highly scrutinized by Commissioner Landis. Cambria enjoyed the day-to-day interaction with the players and had only a rudimentary knowledge of the myriad operational rules of baseball, especially contracts. On more than a half-dozen occasions, Landis censured Cambria for business irregularities (e.g., Tony Citrano) and had many other complaints, so much so that he threatened to kick him out of baseball. On each occasion, Griffith (who had been a masterful arbiter in the formation of one of the first players' organizations) would assuage Landis and temper his ire. Griffith had always maintained a great relationship with Landis that lasted until Landis's death in 1944.

Plus, Cambria and Griffith had another common bond: they were equally parsimonious.

For his generosity and largesse, Cambria swore undying fealty to Griffith for the rest of his life.

Win-win for Griff.

Attention must be paid here to the character of Joe Cambria. Be it by strength of will, blind ambition, or sheer dumb luck, Cambria decided to get into organized baseball and begin a farm system in the absolute teeth of the greatest economic collapse of the 20th century. Speculation insists that Cambria's laundry business must have been profitable and secure in order for him to consider a business venture of this magnitude during the Great Depression. It is possible this could be the offshoot of the great immigrant spirit that pervaded the start of the century. In any event, throughout his career in building his minor-league dynasty and his scouting ventures, Joe Cambria always seemed to be in the right place at the right time.

Starting a farm system came with its own inherent problems, not the least of which was the ire and condemnation of Commissioner Landis. One of the tenets of Landis' commissionership was that the minor leagues were to be a separate, independent entity, and he fought not to have them eaten up by the major leagues. The person with whom he fought the most was Branch Rickey.

Landis felt that if the major leagues took over the minors, it would become a form of indentured servitude, which he felt was evil. In a famous quote, he stated in the third person:

> From the beginning, the commissioner has regarded the farm system as evil; evil not because ownership of several non-competing clubs is bad in itself—although unquestionably is preferable that every club be independently owned and operated—but evil because such ownership is operated to control great numbers of players, imperiling their essential rights, if the rights do not prevent such operation, and also because it reduces minor league clubs to subservience....
>
> Instead of being free to advance as rapidly as their ability merits, and to advance to and through any and every club in baseball, players are unjustly restricted to "grooved" advancement through one system which controls them and solely as that system may conceive to be in its interest.
>
> To this there is but one exception—the remote possibility that the player may be drafted.[35]

"Grooved advancement" was Landis' term for what he called "covering up" players, and the executive who did this the most was Branch Rickey. By the end of the 1920s, Rickey had an octopus of teams scattered throughout the Midwest and would regularly hide his good players by bouncing them from league to league and, in some cases, from team to team within a single league, which would incur the wrath of Landis. "Aside from ideological difference with the St. Louis General manager," writes David Pietrusza, "Landis' skin crawled at the moralistic weeping on the one hand and his [Rickey's] penurious chicanery on the other. 'That hypocritical preacher,' and 'that Protestant bastard [who's] always masquerading with a minister's robe' were two of the Judge's kinder epithets for the Mahatma."[36]

In March of 1929, Landis went so far as to free 10 players from the Pirates, Senators, Tigers, and Athletics from illegal contracts. Most of the players freed were little more than backup players, with the exception of catcher Rick Ferrell, a .300 hitter with Columbus in the Tigers' farm system. Thanks to Landis' intervention, the future Hall of Famer and seven-time All-Star signed with the Browns for $12,500 and a $25,000 signing bonus.[37]

Landis continued fighting major-league control of the minor leagues, freeing minor leaguers on a case-by-case basis, either individually or by the carload. In 1938, he freed 73 St. Louis Cardinals farmhands. In 1939, he freed 90 players in the Detroit Tigers' farm system. His most famous case, though, involved a young sandlotter from Van Meter, Iowa, one Robert Feller.

Feller was signed by Indians scout Cy Slapnicka to the Class-D Fargo-Moorhead Twins in 1936 but knew he would be obtainable by anyone should he appear there. Consequently, on the ruse that he had a sore arm, Slapnicka brought him to Cleveland. While Feller's arm "healed," Slapnicka arranged for him to pitch for the best semi-pro team in the city, the Rosenblums, so he wouldn't technically appear on a professional roster. Slapnicka then arranged for him to appear with the Indians in an exhibition game against the St. Louis Cardinals, where he fanned seven out of eight batters he faced. Slapnicka arranged for Fargo-Moorhead to "transfer" his contract to New Orleans, who conveniently "transferred" it over to the Indians the same day. The Indians had clearly covered up Feller in violation of the minor-league agreement prohibiting a major-league club from signing a player directly off the sandlots. Landis attempted to take action against the Indians, but the action was thwarted when Feller and his father insisted that "Rapid Robert" play in Cleveland and threatened legal action against Landis should he free Feller from his contract. Landis eventually acquiesced, much to his chagrin.

Griffith was far too ethical to be involved in this type of tomfoolery. Cambria had established a good pipeline of sorts: he would find good high school or sandlot players, along with former minor leaguers, use them on the Bugles until they were seasoned enough to go to one of his myriad minor-league teams, where they would be seasoned some more, and then sell them to Griffith or another team, with Cambria making a nice profit in the exchange.

Who doesn't want to make a buck?

With the 1931 season over, Mr. "ADHD" Cambria needed something else to do. He once again promoted football and boxing matches at Bugle Field. He and Ed Brockman, a well-respected Baltimore fight referee, owned and managed the Homestead football team in the local sandlot league. They team fared well, and Cambria made a few dollars on the deal.

And as if he *still* didn't have enough to do, Cambria branched out once again into the world of hockey, and he set his sights on Carlin's Park.

Started in 1919 by John J. Carlin, Liberty Heights Park, as it was first known, quickly became Carlin's Park to thousands of happy children and adults in the greater Baltimore area. Like Glen Echo Park in far northwest Washington, D.C., Carlin's became one of the most beloved amusement parks, not only in Baltimore but also on the East Coast. Carlin was an inveterate tinkerer, always pushing to improve. Every season, new rides and attractions were added or refreshed, and the improvements attracted large crowds. In one warm weekend in May 1921, the park had nearly 20,000 visitors, and Carlin's continued to grow into the 1930s and 1940s. From teacups to swings to shooting galleries to milk bottle tosses, there was a ride or a game to delight everyone.[38]

In 1931, Carlin opened *Iceland,* the city's first indoor ice skating rink. At first a ballroom and roller skating arena, Carlin turned it into an ice skating rink with a seating capacity of 3,000 to promote winter attendance. It became one of his biggest attractions. A Prep School hockey league was formed, featuring schools like Mt. Saint Joseph's, McDonough, and Gilman competing on a bi-weekly basis. On several occasions, the legendary Sonja Henie performed there to sellout crowds.[39]

Another major drawing card for Iceland was the play of the semi-pro Baltimore Orioles, named, of course, after the hometown International League O's. Playing the likes of the U.S. Coast Guard Cutters, the Baltimore Blades, and the Clippers, this "rough and tumble" style of hockey became a huge gate attraction on one hand and a big headache on the other. On one memorable night in 1933, an Orioles game ended in a huge fist fight. The police were forced to use fire extinguishers on both the fans and the players. The fights became all too common an occurrence at these upper-level games.

Cambria was asked to be the president of the inaugural Iceland Hockey League, which he accepted with gusto. The teams were made up of predominantly college level players. Meetings were arranged with the team managers to set up the rules to govern the new league. The rink was smaller than regulation, so allowances needed to be made for shooting.[40] Teams were made up from Walbrook, University of Maryland Dental School, Forest Park, Green Springs Valley, Johns Hopkins, and Mt. Washington. With practice beginning in November 1931 and Walbrook beating Green Springs Valley, 7–1, in the opening game on Monday, December 15, the season ran through April 1932. The level of play was fast and spirited, with some fisticuffs, but nothing to rival the level of animosity of the pro teams.

All seemed to go well. For a while.

President Cambria was forced to sing for his supper when in late March 1932, he received a formal protest from the University of Maryland Dental School team of a game won by Walbrook. Maryland alleged that an official interfered with one of their goals. In a letter sent to both teams, Cambria ruled that both Walbrook and Maryland had signed an agreement letter that stated both teams would abide by the decisions of the referee and, as such, he (Cambria) had no authority to overturn the decision.[41]

Cambria's literary skills were tested once again as he weighed into the fray concerning Baltimore's blue laws. In April of 1932, in a resolution sent to all the members of all the teams and their representative clubs, Cambria stated:

> Ice Hockey league competition, as conducted by the Iceland Hockey League during the past winter, provides Baltimoreans with clean sport. Other cities where the ice game flourished permit Sunday matches and I can think of no sane reason why Baltimore should be denied the privilege of doing the same. Of course, the Iceland League's plans for next winter are indefinite at this time, but we will be back on the ice and the members will show by their ballots that they favor the repel of the present law.[42]

Cambria didn't have long to wait. The vote to repeal the Sunday blue laws took place on May 2 and passed by a resounding margin on May 3.[43]

And, as if he *still* didn't have enough to do, Cambria was approached by Baltimore officials wanting to establish a box lacrosse team to play in an East Coast circuit. He thought better of it.

1932

At the winter meetings in December of 1931, Joe Cambria applied for and was granted entry into the Class-B Central League. He adamantly told the *Baltimore Sun*, "If I'm not in the Central league, I won't be in the Middle Atlantic league."[44]

Always looking for a greater revenue stream, in the Central League he was assured of a larger audience. The league officials welcomed him with enthusiasm because, in a frightening parallel to the coronavirus pandemic of 2020, the Depression forced almost all the major-league teams to end their affiliations with and financial support of minor-league teams. When Joe Cambria started in 1929, there were 26 leagues with 183 teams. By 1933, it had shrunk to a meager 14 leagues and only 101 teams. The minor leagues would suffer further losses during the peak war years of 1943 to 1945.

Ever optimistic, Cambria put a good team on the field. He named Tony Citrano (!) manager of the now Youngstown Buckeyes. Led by the league-leading Babe Phelps once again (.372 batting average, 199 hits, 26 home runs), the Buckeyes placed fourth in a six-team league. By the end of the year, two teams, Akron and South Bend, would disband, and Cambria would sell the Youngstown club.

Nineteen thirty-two would neither begin nor end well for Cambria with his relations with Commissioner Landis. In January, Cambria was called on the carpet by three young players—Charlie Dingler, James Boswell, and Jimmy Wallach—who claimed Cambria and the Youngstown team owed them two months' salary. Clark Griffith acted as a witness for Joe Cambria in the case.[45]

James Boswell, pitching for Hagerstown in 1931–1932, claimed that Cambria illegally suspended him and did not pay him from June through September. The synopsis of the case was this:

For unknown legal reasons, Boswell was unable to play in West Virginia. Cambria knew this when Boswell was contracted in 1931 and was assigned to play in York with the White Roses. York returned him to Cambria. Since six of the 12 teams in the league were in West Virginia, and there were negotiations in effect to move the team to Parkersburg, Cambria had no alternative but to release him; however, he did not "release" him from his contract. He claimed that he suspended Boswell and then released him three days later, telling his team secretary to notify the proper authorities.

No such notification occurred, according to league records.

Boswell further charged that his contract originally stipulated he be paid $225; however, Cambria claimed he didn't have a fresh contract at the time, used a contract from some other player, changed the money amount to $200, and both parties agreed and signed the contract; however, Cambria neglected to have Boswell initial the money change, thereby making the alteration null in court.

Cambria did not want to give Boswell an outright release because, he claimed, "he had a lot of money tied up in him" (which was later found to be false), and Cambria was hopeful that Boswell's legal situation would resolve itself and Boswell could continue to pitch for him because "he was a pretty fair player."

None of this sat well with Landis, who reprimanded Cambria and made him pay back salary to Boswell for the aforementioned months of non-service at the $225 price tag.

Cambria, playing the aggrieved owner, stated in a letter:

> I have been associated with baseball since 1911 and I am ready to take the downs with the ups. I think my record shows that. But Judge Landis has certainly made it hard for me. First of all, in 1931, my club was fined $100 for not answering letters promptly; then when South Bend blew up with salaries unpaid, four of us club owners had to attend to the matter of $1200 in salaries, and now, to cap the climax, the Judge rules that I owe pitcher Jim Boswell salary from June 27 to September 13 after I suspended him.
>
> I won't go into each case separately—but I will say that Landis, who is reported to have said that "the minors would have to shift for themselves" is adding to their troubles, at least he has to mine. A minor league owner who sticks now deserves a Carnegie medal, but this rule seems to be to award him with a stiff fine or tack an assessment on him of some kind. It is downright discouraging.[46]

More run-ins with Landis were yet to come.

So Cambria runs a hockey league in the winter of 1931–1932, runs a semi-pro basketball team in 1932, owns and manages two baseball teams simultaneously, and in the winter, runs a football team while promoting boxing, wrestling and soccer matches at Bugle Field. What's left to do?

Buy another baseball team!

Making good on his "if you can't beat 'em, join 'em" promise, Cambria bought the Negro League Baltimore Black Sox from part-time saloon owner George Rossiter and took over as owner and general manager in April of 1932. They were to compete in Cum Posey's newly formed East-West League.

One of the first things he did was to completely renovate neglected Bugle Field. With the aid of steam shovels,[47] Cambria leveled out the infield and outfield (making it better for football and soccer) and built a bigger covered grandstand to seat 3,000, a clubhouse with showers, a press box, and for the *coup de grace*, installed lights for night baseball.[48]

As they say in gangster movies, Joe Cambria probably "knew a guy" because he was able to get the State Highway authorities to make repairs to Loney's Lane, which was renamed Edison Highway, repave Federal Street, and expand his parking capacity, making it more palatable for auto traffic and public transportation.[49]

Always the inveterate showman, Cambria went out and purchased a pair of ponies, outfitted them with signs announcing the Sox's home games, and paraded them around downtown Baltimore.[50]

It was propitious that he took care to revamp Bugle Field because it got a lot of work. The Buckeyes, the Bugles, and the Black Sox all worked out at the field. The Bugles and the Sox regularly worked out and fraternized together, something unheard-of at the time.

Even before Cambria came on board, changes occurred. George Rossiter fired manager Frank Warfield and hired Dick Lundy to pilot the team. Even though the Washington Pilots hired him to manage their team, Warfield was understandably miffed and vowed revenge.[51]

Cambria, with the aid of new manager Dick Lundy, set about to put a competitive team on the field, but it was tough going at first. Lundy would play shortstop, and several other holdovers from last year's team stayed on. Adding to Lundy's difficulties, the team could not acquire players by trade. The best players in the East were under contract, and the best professional teams not in the East-West League had formed the Southern League. It was next to impossible to pry players away from other East-West or Southern League clubs.[52]

Nonetheless, Lundy worked diligently to field a competitive team for their newly minted franchise. Lundy, relying on his connections in the Negro Leagues, and Cambria, relying on his knowledge of the independent and sandlot teams, cobbled together a team of hustling rookies and wily veterans. Lundy was able to lure away players from the Brooklyn Royal Giants, the Pittsburgh Crawfords, and the Harlem Stars. Cambria and Lundy discovered Lefty Holmes, pitching for the Cuban House of David, and Dizzy Cooke, starting for the Norfolk Pennsylvania Red Caps.[53]

Things went well for Cambria and the Black Sox for the first half of the season. For the week of May 16–21, the Black Sox led the East-West League, Youngstown led the Central League, and the Bugles led the Baltimore Semi-Pro league.[54] Frank Warfield, ex–Sox manager, exacted his revenge upon the Sox by winning the first series against them, but the Sox settled down and began winning. Even with young and relatively inexperienced players, the Sox managed to play respectable ball. They were third in stolen bases, second in home runs, but fifth in runs scored. They were second in fielding percentage and committed the fewest errors in the League.[55] By the halfway point in the season, they were 15–6, in second place behind Detroit, who were 20–6.[56]

Then the bottom fell out.

The Depression had taken its toll on everything in America, including baseball and especially the Negro Leagues. By June 1, the league was on the verge of collapse. The *Baltimore Afro-American* stated: "Lack of patronage has hit the entire circuit from Detroit to Washington and not a single club has been able to cover up on the expenses necessary to promote the games."[57]

Consequently, in the first week of June, in an all-night session in Philadelphia, the club owners were forced to institute some rather Draconian measures to try to ensure the survival of the league.

The club owners instituted three strong measures:

1. The clubs would make "drastic cuts in salaries and overhead operating expenses." Players would be paid from shares of the gate receipts, and all players were free agents.
2. The team's schedules would be revised, meaning the "discontinuance … of everyday baseball."
3. The league would no longer employ "monthly salaried umpires."[58]

The Detroit Wolves merged with the Homestead Grays, the Pittsburgh Crawfords entered the league to shore it up, and the Cuban Stars left the league and played independent ball for the rest of the season.[59] Since everyone was unsure of when any games would be played next, weekly averages and statistics were discontinued.[60]

Joe Cambria's Black Sox were in the lead by the time this whole brouhaha was resolved and were declared the winners of the first half at the end of June. But that did little to salve the wounds. With the contracts in essence torn up, players jumped to other teams with abandon, trying to eke out an existence for the rest of the summer. With no real organizational structure, the East-West League folded, and the Homestead Grays were given the championship.

None of this deterred "Mr. Never Say Die" Cambria. He was determined to see the season through to the end. Even without the attraction of a bona fide star, the young, hustling team Lundy and Cambria had put together were accomplished enough to survive financially, predominantly by barnstorming. (It also helped tremendously to have rent-free Bugle Field on which to play.) With Cambria's myriad connections, they played numerous semi-pro teams up and down the East Coast. They came back home July 6 for the much-anticipated yearly match with the traveling House of David team. Always a gate attraction, the Davidites, stacked with a cadre of former major leaguers like "Pepper" Martin and "Jumbo" Barrett, easily dispatched the Sox, 12–9, to the delight of a respectable crowd.[61] *The Baltimore Sun* couldn't help but have a field day with the game: "Joe Cambria assured us last night that the Davidites will bring their beards and everything with them. There should be a special clause in the rules to the effect that any bouncing ball that becomes lost behind a set of face foliage will go simply as a two-base hit."[62]

Cambria ended his first year of black baseball ownership in grand fashion. In mid–September, he arranged for a three-way series with the Washington Pilots and the New York Black Yankees to decide who would be the strongest black team in the country.[63] Although the Sox did not possess a name player like Mule Suttles of the Pilots or George "Tubby" Scales (who became a player/coach/manager for the Baltimore Elite Giants), the youthful Sox played with determination, spirit and cohesion. When Dick Lundy took over the Sox, he told Bill Gibson of the *Afro-American* that "he would have probably one of the youngest clubs in the game, but that it would be a club of hustlers."[64]

And hustle they did!

In the September three-way series, they beat the Yankees three games out of four, and the Pilots two games out of three to lay claim to the "championship."[65]

If that wasn't enough, P.T. Barnum Cambria pulled out all the stops. He expanded the seating in Bugle Field by 1,000 seats and instituted "premium" seating: 500 seats at $1, 400 seats at 75 cents, 2,000 seats at 50 cents, and another 1,000 seats at 35 cents.[66] All of this was for his annual series with his white "All-Star" team playing against the Black Sox. He even hired a "rodeo" and a "cow-girl band" to perform between innings and before the games. Needless to say, a capacity crowd jammed the ballpark.[67]

Emotions ran high for this seven-game matchup. However, an unhappy crowd of Sox fans watched as the All-Stars confounded them in the opening doubleheader, 9–6 and 7–4. The fans began to doubt almost immediately. Cambria had stacked the All-Stars with such big names as future Hall of Famer Hack Wilson (Cubs), Boston Braves ace Fred Frankhouse, and the mellifluously named Van Lingle Mungo (Dodgers).

Dick Lundy went out and stacked his own deck by enlisting the aid of future Hall of Famers Mule Suttles (Pilots) and Jud Wilson (Crawfords). These two fence busters were just what the doctor ordered. The Sox came back to win the next five games in convincing fashion, while the Stars won the season's final game, 13–9. Everyone went home happy, and everyone made a few bucks in the deal.[68]

For his Herculean efforts on behalf of baseball in Baltimore, the *Afro-American* gave Cambria a ringing endorsement:

> Few fans know that had it not been for the rescue work of Manager Cambria, Baltimore would have been without a baseball team during the season past. If members of the group ever go into sports promotion on a large scale they can learn many valuable lessons from this man, whose dealings with athletes and the paying public, as far as this writer can ascertain, have always been above board.[69]

All of this stemmed from an incident that occurred the previous July. Joe Cambria was promoting a boxing and wrestling match at Bugle Field. When showtime arrived, the crowd was paltry at best. People were just not coming out to watch sporting matches of any kind in 1932. But instead of canceling the matches as he was advised, Cambria opened up the gates and gave the matches away for free. He paid the athletes out of his pocket, Uncle Sam didn't get any tax money, and the crowd went away happy. In his column, Bill Gibson wrote, "More promoters of the Cambria type would be a boon to local sports. Call it showmanship or what you will, it's a refreshing note in times like these."[70]

Lest we forget, Joe Cambria had a lot of balls in the air besides the Black Sox. The Bugles team was still his baby, and they continued to play well throughout the season.

He still had the Youngstown team to look after, although he would soon unburden himself of that. He was able to officially sign Gordon "Babe" Phelps to a big-league contract with the Senators. Phelps took his .382 batting average to spring training and was traded to the Cubs in 1933.

Of greater significance was his signing of Ysmael Morales, outfielder for Alex Pompez's New York Cuban Stars. Since his beginnings in organized ball, Cambria was keenly aware of the talent that resided in the Negro Leagues and the traveling "Cuban" teams, having played against them with the Bugles for the last four years. The Cuban Stars were the most solid of the many "Cuban" independent teams, and Alex Pompez was surely Cambria's promotional counterpart in the Negro Leagues. Morales would be his first big Cuban find.

Joe Cambria signed him from Pompez in April of 1932 and allowed him to finish out the year with the Stars in order to work on his English language skills. Morales was sent directly to the Senators for spring training in 1933.[71] Morales did not stick with the parent club and was assigned to the Albany Senators. He became a loyal friend and "bird dog" for Cambria, recommending that he sign Roberto Estalella out of the sugar cane fields of Cuba.

1933

Nineteen thirty-three dawned like the same nightmare of the year before. The Depression was the worst it ever was. Lines of people waiting for food had grown longer. Hundreds of farmers, angered by Congressional inaction, gathered in the countrysides. And Congress was as divided as ever with gridlock.

Hope arrived in the form of President Franklin Delano Roosevelt, who won in a landslide over incumbent Herbert Hoover, whom everyone blamed for the Depression. Sworn into office on March 4, the very next day he declared a "bank holiday," freezing transactions and giving institutions a week to regroup. The following week, he initiated his promised "New Deal," which established programs that would put thousands of able-bodied men and women back to work again, which provided integrity and self-worth to everyone.

The ever-optimistic Mr. Cambria, seemingly nonplussed by the economic chaos, doubled down yet again. In February, he took $7,500 of Bugle Coat and Apron Company profits to complete a deal with Chicago Cubs owner Bill Veeck, Sr., for the ownership of the AA Albany Senators of the International League.

Cambria was in the deep water now, and sportswriter C.M. Gibbs of the *Baltimore Sun* said as much: "So, Joe Cambria of Baltimore becomes the new owner of the Albany (N.Y.) club of the International League. That's quite a jump up the ladder for Joe and he will find the job somewhat different from that of Bugle Field. Cambria is going into the affair with his eyes wide open and so he will have no complaint to make if the going becomes rough."[72]

Joe Cambria cemented the relationship with Albany by signing a working agreement with his friend Clark Griffith, but still ran the club independently. Knowing this was going to take a lot of work, Cambria officially divested himself of the Youngstown club.

First, he set about to refurbish aging Hawkins Stadium, home of the Senators. The seats got a new coat of paint, the infield was reconditioned, and new money-changing machines were placed outside the park for the fans' convenience.[73]

Second, he announced that they would have two separate training camps: one in Norfolk for the veterans and one at Bugle Field in Baltimore for rookies and others. Cambria transferred many of the old Youngstown players over to Albany, at least for a tryout.[74]

Third, Cambria was served with a big dish of reality. He thought he could offer all the returning veterans lower-class money. That did not fly. Over a dozen players refused to sign unless they received either the new league minimum or substantially more money, and many wished to be traded outright. Cambria and his manager, Bill McCorry, received immediate player help in the form of first baseman Harry Taylor from the Cubs and promises of help from several other major-league clubs.[75]

By way of recap, let us remember: Joe Cambria has a basketball team to manage and a hockey league to oversee. What more could he do?

Boxing.

For someone as prolific as Cambria, this would have been an easy call. Boxing during the Depression was one of the biggest and more affordable forms of entertainment for the weary, job-starved populace. Popularized by the great "theater of the mind," radio, boxing had always been a big draw for the working class, and Baltimore was and has always been a working-class town. The St. Louis Browns' famous slogan, "first in booze, first in shoes and last in the American League," was more so praise to the health of their commerce, rather than the lackluster performance of the perennial cellar-dwelling Browns.

Baltimore, by the same token, from the turn of the century through the 1930s, exuded the same pride in its commerce. Thousands of people toiled in the Bethlehem Steel and Standard Oil processing industries. The Port of Baltimore was and still is in the top 20 percent of major ports in the United States. Before and after Prohibition, Baltimore had literally hundreds of breweries and distilleries. Where St. Louis had the corner on beer and shoes, Baltimore was number one in whiskey and straw hats. General Motors had a major vehicle manufacturing plant in Canton from 1935 until 2005.[76]

But Cambria was in a bind as to where to host his boxing promotions. He was renting out Bugle Field to almost everyone in the city, and it was a little overstressed. During the winter months, it hosted soccer, some boxing, and prep school lacrosse. Starting in April, Albany would be there for spring training, along with his Black Sox, which he still owned. Once the baseball season started in May, the field was in constant use between his Black Sox and a full schedule of sandlot teams. In the winter months, the field became a football Mecca. (Research in all of the Baltimore newspapers indicates that Cambria did not have his Bugles baseball team in 1933.)

Consequently, his fighting promotions, which he had begun several years earlier, had to be expanded. He bought a new indoor ring being built called Charlotte Hall, at Greenmount Avenue and 25 Street. He would sometimes reschedule his boxing matches from Bugle Field to Charlotte Hall when the weather was too cold or rainy. Up until the season fully got underway, he confined himself to promoting amateur bouts, along with a few "rasslin'" shows, and made a bit of a profit in the deal.[77]

Cambria, along with manager McCorry, worked hard to cull together a respectable Senators team for their April opener. But try as they might, they struggled. Albany ace Johnny Prudhomme's debut performance drew a lukewarm response from the Baltimore public and press alike, many feeling he just "didn't have much on the ball."[78]

Cambria did everything he could to attract customers. He instituted a Ladies' Night with free admission for the girls. He went so far as to give away a car on the last night of the Senators' first homestand,[79] but to no avail. A bright spot did appear in the firmament in August, when the Senators fired on all cylinders to trounce Rochester, 22–9. But wins were few and far between. The Senators limped along to a dismal seventh-place finish, going 80–84, 22 games off the lead.[80]

In April, the Central League, which Cambria had just left late in December, disbanded and, in a move of either magnanimity or stupidity, Cambria agreed to take over the Springfield club of the Class-C Middle Atlantic League. The MAL had agreed to take in two orphaned teams from the Central. Springfield at least fared better than the lowly Senators, going 67–64 for a respectable fourth-place finish.

The Eastern Colored League had disbanded late in 1932, and plans were underway to begin a new league. Joe Cambria's nightmare 1933 season would begin with a snub. He was not invited to the new owners' meeting spearheaded by Cum Posey and Gus Greenlee for the establishment of this new "association."[81] Rumors circulated that Baltimore was "out."

"Black Sox Not to Disband" shouted the headline of the *Baltimore Afro-American* in February. Cambria made it clear that he would "continue to stay in Baltimore and will put a hustling Black Sox team on the field."[82] To further dispel the rumors, he set about work once again to refurbish Bugle Field. Maryland Park, the Sox's former home, was being dismantled. Cambria quickly bought up all he could from the park and used it to enlarge the grandstands and the bleachers. He also added showers in the clubhouse and a press box.[83]

Having shown that he was serious, Joe Cambria was able to arrange a meeting in May with Posey and Greenlee to iron out their differences. The meeting was successful, and the Sox were admitted to the new Negro National league.[84]

With only a week to put together a team, Cambria got busy fast. His old manager, Dick Lundy, jumped ship to take over the Philadelphia Stars. So Cambria acquired the services of former Brooklyn Royal Giants great Jess Hubbard. They did their best, but in the end they could only cobble together an aggregate of older players a little long in the tooth, as it were. One veteran in particular, Joe Lewis, was the last active member of the 1913 Black Sox.[85] At least they had a team.

Things were going well … temporarily.

Cambria received a poisoned epistle in the form of an injunction, filed by lawyer E. Everett Lane on behalf of a group headed by former Black Sox catcher James B. Hairstone. Evidently, former owner George Rossiter (and, by association, new owner Joe Cambria) had failed to file income taxes for 1930; consequently, his group charter, known as the Baltimore Black Sox Baseball and Exhibition Company, was forfeit. Hairstone's suit was granted, and he took over usage of the name "Baltimore Black Sox."[86]

Joe Cambria no longer had the use of the team name. "The Black Sox" would play independent and semi-pro ball, while he renamed his team "The Sox." For the summer of 1933, Baltimore would have two Sox, explained with tongue firmly in cheek by Bill Gibson of the *Afro-American*:

> In answer to a half a hundred inquiries regarding the identity of Baltimore's two professional baseball teams, the pillar explains that the city literally has a pair of sox.

The local entry in the National Association of Baseball Clubs is the Baltimore Sox team, sponsored by Joe Cambria, local sportsman and businessman. This club has Bugle Field on the Edison Highway as its home park and is managed by Jess Hubbard. The Baltimore Black Sox (notice the black) are not affiliated with any baseball organization and operates at Maryland Park. The Club is incorporated with James B. (Harry) Hairstone as president and general manager. The club revives the tradition of the original Black Sox, which passed out of the hands of George Rossiter two seasons ago.

So, you see, the city has two clubs—the Sox and the Black Sox. You're welcome, I'm sure.[87]

The 1933 season was dismal at best. Because of the lack of contracts, players kept jumping to other teams in the middle of the season, and teams were stealing players outright with monetary enticements. Teams were having a very difficult time booking games due to the unscrupulous nature of two booking agents, Nat Strong and Ed Gottlieb. These two men controlled all the bookings between both the Eastern and Western Negro Leagues and some of the white leagues as well.

Cumberland Posey, Hall of Fame manager and owner of the Homestead Grays and one of the most respected men in the Negro Leagues, penned a letter to the *Pittsburgh Courier* excoriating these two pariahs:

> It is said that Strong and Gottlieb control the booking of all the white clubs of the East, and any club not wanting to deal through them are blacklisted East of Harrisburg.
>
> No Colored clubs are making any money under the present arrangements. Colored players playing co-plan ball are not averaging $125 a month. They are paying their own room and board on the road. Such men as Joe Cambria … who owns the Baltimore Sox are disgusted with seeing the first ten percent of their games go into the pockets of men who do nothing but ridicule colored baseball. There is no defense for any who seek to uphold these men.
>
> When has a colored club in the East made $1000 on a Sunday since Strong and Gottlieb controlled it? When have they made $500?[88]

The last shining hope for this tepid season came with the annual Sox-All-Stars game held at Bugle Field. The All-Star team was an amalgam of players taken from the Orioles and Joe Cambria's Albany club, peppered with a few big-league players. Cambria called in home run slugger Hack Wilson from the Brooklyn Dodgers and another big hitter, Babe Phelps. Phelps had just finished the 1933 season with Albany and was sold by Cambria to the Cubs for $10,000.

The games were all played on Sundays to bring in the most fans. As the series went on, Cambria continued to shore up the All-Stars with talent. He got his friend, Clark Griffith, to let him use Joe Kuhel, Buddy Myer, and Cecil Travis, although Travis pulled out at the last minute. In lieu of Travis, Cambria got Julius "Moose" Solters from the Orioles, who almost pulled out the International League batting championship with a stellar .360 average.

For the third series, Cambria pulled out all the stops to bring in a gate attraction, and he found it in the form of the legendary Honus Wagner. A legend of the Deadball Era, the 59-year-old Wagner still had a sparkle in his step. "Hans" would play a couple of innings at his customary shortstop position, then retire to pilot the club.[89]

Cambria almost pulled off one of his greatest *coups*. The *Baltimore Sun* reported that he managed to draft one of the all-time greats of the game, future Hall of Famer and center fielder Oscar Charleston, and pitcher Jim Willis to play part of the series; however, box scores from the series indicate that neither of them made it into the series.[90]

With Dickey Seay and Jack Dunn sparking the offense, the Sox fought hard throughout the series. The two clubs seesawed back and forth, with the All-Stars taking a 5–1 advantage by the first of October. But the Sox rallied back to knot the series at five apiece, eventually winning the series, seven out of 12 games.[91]

Cambria ended 1933 on high notes. Through trading and selling players throughout the year, he managed to end his first year in high class baseball with only a small deficit, which he quickly erased by selling four players in December for $14,000.[92] He was enjoying everything baseball. Richard Conners of *The Sporting News* said, "He can best be described as a cross between a practical baseball man and a red-hot fan…. He roots like a leather-lunged bleacherite and is in seventh heaven when his team wins."[93]

After only one season, Joe Cambria received offers to buy the team. Interests in Albany made him a $40,000 offer, which he refused, placing his price firmly at $75,000. Al Mamaux, manager of the Newark Bears, patched together a conglomerate of himself and five others to pool $3,000 apiece and offered Cambria a down payment, with installments for the remainder of the year. Cambria, of course, flatly refused, insisting on a lump sum payment. Mamaux's $18,000 offer was almost twice what Cambria paid for the team, but he was unwavering in his commitment to producing a winner.[94] Throughout the winter months, he continued to wheel and deal players and reappointed Bill McCorry as manager for the 1934 season.

1934

The year 1934 dawned tremulously in the United States. A year's worth of Roosevelt's New Deal saw unemployment lowered to 21.7 percent, down from the all-time high of nearly 25 percent the year before. The Dust Bowl would kill millions of livestock and displace millions of people. Adolf Hitler was ominously proclaimed *Führer und Reichskanzler* of Germany.

The year would also not bode well for baseball in general and for our Mr. Cambria in particular. Those people lucky enough to procure jobs within the New Deal programs were keeping their noses and shoulders to their respective wheels. Baseball games became the weekend diversion from their weekday toils, and the radio would be their only affordable ticket to the ball parks. Attendance figures at sporting events plummeted, and nowhere was this more evident than in Negro League baseball.

Determined to keep Black baseball going during the Depression, the club owners of the Negro National League met in Philadelphia on Saturday, February 17, 1934. However, Cambria failed to show up. In a letter to league organizer Gus Greenlee, he maintained that he was never notified of the meeting place or time. Cambria was sincere in his desire to join the league, saying, "the League can be organized to get everybody going along together. I feel that we should be all through with losing money now, and we ought to have a fine organization."[95] He submitted his application to join the league, only to find out that the majority of his best players had decided to join other teams. He immediately suspended his application until he could ascertain the claims of all the players.[96] A special meeting was then called on April 21 for the purpose of listening to Baltimore's application; again, neither Cambria nor any of his management attended the meeting. Consequently, his application was rejected. The league declared that all of the members of last year's teams were free agents and magnanimously allowed them to play on a Baltimore team, providing their games did not interfere with any officially sanctioned League games.[97]

Cambria did what he always did: he took those players who had remained loyal to him from last year's team and again cobbled together a team with promising semi-pro and sandlot players. The experiment was a disaster. The team lost their first game to the white Harrisburg Senators, 20–1.[98] With the writing firmly etched on the blackboard, Cambria had no choice. He sold the team to Chester, Pennsylvania, boxing promoter Jack Ferrell, folded up his tents, and walked away.

As the old saying goes, "when one door closes, another one opens." It may have been propitious for Cambria to give up the Black Sox, for he needed to pay attention to his Albany team. "Salesman Joe," as he was being called by the scribes, had developed a great reputation within the community. They hailed him as "one of the most amazing newcomers in the ranks, a man who stepped into the leading minor league and [made] money his first year. And in a Depression year at that."[99]

Evidence of Cambria's trading legerdemain was found in the Babe Phelps saga. He found Phelps on the sandlots of Odenton, MD, a suburb of Baltimore, and gave him to Clark Griffith for $0, as per his original unwritten agreement with Griffith. Phelps played with Hagerstown and Albany until Cambria traded him to the Atlanta Crackers for $1,500. When the Cubs started showing interest, Cambria bought him back, then promptly sold him back to the Cubs for $10,000 and first baseman Harry Taylor, whom Cambria immediately sold to the Hollywood Stars for $8,000, for a grand total of $18,000 in money for a player he had originally signed for $1,500![100]

Cambria continued his commitment to talent development. During the season, he formed a school for young talent in Albany. High schoolers and other rookies would train in the town's Hawkins Stadium while the main team was on the road.[101] He started this trend early on, in spring training, when he sent the veterans to Martinsville, VA, and the younger players, under the supervision of coach John Weiland, to Barnwell, SC.[102]

The Albany Senators played well and had a respectable season in 1934. They placed fourth in the league (81–72) and made it to the playoffs, losing to Rochester, four games to one. Their lone standout was Fred Sington, who drove in a league-leading 147 runs.

Always a masterful promoter, Cambria found a way to make money even if it meant slaughtering lambs. Call it chutzpah, moxie or just pure salesmanship, he was able to convince the mighty New York Yankees to play a late–April exhibition game against his Senators. The 2,585 excited fans packed into Hawkins Stadium that April 23 to watch Babe Ruth and his Yankees destroy the Senators, 22–6. Ruth hit two home runs and a double, the crowd went wild, and Joe Cambria made money.[103]

Cambria once again garnered the favor of the fans and the national scribes to boot by a show of generosity. Bill Dooly, writing for the *Philadelphia Record* and quoted in *The Sporting News,* stated:

> In remembrance of the times he loitered at the ballpark entrances, without money enough to pay his way in, Cambria is giving the youngsters of Albany a weekly free day. He is throwing the gates open to the kids between the ages of 10 and 13 with no restriction as to numbers every Tuesday. While Cambria is following in the footsteps of many others, the great majority of club owners have been slow to realize that the growing generation offers an easy field

for missionary work. Cambria, therefore, is to be complimented in that while being relatively inexperienced as a magnate in Organized Baseball, he has followed where the vast majority are either too reluctant or too dense to see the need.[104]

Joe Cambria continued to make money with the team, wheeling and dealing players throughout the season. His penchant for exaggeration seemed to grow yearly. It seemed the kids he peddled to the big-league clubs were all "can't miss" or the second coming of Walter Johnson. Two deals stood out, one of which gained him a national reputation.

Mark Filley was a "can't miss" prospect out of diminutive Williams College, a small liberal arts college in Massachusetts. After a three-year varsity record of 20–6, and with an impressive seven-hit shut-out over Williams' nemesis, Amherst College, to win the Little Three crown, Filley was signed by Albany Senators manager Bill McCorry in early 1933. Filley pitched in 16 games with Albany and went 7–4 with seven complete games and a 3.31 ERA.

Spring training of 1934 had not even started when Clark Griffith got word of Filley from none other than enigmatic catcher Moe Berg. Berg had been a Princeton teammate of Filley's college coach, Charlie Caldwell, who alerted Berg of this up and comer. Five thousand dollars was enough to secure his service from Cambria, and off he went to the Nationals' training camp in Biloxi, Mississippi. For a brief time, Filley, who taught Latin, geometry, and algebra at Burr and Burton Seminary in Vermont, and Berg, who was famously fluent in several languages and read newspapers voraciously, could enjoy some intellectual equality and perhaps converse in Latin together!

Filley's one and only appearance in a Nats uniform came on April 19, 1934, against the Red Sox. He pitched to three batters, gave up two hits, threw one wild pitch, and retired one batter before being taken out. With one run scored against him, he left the big leagues with a 27.00 ERA. Filley was sent down to Chattanooga but refused to go down to A ball. He went home instead to begin law studies. He briefly returned to the 1935 Albany team; however, in November, he received a letter from Cambria which said, "Dear Mark; We have made a deal with Galveston of the Texas League, and you are now the property of that ball club. Your release notice is enclosed."

Filley refused again to report, focusing instead on his new law career. Passing the bar exams in 1937, Filley began his practice in Troy. He won the election to become Judge of the Children's Court of Rensselaer County in 1954, spent more than 50 years as a member of the New York State Bar Association, and loved every day of his baseball life.[105]

Whiskers

As mentioned before, Joe Cambria loved a good promotional scheme: Ladies Day, kids' day, car giveaways, advertising ponies, and circus clowns. (One wonders why he never thought about skywriting!) However, one gimmick in particular started him on the road to "P.T. Barnum-ville."

Cambria was always aware of the attraction of the barnstorming teams. He promoted games with his Bugles against the likes of an all-girl baseball team, a Harlem Globetrotters–like Negro leagues team, and of course, the granddaddy of them all, the traveling House of David ball club. In late spring of 1934, Joe Cambria discovered a young pitcher by the name of Allen Wilbert "Bullet Ben" Benson twirling for the Davidites against his Bugles. Benson, who had gone 18–5 for the Davids, was no stranger to organized ball. He had stints with minor-league teams in Waterloo, Akron and Minneapolis between 1927 and 1930, before returning to his first love of farming. But a drought and the Depression had left his South Dakota business unprofitable, so he needed to supplant his income by returning to baseball.[106]

Joe Cambria squired the young man to a private pitching session with Clark Griffith and manager Joe Cronin, who approved of what he saw and bought Benson from Cambria on the spot, making him Cambria's first official outright signing.

Griffith was no stranger to the circus of baseball, and he felt the bewhiskered Benson would be a good gate attraction. Griffith had used the clowning talents of Al Schacht, Nick Altrock, and Germany Schaefer to his advantage for over a decade. Joe Engle, the "P.T. Barnum of the Bushes" at the Nats' AA affiliate in Chattanooga, had famously traded a pitcher for a Christmas turkey, put singing canaries in the grandstands, and once signed a girl pitcher, Jackie Mitchell, who purportedly struck out Babe Ruth and Lou Gehrig in an exhibition game.[107]

Also, Griffith had nothing to lose. He needed more pitching help and was willing to give almost anyone a tryout. The 1933 pennant-winning Senators were now mired in the second division and would end the year in seventh place.

Benson got his first start against the White Sox on August 19, to the derision of the national press. With a beard about a quarter as large as those of Jason Werth and Bryce Harper, he was labeled "pink whiskers," "flowing pink weeds," "mattress-chinned," and "spinach faced." Frank Young, writing in the *Washington Post,* said, "No protests have been made by the Sox yet, but it is expected that Manager Jimmy Dykes will ask that Benson not be allowed to use his whiskers for the hidden ball trick."[108]

Benson went 7⅔ innings before a blister popped on his pitching hand. He gave up nine hits, seven earned runs, and five walks, and recorded four strikeouts. His second outing against the St. Louis Browns on August 26 was a disaster. In two innings, he gave up seven runs, 10 hits, no walks or strikeouts, and one wild pitch before being lifted in the second inning. His major-league career consisted of 9⅔ innings, 19 hits, 13 earned runs, five walks, four strikeouts, an 0–1 record, and a 12.10 ERA.

Needless to say, he was released back to Cambria and the Albany Senators on August 27, but he decided he needed to get back to his wife and his farm. A disappointed Benson told the *Washington Post:*

> I believe I could have made the grade with the Nats but for these danged whiskers. I want to cut 'em off right now, but Mr. Cambria says they make me a drawing card—a sorta circus attraction—and that I've gottah wear 'em for the rest of the season. But I'll tell you one thing, they're comin' off just as soon as the season ends and when I report to Albany next spring, I'll be looking like the rest of the gang. I know how it is. The players thought I was trying to break in their game on account of my whiskers instead of my merit. I had to wear the beard to play with the House of David team—and jobs were hard to get when I landed that one—and, when Mr. Griffith brought me here, he insisted that I keep my whiskers, for a little while at least.[109]

Benson returned to Albany in 1935 but was assigned to the Harrisburg Senators in the NY-Penn League. On August 10, he suffered a fracture at the base of his spine in a collision at home plate against the Binghamton Barons, and to add further insult to injury, lost the game in a 3–1 decision. Benson never played ball again after that. He retired to his farm in Hurley, South Dakota, where he passed away at age 94 in November 1999.[110]

Hoping to make up for Allen Benson's shortcoming on the hill, Cambria decided to send Griffith another "can't miss" prospect in the form of an 18-year-old phenom in the Blue Ridge League named Reese Diggs. ("Faster than Walter Johnson" was one of Cambria's favorite expressions.) Griffith liked what he saw, signed him to a contract, then sent him out west to pitch batting practice and get "seasoned up."[111]

Aside from Diggs' wildness, acting manager Nick Altrock thought he had "the right stuff," and the Nats were in desperate need of relievers. But alas, it was not to be. Diggs pitched four games for the Senators late in September. Officially, he went 1–2, with a 6.75 ERA, 26 hits, 17 runs, 16 earned runs, three home runs, 15 walks, and two strikeouts. As with Benson, Diggs was sent back to Joe Cambria in Albany, who, in turn. sent him down to Harrisburg. He pitched in four games in the 1935 season and retired from organized ball.[112]

Cambria had his annual pilgrimage to Commissioner Landis's courtroom carpet in August of 1934. Albeit for an act of generosity, he nearly blew the deal with his big mouth.

Cambria had signed a young player to a $250 contract with Albany. The young man didn't have enough money to move himself and his mother to New York and appealed to Cambria, who magnanimously gave him extra money to assist in the move. For some unknown reason, the young player spilled the beans about the extra money, and Cambria was summoned by Landis to explain. Upon hearing the argument, Landis conceded that the young man was indeed ungrateful, but Cambria had overpaid him nonetheless, which was against the rules, and he fined Cambria $500.

Cambria felt he was the aggrieved party in this suit and began to harangue Landis, pleading that "he wasn't a baseball aristocrat rolling up in a Rolls-Royce but just a 'covered wagon man.'" He wanted his punishment tempered with some mercy; however, he went on to intimate that Landis had a good car and a good salary and all that goes with it. Pausing to catch his breath was all that Landis needed. Landis promptly rose from his chair and informed Mr. Cambria that his statements were "irrelevant, immaterial and incompetent" and fined him the $500 anyway. The "covered wagon man" reference made it into the *New York Times* and stuck with Cambria for the rest of his life.[113]

Despite all of Cambria's run-ins with Landis and his questionable prospects, he was beginning to get an outstanding reputation within the baseball community. Joe Donovan of the *Newark Ledger,* quoted in *The Sporting News*, intimated that Joe Cambria was destined for a spot in the majors:

> Cambria hasn't been in baseball as long as some of his league competitors, but he is no sap who [is] tossing money about, paying wild prices. To be more specific, he's giving other high-finance executives a lesson in operating a Double-A baseball club. With all his clowning, Cambria is a serious-minded, hard-boiled baseball businessman—a man who gets what he wants, whether it's cleaning dirty collars or a hustling ball club. This year he bobbed up with a flock of players, starting the season with a club that couldn't finish 7th in a Married Men's league. After a month of playing, Cambria snatched players from Pittsburgh, Brooklyn, Washington, Boston and even the Giants. He made the most of the job and today his club is in fourth place with a good chance of making the play-off grade.[114]

Cambria's reputation got around the majors, so much so that by September, he had received offers from two clubs, one as an executive and one as a scout. Baseball was still a sideline for him, though, as the laundry business was expanding and getting more profitable.[115] However, that was all about to change.

Before the end of the season, Joe Cambria would always wander back to Baltimore for his annual Black Sox-All-Stars series, and this year, he went out of his way to make it a spectacular event. The Black Sox relied on the arms of Laymon "Corner Pocket" Yokely and Phil "Fish" Cockrell for their moundsmen, whereas Cambria, managing the All-Stars, stacked the team with a ton of major-league talent. He called upon his former players Babe Phelps, Jake Powell, and Hack Wilson to add the needed punch to the batting order. He enlisted the aid of Cliff Melton, Baltimore Orioles and future New York Giants pitcher, to be his ace of the staff, and acquired the service of New York Yankees second baseman Don Heffner. He also hired "the Clown Prince of Baseball," Nick Altrock of the Washington Senators, to perform his zany acts for the crowds.[116]

But he saved the best for last.

Always the showman, Joe Cambria was able to convince the Dean Brothers, Dizzy and Paul, to pitch the entire October 18 night game. The Deans (who, like Cambria, had endured their share of run-ins with Landis) were fresh off the St. Louis Cardinals' breathtaking 1934 World Series win against the Detroit Tigers. Charter members of the notorious "Gas House Gang," the Deans did not disappoint the crowd, beating the Black Sox handily.[117]

The biggest announcements of the 1934 season came from Griffith himself. Cash strapped and sinking to the bottom of the division, Griffith knew it was time for a change: "We have gone far enough with veteran material. The time has come when our ball club must be gone over in virtually every respect. We need at least two new outfielders, perhaps two young catchers and a host of young pitchers. Picking up something worthwhile will be difficult, but we must acquire the youngsters."[118]

Just like the pre–COVID 19 Baltimore Orioles, Griffith decided to "clean house," dump the aging, high-priced veterans, and head to the farm. Griffith looked to both Engle and Cambria to supply him with fresh, young players eager to play and hustle. Cambria responded by sending him outfielders Jake Powell and Fred Sington from Albany, and Engle sent three pitchers—Orville Armbruster, Leon Pettit, and Sammy Cohn—a catcher, Sam Holbrook, and a second baseman, John Mihalic, from Chattanooga. Much to everyone's surprise, all with the exception of Armbruster stuck with the parent club.[119]

The most surprising factor in Griffith's change in direction, however, came from Adolfo Luque. Luque is considered one of the greatest pitchers in the history of Cuban baseball and is enshrined is every Hall of Fame except Cooperstown. "Dolf" began his career in the Cuban National Leagues in 1911. Word of his pitching prowess quickly spread, and he was signed to the Boston Braves in 1914. He spent 20 years in the big leagues, all in the National League. In 1923 he went 27–8 with an astounding 1.93 ERA. He also spent almost 40 years playing, coaching, and managing in the Cuban winter leagues and often in the Negro Leagues. Fiery and pugnacious, Luque would often respond to racial taunts with vicious beanballs. After his major-league career was over in 1935, he spent time mentoring some of the greats of the 1950s, such as Sal Maglie and Camilo Pascual.

Handcuffed by "King" Carl Hubbell's stupefying screwball and "Prince" Hal Schumacher's deceptive speed, Washington eked out only one win against a dominant New York Giants team in the 1933 World Series. But it was the pitching performance of Luque in the deciding game that set Griffith to pondering. *The Sporting News* said: "Adolfo Luque, the venerable Cuban, proved a superb pitcher in need for the Giants at the finish. Sent in when the Senators for the first time in the series threatened to surge at bat, as they often had during the League Championship campaign, Luque, with his sweeping curve, stopped them cold to get credit for the victory in the decisive contest."[120]

Luque was dominant in relief of Hal Schumacher, giving up only two hits and two walks and striking out five Senators in his 4⅓ innings pitched.

Griffith was not unaware of the prowess of the Cuban players. Every biography of him attests to the fact that in his youth, Griffith managed the first two Cuban players to play in the modern era, Armando Marsáns and Rafael Almeida of the 1911 Cincinnati Reds. Playing for Almendares in 1908, both players were integral in a four out of five-game series win against the Reds in Cuba. Griffith knew also that there was a wealth of talent to be had cheaply on the island, and in 1934, he officially sanctioned Cambria to find him good Cuban players.

The second announcement was sincere but publicity-laden. Babe Ruth had made it known that he wanted a managerial position. Rumors abounded that the Senators, in need of a new manager, were in negotiations. Word on the street was that Ruth was offered $15,000 and a cut of the gate but was holding out for $30,000. Clark Griffith, however, was quick to squelch those rumors, saying, "No, I did not invite [Ruth] to talk over the situation with me today. He came as a casual visitor. Ruth never has been regarded as a managerial possibility here by me, nor will he be so regarded. I greatly respect the Babe as a man and for his great work in the game. He is of managerial timber, I believe."[121]

1935

Nineteen thirty-five started with a flurry of activity for Joe Cambria and for Western Maryland in particular. Thirty baseball men convened at the Hotel Frederick on January 27 to discuss and possibly reorganize the dormant Blue Ridge League. Lying fallow since the Crash of 1930, the Blue Ridge League was one of the oldest organized leagues in baseball, having started in 1915. Cambria was, of course, very familiar with the league, having bought the Hagerstown franchise in 1928 and then moving them to the New York–Penn League in 1931, after the Blue Ridge disbanded.

However, the odds against the reformation of the league were insurmountable. The major stumbling block was the schedule: most of the team owners only wanted to play three days a week. Most of them felt the area was not economically ready for daily baseball. All of the old major-league affiliates were adamant that they play a six-game weekly schedule; consequently, several of them dropped their financial support of the teams.

Joe Cambria, who had promised some support for this old Hagerstown club, had to face some harsh economic reality: he couldn't support Hagerstown along with his Albany and Harrisburg clubs. At a March 3 meeting, the league's fate was sealed. It could not survive. In an op-ed piece in the *Frederick News*, Harry Grayson summed it up:

> Blue Ridge League baseball officials may as well face the issue—the circuit can't go in organized ball this year. Even with a fourth club we can't possibly see how the league can survive. Frank Colley, president of the loop, has pulled every string possible in an effort to get the league back into organized ball, and is firmly convinced it can't be done at this time. [This]

writer has felt from the beginning that the venture was doomed to failure because this section isn't ready economically for professional baseball on a full week basis.[122]

Martinsburg, Frederick, and Hagerstown decided to play independent ball on a three day a week basis throughout the late spring and summer; however, the old Blue Ridge League, which had given Cambria his *entrée* into organized baseball, would be no more. A new Blue Ridge League would organize from 1946 through 1950, but it would be located in North Carolina and Virginia.

Cambria, the quintessential "cockeyed optimist," faced the new season with the same delight as a kid on Christmas morning. Undaunted by the fact that the majors were not going to unlock their optioned players, he stated: "We are not so bad off. We will have a very young ball club, with several fine prospects, and we have, in Al Mamaux, a smart manager. All we need is one big hitter and a second basemen."[123]

New manager Al Mamaux was a Cambria favorite and came with great provenance. He pitched 12 years in the majors, then another nine years with the Newark Bears, Albany rivals in the International League. He led the Bears to the championship in 1932, then was unceremoniously fired in 1933. He sat the year out of baseball, but not before trying to put a consortium together to buy the Albany team in 1934. Mamaux was hired as player/manager in 1935.[124]

Joe Cambria went even further to try to ensure a winning season. He hired Johnny Evers, he of the famous Chicago Cubs "Tinkers to Evers to Chance" double play combination, as the team's new general manager. Evers had been running a sporting goods store in Albany and was looking for another chance to get back into baseball.[125]

Cambria abandoned his "youth movement" idea quickly when was able to sign veteran catcher Eddie Phillips from the Cleveland Indians to shore up his battery, as well as a veritable cadre of past and future major-league players, such as Frankie Hayes, Taft Wright, Hugh Mulcahy, Johnny Rigney, Bob Wieland, Milburn Shoffner, Ray Prim, Pete Susko, Bob Reeves, and Joe Krakauskas. Krakauskas would soon find his way to the Washington Senators.

However, Joe Cambria had one other "big fish" to land, his big hitter.

Lewis Robert "Hack" Wilson was one of the biggest fish Cambria would ever land. The whole sporting world of the 1920s and 1930s was aware of Wilson's lethal prowess with his bat. After yo-yoing up and down with John McGraw's Giants from 1921 to 1925, Wilson found his power with the Chicago Cubs. Between 1926 and 1930, his offensive numbers were staggering. He led the National League in home runs (as well as strikeouts) four out of those five years, capped off by his legendary 1930 season, when he led the league with 56 homers, 191 RBI, 105 walks, a .723 slugging percentage, and a 1.177 OPS, all while posting a .356 batting average. Wilson held the distinction of being the first National League player to hit two home runs in one inning, on July 1, 1925. All of this success, however, belied a deeper, more sinister problem.[126]

Curiously built like a fire plug with feet, Wilson stood only 5'6" tall, with a huge torso, short stubby legs, and a very large head. His bat handles all had to be shaved down to accommodate his tiny hands, and his size 5½ feet made him look more like a ballerina in a beer barrel. Modern medicine has now found out that these are all manifestations of Fetal Alcohol Syndrome. Both of his parents were alcoholics. His childhood was extremely rough for a young boy, and by the time he made it to the big leagues, he had already found solace in the bottle.[127] After 1930, however, Wilson's career took a precipitous nose-dive, due in large measure to his drinking. Albany became his "last good year in the sun."

Hack Wilson's big-league career ended ignominiously with him playing only 74 games between the Dodgers and the Phillies in 1934. In September, Phillies manager Jimmy Williams told him he could have his old job back if he could shed about 40 pounds. To his credit, Wilson made a valiant effort to reform. In December, he went home to Martinsburg determined to "hit the gym." After being signed by Cambria in January of 1935, he spent six weeks in Hot Springs, Arkansas, which had become the health Mecca of the U.S. He dropped 21 pounds and promised to curtail his drinking as well. Manager Al Mamaux had Wilson running the outfield in a rubber suit to keep the pounds off. He would also keep Wilson in all of his games until the ninth inning to keep him hot, sweating, and sober. Both knew this was Wilson's last stop.

Wilson gave it the "ol' college try" as they say, but he was already an "old" 35 years old. The legs didn't have the elasticity, and the batting eye had waned. By June, he slumped badly, and the team was doing poorly. Cambria had no choice but to try and find another big bat.

The "Alabama" Pitts Saga

In a scene rather prescient to that of the great 1989 baseball movie gem *Major League,* in which Ricky "Wild Thing" Vaughn confesses to playing for the California Penal League, Joe Cambria found Edwin C. "Alabama" Pitts hitting a ton for the Sing Sing prison team in Ossining, New York.

The meteoric rise and fall of the briefly legendary Alabama Pitts is a saga that was played out in dozens of old black and white films during the 1940s and 1950s. Born into poverty in rural Alabama in 1910, Pitts lost both his biological father and stepfather before he was five years old. Poorly educated, he left home at 15 to join the Navy, served honorably for three years, and was transported to New York City at age 18. Destitute and hungry, he fell in with the wrong crowd, robbed a grocery store, and was caught while using a taxicab as a getaway car. Pitts had been suspected in five previous robberies, but the police had failed to implicate him.

His trial was pretty much open and shut. Even after penning a poignant and penitent letter to the judge before his sentencing, he could not catch a break. His pleas for leniency were denied and he was sentenced to 8 to 16 years in Sing Sing prison. Here, however, is where Pitts caught a big break. Warden Lewis E. Laws had instituted a series of meaningful reforms to the prison upon his arrival in 1919. He was a big advocate of reformation through athletics, and Pitts excelled in three—football, basketball, and, in particular, baseball.

Playing in exhibition games against the Yankees and Giants, Pitts shined in the outfield. He batted .500 with eight home runs in all his documented prison games. He even worked out with several pro football teams and was offered a contract with the Philadelphia Eagles. Never one to shun a publicity stunt, Joe Cambria instructed Johnny Evers to go sign him to an Albany contract. In May of 1935, Cambria offered Pitts $200 a month, which he signed for quickly. Because of all the press he was garnering from the national media and for his exemplary prison behavior, Pitts was granted an early release on June 6, 1935.

And then the firestorm began.

Seeing the snake in the woodpile, International League president Charles H. Knapp refused to recognize Pitts' contract. His decision was upheld by minor-league president W.G. Bramham, who recognized Cambria's attempts to use Pitts as a publicity stunt. Almost overnight, a maelstrom of publicity and sympathy in papers from Los Angeles to New York quickly followed, the majority of which was pro–Pitts. Pitts and Cambria appealed the decision to Commissioner Landis. Evers and Cambria tried to request an official pardon from the Governor, which would have nullified any actions taken by the league. They received backing from Congressmen Raymond Cannon of Wisconsin. Even the clerk at the store robbed by Pitts weighed in his support for "Alabama" to get his chance.

On June 17, Commissioner Landis ruled that Pitts could play, but only in regular season games. Landis had also seen the snake and knew that Cambria would try to make a boatload of money playing exhibition games with Pitts at the plate. Pitts made his debut with the club in a doubleheader on June 23, getting two hits and playing spectacular defense in center field.[128]

Despite Pitts' outfield prowess, he was "weak with the willow." Pitts batted a mere .233 for the year. Cambria tried to explain this away by telling the papers that Pitts was only allowed one short wooden bat when playing at the prison. The warden would not allow the usual row of bats in front of the dugout, lest the boys decide to bat their way out of prison.[129]

Pitts was also plagued by a plethora of injuries throughout the season which robbed him of precious playing time; however, due to the tremendous support and respect garnered from crowds around the league, Cambria and Evers offered him a contract with Albany for 1936.

Pitts did not do well in AA Albany in 1936, so Cambria sent him to the York White Roses in the NY-Penn League, which was forced to relocate to Trenton when its home field was flooded out. Tiring of being used as a "circus freak," Pitts left the north after his last game with Trenton in July 1936 to play in the outlaw Carolina League. By this time, he was insistent on being called just Ed Pitts instead of "Alabama," and he shunned both publicity and spotlight. Now just one of the boys, he got married, had a daughter, and bounced around in the low minors and mill teams from 1937 to 1941. After playing a game one night with a Valdese, North Carolina, mill team, Ed Pitts went to celebrate with his team in a rather notorious roadhouse. "Over served" at the bar, he tried to cut in on a man who was dancing with his girlfriend. The man, Newland LeFevers, took exception and slashed Pitts. The wound was serious enough to kill him at the age of 31.[130]

Back in Albany, Cambria had to let Hack Wilson go to make room for Pitts in June of 1935. Rather than ship out to the Portland Beavers in the Pacific Coast League, Wilson called it quits. He went back home to Martinsburg, played with the local semi-pro town team, opened up a pool hall and bar, and slowly faded into obscurity until he was elected to the Baseball Hall of Fame by the Veterans Committee in 1979.

In spite of Wilson, Pitts and the cadre of other good major-league-caliber prospects on the club, Albany sank to the bottom of the league with a woeful 49–104, 42½ games behind the league champion Montreal Royals. There was, however, one, brief shining Camelot moment for the year. On June 3, in a more than three-hour slugfest under the lights, Albany shellacked the Syracuse Chiefs 23–11. Bud Hafey and Taft Wright, both destined for major-league careers, drove in six runs apiece.[131]

CHAPTER 4

1935–1939:
The Cuban Connection

Clark Griffith was in need of players who could play at the big-league level, and the only way he could do that required a two-fold approach: grudgingly expand his farm system and find cheaper talent. Grievously in debt to the tune of $125,000 (close to $2.5 million in today's money), Griffith famously sold his manager, shortstop, and son-in-law Joe Cronin, who had piloted the team to the 1933 pennant, to the Boston Red Sox for $350,000 in order to pay off his debts and make his payroll.

So eager was he to expand his farm system, Griffith promised to meet half the payroll of the newly formed Selma, Alabama, club in March 1935. However, the Southern League failed to organize on time. Consequently, Griffith took his business north. Joe Cambria had taken control of the Harrisburg (PA) Senators and the Lancaster club in the Keystone League. Griffith bought a controlling interest in both clubs. Per his usual agreement with Cambria, Griffith would have first claim on any player found worthy of consideration. In turn, Griffith would funnel players from Chattanooga to Cambria who needed more seasoning in the lower minors. This expanded the Senators' farm system to five teams: Chattanooga (A, Southern Association), Albany (AA, International), Panama City (D, Florida State), Harrisburg (A, NY-Penn) and Lancaster (D, Penn State). The 1933 pennant-winning Senators were certainly in need of better-quality players. The team would place in the first division of the American League only once between 1934 and 1939.[1]

By now, Cambria had developed an army of "bird dogs," friends, former players, ex-managers, and the like, who would alert him to new talent. This could be the only reason he found out about another "can't miss" phenom, 19-year-old John Benninghoff. Pitching for his Jenkintown, Pennsylvania, high school team, Benninghoff had garnered a reputation by pitching in 11 games and allowing only one run, a staggering accomplishment in anyone's league.

Benninghoff left his home on July 9, with a man his mother understood to be a scout for the Baltimore Orioles. After 24 hours, his mother, becoming frantic because she hadn't heard from him, called the Philadelphia police, asking that they search for him. Authorities contacted Baltimore and Buffalo, where the Orioles were playing, but found no trace. That is until young Johnny Benninghoff walked into his house on Friday the 12th with a big grin and a contract signed by Cambria. Somehow, he tried out in front of Cambria in Baltimore, who instructed him to go home, pack his bags, and head to Charlotte. Benninghoff spent one year in D ball in the North Carolina State league and retired from baseball altogether.[2]

Alabama Pitts, Hack Wilson, and Johnny Benninghoff were mere distractions to the real saga that was about to begin in 1935. This was the year Joe Cambria made good on his promise to Clark Griffith—that he would find him good, inexpensive ballplayers in Cuba.

Ysmael *"Mulo"* Morales was the first Latin player that Joe Cambria signed. He bought him from New York Cubans owner Alex Pompez in June of 1932 but allowed him to finish the season with the Cubans to work on his English language skills. Morales was a journeyman minor leaguer, bouncing up and down between AA and D ball throughout his 12 years in organized American ball. However, Morales became one of Cambria's trusted bird dogs. He recommended that Cambria look at a young slugger who was terrorizing the Cuban winter leagues and the sugar cane plantation teams as well.

Roberto *"El Tarzan"* Estalella Ventoza was found by Cambria playing in the Cuban Amateur Leagues for Deportivo Cardenas and the Central Hershey clubs, hitting at a reported .760 batting average. Utilizing a swing he developed from cutting sugar cane, Estalella had played for Havana Leones of the Cuban amateur leagues, hitting .351 in 1931–1932 and .317 in 1932–1933. Estalella was a muscular 5'7", and his playing weight was around 200–210 pounds, hence the nickname *El Tarzan*. He is described by Roberto Gonzales Echevarria in his book *Pride of Havana* as "a very light mulatto, a *mulatto capirro* (red *mulato*). He was white enough to play in the Amateur League and in organized (American) baseball."[3] Using Morales as his interpreter, Joe Cambria offered Estalella $150 a month. His job as an apprentice machinist paid him $1.20 a day, so the offer, to Estalella, was a no-brainer.[4]

"Tarzan" played out the 1934 season with Cambria's Albany Senators, used sparingly. In 1935, Cambria sent him to the Class-A Harrisburg Senators in the New York–Penn League, where he batted .316 in 118 games with 18 home runs. Those numbers were hard to ignore, so on Saturday, September 7, Estalella made his major-league debut with the Washington Senators against the St. Louis Browns. He played the entire game at third base, had one hit, a double in his first at-bat, and flied out his next three times at the plate.[5]

Estalella could hit a ton, but his liability was his glove. Why he was positioned at third base is a mystery because he had a penchant for knocking down hard grounders with his chest, arms, and sometimes his head. Too short for first base, he was moved to the outfield for his own protection, becoming an adequate center and left fielder with a great arm.

Roberto Estalella seesawed through the minors throughout his career. He wound up playing nine years in the majors and nine in the minors. He finished his major-league career with a .282 batting average with 44 homers, 33 triples, and 106 doubles. Just like Roy Sievers of the 1950s Senators, he had the unfortunate distinction of being a right-handed pull hitter in Griffith Stadium with its 407-foot left field line.[6]

With his effervescent smile, his all-out hustle style of play, and his endless chatter on the base paths, Roberto Estalella became a fan favorite. Shirley Povich of the *Washington Post* reported in 1949 that fans would call the box office regularly to see if he was playing before buying their tickets.[7] Griffith was derided for using the Cuban players as a "circus act" like Allan Benson, but he did not care. He knew good gate when he saw it and utilized Estalella to his advantage.

The nature of Estalella, like all the Cuban players, is eloquently summed up by Joanne Hulbert in her essay-length SABR biography of Estalella: "It was not just language that set Roberto Estalella apart from his teammates. He was a different sort of player than what Americans were used to. Exuberant at the plate, irrepressible on the field, and relentlessly noisy in the clubhouse, he arrived in the US bringing with him a style of baseball that was lost in translation by the American managers, magnates, and teammates."[8]

Estalella endured racist taunts from both his own and opposing players, physical abuse from opposing players, ostracization by his own teammates, and endless beanballs, all the while paving the way for a host of his "tan skinned" brothers to make their way to American major-league baseball.

Cambria wasted little time in filling the Senators' roster with Cuban talent. He found Fermin "Mike" Guerra playing with the Habana Reds of the Cuban Amateur League in 1936, and quickly signed him as a catcher. Fermin would play 19 seasons in organized American baseball and return each winter to play Cuban league ball for 20 years. Guerra played five years total with the Senators, most notably during the war years.

Roberto Estalella, Joe Cambria's first Cuban signee for the Senators, was playing for a sugar cane factory team and hitting over .700! His infectious smile and all-out brand of play made him a fan favorite in Washington. Estalella would be the first of nearly 400 Latins signed by Cambria (National Baseball Hall of Fame and Library, Cooperstown, New York).

Another acquisition from Alex Pompez was Tomas de la Cruz. Cambria signed him to Albany in 1936. A good right-handed pitcher, de la Cruz bounced up and down the high minors from 1936 until 1944, when he played his only year in major-league ball with the Cincinnati Reds. It was here that he became the first Latin American pitcher to throw a complete-game one-hitter on a big-league diamond.

Rene Monteagudo, left-handed pitcher and outfielder for Habana in the Cuban Leagues, came to the Nats in 1938. He played four years with the Senators and nine years in the minors. In 1945, he was one of several Latin players to jump to Jorge Pasquel's new Mexican League and was consequently blackballed from American baseball by Commissioner "Happy" Chandler. Joe Cambria often referred to him as "Ray Montague."

Alejandro Carrasquel, the first Venezuelan-born player in major-league baseball, debuted with the Nats in 1938 after having pitched for almost eight years in Venezuela and Cuba. His name, a mouthful to everyone in America, including Cambria and Griffith, cause them to change it (for a while) to Al Alexander. But after several superb outings against the Yankees and the Browns, Griffith demanded that the press—and everyone else—use his real name.

Nineteen-year-old Gilberto Torres was signed by Cambria in 1935, originally as a pitcher, and sent to the AA Milwaukee Brewers. A good infielder as well, Torres did not come up to D.C. until 1944, but he became an integral part of the wartime Senators squads, as did Roberto Ortiz.

Roberto *"El Gigante"* Ortiz was signed by Cambria in 1939. He and Gilberto Torres were teammates in Charlotte in 1939 and 1940, along with Roberto Estalella and future Hall of Famer Early Wynn. Ortiz would become a legend in Cuban baseball with the Almendares club.[9]

All of Joe Cambria's early signees went on to have excellent careers in both the major and minor leagues, as well as some in the Mexican League. All of them also went home to Cuba to play winter ball for many years.

Alejandro "Alex" Carrasquel, Joe Cambria's first Venezuelan signee, was already a veteran by the time he came to Washington. MVP of the 1938 Cuban Winter League, Carrasquel was quickly snapped up by Cambria and debuted with the Senators in 1939, facing Joe DiMaggio, Lou Gehrig and Bill Dickey in his first game. He retired them all (National Baseball Hall of Fame and Library, Cooperstown, New York).

Joe Cambria was certainly a busy guy in 1935 with his laundry business, three ball clubs to oversee, his promotions in Baltimore along with the sandlot team, and now his frequent trips to Cuba. In August, he found some time, however, to have a bit of enjoyment for himself. In what was billed as a "Sandlot Extravaganza," Cambria, along with a cadre of old minor-league, semi-pro, and sandlot veterans, "put on the monkey suit" one last time to play an Old Timers Game against the Dickey Athletic Club of the Western County sandlot league at Bugle Field on August 6. A good time was had by all.[10]

Francis Stan of the *Washington Evening Star* gleefully proclaimed, "Joe Cambria is Master Showman of Baseball" and chanted about Cambria's "P.T. Barnum"-like antics. The signing of Allen Benson was first, followed by "Alabama" Pitts and, in 1935, Roberto Estalella. They were amazed that this "laundryman" could buy a AA ball club, have it sink to the bottom of the league, and still make money with it. Most of all, they loved the "color" of his team in Harrisburg. Like a mini–United Nations, he had Estalella, a Cuban; Ed Romorenko, a Russian; Heinie Hentalel, a German; Del Young, a Scotsman; Bill Starr, a Jew; Bucky Lai, Chinese; and the *coup de grace*—Joe Krakauskas, the world's only Lithuanian-Canadian, whom Cambria playfully referred to as "park-yer-carcass." Of them all, only Estalella and Krakauskas would have an impact on the majors.[11]

1936

"I want to know what club looks better than ours on paper at this time?" said Joe Cambria to *Baltimore Sun* reporter Jesse Linthicum in a February 1936 *Sun* article. Then again, that was Joe Cambria—effervescent and irrepressible about his Albany club. He went on the talk about all the great talent he had assembled and predicted that they would end up in the first division.[12]

In the immortal words of George H.W. Bush: Not gonna happen.

Cambria would wheel and deal throughout the winter months and into the early spring, putting an Albany team together that would, on paper, look pretty good. There would be promising rookies (Johnny Welaj), one gate attraction (Alabama Pitts), and several Cubans (Estalella, Reggie Otero, Fermin Guerra, Tomas de la Cruz). However, as with Hack Wilson, Cambria had a penchant for cheap players who once were great but were now on the tail end of their careers. This year, he signed two doozies, Smead Jolley and Frank Hogan.

Cambria signed Smead Jolley from the Hollywood Stars of the Pacific Coast League for very little money. Jolley, the fabled "big, strong farm boy" from a family of nine in Arkansas, was the quintessential "good hit-no field" player, amassing tons of homers and tons of fielding errors. He spent eight years in the minors from 1922 to 1929. He had four tremendous years with the San Francisco Seals, hitting .346, .397, .404, and .387 from 1926 to 1929, winning the league's Triple Crown in 1928. Jolley was called up to the Show with the White Sox in 1930. After four years in the majors (521 hits, 46 HR, .305 BA) he was sent back to the PCL to the Hollywood Stars.[13]

The Sporting News said Jolley "fielded like a kid chasing soap bubbles."[14] Jolley always retorted to those statements by saying, "I don't get paid for fielding. I get paid to hit."[15] Regardless, Jolley led the International League in 1936 with a .373 batting average, 221 hits, and 53 doubles, as well as posting the worst fielding percentage, .951. The *New York World-Telegram* called him "the Babe Ruth of the Minors" but it still didn't help the Albany Senators, who finished eighth with a 56–98 record.[16]

Equally colorful is the saga of Frank "Shanty" Hogan. For those who have attended an Orioles minor-league baseball game, there is one funny mid-inning entertainment they like to play, where two kids dress up in plastic, blow-up Sumo wrestler suits and try to knock each other down. That's sort of like what Shanty Hogan looked like. Listed as 6'1" and weighing 240, he was definitely in the Ernie Lombardi category (6'3", 230). However, he had a fatal flaw: he was a switch eater.

"He was the greatest two-fisted eater since the invention of the cow," said Casey

Stengel. "He was only a kid, but he ate like a half a dozen men."[17] In an effort to keep Hogan's weight down, famed Giants manager John McGraw waged a running battle with Hogan, going so far as to inspect his meal orders every day. But Hogan defeated him. As Stengel told it: "He had a favorite waitress and they rigged up a set of hand signals. One finger meant a double order of roast beef. Two fingers meant seconds all around. Three meant spaghetti and meat balls. Four meant rolls and plenty of butter in a covered plate. Five meant potatoes: fried if he made a fist."[18]

Despite the endless stories of his prolific prowess with the knife and fork, Hogan was a solid ball player. In his 13-year big-league career, he hit .295, drove in 474 runs, had 939 hits, and hit 61 home runs. Playing with the Giants from 1928 to 1931, he hit over .300 six out of his 13 years in the majors.

But his weight was his undoing, ballooning up to as much as 260 pounds. After stints with the Boston Braves and the New York Giants, he finally wound up with the Washington Senators in 1936; however, after only 19 games, he was sent down to Cambria in Albany. Hogan became a fan favorite in Albany and a productive hitter, batting .359 with 56 hits. He made it back to Washington for 21 games in 1937 but was sent to Toronto in the International League and never returned to the majors.[19]

Joe Cambria continued to play fast and loose with his business, and the beginning of 1936 was no exception. Cambria found himself in Dutch again with the sale of one Claude Linton. Papers in St. Paul announced that Cambria had swapped five players to acquire Linton, the leading catcher in the Texas League, and sold him to St. Paul in a cash deal.[20]

The St. Paul Saints and the Toledo Mud Hens, both of the AA American Association, claimed they had both bought Linton from Cambria. Mud Hens manager Fred Haney claimed that they struck a deal with Cambria for Linton and wired back their acceptance, whereupon Cambria sold Linton to St. Paul. Research showed that National Association President W.G. Bramham, arbitrating the case, awarded Linton to the Mud Hens.[21]

By now, Cambria had constructed his Cuban pipeline. It was not uncommon for between 12 and 20 Cubans to come to the Washington Senators' training camp, which continued throughout the 1940s and 1950s. In 1936, he had eight new players up from Havana. To make their transition easier, Cambria signed an agreement with the Chamber of Commerce in Winter Garden, Florida, to become the new spring training site for the Albany Senators. He brought in the Spanish teacher from a local high school as an interpreter for the new youngsters. Winter Garden was only a short car ride to Orlando, the spring training site for the Washington Senators; consequently, if some of the youngsters made the grade, he could shuttle them back and forth easily.

Cambria brought eight players with him from Cuba to Winter Garden that year: Fermin Guerra and Ramon Cueto, catchers; Regino Otero, first base; Raul Sanchez, Alejandro Zabala, Jorge Comellas, Tomas de la Cruz, and Manuel Forti, pitchers. With the exception of Forti and Zabala, all of them made it to either Albany or Harrisburg/Trenton that year. They would all go on to make it into a big-league uniform, but not for a very long time.[22]

The Island Park Saga

Even before the 1936 season got underway, Joe Cambria's Harrisburg club became wandering vagabonds when disaster struck.

William H. Shank, author of the book *Great Floods of Pennsylvania*, wrote:

The winter of 1935–36 had been one of the most severe that Pennsylvania had seen for years. Huge quantities of snow fell in January and February throughout the state, and prevailing low temperatures preserved it well.

In late February, the cold spell ended with remarkably warm weather and light rains. This resulted in the rapid melting of two months accumulation of dormant moisture throughout the state, all of which was turned loose on the streams and rivers within a period of about 10 days.

An early effect of the warm spell was the thawing of the heavy layers of ice, fifteen to twenty (or more) inches thick, formed on the rivers during the intense cold period. As this ice melted, and as the rivers raised, the ice "gorged" or jammed at various points, forming temporary dams, with resulting high "back-up" water. The heavy ice cakes, borne in-shore by the high water, resulted in great damage to properties or communities where the jams occurred.[23]

Once the ice dams broke, all hell broke with it. Between March 16 and 19, all the major rivers in western and middle Pennsylvania, including the Susquehanna, Monongahela, and Allegheny, swollen by that snowfall during the winter, overflowed their banks, devastating cities throughout Pennsylvania and eastern West Virginia. The St. Patrick's Day flood, as it was called, caused hundreds of millions of dollars in damages and approximately 69 deaths.

Pittsburgh was left without power and faced a $250 million price tag in damages. The National Guard was brought out to stop looting in Johnstown. President Roosevelt pleaded with the nation for flood relief. Residents of Harrisburg were literally running for the high ground to escape the rising waters.[24]

Island Park Field was the home field of the Harrisburg Senators, and it was just that. It was built on an island between two bridges in the middle of the Susquehanna that passed through Harrisburg. It was submerged under 30 feet of water and almost completely destroyed, especially the light towers.

If he wanted to have a season, Cambria had no choice but to look for another place to put his ball club. York, Pennsylvania, was close by and had been without a franchise since 1933. He negotiated a deal with the Chamber of Commerce and transferred the team to York and into the New York-Penn League, becoming the White Roses. He initially indicated that the move would not be permanent and that he was willing to return to Harrisburg if the city made the necessary repairs to Island Park.

That would not be the case.

Both Cambria and the city authorities agreed that there were more pressing matters of concern to the city than the renovation of the baseball field. Consequently, Cambria stayed in York for the first half of the season. He had been hopeful that by moving to York, it would be close enough for the residents of Harrisburg to travel to attend games.

That would not be the case.

Attendance waned in York, exacerbated by the fact that the team, even with all of its colorful players, played poorly, going 29–69 for the first half and languishing in the cellar. Cambria could not meet his payroll adequately. He needed to move the club to a city that could support it, and that is when he found his ace in the hole.[25] Twenty-year-old pitcher/outfielder George Washington Case, Jr., coming off a tryout with the Philadelphia Athletics, had been recommended by Connie Mack to Clark Griffith, whose Washington outfield was lacking in depth compared to Mack's. Trenton native Case was the half-brother of Clifford Case, who had taken over the pork packing business and backed the semi-pro Packers. Clifford Case and a committee of Trenton business leaders soon met with city officials and Joe Cambria, and on June 30, 1936, Cambria signed a one-year lease from the Trenton Cathedral Parish on Dunn Field, a soccer facility, to be converted to baseball use. The announcement came the next day, July 1, that the York White Roses would become the Trenton Senators and play the second half of the season in the New Jersey state capital.[26]

Consequently, on July 2, Joe Cambria moved the team to Trenton, New Jersey, and renamed them the Senators. It was the first time New Jersey ever had a team in the NY-Penn League. Cambria signed Case to an Albany contract with the condition that he would become Washington property soon. Cambria was confident that the addition of Case and the larger population base in Trenton would attract more paying customers to Dunn Field.

This would not be the case.

Even bolstered by local hero Case, as well as two other local standouts, Alex Sabo and Johnny Welaj, the Senators could not catch a cold. They wound up in last place with an overall record of 40–99. The one bright spot in the saga was the acquisition of George Case, Jr.

As mentioned, George Case, Jr., was born and raised in Trenton and inherited his father's blazing sprinter's speed. He was a standout pitcher on his Trenton High School team; however, his legendary running abilities were soon noticed by scouts everywhere. The story goes that Cambria saw Case at one of Connie Mack's tryout camps and "stole" him away from Mack. Such is not the case, as elucidated by his son, George Case III.

I'm not so sure if he was "stolen." Connie Mack had a tryout camp at Shibe Park in 1936. And my dad went there as a pitcher! And when he got there, Connie Mack saw him run and saw him hit and he said, "Son, your future in baseball is going to be in the outfield, not a pitcher! And we're stocked with a lot of outfielders so I'm gonna recommend you sign with Washington." And that's how he got hooked up, so Connie Mack actually gave my dad the advice to move from the pitcher's mound to the outfield. And Mack at the time had a lot of outfielders and Clark Griffith needed outfielders because Griffith Stadium was so big, he needed somebody with speed. So, Mack told Griffith (they were good friends), my recommendation is we got a young kid named Case, he said I would go after him, if you can get him, all the more power to ya. I think he'd do better with Washington than in Philadelphia. So, Mack really discovered my dad! As far as his abilities. So, it wasn't really that my dad was "stolen" from under his wing, it was more or less Mack making the decision he would have a better future in Washington than in Philly.[27]

Case was tutored on the basepaths by none other than Clyde Milan, whom Griffith brought out of retirement just for Case. Milan, who had been a disciple of the great Ty Cobb, actually beat out Cobb twice for the American League stolen base crown, in 1912 and 1913. Case went on to become a six-time stolen base leader and a three-time All-Star in his 11-year career, all with the Senators, from 1937 to 1947, posting a lifetime .282 batting average and an impressive .341 on-base percentage.[28]

In the middle of these colorful player acquisitions, funny money dealings, and his teams' wandering ways, what would make Joe Cambria want to start a hockey team, build a stadium and move to another city?

Maybe it was his peripatetic nature or possibly a severe case of Adult Attention-Deficit/Hyperactivity Disorder. Maybe he saw the success in Baltimore of the Iceland

George Case, Jr., six-time American League stolen base leader, was signed by Cambria upon the recommendation of Philadelphia A's owner Connie Mack. His blazing speed made him a terror on the diamond, and his gentlemanly demeanor made him a favorite of players and fans alike (private collection of son, George Case III).

Hockey League and their star attraction Orioles hockey team. Whatever it was, Joe Cambria decided around July 1936 to become a hockey entrepreneur. He entered a team in the Eastern Hockey League despite the fact that (A) he did not have a team, and (B) he had no place to play!

The Eastern Amateur Hockey League, started in 1933 by Thomas Lockhart, would become one of the most successful amateur hockey leagues of all time, continuing with one brief interruption, between 1948 and 1949, until 1972. The title of "amateur" in their name did belie the nature of the league's play. Players were recruited and paid like the pros. The level of play was fast and intense, and their fights were real. Being amateur in status only meant they played under the rules of the Amateur Hockey Association of the United States, and the players were outside of the rules of the National Hockey League and their affiliates.[29]

The League consisted of teams from Hershey, Pittsburgh, Atlantic City, New York, and Baltimore. Cambria wanted to take advantage of the "Washington–Baltimore" rivalry that existed between two cities just 30 miles apart and felt a Washington-based hockey team would enhance the competitiveness of the league. But ol' "never-satisfied" Joe Cambria didn't want just a team; he wanted a place of his own. His Bugle Field was being used night and day, and it is safe to assume that he was making money renting out his ball field to all comers. On Sunday nights, it was necessary to wait in line to get onto any ice rink in Baltimore, and he wanted a piece of that.

Cambria "do-see-do-ed" around Washington for a location and found one at the bottom of Wisconsin Avenue and M Street. For anyone who has been to Washington,

D.C., and is familiar with the area, this would have been in the heart of the famous Georgetown entertainment district.

Joe Cambria's proposed hockey location could possibly have been in the vicinity of what is now called The Washington Harbor, a mixed-use mall type area known for boutique clothing and fine dining restaurants. The location, however, would have been almost between the banks of the Potomac River and the old C & O Canal tow paths and in the middle of a flood plain. Consultation with the city engineers became inexorably slow, and by the time they had settled on the building size, seating capacity, parking and other matters, it was already October, and time ran out to begin the season. Once again, bureaucratic red tape reared its ugly head.[30]

This was Washington's square dance, and they called the tune. Joe Cambria vowed to get it all on track for the second half of the season, but it did not come to fruition. Washington did not get a hockey team until 1939, when the Washington Eagles joined the EAHL. Had Cambria been able to acquire the land in question, it would have been worth a fortune.

Back in Albany, Cambria was beginning to see some handwriting on the wall. In a *Sporting News* story, he claimed that forces within the International League were "ganging up" on him to force him to sell his Albany franchise so it could be relocated to Jersey City. He claimed they were trying to "starve him out" from playing his share of night road games, which were a significant cause of his money losses. (That and the fact that the team had been dead last for two seasons running.) Several of the other owners were openly critical of Cambria's business methods, and he cited them as being the instigators of the move.[31]

According to Cambria's business model, he had been pretty much shooting himself in the foot for years. All of his decent players like George Case, Jake Powell, Taft Wright, Johnny Welaj, Ben Chapman, Joe Krakauskas, and Roberto Estalella, and many of his new Cubans had all been sold to Washington or other minor-league clubs for money. Even his gate attractions like Hack Wilson, Alabama Pitts, Smead Jolley, and Frank Hogan turned out to be duds, leaving the fans with less reason to come to the ballpark.

By October, Cambria was reading the writing on the wall. He began to advocate for shorter series in 1937 between Albany and the other weak clubs in the league, who were having the same amount of trouble attracting fans. *The Sporting News* said: "Shorter engagements would quicken interest among fans, especially in smaller cities like Albany and Syracuse. Their teams are less likely to be pennant contenders and a club not in the running cannot pull patrons through the turnstiles for 18 to 20 day stands. Also, cash customers tire of seeing the same visiting clubs for more than three contests."[32]

Joe Cambria needed to do something spectacular, and he needed to do it fast.

Enter Babe Ruth.

By late November, papers from Los Angeles to Tampa to Boston were burning up the wires with the reports that Babe was in negotiations with Joe Cambria to manage the Albany Senators: "Ruth said he would like to get a manager's job in the major leagues," said Cambria, "but I think he's interested in the offer I made him. He's going to talk it over with Mrs. Ruth. If he accepts the job, I will go up to New York to sign the contracts."[33]

Of course, with something this spectacular, a firestorm erupted in the papers. The *Baltimore Sun* reported that Ruth was not approached by Cambria and he was not interested anyway.[34] The *New York Times* said Ruth *was* talking to Cambria but would not make a decision until the major-league winter meetings in December.[35] The other International League owners, eager for the publicity and attraction Ruth would bring to them and their league, vowed to back Cambria and offered financial help to make up any salary difference.[36] However, International League president Frank Shaughnessy quickly squelched those rumors at the minor-league meetings in Montreal: "We are not going in for syndicate baseball or any kind of circus performance. No, we are not doing anything like that even to get Babe Ruth into our league. But I will say that if the Babe wants to become the manager of a big-league club, he must start in the minors. He must prove himself first."[37]

The greatest rumor abounding was that Clark Griffith was the puppet master in this whole affair. The *Washington Post* conjectured that Griffith was grooming Ruth to become the Washington Senators' new manager in 1938—if he cut his teeth in Albany in 1937 and was willing to sign an ironclad contract to do so.[38]

By December 9, however, all of the major news services printed this terse statement from Babe Ruth: "I appreciate Joe Cambria's offer, but I'm not interested in going to the minors and that's that."[39]

One would think that just getting the great Babe Ruth to consider a minor-league managerial contract would be spectacular enough! One would be wrong.

By the end of December, Joe Cambria saw the writing on the wall. He had little choice but to cut and run, and his savior came in the form of New York Giants owner Horace Stoneham.

The Giants had also read the proverbial writing, and it read "farm system." They were eager to begin its development and initiated negotiations with Cambria for his Albany club. In a *New York Times* article, Cambria, talking to the *Albany Evening News*, said, "I am not crazy to sell, but if there are any men who think they can do a better job with the Albany club than I have, I'm willing that they take over the club."[40]

Joe Cambria met with Stoneham in mid–December, and, in a nutshell, it went like this: The Giants offered him $30,000 for the team. Cambria said that was ridiculous, said he wanted $50,000. Stoneham said $40,000 was his final offer. Cambria said, I'll get back to you. He made a vow to Albany businessmen that he would sell the team to them first. Cambria complained to the press that the deal was about $15,000 short. Stoneham said, okay, $65,000 then. Cambria said, I'll get back to you. He went to Albany one more time and asked what's your decision? Evidently, they said yes, but Cambria hedged when he told the *Baltimore Sun*: "Albany's a small town but there are real fans up there and I hate to sell them out of International baseball. But I guess if the Giants meet my price, I'll have to let the club go. After all, talk about being in baseball for the sport is all right but the thing most of us have to consider is the money angle."[41]

Cambria went back to Stoneham and said yes. Controversy yet abounded. The Associated Press said the price was $50,000. Shirley Povich in the *Washington Post* said it was $60,000. Joe Cambria stated unequivocally in the *New York Times* that the price was $70,000. Whatever the price, he made a boat load of money on a team for which he paid $7,500. If we go with the $60,000 price tag, that would mean a gross profit of $52,500. Add to that another $40,000 in ballplayers he sold at the end of the season for a grand total of $92,500. In today's money, that would give him the equivalent of over $1.7 million, give or take a few thousand. It took a few weeks for all the paperwork to be finalized, but Cambria inked the deal officially on January 12, 1937.

Joe Cambria tries to convince Babe Ruth to manage the Albany Senators with the *possibility* of becoming the manager of the Washington Senators. Rumor had it that Mrs. Ruth did not want to move to Washington, D.C., and convinced her husband to decline the offer! (private collection of Jim Castetter).

1937

Well, it wasn't spectacular for Albany.

Hearing that the team was sold and was to be relocated, the Albany Senators fans were seething with indignation and felt they had gotten the shaft, especially after they had shown their loyalty to a team that finished dead last two years in a row. Many business owners, who were willing to pony up the money necessary to keep the club in their city, were indignant with Mayor John Thatcher, who had assured them that Cambria had promised to keep the club in Albany for the 1937 season. One businessman in particular went searching for Cambria from Baltimore to New York with a certified check already made out to him but was unable to track him down.[42]

In an editorial, *The Sporting News* praised International League President Frank Shaughnessy for the adroit way in which he handled the Albany/Jersey City situation and pretty much exonerated Cambria, saying his "experimental melting pot" of players did not work out as planned. They said Cambria had no choice but to cut and run and laid the blame for the whole affair at the feet of the Albany public, whose interest in the team had "[fallen] to nil."[43]

Charles Young, sports editor of the *Knickerbocker Press*, loudly cried foul. In a scathing rebuttal to the *TSN* editorial, Young asked their editors a series of rather pointed questions:

1. Does it not think that International League President Frank Shaughnessy should have inquired into conditions in Albany before he, according to Joe Cambria, forced the sale of the Senators to the Giants?

2. Does it not think that Cambria, after promising Mayor Thatcher and the newspapers of Albany, that he would operate the club in Albany this year, or give Mayor Thatcher the first chance to buy the franchise, was morally bound to carry out these promises before the club could be transferred?

3. Wasn't it the duty of President Shaughnessy to see that these promises were kept?

4. Does *The Sporting News* know that Joe Cambria told [this] writer that he did not want to sell to the Giants, that Shaughnessy forced him to do so, and that Shaughnessy, when informed of Cambria's charges, was not inclined to deny them?

He further pointed out that other International League teams had been working in the red and going begging for loans and further intimating collusion on the part of Shaughnessy to utilize bankruptcy to pay off teams' debts.[44]

The Sporting News replied eloquently and succinctly to Young's charges, saying it was unfortunate that Albany had to suffer because of this situation but basically, it was Cambria's team, it's a free country, and he could do with it whatever he wanted.[45]

The deal with Albany was consummated, and the Giants quickly whisked the team to Jersey City to be in direct competition with the Yankees' Trenton farm club. Cambria, possibly feeling a little guilty about reneging on his promise to his Albany business friends, just as quickly sought a replacement for the city. He packed up his car in the dead of January and went to Toronto to make a bid for their Maple Leafs baseball club. But he must have been a little slow on the trigger. Cliff Oakley, who had succeeded his father George as team president after his father's untimely passing, quickly cobbled together a group of local investors, spearheaded by former Lieutenant-Governor of Ontario William Donald Ross, who bought the Leafs before Cambria could finish his negotiations.[46] Cambria just took his lumps and moved on.

"Goin' Downey Ocean"

For those of you unfamiliar with a unique dialect of Maryland called "Baltimorese," "goin' downey ocean" is their way of saying one is going to the beach, usually Ocean City, Maryland, one of the most beautiful resorts on the East Coast. With its snow-white beaches and fabled Boardwalk, Ocean City was and still is one of the largest summer seaside attractions, drawing people from up and down the East Coast to cavort in the warm waters of the Atlantic. This is where Joe Cambria decided to try his hand once again. Well, almost.

America and minor-league baseball were both inching their way back from the precipice of the Great Depression. Wages, profits, and production had recovered to their 1929 standings, unemployment was still high but nowhere near the 1933 25 percent level, and farms were flush with food again. Minor-league baseball's disastrous 1933 season, which saw only 14 complete leagues and 101 teams, had climbed its way back up as well. By the end of 1937, there would be 37 leagues, over 250 teams, and hundreds of employed young ballplayers.[47]

The Eastern Shore League, comprised of teams from Delaware, Maryland, and Virginia, started in 1922 and had lain fallow since folding in 1928. It was revived for the 1937 season as a Class-D league. While Cambria was in the thick of his Montreal negotiations, he instructed his dear friend and former Harrisburg Senators manager John "Poke" Whalen to attend the ESL's opening conference in Salisbury, Maryland, on January 14. Agreements were met and arrangements were made quickly. Officials were appointed posthaste. Teams from Salisbury, Centreville, Crisfield, Pocomoke City, Cambridge, Easton, and Federalsburg in Maryland, and Dover, Delaware, all pledged to play in the league pending affiliation with a major-league team and other financial matters.[48]

Flush with cash from the Albany sale, Cambria became the sole owner and operator of the Salisbury club, named the Indians. He once again signed a working agreement with his friend and mentor, Clark Griffith, and named "Poke" Whalen business manager and Jake Flowers field manager. He bought Gordy Park, the old ballpark of the previous Salisbury club, and immediately did what he did best: refurbished the field and grandstands and installed new lighting for night games.[49] Cambria and Whalen scouted and traded their way to a team that could have easily been a Class-A team. He also brought with him a few of his Cuban players from his Trenton team as well. The league was young, fast, strong, and well-organized. Each team was well-owned, financially solid, and managed by knowledgeable baseball men, and the majority of them were affiliated with a major-league team.

Cambria was once again in clover. Salisbury was the seat of the county government and had a population well over 10,000 people. Although situated in the heart of Maryland's bucolic corn fields and chicken farms, it had the most rabid of baseball fans, born that way due to their isolation on the Eastern shore. If they wanted to see a major-league ball game, they had two alternatives: travel several hours up Route 13 to Philadelphia or take the Claiborne-Annapolis Ferry, the only connection between the eastern and western parts of the state, and travel to Washington, which took several hours, to see the Senators. Consequently, the Eastern Shore populace were very happy to support the Eastern Shore League from 1922 until its eventual collapse in 1949.

Joe Cambria was in heaven. He had a good team, a fine manager in Jake Powell, support from the community and from the press, and the money necessary to make a good franchise. What could possibly go wrong?

The ESL got off to a great start in 1937. Attendance was up, especially for night games. Five out of the eight teams were equipped with lights and were doing land office business. Support for the league was at an all-time high, as were the spirits of the baseball fans.

Murphy's Law: If something can go wrong, it will. And by mid–June, it did.

The Indians played like a team of destiny. Led by the arms of ace Joe Kohlman (25–1), Jorge Comellas (22–1), and Leon "Bobo" Revolinsky (13–2), the slick fielding of second baseman Jerry Lynn, clutch hitting by shortstop Frank Treschock and center fielder Bill Luzansky, and captained by catcher Fermin Guerra, the Indians could scarcely be beat. They would win a few, lose one, then win a few more, and by June they were in first place. (Curiously, Kohlman lost his first game of the season, then proceeded to win 25 straight after that.)

On June 19, they were 25 and 1. On June 20, they were 0 and 26.[50]

A controversy erupted around player eligibility rules. ESL Class-D rules stated that a team was permitted to carry 10 rookies, two non-"class" or players with one year of experience, and two "classmen." A "classman" was a player who had experience playing in a class higher than the one in which they were playing.[51] Word got back to the ear of J. Thomas Kibler, president of the ESL, that Salisbury was employing one too many "class players."

Evidently, Cambria had signed a young first baseman, Robert Brady, who had signed a contract three years earlier to play with Class-B Harrisburg in the NY-Penn League. Brady claimed that the contract he signed in 1931 was illegal because he was an 18-year-old minor and his parents had not signed the contract. Cambria and his business manager, M.E. Murphy, stated that Brady had letters from the defunct Harrisburg club saying that he was under contract illegally.[52] Manager Jake Flowers, himself a major-league veteran with the world champion St. Louis Cardinals in 1926 and 1931, was well aware of the shenanigans engaged in by major-league owners (Branch Rickey in particular) concerning their minor-league players. He stated that Brady had been covered up by the Boston Braves, who apparently owned Brady's contract at the time. Brady said he had been verbally "released" by the club, then marked as suspended. Brady further stated that he never played a game, never put on a uniform, and never received a dime of payment.[53]

Kibler, a former World War I Army colonel and a stickler for rules, demanded a full Indians roster and vowed to investigate. Upon his investigation, Kibler, in what could only be considered as a most Draconian of rulings, found that Brady should be considered an experienced player and, according to the league rules, made the Indians forfeit all 25 of their wins.[54]

Cambria was incensed. He immediately appealed to Minor League Commissioner William G. Bramham. Before the season opened, Cambria and the Salisbury club submitted a list of players to the league president. Kibler okayed the list. "Kibler had as much knowledge about Brady as Salisbury did," said Cambria.

Bramham upheld Kibler's decision.

Cambria said, "We're floored, but we'll never quit. I've instructed my manager and the team to carry the fight on and off the ballfield."[55] He vowed to appeal to minor-league baseball's Executive Committee, who were the final arbiters of these matters. Cambria was hopeful that, instead of forfeiting all 25 games, they would forfeit just the 12 in which Brady played.[56]

Research indicates that that did not occur, and the whole 25-game forfeiture stayed in place. Jake Flowers, being a major-league alumnus, told Cambria this was really a major-league matter and took it to Commissioner Landis. Landis said no, this was a minor-league matter and refused to intercede in the case.[57]

Jake Flowers refused to pursue the matter any further for one reason: loyalty.

Colonel Kibler had been Flowers' coach and mentor during his playing days at Washington College in Centreville, Maryland. Flowers picked up the team, wiped away the dust, and vowed they would be back in the first division by Labor Day.[58]

And they did just that. Undaunted and undeterred, the Indians, starting on June 21, put together winning streak after winning streak. In what can only be described as a made-for-TV movie script, the Indians roared back to take the league lead on September 3, three days before Labor Day, and didn't stop until the end of September.

Clark Griffith was the guest of honor at a standing room only "Indians Boosters" game on September 1. The team was showered with gifts and prizes, and monies were raised for local charities. The *pièce de resistance* was Griffith signing Kohlman, Comellas, Guerra, Lynn, and Trechock to Senators contracts.[59]

September 7 saw the Indians play an exhibition game with Cambria's Trenton Senators, where pitcher Joe Kohlman was awarded the Most Valuable Player trophy for his amazing 25-win season.[60] By September 11, the Indians defeated the Cambridge Cardinals in the playoffs and faced the Centreville Colts for the Championship. The Colts took the first two of the best-of-five series and things looked bleak. Then the Indians hitched up their pants and won the next two games to force a final game five on September 19. The team's fate was in the hands of their ace, Joe Kohlman, who proceeded to show why he won the MVP award. Kohlman threw a no-hit 7–0 shutout, facing just 29 batters, allowing only one walk and one runner due to an error, and the Indians were the Champs![61]

Throughout the entire stretch run, Joe Kohlman and Jorge Comellas were unhittable. Second baseman Jerry Lynn, shortstop Frank Trechock, catcher Fermin Guerra, and center fielder Bill Luzansky tore up ESL pitching, busted down the fences, and stopped every ball that came through the infield. The team that was 0–26 on June 20 won the league championship by going 59–11. Kohlman led the league in wins (25), strikeouts (257), and winning percentage (.962). Jerry Lynn led the league in batting average (.342), and Frank Trechock led the league in hits (131) and RBI (84). Concerning their big-league careers, all of them got to play in at least one game for the Nats. They were sent back down at the end of the season and, with the exception of Guerra, none of them never made it back up to the bigs.

For his Herculean efforts, manager Jake Flowers, who nursed his team back from the edge of death in June, was awarded Minor League Manager of the Year by *The Sporting News*, the first time a rookie manager and a Class-D manager ever won the award.[62]

More Yet to Do

With the ESL season over, ol' "use 'em till they're done" Cambria gave the team a little fun and made a few bucks in the meantime. He arranged an exhibition game between his Indians and the Philadelphia A's in Salisbury on September 20. The Indians won in a nail-biter, 3–2, playing against the A's regular lineup.[63] The next night, Cambria arranged a two-game series with his old pals from the House of David. The Indians won the first game of the charity event, 7–4, but lost the second game in Baltimore's Orioles Park by a score of 7–6.[64]

Unquestionably, Cambria's Cuban players were a large part of the success of the 1937 Indians. Jorge Comellas pitched magnificent ball, going 22–1 and adding a few hits in his 88 plate appearances. Fermin Guerra handled the pitching staff with big-league efficiency and tore up ESL pitching with 93 hits, including 16 doubles and 14 homers for a very respectable .296 batting average. Juan Montero was a late-season addition from Trenton and was used primarily in relief.

The boys played with confidence and enjoyment, due in great measure to the love and care they received from "Pappa Yo,'" a sobriquet Cambria received from Roberto Estalella. He took pains to see to their welfare, providing them with their favorite Latin albums, encouragement, advice, as well as a little money when necessary. Cambria urged them to stay out of trouble, to which they assured him "we no revoloosh," meaning they wouldn't "revolt" or cause trouble.[65] Cambria would shuttle his Cuban "ivory" between Trenton and Salisbury, both Northern cities where racial prejudices were considerably less than in the South.

"This is the best Class-D team ever formed," gushed the ever-optimistic Mr. Cambria to the *Baltimore Sun*. "We finished on top at the close of the regular playing season despite the fact that 21 games were taken away from us. It took men with hearts of steel to work their way from the cellar to the top position. This is a great ball team and Salisbury is a great ball town. We will rebuild for next year. Salisbury must have a winner. It is the best drawing town in the United States."[66]

Hyperbole was always Joe Cambria's stock in trade; however, he really did love the beautiful little town. So much so that he decided to open a laundry business, the Eastern Shore Linen Supply Company, a rental business that would supply restaurants, barber shops, and hotels with linens, jackets, and towels. He temporarily headquartered the company at Gordy Park Stadium until he was able to find a suitable off-site location. True to form, he had his friend and business manager, Melvin E. Murphy, and his secretary, John Milton, run the operation for him.[67]

Besides the laundry business, Cambria wanted to give back to the town. In late December, he decided to give the town a special Christmas present. To the papers he said, "Salisbury stuck by the Indians when everything seemed lost last summer and [this is] the best way I can repay them—to give them the best team possible in 1938. Salisbury will get the pick of all the rookies signed by the Indians, the Trenton Senators, Greenville, South Carolina, or St. Augustine Florida."[68]

Joe Cambria would play Santa a lot in the coming months.

1938

This would turn out to be a pivotal year for Cambria. On an unknown date during 1938, he sold his lucrative Bugle laundry business to the Industrial Laundry Corporation. The new owners chose to retain the name. Baltimore City archives indicate that Cambria, referred to as "manager" of both Bugle Laundry and Bugle Athletics, was now simply referred to as a "sports promoter."[69]

Now, sportswriters would refer to him as the "former Baltimore laundryman" or some such sobriquet that he would never shake. However he was described, it was clear that he had decided to make baseball his full-time profession. It is safe to assume that selling the laundry business unburdened him of myriad day-to-day problems inherent in running a seven-day-a-week business. It can also be safe to assume that, from the plethora of baseball dealings in which he was involved starting in 1929, Cambria was not paying much attention to the laundry business anyway, more likely than not leaving the business in the hands of his wife and his shop managers. Cambria was probably making as much if not more money buying and selling baseball franchises and players, and he delighted in it. He had found his true calling, and he was anxious to make the most of it.

Joe Cambria always seemed to save his big news for late in the year. "Joe Cambria, Baseball Santa!" exclaimed the headline in the December 20 *Greenville News*.[70] Greenville, South Carolina, would become the next stop in the ever-expanding Cambria-Griffith farm system. Ripe with cash from the Albany sale, as well as his success with the Salisbury team and his laundry businesses, Cambria was looking for the next big advantage and believed he saw it in Greenville.

The South Atlantic League, commonly called the Sally League, had a storied history. Started in 1904 as the South Carolina League, it did not officially become the Sally until 1919. Game attendance, fan, and municipal support were all outstanding, and the league turned out good profits and good players. Some of the greats to play for Greenville included Shoeless Joe Jackson, Dixie Walker, Harry "The Hat" Walker, Pepper Martin, Tommy Lasorda, Clem Labine, and a skinny kid Joe Cambria found at Villanova College, Mickey Vernon.[71]

The populace was in a tizzy. The mayor, city council and local media were tumescent with anticipation. Cambria penned a letter to the powers that be expressing his gratitude, outlining his plans, and explaining his farm system:

> Dear Mr. Latimer:
>
> Mr. Whalen and Mr. Hering have just returned from your city and this is just to thank you for the courtesies extended them during their visit.
>
> In addition to Trenton, we also operate Salisbury, Md., in the Eastern Shore (Class D) and St. Augustine, Fla., in the Florida State league (Class D). Trenton is Class A and Greenville will be Class B. We work with Mr. Clark Griffith, president of the Washington club which owns the Charlotte, N.C. franchise in the Piedmont league (Class B). So, you see we have quite a hook-up and we will do our best to give Greenville a fine ball club.
>
> Right after the first of the year, we will want to get started building the ballpark. All Greenville help will be hired for erecting the ballpark. [We] will send down a couple of local men to help supervise the job; these men have had considerable experience building ball parks and know the set-up. Mr. John Milton will act as business manager for the time being.
>
> With your support, we hope to have a fine club for the South Atlantic league and want to thank you for your continued cooperation.
>
>   Yours very truly,
>   Joe Cambria, President
>   Trenton N.J. Baseball club[72]

Cambria neglected to mention the AA Chattanooga team, which would have shown that the organization was controlling teams in almost every classification. The Washington Senators' farm system was indeed shaping up, with Cambria owning outright four of the franchises.

Like Caesar returning to Rome after a battle, Cambria came to Greenville with his army before him. In early January, he sent his loyal lieutenants, Poke Whalen, Fred

Hering, Matt Reinholt, Henry Buck, and John Milton to the city, where they were received a hero's welcome by the chairman of the city council and the president of the Parks Commission. All parties inspected several sites around the city for the new stadium and settled upon an area known as Meadowbrook Park. John Milton would oversee the business matters, Matt Reinholt the construction, and Whalen acted as spokesman for the group and the team. He announced that, since the stadium was to be built between February and April, the team would train in St. Augustine, Florida, along with the Trenton club.[73]

Diving right into his new ownership of the Greenville club, Joe Cambria did as promised and started building the new 5,000 seat stadium for the Spinners. Floodlights and a public address system were to be installed. Road access was changed. Parking lots were plotted out. A boosters club was started. So confident was he in the quickness of construction, John Milton announced that the Spinners would hold open tryouts starting April 4, lifting further the spirits of the local community. All papers were dutifully signed and, before they left, Cambria and his lieutenants were fêted at a sumptuous banquet in his honor.[74]

Feelings were very positive, and spirits were soaring.

Cambria was just doing what he had always done and stayed true to his original business model. He would find franchises that had lain fallow in leagues that had all but disbanded, buy them up for a song, shore them up with young, hungry ballplayers, eager for major-league dreams and, after 1935, young, hungry Cuban players seeking the great American Dream. In many instances, he was looked upon as a Messiah willing to invest his own money into derelict minor-league franchises in the middle of an historic economic collapse. A quintessential Horatio Alger story.

With Harrisburg in 1929, he helped revive the Blue Ridge League. With Salisbury, he again helped to revive the Eastern Shore League, another league that had been dormant for some time. Now with Greenville, he was reviving once again another league, the South Atlantic League, that had been silent for seven years. In St. Augustine, he would be instrumental in reviving the Florida State League. The majority of these leagues had been forced to shut down either before or during the Great Depression.

With his radiant smile and his unbridled optimism, Cambria brought not only hope to baseball-starved cities up and down the East Coast, but also the pure excitement of baseball to these rural communities. Remember: this was 1938. There was no television. In towns like Greenville and Salisbury, there may not have been running water in every household, let alone a radio. Their only forms of information and entertainment were the newspaper, movie theater, and the barber shop. Baseball teams brought diversion, acculturalization, entertainment, and the chance for kids young and old to see young men make their own dreams come true.

Joe Cambria's first foray into Florida baseball ownership began in St. Augustine, where he took over ownership of the Saints in the Class-D Florida State League from local baseball legend and businessman Fred Francis. The city helped finance a new ballpark for the team, which included lights for night games. Francis Field at San Marco Park was built quickly to accommodate spring training schedules. Cambria arranged for his Trenton and Salisbury teams to do spring training there starting March 15.[75] His Florida teams became an important part of his Cuban pipeline.

Cambria was not the only one to see the value of Florida real estate. Clark Griffith had been in and out of the Sunshine State for years. In the first two decades of the century, the Senators wandered all around the Virginia Tidewater area for spring training. Not until 1920 did they settle upon Tampa, for nine years. After a brief five years in Biloxi from 1930 to 1935, the Old Fox decided finally to make Florida his spring training home. They moved to Orlando's Tinker Field in 1936 and, with only a very brief two years at College Park, Maryland, during the war years, remained there until 1960, moving to Pompano Beach during the expansion years.[76]

Joe Cambria knew that Florida would be a major help to him in his Cuban endeavors. He was regularly bringing a dozen or more Cuban players to the U.S. to try out with the Senators, usually farming out the good ones and sending the others back home. Florida made for easier entrance and exit to the mainland and there was a small but thriving Latin community around the major southern Florida cities, making the boys a little more comfortable with their surroundings.

Griffith was so sure of the Orlando connection that at a special Chamber of Commerce luncheon on March 7, he outlined a two-point proposal, where he hoped:

1. The Washington Senators would be able to take over control of the Orlando team in the Florida State League and,
2. Washington would conduct a huge baseball school there.

Griffith stated to the assembly:

> If Washington takes over the Orlando franchise, I would conduct a baseball school free of charge to any and all youths who think they have talent. I believe that we would have an enrollment of several hundred under the best instruction we could provide. I have always been opposed to charging tuition for these baseball schools as is the common practice.[77]

Florida would be the site of many successes and challenges for Griffith and Cambria.

All of Cambria's efforts in scouting and signing were now beginning to pay off. Several of his discoveries were now on their way to successful big-league careers.

Originally from Cambria's Albany club, Joe Krakauskas pitched five games and went 4–1 with a respectable 3.15 ERA for the Senators in 1937. In 1938, Krakauskas was plagued by wildness in the first half of the season and was sent down to Trenton in May. He vehemently protested to Griffith about the transfer, saying: "Anywhere but Trenton—riding busses all night and eating on the fly. It's a terrible life for a ball player."[78]

The pitcher eventually got back up to the parent club and finished the year with a 7–5 record and a 3.12 ERA.

Another Albany alum, Taft Wright, came up to the Senators in 1938 and put up a very nice .350 batting average with 92 hits, but only two home runs. Wright had a fine nine-year major-league career.

Cambria's second Cuban "gold mine," Roberto Estalella, was once again seesawing through the minors, working on his fielding and trying not to get beaned every time he came to the plate. He tore up the Piedmont League with the Charlotte Hornets, beating out Phil Rizzuto of the Norfolk Tars for the league MVP honors. Estalella hit a monstrous .378, with 38 homers, 163 hits, 140 runs scored, and a dizzying .754 slugging percentage. All of this happened in spite of the fact that he was hit in the face with a fungo bat and suffered a broken jaw on August 21 and was out for the rest of the season. Estalella would return to the Senators in 1939 and 1942.

George Case, Jr., played his first full season with the Senators, posting a fine .305

batting average with 11 steals, on his way to leading the American League in stolen bases six times in his injury-shortened 11-year career.

Rene Monteagudo, one of Cambria's many Cubans, made it up for a late September cup of coffee in 1938, playing in only five games. Rene would go on to be a big help to the Senators lineup during the War years.

Joe Kohlman, after going an astounding 25–1 with the Salisbury Indians and named League MVP, got his shot at the "bigs" in 1938. In 14⅓ innings pitched, mostly in relief, he posted a disappointing 6.28 ERA with no strikeouts, 11 walks, and 10 earned runs. He would spend the remainder of his nine-year baseball career in the minors.

Cambria's biggest catch, however, would be a tall, skinny kid from Villanova University named James "Mickey" Vernon. Vernon started his career in 1937, playing with Easton of the Eastern Shore League. Cambria got to see a lot of Vernon during Salisbury's magical comeback year, and his Indians actually defeated Easton for the league championship. Easton was affiliated with the St. Louis Browns. At the end of the year, Browns ownership decided to pass on Vernon and everyone else on the Easton team. Cambria got wind of this and convinced the Senators to buy up Vernon's contract for $500. He took Vernon to St. Augustine in February of 1938 to work out with his Tren-

ton team. After camps broke, he took him with Trenton up north; however, they decided along the way to stop in Greenville, South Carolina, to play an exhibition game with Cambria's newest team, the Spinners. Cambria liked what he saw and left Vernon with the Spinners for the 1938 season. The Spinners stank, ending dead last with a 53–83 record, but Vernon played respectably, hitting .328, driving in 72 runs and scoring 84. After Vernon's call-up the next spring, he remained in the majors for good.[79]

In his biography, *The Gentleman First Baseman*, Vernon recalls how cantankerous Cambria's Cuban players had become: "At camp that spring (1938) there were 12 or 14 Cuban players. One of them, Gil Torres, called a strike for more meal money. Just the Cubans went on strike. It lasted for a couple of days. [Finally] we all got another 50 cents."[80]

Evidently, the spirit of

When the Browns neglected to pick up young Mickey Vernon's option after his first professional season, Cambria swept in to sign the 19-year-old. Vernon, shown here in 1954, blossomed into one of the best first basemen in the American League (National Baseball Hall of Fame Library, Cooperstown, New York).

"revoloosh" may have been growing in the Cubans. Cambria got a bothersome telegram from his Salisbury business manager, Melvin E. Murphy, informing him that catcher Fermin "Mike" Guerra had deserted the team. When Guerra found out that his last remaining Cuban friend, pitcher Jose Salazar, had been released from the team, he told his teammates, "no good for them [other Cubans] no good for me," and left on the same bus with Salazar. Cambria had no recourse but to promote his utility catcher, Fred Thomas, to starting catcher and called up rookie John McCormick from Trenton to serve as back-up.[81]

Isolation was only one of the many tribulations facing Cambria's Cuban players, and in rural Salisbury, Maryland, the Cubans were both isolated and vulnerable. As with any immigrant class, they craved the companionship and camaraderie of their countrymen. Cambria did his best to have at least two Cubans on any of his myriad teams, but sometimes it just did not work out.

Guerra's departure was my no means his only headache with his Salisbury club that year. Before the season started, he had to assuage the ego of his championship manager, Jake Flowers.

After the Indians were penalized 21 games due to a rules violation, it was Flowers who piloted the club to the championship in one of the most amazing comebacks in baseball history, and he was named Minor League Manager of the Year for his efforts in 1937. Flowers obviously felt his time had come, and he wanted to move up. He refused to sign his contract for the 1938 season after he heard the news about Greenville. Flowers wanted to advance. When Cambria got the franchise at Greenville, Flowers was led to believe that he was to be the manager. He felt he had earned the promotion to a higher-ranking league and was waiting for confirmation from Cambria. Flowers said, "Cambria signed Jiggs Donahue for the job and I believe he is expecting me to return to Salisbury. My one and only reason for choosing the Greenville job was the opportunity for advancement. Now that Cambria has decided it will be Salisbury for me, I am forced to wait for him to meet my terms."[82]

Flowers had to wait two weeks before he could meet with Cambria. Finally, after a long "heart to heart" with Cambria, Flowers signed his contract. Making the announcement, Cambria said: "[Flowers] will be the highest paid manager in Class D baseball this year. I know of no manager in minor league baseball who will approach Jake's ability. He has proven himself a real manager. I see nothing but sunshine for the club this year; if it starts raining, Poke has been instructed to grab the umbrella and keep the rain off Salisbury."[83]

Research shows that Cambria was a master of hyperbole for effect. Every one of his prospects was either "can't miss" or the next great somebody; every team would finish in the first division or contend for the championship. He was, by his Italian nature, ebullient and optimistic.

In the case of Salisbury in 1938, he was justified. Jake Flowers did what he said he would do and brought another pennant home to the Eastern shore. Facing the same Cambridge Cardinals as in 1937, the Indians beat them in four games. Jorge Comellas was the hero of the hour, pitching a 3–0 shutout even after his pitching hand went numb in the fourth inning. Using the only pitch he had left, a wide-breaking curve, Comellas kept the Cardinals off-balance, getting into trouble only once in the seventh inning. He gave up only five hits, walked two, and fanned four.[84]

Joe Cambria finished the year off by wheeling and dealing. In November, Cambria increased the size of the Senators' farm system by one more when he and Clark Griffith's nephew, Calvin, signed a deal with Shelby in the old Class-D North Carolina State League. The team had originally started operating in 1936 in the independent Carolina League, but lack of finances forced them to fold midway through the year. The St. Louis Cardinals took control of the franchise in 1937, and the team was admitted to the Class-D North Carolina State League. That team eventually moved to greener pastures in Gastonia.

When Cambria and Griffith took it over in November of 1938, they renamed the franchise the Nationals and became charter members of the Class-D Tar Heel League. The team ended the year in fourth place with a 50–59 record, losing to Gastonia in the playoffs.

The Senators now had five links in their chain operated by Cambria: Trenton (A, Eastern), Charlotte (B, Piedmont), Greenville (B, Sally), St. Augustine (D, Florida State), and Shelby (D, North Carolina.) Shelby would be short-lived, however. They played so poorly in 1940 that they dropped out of the league midway through the season.[85]

The kicker for the year came in late December–early January when Cambria officially moved his Class-A Trenton club to Springfield, Massachusetts, where they were renamed the Nationals. Playing in venerable Pynchon Park, the Nationals finished a very respectable third in 1939, with Rene Monteagudo tying with his own teammate, Newton Jacobs, as league pitching leaders with 18 wins apiece. The team would start a steady decline into the bottom of the league and fold up in 1941 due to the War.[86]

1939

Nineteen thirty-nine dawned ominous. War clouds were forming in the east. But all was sunny in Florida. On February 1, Clark Griffith began spring training in Orlando, two weeks before the usual start date and a full two and a half months before the opening of the season. Vowing to put "good money" back into the team, Griffith was wholeheartedly committed to a complete rebuild, a "youth movement" for the Washington Senators.

> The idea behind this program is to develop players instead of trying to trade them or buy them. It is easy to talk about going out and buying a couple of pitchers, but it isn't easy to do. There simply aren't any ready-made pitchers for sale. The only way, as I see it, is to develop young players. That's what we're trying to do by starting so early. I look for three or four of those first 16 youngsters to come around and make the team. We are going to rebuild on youth, particularly in regard to the pitching staff. We saw what the old pitchers did last year, and it wasn't good enough.[87]

Griffith cut up his team into four different segments, each one reporting at a different time. The "first 16" he was referring to would be the young pitchers and catchers he was going to build into his "army of arms." The kids would be overseen by manager Bucky Harris and live together in a private boarding house paid for by Griffith.[88]

Griffith was expecting the dividends he had paid out to Joe Cambria would be repaid, and Cambria, as ever optimistic, knew he could come through and nearly did. But this story did not have a happy ending.

Cambria, who also believed in early talent development of young players, started a baseball training school in St. Augustine in 1937 under the auspices of his trusted manager, Poke Whalen, and his general manager, Fred Hering. In 1938, he brought down his Salisbury and Trenton clubs to utilize it as an ersatz spring training camp for them as well. On a sunny spring morning in 1938, a ruddy-faced local phenom, 18-year-old Forrest "Lefty" Brewer, and his friend Faulene Kirkland walked into camp for a tryout. With his silky-smooth delivery, blazing fastball and his "fall off the table" curve ball, Brewer was offered a contract with the St. Augustine Saints on the spot.[89] "He's a sure winner," exclaimed Cambria. "I'll stake my reputation on it."[90]

What happened next was the stuff of Hollywood legend. Brewer completed 28 of his 41 starts, won 25 games, led the league in wins and strikeouts, threw four shutouts, and was named an All-Star. In 1939, he was one of the "first 16" in the Senators' early spring training. Here, the harsh realities of major-league baseball were exposed. Needing further seasoning, Brewer was released to Cambria's Class-B Charlotte Hornets for the season. After Brewer won just one of his three starts, manager Calvin Griffith justifiably saw he was not ready for Class-B ball and sent him down to the Class-D Shelby Nationals. Plagued by arm troubles from overuse, Brewer recorded only five wins in 19 starts with a terrible 5.25 ERA. That bought him a ticket back to Orlando in the Florida State League in July, where he fared better, going 7–11 with a 3.85 ERA.[91]

Brewer was back with the Hornets for 1940 and became a fan favorite. One of the team's better pitchers, he went 11–9 for the year with a 3.68 ERA, which earned him a recall with the Senators for the 1941 season.

But Brewer did not report to his Uncle Clark in 1941, he reported to his Uncle Sam at Camp Blanding, Florida. Brewer chose to go to parachute jump school at Ft. Benning, Georgia, and was attached to the 508th Parachute Infantry Regiment. He played ball, of course, with the 508 "Red Devils," which won the Camp Mackall championship with a record of 26–4. Unfortunately, a regimental order disbanded the team because they felt it interfered with their training. Had the team stayed together a little longer, Brewer might have had a chance to pitch against Ted Williams and the North Carolina Pre-Flight Cloudbusters and the Norfolk Naval Training Station with Phil Rizzuto and Dom DiMaggio.

In March of 1944, he was deployed to England in preparation for the final push of the war. He participated in Operation Overlord on June 5 and 6, in preparation for the D-Day invasion in Normandy. They were supposed to secure the town of Sainte-Mere-Eglise but were dropped in at the wrong place. They encountered heavy German forces between Picauville and Mere-Eglise, where a terrible firefight ensued. It was there that Forrest Brewer lost his life, one of the many minor-league ballplayers to serve and die for their country.[92] We will never know if Cambria's prophecy could have come true.

For the first time in a long time, there was an air of excitement in the Senators' spring training camp in February of 1939. Besides his cadre of green Cuban players, Cambria brought four Cubans with him to camp, sort of "something old, something new," which brought immediate attention from manager Bucky Harris and owner Clark Griffith.

Once again, Roberto Estalella and Rene Monteagudo were back in camp to see if they could stick with the team this year. Roberto did, Rene didn't; however, both would be integral as wartime replacement players in the 1940s.

The two other newcomers who were turning heads were Alejandro "Paton" (or "big foot") Carrasquel and Roberto "El Gurajiro" (the "farmer") Ortiz.

Carrasquel, the first Venezuelan to play in the major leagues, was already a seasoned veteran when he was signed by Cambria. After Carrasquel won the MVP award in the Cuban winter league in 1938, his manager, Jose Rodriguez, alerted Cambria about his pitching prowess. Shirley Povich, in a famously told story, said that Cambria "trailed him from the Havana [ballpark] park one day and got his name on a Washington contract while they were sitting on a park bench with an interpreter in between."[93] Carrasquel had little trouble with spring training batters, and the arm-starved Griffith had no recourse but to sign him to the team. "Al Alexander," as he was surreptitiously named by the press, made his debut in the majors in another oft-repeated saga. On April 23, 1939, Carrasquel made his first appearance in a Senators uniform in relief in the fourth inning of a 6–3 game with the dreaded Yankees. The first three batters he faced were Joe DiMaggio, Lou Gehrig, and Bill Dickey. He retired them all.[94]

Carrasquel went 5–9 in 1939, with seven complete games and a 4.69 ERA. He became a mainstay on the Senators' pitching staff for seven years from 1939 through 1945. He became one of the famous "Mexican Jumpers," going to Jorge Pasquel's banned Mexican League from 1946 through 1948. Coming back to the majors for a year in 1949 with the White Sox, he finished his career in the Texas League in 1956.[95]

No, the big news in the Senators camp that winter was Roberto Ortiz. Known as "The Giant from Central Senado," Ortiz stood 6 feet 4 inches tall and weighed 210 pounds in his prime. With brown hair, blue eyes, and thick biceps, he was the complete antithesis of the short, squat, black-hair-dark-eyed Estalella type. He was described by noted author Roberto Gonzalez Echevarria as "the very image of the *guajiro*, symbol of the fatherland."[96]

Cambria, another "giant" of verbiage, could not say enough about the kid: "He really is a great ball player. He's so good it was only the other day that I decided he was a pitcher. You see he can play center field like [Tris] Speaker used to do, and when he gets a hold of the ball with his bat, he drives it as long as Ruth. But, because he is faster than Feller and because he has a swell curve ball like Tommy Bridges, I decided he was a pitcher."[97]

Cambria, in Havana looking over Carrasquel, got wind of this huge guy in Camaguey, 400 miles southeast of Havana, and traveled all day to look him up, playing pick-up ball in the sugar cane. He had almost no formal baseball training whatsoever. He didn't know how to wind up or toe the pitching rubber, didn't know how to grip the ball. But his pitches had blazing speed and he hit a ton, so Cambria signed him on the spot.

Once Cambria brought Ortiz into camp, manager Bucky Harris had no idea where the man wanted to play or what he could do, and Ortiz was totally unconversant in the English language. Through many wild gestures like bat swinging and throwing a ball, they kind of figured it out. He told Cambria, who he thought knew some Spanish, to figure out what the boy wanted to do. Cambria went up to Ortiz and shouted in his face, "YOU PEETCH? YOU CATCH?" Harris said to Cambria, "Get out of here! You don't know any more Spanish than I do and all you're doing is yelling the same thing I've been saying only louder! That doesn't help!"

To alleviate the language problem, Harris asked permission from the Boston Bees to bring catcher Al Lopez down to Orlando to tutor Ortiz and help interpret. After a few days, Lopez was effusive in his praise: "There has been a remarkable improvement in his style. He's quick to learn and he's eager. At the rate he's progressing he can be quite a pitcher by the time the season opens, and he'll improve steadily after that. With an arm like he has there's unlimited possibilities. I don't blame Mr. Griffith and Bucky for getting excited about him."[98]

Ortiz was too green to make the club in 1939. He was sent to Cambria's Class-B Charlotte club for two years, where they tried to teach him to pitch; however, his bat was too lethal. He hit over .300 each year. Debuting with Washington in 1941, he stayed with the club through the war years, jumped to the Mexican leagues from 1945 through 1948, and returned briefly to Washington in 1949.

It would seem that all of Cambria's work was paying off. The 1939 Senators boasted eight players who were directly signed by Cambria: Alex Carrasquel, George Case, Roberto Estalella, Joe Krakauskas, Mickey Vernon, Johnny Welaj, Taft Wright, and a youngster named Walt Masterson.

Walt Masterson was a standout pitcher with North Catholic High School in Philadelphia who was famously "signed in the showers" by Cambria. He was also one of the "first 16" to go to Orlando in 1939. Clark Griffith asked in the *Washington Post*, "Ever hear of Walt Masterson? Well, we signed him off the Philadelphia sandlots right under the nose of Connie Mack. Ira Thomas, the A's scout, was ready to give Masterson a $3,000 bonus for signing. But Mack was in a bad humor that day and wouldn't listen to Thomas. So, we got Masterson. If anybody can throw a ball as hard as Feller, he can!"[99]

Despite veterans Buddy Myer and future Hall of Famer Rick Ferrell and the host of Cambria proteges, the Senators came in sixth in the league with a 68–87 record.

The press was having a field day with the Washington team in 1939. *The Sporting News* headline on March 30 read, "Cubans Turn Washington Spring Camp into Circus." Joe Williams of the *New York World Telegram* wrote:

> By opening day Washington will be known as the Cuban Giants. What is worse, they'll probably be playing like 'em. There was a time when old Griff used to try to build up his club, that that time is gone. All the Cubans, except possibly Estalella, have been over-ballyhooed. In short, old Griff seems to have reached the point where, like Connie Mack, he is satisfied if the club takes in enough at the gate to pay him a salary and meet expenses.[100]

Anything out of the ordinary was cause for derision, and the press was quick to pounce on anything for a headline or a story, anything that could make copy. Griffith was trying to put a competitive team on the field with very limited means and was relying on anything and anyone he could to put together a team, Cambria in particular. Sometimes Cambria would bring him talent. Sometimes he just brought him bodies.

What Griffith needed, unfortunately, was healthy bodies. Despite the early start to spring training and all of the platooning Griffith did, he was always short one or two men at a time. Taft Wright went down with an ankle sprain. When he was on the mend, George Case pulled a hamstring. When Case got back up, shortstop Cecil Travis had to be hospitalized with the flu. Next came third baseman Buddy Lewis, who strained a knee in an exhibition game, and before he could get back, Taft Wright went out again with a neck strain. The outfield of Estalella, Case, and Wright didn't play a game together throughout the spring. The pitching staff was Joe Krakauskus, Ken Chase, and whoever else Griffith could bring in after that.[101]

The Dave Hollidayoke Saga

By now, word of Cambria's scouting proclivities was legend, especially throughout Maryland's eastern shore. Word came from Annapolis, the state capital, of a tremendous pitching prospect who was burning up the Maryland sandlots.

William David Hollidayoke was the talk of the town around Annapolis. In 1938, he went 21–24 pitching for the Columbia Athletic Club in the Western Athletic league.[102] Playing for the Skipper Electric Athletic Club in April of 1939, he began the season by pitching a 2–0 shutout, striking out 23 batters. In his first five games, he pitched four shutouts.[103]

At six feet tall and 175 pounds, the 19-year-old was a pillar of confidence. Word of his exploits finally got around to the ear of Clark Griffith, who sent a detachment of his players to look over the youngster. After one of the Senators catchers caught him in his backyard in Eastport, Cambria was immediately dispatched to acquire the lad's services. Cambria watched him mow down 15 batters in a game and remarked how he was one of the best prospects he had looked at in many a day. "This kid will be in the big time before you know it," he said.[104] The overly ebullient Mr. Cambria didn't realize that this would be a case of just too much too soon.

Hollidayoke was signed by Cambria, then assigned to play just a few hours away from his home with the Salisbury Indians in the Eastern Shore League on June 14, 1939. Baseball reference has no actual statistics on Hollidayoke, but by all accounts, in the newspapers, he just fell apart. In the second game of a doubleheader with Milford on July 6, Hollidayoke pitched just 1⅓ innings in relief, giving up three walks, one strikeout, one wild pitch, and one hit batter.[105] In his next assignment, he also was credited with the loss, surrendering four hits in three innings, with one wild pitch and one hit batter.[106] "Wild Bill" Hollidayoke was then relegated to pitch batting practice for the Indians until he found his control. Evidently that did not help, and newspaper reports say he jumped his contract July 28, was released by the team, and played out the summer back in the Annapolis semi-pro leagues.[107]

Hollidayoke returned to Salisbury for the 1940 season and fared no better. Against Federalsburg on July 18, he struck out four but walked nine, gave up three hits in 4⅓ innings, with one wild pitch, but he didn't hit anyone. He did not do much better against Dover on June 29: five walks, four strikeouts, eight hits in three innings, and this time he did hit someone.[108]

The writing being firmly pasted on the wall, Hollidayoke put his baseball career on hold, joined the Naval Reserves, and was assigned to Guantanamo Bay, Cuba. His commanding officer got wind of his pitching experience and promptly assigned him to the division's team. In one game, he did well, striking out eight but walking six in a 2–0 loss to the Marines.[109]

Surviving the War, Hollidayoke returned home, tried out for and made the Seaford, Delaware, team in the Eastern Shore League. In the five games and 14 innings he pitched, he had two losses; he gave up 15 hits and 12 runs, had eight strikeouts, and issued 19 bases on balls. He played no more in organized ball after 1946.[110]

The whole Dave Hollidayoke saga is just another case in point in the desperation of the Senators organization. Cash-strapped and poor, unable to buy or trade for any type of quality players, they resorted to signing anyone who showed any prospects at all. Sandlot is sandlot and the big leagues are the big leagues, and hardly ever do the twain meet. Joe Cambria had much better luck with bush leaguers, who could actually produce, scouting in Cuba, and during and after the War, he almost exclusively spent his time and energies there.

Dave Hollidayoke became a minor player in a different sort of tragedy that would plague Cambria for the rest of the year.

Cambria was a bit too transparent with his dealing with his players. It was known all over the circuits how much he bounced his players from one team to the next, from one class and division to the next, without regard to their contract. This was especially true with his Cuban signees.

Bob Loane, a reserve infielder for the Senators, evidently got tired of being bounced around and sent an appeal to Commissioner Landis. Research indicates that he was assigned to six teams in three years, several of which were Cambria-owned. Cambria's whimsical transferring policies were coming under scrutiny by many of the club owners. On June 11, Landis, sensing a snake in the woodpile, ordered Cambria to produce his books on his players in Springfield, Greenville, and Salisbury. Cambria was unable to do so in a timely manner. After an investigation which stretched into August, he was slapped with some severe restrictions. He was forbidden to bring in any more players into organized ball teams or to make any more transfers for the remainder of the year. Springfield players Johnny Welaj and Bob Prichard were sent back to Washington, infielders Doug Dean and Ben Geraghty were ordered back to their original clubs, and Dave Hollidayoke's release was disapproved.[111]

Clark Griffith came to Cambria's defense, albeit in a rather back-handed manner, saying, "As far as I'm concerned, Cambria was negligent in producing his records. Joe has a bad organization. He has one girl to handle the pay rolls, contracts, transfer and that sort of thing for three teams—Springfield, Salisbury and Greenville. She can't possibly do it all, and she is a very competent person."[112]

Cambria was equally defensive talking to the Salisbury Times: "You can't get four years of records together in no time when you've got ball clubs to run too. He hasn't got anything on me and he won't have. I don't run things that way."[113]

Cambria eventually got his act together and produced his records to the satisfaction of the Commissioner. The ban on player transfers was lifted. Bob Prichard was sent back to Springfield, but Johnny Welaj remained in Washington. The other players were taken care of on a case-by-case basis. Hollidayoke, who had jumped his contract and was released on July 28, was approved and finally released.[114]

From then on, Commissioner Landis was all over Cambria like a bad suit. In September, Landis stripped Cambria of control of the Saint Augustine Saints in the Florida State league. Reason? Clark Griffith owned the Orlando Senators in the same league. It was against the rules; no major-league team could have an interest in two clubs in the same league.[115]

In November, Landis declared eight Salisbury players free agents and prohibited them from playing on any Cambria-owned club for between one and three years because of Cambria's mishandling of their contracts.[116] None of the players affected by the release ever made it into the big leagues or lasted very long in the minors.

However, to paraphrase ol' Blue Eyes, "the worst was yet to come." Cambria finally got caught with his hand in the cookie jar once too often, and even his dear friend and mentor, Clark Griffith, could not get him off, even for old times' sake. Cambria was slapped with a $1,000 fine ($18,640+ today) for signing young William J. Donovan to a desk contract, which was essentially a blank contract. This practice had been used rampantly by scouts and owners for years, and Commissioner Landis was vehemently opposed to it.

The synopsis of the story is as follows: Donovan was signed by Cambria to a blank contract of the Salisbury Indians. The young man sat on the bench for a week and was subsequently sent to another club without a contract. When one was produced, it was pre-dated and called for a cut in salary because he had not participated in any games in Salisbury, which is not permitted in the case of a first-year player. He was also not paid for his time at Salisbury, had to pay for his own travel to the other club, arrived at the other club penniless and wired Cambria for $10, which was refused. Court testimony revealed that Cambria and others had fudged the dates on his contract to reflect that he had been acquired correctly, but it did not jibe with Donavan's testimony.[117]

This would not be the last time Joe Cambria would get into trouble with the league officials.

CHAPTER 5

1940–1945: Washington at War

In 1940, the Blitzkrieg raged, France fell, bombs rained over Britain, and America was nervously looking over its shoulder.

"For everything there is a season, and a time for every purpose under heaven." Two major events started the year 1940, both involving Joe Cambria, one directly and the other indirectly, but both would have enormous significance to his career.

First, in June of 1939, Cincinnati Reds general manager Warren Giles announced that the Reds had entered into a deal with the Cuban government. The Cubans would provide four of their "best and brightest" to the Reds annually for a full major-league tryout, all expenses paid by the government and *Carteles* magazine (the *Life* of Cuba) as a show of appreciation for the many years the Reds had allowed Cuban players to "make good" in the American major leagues.[1]

The guiding factor in this development was one Lieutenant Colonel Jaime Marine, head of Cuba's *Direction General Nacional de Deportes*. The D.G.N.D. in essence functioned as the Cuban Sports Commission, similar to major-league baseball's governing body; however, its focus was on establishing guidelines and procedures for Cuba's burgeoning amateur baseball leagues. Colonel Marine, President Fulgencio Batista's number-two man in the government, was tasked with the job of organizing the pro and amateur leagues, building ballparks and enticing American baseball and tourists to come to Cuba. He also built Cuba's first baseball museum and Hall of Fame.[2] Herman Canal, sports editor of Tampa's Spanish language paper, *La Traduccion*, represented the Cincinnati club and negotiated the arrangements. The Cuban players would be named by a committee headed by influential sportswriter Jess Losada, who was associated with both *Carteles* magazine and the *Pueblo* daily newspaper. Losada was to Havana what Shirley Povich was to Washington, D.C. Both men were extremely knowledgeable about baseball talent, and their words had weight.[3]

The Reds had been in the good graces of the Cuban government for a long time. They were the first major-league team in the 20th century to scout and hire Cuban players, starting in 1911; however, this was not the only guiding notion in this agreement. All the teams in the American majors were aware of the successes Joe Cambria had over the past five years with signing good quality Cuban players for next to nothing, and all of them having a significant impact on the game. The Reds and Jess Losada saw this agreement as a way to cut down on Cambria's monopoly with all of the best of Cuba's amateur leagues. Losada had been openly critical of Cambria's shady signing practices.

Tryouts were held throughout the island, and 16 boys were originally selected. Of them, four players were selected and were set to travel to Tampa, Florida, in early March of 1940 to attend the Reds' camp. For several days, Reds management, the mayor of

Tampa, and officials from the Cuban settlement in Ybor City waited for the players to arrive. With a brass band waiting on the docks, all was going along swimmingly until the Cuban gunboat arrived in Tampa. There was no trace of any ballplayers. Those waiting were informed that Joe Cambria had already signed them to contracts with the Senators. The mystery was summed up by George Kerksey, UPI sportswriter for the *Miami News.*

> Cambria, a swarthy individual who moves in strange and inexplicable ways, hied himself off to Cuba last winter as soon as he heard the Reds had signed an agreement with the Cuban government to get the four best ball players from the land of the Bacardi.
> "I went right to the captain of the regiment who was in charge of the situation and told him that the Washington club had given Cuba a million dollars' worth of publicity on the players they brought up last year—Ortiz, Carrasquel and Monteagudo. And I asked him what had the Reds ever done for the Cuban players. The captain saw it my way. He called in the outstanding players and gave me my pick. I picked Lou Minsal and George Torres. They are willing to sign up because the Reds hadn't given them anything.[4]

It was an amazing display of both chutzpah and *cojones*. It is also not outside of the realm of possibility that money exchanged hands between the captain and Cambria.

Cambria had been down in Havana since early January, already scouting the winter leagues. He saw all four of the players picked out for the Reds: Louis Minsal, Natilla Jimenez, Agapito Mayor, and Chico Suarez. Cambria had signed them all, George Torres and a pitcher named Gonzalez. He picked Minsal and Torres to come to the Senators' spring training camp and left the others to season up in the Cuban Leagues until he was ready to bring them to Washington.

Needless to say, Jess Losada, who had spent months organizing the deal, was incensed and let his feeling be known to the press.

> I returned to Tampa thinking about the odyssey of these enthusiastic boys. They had signed with a poor club [Senators], at *infimal* prices. Joe Cambria, former "lavandero" [laundryman] and current scout from Washington; he had seduced them with "vulgares sinerismos" [insidious tactics]: a contract in the big league, a handout to sign and a salary lower than one is accustomed to in the big leagues of baseball. The boys on our soil go crazy before the possibility of getting into the big leagues … and so they sign whatever contract that is presented to them without understanding that they are offering their "juventud beisbolera" [literally their younger years of playing baseball] for a petty salary, on a team with few possibilities, that will send them to their mediocre branches in the minors, for the rest of their youth (juventud).[5]

Losada and several other writers delighted in referring to Cambria as a "laundryman," "tub thumper," or "wash tub man" as a means of deriding his business acumen about signing ballplayers.

Also displeased with the outcome was the Senators' manager, Bucky Harris, who exclaimed to writer George Kerksey, "Bah! Haven't I enough troubles without Cambria bringing me some more of those rhumba dancers to look over!"[6] Harris was not shy about his contempt for Cambria and his never-ending parade of Cubans into spring training camp. But Cambria, ever optimistic, cautioned Harris in the press, saying, "Someday we are going to get another Luque, Marsans or Gonzales out of Cuba. It's just a question of time. And I couldn't afford to let the Reds walk right in and get the cream of the crop."[7]

All of this craziness was for naught: All of the aforementioned players had excellent careers in the Cuban leagues, but not one of them made it to the major leagues.

Second, in December of 1939, at baseball's winter meetings, Commissioner Landis had had enough of the mishandling of minor-league players, their being covered up in multiple teams, and the general disregard for the players themselves. He decided to "go to the mattresses" with major-league owners. Perhaps it was Cambria who was the catalyst; we cannot be sure. However, Landis surely had grown tired of not only Cambria but also others like Cy Slapnicka, Branch Rickey (in particular), and a host of other scouts and owners for their blatant disregard for the baseball rules, and in particular the Detroit Tigers.

Landis, flexing his muscles for possibly the last time, asserted his power by declaring, once and for all, his eight rules concerning dealings with the players:

1. Players must not be signed to blank contracts and a true copy of the contract must be delivered to and left with the player.

2. Players must not be signed for other clubs, directly or indirectly, whether owned, affiliated or independent.

3. Players must not be placed with other clubs, except under proper transfer agreements, duly filed for promulgation, which agreements must be optional assignments if the assignor desires to retain a right of acquisition exercisable before the player has passed through a selection period at which he is subject to selection.

4. "Working agreements" must truthfully set forth in the officially filed document "the actual consideration, terms and conditions" of that agreement and there must be no "agreement not embodied in the document as filed."

5. "Working agreements" must be executed by the club actually making same and must not be executed in the names if affiliated or subsidiary clubs to whom the major or other higher-classification club supplies the necessary funds therefor by loans, advances, capital stock subscriptions, player purchases, or other methods whatsoever.

6. In every instance of secret player transfer hereafter effected, the player concerned will be declared a free agent, each club concerned will be fined $500, and each club official or employee participating therein will be placed on the ineligible list.

7. In every case of certificate of club relationship, affiliations and connections hereinafter filed, which is found to be misrepresent or untruthfully report any material fact, the club will be fined $1000 and the official executing such certificates will be placed on the ineligible list.

8. No contract can be pre-dated, and the salary of a first-year player cannot be reduced during his first season, regardless of the classification to which he is sent.[8]

The entire transcript of the case was printed in the December 14 and the January 18 edition of *The Sporting News* and is very revealing as to the lengths to which Landis was going in trying to control the covering up of players and other practices by the scouts and owners that he viewed as abhorrent. The commissioner had come to the aid of the player several times.

In his memoir, Leo Durocher summed it up nicely: "He was always on the side of the ballplayer. He had no use for the owners. 'Don't worry about them' he would tell me, 'They're not out to help you. You know where your friend is. Right here, **I'm** your man!' The only way a player could lose with him was to be daft."[9]

Landis was vehemently opposed to the minor-league system and, if he had his way, would have banned the whole thing. He felt it a form of slavery with the ballplayers held prisoner by the major-league clubs:

> From the beginning, the Commissioner has regarded the farm system as evil. Evil not because ownership of several non-competing clubs is bad in itself—although it is unquestionably preferable that every [minor league] club be independently owned and operated—but evil because such ownership inevitably are [sic] and will be operated to control great numbers of players, with consequent imperiling of their essential rights, if the rules do not prevent such operations, and also because it reduces Minor clubs to subserviency.[10]

He further believed that a draft system would help ameliorate the basic illegality and unfairness of the reserve clause, and that major-league ownership of minor-league affiliates was the cause for the precipitous drop in attendance in minor-league games.

Landis, in essence, was very much akin to Clark Griffith and Connie Mack: they were all 19th-century minds in a 20th-century world, each secretly longing for the "simpler days of baseball," as Landis stated so eloquently:

> I am convinced that I am right when I say that we ought to return to the system of one ball club under the control of one interest only. How can you expect a man to go out and root for a team when he knows that the team is owned by someone 1,000 miles away and he is cheering and backing their interests and not those of his own community? We ought to get back to a situation where a man can think about his town's club as his own and there is the old-time traditional rivalry between the towns.[11]

Landis hated what he termed "chain-store" baseball and said he was going to "keep hammering at this thing until something was done about it." This cause would be his *raison d'être* until his death in 1944.

The commissioner's justice came and that right soon. After a lengthy investigation preceding the announcement, the commissioner granted free agency to 91 players in the Tigers' organization, and 15 others were given the amounts paid for their contracts. Most of those players were in the Tigers' minor-league system, but four of the players had made it to the major leagues. *The Sporting News* reported: "A bewildering maze of interlocking connections between clubs [was] revealed by the commissioner in his findings, involving Detroit at the top and penetrating through various classifications down to Class D leagues, bringing to light secret agreements, under-cover shifting of players, control of as many as three clubs within one circuit and deliberate violation of known rules."[12]

The firestorm that erupted following the announcements was obviously mammoth. Even though Landis really could not enforce the decrees, the club owners knew he had enough power to make it uncomfortable for them to continue as they had. The owners begged for more time to reconsider. Ford Frick, president of the National League, and William Benswanger, owner of the Pittsburgh Pirates, both suggested that the minor-league rules needed to be rewritten or at least reviewed, and a lot of the turn-of-the-century rules repealed or reworked.[13]

After a meeting of the owners and the rules committee at the Belleair Hotel in Florida on February 12 and 13, 1940, Landis relaxed some of his demands, agreements were reached, and the system went back to nearly the same as before, but with several changes in place. Landis had succeeded in smacking the puppy with a rolled-up newspaper and got its attention.

The Landis decrees forced Cambria to watch his signing practices much more closely.

"Desk contracts" were now taboo, as was bouncing players from league to league, team to team to keep them covered up from other teams. Players had much more say in their treatment, and they knew they had a staunch ally in the commissioner. Unfortunately, the commissioner passed away in 1944, and when that happened, the full force of the reserve clause came into effect. The players were forced to fight for their salaries until the advent of Marvin Miller.

The Landis decrees made Cambria clean up his act in the present, but he would find ways to get into trouble in the future. Once Landis's initial ire about "chain store baseball" wore off, the Senators, with help from Cambria, developed a small farm system. Teams like the Cardinals, Yankees, Tigers, and Giants had literally dozens of farm teams scattered throughout the country. The Senators, probably for the sake of expediency, concentrated their system more to the East Coast. It consisted of the Trenton/ Springfield (NJ/MA) Senators (Class A), Greenville (NC) Spinners (Class B), Salisbury (MD) Indians (Class D), St. Augustine (FL) Saints (Class D), Orlando (FL) Senators (Class D), Sanford (FL) Greyhounds (Class D), Charlotte (NC) Hornets (Class B/C), and Chattanooga (TN) Lookouts (Class AA), and in 1941 they added the Tampa (FL) Smokers (Class D). Of these nine, four were operated by Cambria (Trenton, Salisbury, Greenville, and St. Augustine), while the others were affiliated outright with the Washington Senators and Griffith. Cambria was forced to sell St. Augustine and Salisbury in 1940, but they remained affiliated with the Senators nonetheless.

With the preponderance of Class-D teams, it was more "dime store" than "chain store" baseball.

Landis's minor-league decrees probably did not really affect Cambria all that much. His "working agreement" with Griffith was a handshake, a "wink and a nod" if you will. He was pretty much an independent operator from the beginning. He paid almost all his own expenses and only got money from Griffith if a prospective player made good or through player sales, either with the Senators or a farm team.

Add to that the fact that Griffith was one of the most influential owners in either league and could assuage the commissioner in most matters. Landis held Griffith in high respect and would be assured on many occasions that he would keep Cambria in check.

Despite all the brouhaha with Commissioner Landis during the winter months, Clark Griffith still had a ball club to put together, and things were looking somewhat slim. The 1939 Senators limped into sixth place in September with a 67–87 record, with little but Buddy Lewis's .319 batting average and George Case's 51 steals. Griffith needed arms, bats, and almost everything else and called upon everyone he knew to bring him players. Joe Engle, Joe Cambria, and Clyde Milan answered.

Starting on February 19, 1940, the *Washington Post* published "**Nat's Rookie Parade**," short bios on all of the year's "rookies." The term must have had a different connotation than it has today because many of the players mentioned had previous experience either with the Nats or other American League teams. They were "rookies" in the sense that they were trying out for first-string roster spots on the team, and this was their "rookie" tryout. Many of them were recommended by Cambria.

The following synopses provide context for Griffith's sense of desperation about the Senators' system[14]:

Almon Williams, pitcher: A big Texas lad, Williams went from high school to the Philadelphia A's, where he pitched in six games in 1937 and 1938, feasting on the Senators predominantly. Connie Mack sold him to Chattanooga in 1939, where he helped the team win the championship. Joe Engle sent him up to spring training in 1940, but elbow soreness curtailed his career, and he was out of baseball by 1941.

Walter Masterson, pitcher: Masterson was literally signed by Cambria in the showers at Shibe Park after Masterson went to the Philadelphia A's morning tryout camp in 1938. He went 2–2 in 1939 and won a starting job in 1940. In his 11 years with Washington, he went 62–88 with a 3.98 ERA. He went 78–100 with a 4.15 ERA in his career.

Early Wynn, pitcher: While visiting his grandmother, 16-year-old Early Wynn wandered into an open Senators tryout camp in Sanford, Florida. Impressed with his fastball, coach Clyde Milan had to convince Wynn's mother that professional baseball could pay for her son's education. Wynn spent a year in Sanford and three years in Charlotte before sticking with the Senators in 1941. In his eight years with Washington, he went 72–87 with a 3.94 ERA. Traded to the Indians in 1949 and the White Sox in 1958, he turned into a Cy Young Award winner and a Hall of Fame pitcher with exactly 300 wins, 2,334 strikeouts, and a lifetime 3.54 ERA.

Newton "Bucky" Jacobs, pitcher: Jacobs was still trying to make the starting rotation after three tries. He threw 11 games in 1937 and was sent back to Charlotte, later pitching two relief games for the Senators in 1939, and nine games in 1940. For his time with the Nats, he was officially 1–2 with a 4.91 ERA. After his cup of coffee in 1940, he was sent back to Charlotte and stayed in the minors until 1945.

Paul Gehrman, pitcher: Gehrman's only big-league experience was two games for the Reds in 1937. He was sent down to Durham, landed in Albany, and was purchased by the Senators in 1939, but never made it past the tryout camps: his fast ball never made it up to major-league standards. He remained in the minors until 1943.

Joe Mellendeck, Elmer Gedeon, Joe Frank, "Gee" Walker, and Fred Sington were part of a contingent of 11 current and former collegiate football players invited to rookie camp in 1939 and 1940. Looking for strong arms and bats, along with speed to patrol the vast expanses of Griffith Stadium, Griffith thought that perhaps he could find another Lou Gehrig or Frankie Frisch lurking in the gridiron group.

The story of Joe Mellendeck is a combination of serendipity and providence. Looking through the usual baseball reference sites, I found no mention of a Joe Mellendeck and thought there must be an error somewhere. Then fate lent a hand.

While waiting in line in my doctor's office, I was behind a gentleman. When he was finished checking in, the nurse said, "you may go right in Mr. Mellendick." Struck by the eerie similarity of the name, I waited until I was finished my appointment and asked to speak with the gentleman in the lobby. As fate would have it, his name is William G. Mellendick, nephew of Joe Mellendeck.

Bill Mellendick spent many a boyhood summers vacationing with Joe and his seven siblings at Deep Creek Lake in western Maryland and was more than happy to talk about his uncle.

In our interview, the first discrepancy we discussed was his name. Joe spelled it Mellendeck, whereas Bill spells it as Mellendick: "Yea, Joe was born with the Mellendick spelling, but he got razzed a lot playing ball with a name like 'Mellon Dick,' so he just changed it and started calling himself Mellendeck to avoid the razzing."

Born in Trenton, New Jersey, Joe came with his parents to Maryland, where his father found work in the auto factories. Joe first became a standout three-sports star at Loyola High School, one of Baltimore's most prestigious all-boys Catholic prep schools.

Graduating to Georgetown University, Joe became the star running back and a Catholic League All-American for the Hoyas starting 11 in 1937 and 1938, but a busted knee made him sit out his 1939 senior year. Focusing on baseball, he was scouted and signed by Cambria playing for a Glen Burnie, Maryland, semi-pro baseball team; however, he also got drafted by the Washington Redskins, who eventually passed on him after learning the extent of his knee injury.

Mellendeck became well-traveled, playing for parts of three years with Cambria clubs in Greenville, Springfield, Charlotte, Chattanooga, and Memphis from 1940 to 1942. Unfortunately, he had big "trouble with the curve" and a little trouble with the "brew," and he did not make it past the Senators' tryouts in either 1940 or 1941. Unable to afford the cost of an operation he needed on his knee, he took a voluntary year off in 1943 and worked in the Bethlehem Steel plant. In 1944, he talked with Tommy Thomas of his hometown AAA International League Baltimore Orioles, who agreed to pay for his knee operation. Mellendeck was operated on by Dr. George Bennett, who would also care for an ailing Roy Sievers of the St. Louis Browns in 1952.

Joe Mellendeck played three years for the O's, 1945 through 1947, where he averaged 58 hits, 14 doubles, 12 homers, 63 RBI, a .254 batting average, and a .344 on-base percentage. He was sent down to B ball for two years and then decided to hang it up. After his playing career ended in 1949, he and one of his brothers opened a sporting goods store and ran the Churchill liquor distributorship in Baltimore. Joe Mellendeck became a three-sport coach for the Calvert Hall Boys School in suburban Baltimore (archrivals to his Loyola alma mater), worked as a minor-league instructor for his hometown Baltimore Orioles, and along with Eddie Robinson, was a founding member and President of the Maryland Old Timers' Professional Baseball Association. Mellendeck continued to show his love for the game to the littlest of boys. He was instrumental in the development of the Baltimore Metropolitan Area Cub and Little League All-Star Game, held yearly at Memorial Stadium in the late 1950s and early 1960s. Between 30 and 40 boys ages 10 to 12 were selected from teams throughout the Baltimore area to play a yearly championship game. Mellendeck was the manager and coach for the American League team, and former Orioles pitching star Frank Sansosti managed the National League side.

Joe Mellendeck was married to his wife Helen (Pearson) for 35 years, had one son, lived in Catonsville, and died in 1975.[15]

Elmer Gedeon, outfield, was signed from the University of Michigan track team. He made the most of his opportunity in five games with the Senators in 1939, playing 38 innings in the outfield and handling 17 chances without an error for a sparkling 1.000 percent fielding average. Unfortunately, his bat did not sparkle, and he was sent down to Charlotte, then to Orlando, and left baseball in 1940. Gedeon was drafted into the Army before Pearl Harbor and became a B-25 bomber pilot. His plane was shot down on a mission on April 20, 1944, and he and his crew perished in the crash. He is one of only two major-league ballplayers to die in World War II.

Jim Dean, pitcher: Mr. James Harry Dean could not be confused with Mr. Jay Hanna "Dizzy" Dean but relished the similarity in the names. Having spent 1939 with the Sanford Florida team, he got a tryout in 1940 but was sent to Charlotte for more seasoning. He pitched two games for Washington in 1941, facing 12 batters, with two innings pitched, three earned runs, two hits, three walks, one hit batter, and a 13.50 ERA. He was sent down to Greenville, where he played out the end of the season and his career.

Joe Mellendeck of the 1946 International league Baltimore Orioles slides into third base on a close play. Mellendeck was just one of the many young men given the opportunity to forge a good life both in and out of baseball because of Joe Cambria (private collection of his nephew, William Mellendick).

Eddie Leip, second base: Signed by Cambria off the Trenton sandlots in 1936, he spent his first year at Trenton, then was sent to be part of Cambria's 1937 Salisbury Indians "Miracle Team" that came back from a 26-game deficit in June to take the championship. He could not unseat Buddy Myer or Jimmy Bloodworth for the second base job in Washington, so he was dealt to Pittsburgh in 1940. He seesawed through their major- and minor-league system for two years, served in the War from 1943 to 1945, then played in the Pittsburgh minors again from 1946 until ultimately finishing his career in 1950.

Bill Kennedy, pitcher: A local boy from suburban Alexandria, Virginia, William Gorman Kennedy came from the sandlots of the semi-pro Old Dominion league to Crisfield in the Eastern Shore league. Bucky Harris liked him enough in rookie camp to send him to Orlando and Charlotte from 1939 to 1941. He pitched for the Nats in relief in eight games in 1941, going 0–1 with 21 hits, 18 runs, and an 8.00 ERA. Sent back to the minors, he had two more cups of coffee in 1946 (1–2) and 1947 (0–0). In service from 1943 to 1945, he played in the minors from 1947 through 1953.

Louis Thuman, pitcher: Originally scouted as a third baseman by Joe Cambria while playing for an airplane factory team in Baltimore, Thuman was told by Cambria that his money was on the pitching mound. Cambria's prediction was as bad as it was for Roberto Ortiz. Even after Thuman went 8–15 with Greenville in 1939, the Nats still brought him up for a look-see. In three games in relief in 1939, Thuman gave up five hits, six runs, two walks, and had one strikeout in four innings with a 9.00 ERA. He had a two-game cup of coffee in 1940, giving up 10 hits and 11 runs in five innings with a 14.40 ERA. He stayed in Charlotte for the remainder of 1940, served in the war, and never returned to baseball.

Jimmy Pofahl, shortstop: Recommended by both Joes, Engle and Cambria, Pofahl became one of Griffith's more costly mistakes. After Pofahl burned up the American Association with the Minneapolis Millers in 1939, Griffith paid $40,000 and three players to get Pofahl. Touted as an extra-base hitter extraordinaire and a sure-handed shortstop, Pofahl was a true rookie in 1940. In 406 at-bats as the starting shortstop, he had a .234 batting average, 95 hits, 36 RBI, and two inside-the-park home runs. Unfortunately, his run production lagged in 1941 and 1942. He was traded to Philadelphia in 1943 and was sent back down to Minneapolis, but decided to stay with his war job and never returned to baseball.

Of course, the real sideshow of the rookie camp was the Cuban contingent brought there by Cambria. Louis Minsal (third base) and Arturo Castro (pitcher) were two of the four players "stolen" from the Reds. They, along with Jorge Torres (outfield), Roberto Ortiz, Alejandro Carrasquel, and Rene Monteagudo (pitchers), and Gilberto Torres (catcher and interpreter), made for a rambunctious bunch of happy Latins, with whom Bucky Harris was less than thrilled.

In short: Minsal, Castro, and Jorges Torres did not make the team but had fine careers in both the Cuban and Mexican leagues. Roberto Ortiz was sent to Charlotte, where they finally figured out he was not a pitcher but an outfielder who could hit a ton. He seesawed up and down between the Senators and the minors throughout the war years of 1941–1944, jumped to the Mexican leagues from 1945 to 1949, went back to D.C. in 1949–1950, and played out his career between Mexico and Cuba from 1952 through 1956. Rene Monteagudo, one of Cambria's original Cuban finds, pitched 22 innings for the Nats in 1938, was sent down and brought back up in 1940, where he pitched 100+ innings in 27 games, with a total 2–6 record and a 6.08 ERA. He was sent back down at the end of the season and was sold to Philadelphia in 1945, then found success in the Cuban and Mexican leagues from 1946 to 1951. Both Monteagudo and Ortiz were highly respected in Cuba for many years after their careers ended.

Despite all the happy Latins, muscle-bound footballers, and pea-green sandlotters, there was some cream that rose to the top.

After two years playing for Sanford, Sid Hudson became a starter for the Senators in 1940. He became a work horse in the rotation, with 19 complete games, a 17–16 record, and a 4.57 ERA, and was a runner-up for Rookie of the Year. Hudson stayed in the majors from 1940 through 1954, except for 1943–1945 service in the War. He stayed with the Senators, became their pitching coach with the 1961 expansion club, and stayed on when they moved again to Texas. He eventually became their minor-league pitching instructor and later coached the Baylor University baseball team.

Joe Haynes not only became a regular on the Senators' pitching staff in 1939 and 1940, but he also literally became a "member of the family" when he married Clark Griffith's adopted niece, Thelma. Haynes had two good years with the Nats and was traded to the White Sox, where he became a star. He went 14–6 for the 1947 White Sox and led the league with a minuscule 2.42 ERA. In 1948, he became an All-Star. Haynes was traded back to Washington in 1949 and stayed in the rotation until 1952. He became a pitching coach from 1953 to 1955 and then moved into the front office with the team.

Scouted and signed by Joe Cambria out of the Limeport, PA, semi-pro league, Johnny Welaj (Well-Eye) played the outfield alongside another Trenton, NJ, native, George Case, Jr. He made the team in the spring of 1939 but was sent back to Springfield for three weeks. Accused by Commissioner Landis of trying to "cover up" Welaj, Cambria sent Welaj back to Washington. In his 63 games in Washington that season, he had 201 at-bats, 55 hits, one homer, 33 RBI, and a .274 average. He stayed with the team for 1941 and 1942 until he was sent down to the minors in late 1942, then traded to Philadelphia in 1943. After military service for 1944 and 1945, Welaj returned to the minors in 1946 and stayed there until 1956.

The true cream of the rookie crop in 1940 was James "Mickey" Vernon. Signed by Joe Cambria out of the Eastern Shore League in 1937, Vernon originally tried out for the Senators at rookie camp in 1939. Unable to unseat Jimmy Wasdell for the first base job, he was sent back to Springfield; however, when Wasdell went down early in the season, Vernon quickly filled it. In 276 at-bats in 1939, he had 71 hits, 30 RBI, one homer, and a .257 batting average. He played only five games for the Nats in 1940 and was again sent down; however, he won the starting position in 1941 and never looked back. Even with 1944 and 1945 lost to the service, Mickey Vernon was a seven-time All-Star. He hit .286 lifetime with 2,495 hits, 1,196 runs, and a .359 on-base percentage, won the American League batting title twice, and still holds numerous fielding records. He has been constantly mentioned as a Hall of Fame candidate. He became the expansion Senators' first manager from 1961 to 1963 and remained a Washington favorite until his passing.

The sheer volume of players was a bit extraordinary for 1940, but not totally out of the ordinary for any year thereafter. Cambria always had a contingent of between eight and 20 players he brought up for Cuba, many of whom were summarily sent back home or found their way onto one of his many farm teams. There were myriad high school walk-ons who thought they were as fast as Feller but who also left hat in hand. "Bird dogs" and friends would always recommend players that Griffith would dutifully see. Rookie camp was always a way for Griffith and his managers to look over and discuss any prospect who might just make a difference to the Senators and of course, to Griffith's bottom line.

Cuba was not the only place Joe Cambria would go to find raw talent. As fate would have it, to beat the bushes, he only had to go out his back door.

The Joe Stripp School of Baseball was started in Orlando in 1937. "Jersey" Joe Stripp was a third baseman who played 11 major-league seasons with the Cincinnati Reds, Boston Braves, Brooklyn Dodgers, and St. Louis Cardinals. Stripp was known for both his hard-scrabble play and his tremendous proclivity for holding out on his contract. Stripp not only raised the ire of all his managers and owners by holding out for almost every year he played, but also gained their respect as a tough negotiator. He said he learned the business side of baseball from his mentor, Joe Tinker, he of the famous Chicago Cubs double play combination. Stripp also held the distinction of being the last batter to hit against a legally thrown spitballer when he batted against Burleigh Grimes in 1934.

Stripp, like Cambria, had a fondness for showing young men the ropes of the baseball trade. He started the school in 1937 under a working agreement with Griffith: "I have the approval of both Mayor V.W. Estes and Clark Griffith for the use of Tinker Field," Stripp said. "Griffith will be given first chance at any likely looking youngster who are developed."[16]

And youngsters they were! Most of the boys were between 16 and 19 years old. Stripp only took between 125 and 150 boys each year, carefully looking for those who had a legitimate chance at a career: "I'm looking for big league prospects and don't want young fellows without ability. It wouldn't be fair to take their money unless they had an even chance of earning a living on the diamond."[17]

The camp ran from around mid–January until the major-league spring training camps began in late February. From the beginning of his school, Stripp always had a waiting list of eager young hopefuls.

Since this was a fallow time for most ballplayers, Stripp had no trouble attracting some of the best the big leagues had to offer as instructors. His teachers included, among others, Joe Tinker, Van Lingle Mungo, Al Lopez, Bob Weiland, Ducky Medwick, Johnny Clooney, Don Padgett, Dutch Leonard, Earl Torgeson, and many more. Throughout its 18 years of operation, Stripp's school became a haven for major- and minor-league managers and scouts alike.

Griffith typically made an annual pilgrimage to Stripp's school, but when he could not, he would send the redoubtable Mr. Cambria to look over the kids and maybe make a deal or two. For Griffith, this was always a "crap shoot." Early on in their relationship, Griffith expressed his misgivings about Cambria's scouting abilities. In a 1936 *Washington Post* article, Shirley Povich discussed the allegiance between the two: "The paradox of the alliance is that as a scout and judge of talent, Griffith rates Cambria slightly below a blindfolded tailor's dummy. But he gambles heavily on the law of averages that some day Cambria will turn up with a genuine 'find' among the hundreds of youths he shepherds into organized baseball."[18]

History will show that Cambria had a good "baseball eye" (Mickey Vernon, Ed Yost, Camilo Pascual, Tony Oliva), but sometimes his regular eyes may have been myopic. In January of 1940, he went down to Stripp's school in Orlando to look over prospects for the Senators. Cambria watched the drills and practice, then called Stripp over to say he had spotted a bright youngster and wanted to talk deal. When Cambria pointed out the "youngster," Stripp burst into laughter. Cambria had picked out Johnny Cooney, a 38-year-old, 15-year veteran who was, at that time, playing with the Boston Bees and was one of Stripp's instructors.[19]

Cambria would also make his yearly journey to the school to try to round out his own rosters of minor league teams. In 1941, his "keen eye" picked out three young men, all pitchers and all 18 years old, that Cambria said "couldn't miss": Raymond Fancell, Mario Secciani, and Henry Alexander. Fancell played three years in the minors with four years off during the War years, Secciani played two years of minor-league ball in Florida, and Alexander pitched for one year with the Mayodan Millers in the Bi-State League.[20] All three missed.

Perhaps Branch Rickey's "from quantity comes quality" adage held water. From the beginnings of the minor leagues until today, there were and are thousands of young men trying to pluck that brass ring and make it to the big leagues, only to have their hopes dashed by the fact that they could not hit or throw a curveball. Hundreds of both white and tan players came through the Senator's training camps and into the minors and maybe had a cup of coffee in the majors. Cambria is purported to have signed over 400 players out of Cuba alone. The system relies on all those thousands of youngsters to produce a Musial, Mays, Mantle, Aaron, Gibson, or Clemente; however, serendipity plays a part as well. Tom Greenwade just happened to stumble upon "Little Mickey Mantle" playing in Alba, Montana, and the rest is history. The same story is repeated dozens of times with almost all the superstars of the past. The talent is out there: one must find it first. The cream does rise to the top but only if you see it, and if you do not see it, you will not know.

Despite talented yet vastly underpaid Cuban pitchers like Alejandro Carrasquel, Sandalio Consuegra, Conrado Marrero, Camilo Pascual, and Pedro Ramos, and run producers like Buddy Lewis, Cecil Travis, Mickey Vernon, Pete Runnels, Roy Sievers, Jim Lemon, Bob Allison, and Harmon Killebrew, the Senators never won a championship after 1933. From 1940 until they moved to Minnesota in 1961, they placed in the first division only three times—1943, 1945, and 1946.

Cambria's "seat of the pants" business model finally caught up with him during the early spring-training months, causing some major consternation. The Greenville Spiders and the Springfield Senators (both owned by Cambria) were both working out at the Greenville stadium in March. Springfield manager Spencer Abbott and Greenville manager Alex McColl were forced to wander about and ponder for days. Why? Because Cambria had signed so many players during the winter months and had shuffled them more than a Vegas blackjack dealer, so much so that neither he nor the two managers knew who belonged to whom! Both managers had to wait until Cambria could find all the contracts and send them out to the managers.[21]

Business as usual for Joe Cambria, pain in the neck for everyone else!

Perhaps it was the uninspired play of Gee Walker. Walker, who was traded from the White Sox to the Senators for "big hit, no field" Taft Wright and pitcher Pete Appleton, seemed lethargic. Walker was not "phoning it in" (.298 BA, second in steals, third in runs scored, tied for first in homers); he just seemed to be dissatisfied with playing for Griffith. Perhaps it was the lackluster performance of the pitching staff. Joe Haynes was out with a sore arm, and the only two Cubans on the staff, Alejandro Carrasquel (6–2) and Rene Monteagudo (2–6), were working hard to pick up the slack. Griffith was even talking about trading the durable Joe Krakauskas for some better arms. Perhaps it was Bucky Harris's constant complaining of having to listen to the Cubans and their "monkey talk."

Whatever it was, by mid–August, Griffith was bordering on distraught and possibly took it out on Joe Cambria. In a *Sporting News* article, Griffith told Cambria to stop beating the bushes in Cuba, South America, and other places outside of the U.S. "I just think they are pretty well milked," said Griff, "and it isn't worth the trouble for a while yet."[22]

As we shall see, managerial troubles were probably more the cause. However, world trouble would not only make the Cubans worth the trouble, but also a necessity.

There was trouble brewing in Salisbury, and this time it was a lack of communication that got Joe Cambria in hot water.

"We'll get our back pay before we go on the field," said Elwood Hines, catcher for Cambria's Salisbury Indians and team spokesman. The players believed they were not receiving the monies they thought they were supposed to receive for the playoff games. Hence, the Centreville–Salisbury evening game of September 6 was canceled because (a) only two players from Salisbury showed up on the field; and (b) both managers decided that the balmy 70-degree clear night sky was "threatening to rain."

Evidently, neither Cambria nor business manager Melvin Murphy had discussed league rules with the players, which stated that the players received only straight salary through the playoffs but were not owed a cut of the gate. Salisbury was standing fourth in the league and assured of a playoff berth. The players had sent two complaints about delinquent bills to Judge W.G. Bramham, president of the minor leagues.[23]

Cambria made a trip to the Eastern Shore, discussed the situation, all was resolved, and the games went forward. Salisbury still ended up fourth in the league but won the league championship, beating Milford, four games to two.[24]

Who is this guy?

I would like to think the phone call went something like this: "Hey Joe! It's me, Alex. Alex Sparra. Yea, I played for you in Albany '35, remember? Yea. Look, I'm up here in Havre de Grace, Maryland, lookin' over Glen Burnie and Havre de Grace playin' for the semi-pro league championship and boy! Do I have a kid you gotta see! This short-stop, Merton Fennimore, is the cat's pajamas! Throws, hits, runs like a deer, you gotta see him! … Ok, I'll see you when you get here."

So, Cambria hops on a bus somewhere south of Washington, D.C., and travels 150 miles up U.S. Route 40 to see the kid. (Today, with U.S. 95 North, this trip would be less than two hours. In 1940, a good four hours at least.)

"OK, show me this Fennimore," a weary Cambria says to Sparra upon arrival. "Sure," says Sparra, "and if ya want, I'll help get him for ya!" Sparra points out the youngster, and Cambria's countenance just sags.

"You mean that guy? That's Eddie Feinberg from my Greenville Sally League team! Where the hell has he been? And here I spent good money to come and look at my own ballplayer!"

Evidently, young Mr. Feinberg had pulled a fast one on Cambria. According to Baseball-Reference.com, Feinberg played 46 games with Greenville in 1940 and must have failed to report to the team at some point, instead going home to Philadelphia. He somehow wound up playing in Havre de Grace in late 1940.

Feinberg hit the winning home run for Havre de Grace to win the championship, and it was his swan song. After two cups of coffee with the Philadelphia A's in 1937 and 1938, Feinberg languished in the minors. Greenville and Havre de Grace were his last known stops. Another "can't miss."[25]

And Lo! a decree was sent forth from King Mountain of Landis that those who doth scout for a major-league team must henceforth cease and desist from owning any minor-league baseball club. And thus it was that by Christmas, Joe Cambria, who had become officially recognized and hired by Griffith as a scout for the Senators, was forced to dispose of his ownership of all his minor-league teams. He sold his Salisbury Indians to Reuban Levin, a minor-league owner from Bennington, Vermont, and the Spring-field Senators were turned over to his brother John.[26] The Sally League Greenville Spinners were sold outright to Clark Griffith. With all his other teams, Cambria relinquished ownership in the name of other trusted friends and colleagues and became a member of the board or an executive of some sort. He never really left the day-to-day operation completely but kept his fingers in the pie as it were. In the future, he would buy teams, but in the name of Clark Griffith, and become a general manager of some type, but never an outright owner. He used all his teams to shuttle players back and forth, especially his Latin players, still covering them up to the chagrin of Commissioner Landis.

As the Year Ended

Shirley Povich ended his October 13 column with two statements, one of which speaks to the expert timing of Joe Cambria and the poor timing of Clark Griffith:

"The Red Sox offered Joe Cambria $2,500 for Mickey Livingston, his catcher at Springfield, but Cambria demanded $3,000. Two weeks later, Brooklyn bought Livingston in the draft and paid Cambrai $6,000.... Clark Griffith is delaying a $120,000 expenditure for lights at his ballpark until he learns how baseball is going to be affected by the draft and the threat of war."[27]

Griffith should have bought those lights sooner rather than later.

1941

The War

In the spring of 1941, Hitler conquered the Balkans, which was a precursor to the invasion of Russia in June. Also around that time, Hitler announced his plans for the "final solution" to the Jewish "problem," and America was nervously looking over its shoulder.

Spring Has Sprung

February spring training of 1941 dawned sunny, warm and Latin-free. Griffith's late-season edict of "no more Cubans" to Cambria held true. According to Shirley Povich of the *Washington Post*, "The only Latin with the Washington team is Carrasquel, the forbidding looking fellow who looks as if he should be climbing over the side of a pirate ship with a dagger in his teeth. And Carrasquel is not a Cuban but a Venezuelan. The fact that he is still being retained by the Nats is less a tribute to Carrasquel than it is a sad commentary on the state of [Washington's] pitching."[28]

This, of course, was most pleasing to manager Bucky Harris,

> The Cubans were a trial to [Harris], who refused to learn Spanish on the grounds that he was too busy otherwise. More than once the Nats' manager had to step in also to halt the squabbling between the Cubans and the American boys on the squad who resented their presence. Harris demanded that the Cubans be treated with respect as long as they were with the club. But he never did become raptured over the possibility that they would be with the team a long while."[29]

The national baseball scribes always loved to either incite or continue a good controversy whenever they could, and Bucky Harris's distaste for the Cubans was gaining more traction every day. In the major league claiming stakes, the Senators were able to take 14 Yankees into their system. "Just give me 10 of those Yankees and see how quick I [get] rid of 10 of my players," said Bucky Harris.[30]

Whitney Martin of the Associated Press reported, "At that, Harris thinks the Nats' outlook is 'a little better' than it was a year ago, and he is much happier at his work. A year ago, he was knee deep in a choice assortment of Latins whom Joe Cambria had smoked out from the cane fields of Cuba, and Bucky couldn't tell if they were asking him for the correct time or the hit-and-run sign."[31]

This did not deter our intrepid Mr. Cambria at all. He showed up in camp with another crop of "can't miss" pitching prospects. They were Joe Cleary (pitched one game for Nats in 1945), Joe Poydock (no major-league appearances), Louis Thuman (pitched five games in 1939–1940), Alex Zukowski (no MLB appearance), and Bill Zinser (pitched two games in 1944). The only pitcher who was of any significance was a local boy from Alexandria, Virginia, William Gorman "Bill" Kennedy. He pitched in three seasons for the Nats, 1943, 1946 and 1947, primarily in relief. For his big-league career, he went 2–6 in 31 games, 63⅔ innings pitched, 23 strikeouts and a 6.79 ERA. He did not miss. All the rest did.

The Farm Makes Good

Joe Cambria was a happy camper for at least a brief moment in June of 1941. Dispatched to Charlotte to witness a game between Norfolk and Charlotte, he was happy to report: "In the sixth inning of tonight's game, with the score tied 6–6, Outfielder Roberto Ortiz hit a home run over the left field wall. On the next pitch, Outfielder Joe Mellendeck hit a home run over the left field wall. On the next pitch, Outfielder Jim Mallory hit a home run over the right field wall."[32]

It certainly helped that the left field fence in the Charlotte ballpark was a mere 360 feet from home plate, as opposed to the 407-foot left field fence in Griffith Stadium.

Also, during the spring of 1941, Cambria got himself into an imbroglio which did not turn out well for him. In March, Cambria filed a complaint in Baltimore Superior Court for "improper conduct unbecoming to and unworthy of a member of the bar" against his own lawyer, Willis R. Jones, chairman of the Maryland State Board of Corrections. The complaint alleged that Jones received "unduly high" fees, withheld information from clients (Cambria), and acted improperly in connection with the sale of the Bugle Coat and Apron Company.[33] The laundry business had been Joe Cambria's cash cow since he settled in Baltimore and was almost solely responsible for his rise as a minor league baseball mogul. He was not about to let it go without a significant profit.

The deal began in 1938, when Cambria sold his interest in the business to a New York firm for $265,000 ($4.83 million in 2020 money.) Jones, Cambria's attorney, charged a fee of $32,000 for the sale (approximately 12 percent in 1941). Jones contended that there had been no complaint of excessive fees until 18 months after all the fees had been agreed upon and that the figure was arrived at by "an amicable agreement with Cambria."[34]

What is significant about this story is that we have one of a very few accounts where Joe Cambria's wife, Charlotte, is actually involved. Charlotte testified that, although the sale occurred in April of 1938 and was settled in June, she was unaware of the fees until she filed her income taxes in March the following year. She thought Jones' fees were part of another lawyer's fees; however, she knew that Jones was employed as a trustee of the money received from the sale of the company.

The defense introduced an affidavit, signed by Mrs. Cambria, which stated she knew on the day of the sale that Jones was to receive a $20,000 fee for his work to date. Jones received in excess of $32,000 in total for his work on the transaction. After cross-examining Cambria, Chief Judge Samuel K. Dennis stated that in view of the profits made by Cambria on the business sale, the fees were not excessive.

In the end, Mr. Jones was accused of conflict of interest, but was not officially charged. The three-panel court voted to dismiss the petition to discipline Jones in any way. Cambria was probably charged some court costs, but in the end, his parsimony proved his undoing.[35]

It must have been the enormous deal that Cambria made, selling his Albany Senators to the Cubs for thousands of dollars in 1936, that endeared him to boss Clark Griffith. It was, without a doubt, a blockbuster sale. Perhaps Griffith thought Cambria could pull off another one; hence the reason he sent him to Milwaukee to buy the venerable Brewers in June of 1941.

The Milwaukee Brewers were a storied franchise. Beginning as the National League Greys in 1878, they changed their names to the Brewers, and the team became a professional team as a founding member of Ban Johnson's upstart American League in 1901. Relocating to St. Louis, they became the original Browns. The Brewers would re-form, and from 1902 until 1952, would be the longest lasting club in the American Association, becoming champs of the league six times.[36] The American Association was the highest level of the minor league system, and the city embraced and supported the team since its inception.

However, time and the impending war were not kind to the Brewers, and attendance lagged considerably, so much so that by 1941, the team was without an owner. Minor League President George Trautman took over the team with a durable power of attorney and set about to attract a real owner.

Cambria was dispatched to Milwaukee to try and seal the deal. The *Washington Post* reported that they would try to work a deal lower than the $125,000 asking price.[37] Evidently our Mr. Cambria met his match in the form of a young Mr. William Veeck, Jr.

The legend of Bill Veeck, Jr., is one of unparalleled import to baseball and American history, and frankly, why a major motion picture has not been made about his life is a mystery. Books such as *Veeck—As in Wreck* and *Bill Veeck: Baseball's Greatest Maverick* more than aptly spell out the life and career of baseball's greatest promoter. He believed ball games should be fun and invented new and exciting ways to show his fans a great time at the ballpark. From 3-foot 7-inch Eddie Gaedel's one and only at-bat to Grandstand Managers Night to Dixieland bands, exploding scoreboards and players in shorts, Veeck was never at a loss for a new idea to please the crowd. Rather than giving away free beer to the first 1,000 customers, he thought it would be more fun to give one customer 1,000 beers and see what he did with it!

The Brewers would be Veeck's first foray into team ownership. Although dead broke and without any personal resources, Veeck, along with the avuncular, banjo-strumming, ex–Chicago Cubs manager, "Jolly Cholly" Grimm, somehow managed to cobble together a syndicate of Chicago and Milwaukee businessmen who came up with $50,000 for the club and were willing to assume $50,000 of the club's debt of $118,000. Veeck got help from Phillip Clark of City National Bank of Chicago and Lester Armour of the meat-packing family, both old friends of his father's, along with a sprinkling of

Milwaukee investors. The Brewers became Veeck's guinea pig for his myriad crazy promotional schemes, making it up as he went along. For one game, he gave away live farm animals, which actually turned out to be a big hit! After finishing dead last in 1941, Veeck and Grimm managed to turn the team completely around, winning three pennants in five years, with some managerial help from a young Casey Stengel. In 1945, he sold the team for a $275,000 profit.[38]

How much of that profit Veeck saw is unclear. In retrospect, however, Cambria's sale of the 1936 Albany Senators netted him a kingly sum in Depression-era dollars. Cambria may have been a better bargainer, but he never put a Major League championship team on the field.

Perhaps the biggest change to occur with the Senators in 1941 was not Joe Cambria's lack of Cubans but Clark Griffith's change of mind. After seeing the Cincinnati Reds play the first Major League night baseball in 1935, Griffith remarked that the National League was turning into "a circus" and staunchly opposed what he considered a fad. As mentioned earlier, Griffith was unabashedly opposed to baseball being played in something other than "God's own sunlight."

But the growing prospects and uncertainty of the United States' involvement in the looming war in Europe, coupled with the fact that the Reds had drawn five times the number of fans with a night ball game, made him reconsider his options. With an investment of $130,000 (over $2.4 million in 2021 dollars), Griffith erected lights around the stadium. At 8:30 p.m. on Wednesday, May 28, the great Walter Johnson strode out to the pitcher's mound and tossed a perfect strike across the plate as an engineer flipped the switch to turn night into day in Washington, D.C. Twenty-five thousand people shed their coats and hats, rolled up their sleeves, and began to celebrate like it was a Fourth of July picnic. The hated Yankees, however, played ungracious guests and served up a 6–5 defeat, giving Washington its 10th straight loss of the season.[39]

Griffith's investment paid off handsomely, saving the Senators from certain financial ruin during the war years and providing much needed relaxation and entertainment to the weary first shift workers of the Washington, D.C., community.

December 7, 1941

There are certain dates in the modern era that will forever evoke feelings of dread and fear and are often accompanied by "do you remember where you were?" November 22, 1963, in Dallas, Texas, and September 11, 2001, in New York City and Washington, D.C., will be forever etched into the collective consciousness. December 7, 1941, the "day that will live in infamy," became the first great American wake-up call on that sunny Hawaiian Sunday. Not only the United States but also the whole world changed on that day. America was plunged, again, into a global conflict that would have everlasting consequences.

Tradition has it that when Lord Cornwallis surrendered his British troops at Yorktown, Virginia, in 1781, the fife and drum corps played the British ballad "The World Turned Upside Down." Surly it was as such on that infamous day in December. Nothing would ever be the same.

However, there was always baseball.

1942

Less than two months after the attack on Pearl Harbor, the United States sent its first troops to England. However, Germany and Japan made decisive victories month after month. It was General Jimmy Doolittle's raids on Tokyo and Yokoyama that provided a little meat and potatoes to an America that had been living on a diet of bad news. The Battle of Midway was a decisive victory for American Naval forces in the Pacific and a major turning point in the War. The United States was no longer looking nervously over its shoulder but was now standing shoulder to shoulder with our Allied brothers in arms.

> Baseball will help keep our front strong. Not only baseball but all the other sports. Even during these times it must be kept in mind that all work and no play makes John a dull boy. The harder the work, the greater the need for both mental and physical recreation. Americans poses the happy faculty of working hard and then playing hard. That helps make us Americans. And by continuing to be Americans we write a new guarantee on America's survival in this fight to the finish. So in our present troubles and the worse ones which may come, let's don't forget how to live—to live like Americans have always lived and always will live![40]

America was rallying for the war and what could be more American than baseball? The above quote by Red Camp, taken from the *Greenville News*, holds the same poignancy as the famous soliloquy given by James Earl Jones in the Kevin Costner movie *Field of Dreams*: "The one constant through all the years, Ray, has been baseball." Baseball would be the glue, the one thing that would bind America through this horrible struggle. Baseball needed to go on in order to bring calm, sense and repose from the insanity of war.

However, Clark Griffith was in a deep financial bind.

Owning a ball club in one of the smallest markets in the Major Leagues, Griffith knew that a cessation of play would destroy him financially. No one was sure at first if baseball play would go on. He had to show that baseball was vital to the American war effort. He had to do something fast, and he did two things in particular. First, he looked to the past.

During World War I, Griffith became an active fund raiser for the war effort, holding War Bond and other fundraising rallies. One initiative he started was the "Clark Griffith Ball and Bat Fund," which provided servicemen with baseball equipment. Griffith suggested that if every fan contributed 25 cents, balls and bats could be provided for the servicemen in their "training camps" overseas. President Wilson, who wholeheartedly supported this initiative, gave his quarter, and Griffith raised $40,000 for the fund (approximately $886,000 in 2021 money). Unfortunately, when the equipment was finally purchased, the merchant ship carrying it to Europe was sunk by a German submarine.[41]

Less than a week after the bombing of Pearl Harbor, Griffith sprang into action again, starting the Baseball Equipment Fund, based upon his World War I idea. The initial funds of $25,000 were raised at baseball's winter meetings, where both the National and American Leagues plus the Baseball Writers Association of America contributed. Griffith led the way by placing an order for 18,000 balls and 4,500 bats with three of the leading sports manufacturing firms in the country. Funds for both equipment and the ongoing war effort would also be raised during the two All-Star Games that were scheduled for the year, as well as other special games. Griffith worked together with Major Theodore Banks of the Army's athletics and recreation branch to see that the equipment was delivered safely into the hands of the American G.I.'s.[42]

Second, Griffith went a step further to try to ensure that baseball would continue throughout the War. Upon the request of the Commissioner, Griffith hand-delivered a letter from Landis to President Franklin Roosevelt, asking him his intentions as to whether baseball should continue play. Griffith had developed strong relationships with the Washington power elite ever since William Howard Taft threw out the first Opening Day pitch in Griffith Stadium in 1910. Griffith also used all his diplomatic skills to influence Roosevelt's intentions. The entreaties of Landis and Griffith resulted in the famous "Green Light" letter, sent to Commissioner Landis on January 15, 1942, with Roosevelt giving his enthusiastic support for the continuance of baseball games as a way for the American people to relax from the work of the war effort.[43]

The "Green Light" letter also contained a belated Christmas present for Griffith. Roosevelt expressed his desire that night games be played so that the day shift workers could see games in the evening. (Griffith, originally opposed to night baseball, changed his mind in 1939 when he saw the attendance figures at Philadelphia's Shibe Park.) Griffith knew this would be a tremendous boon to his bottom line. He fought to get unlimited night games in Washington but was outvoted by the National League. Still, he pressed on and fought to get 21 night games for the Senators; however, he was not satisfied with just that. He continued to lobby both Landis and the White House. Finally, in July of 1942, citing the needs of the wartime shift workers, Landis granted his wish for unlimited weekday night games. Griffith was able to juggle the team's schedule to allow for 35 night games, which would almost ensure his solvency during the war years.[44]

Yet this was still not enough for the ever-parsimonious Griffith. He worked tirelessly to get the league to lift the restrictions on doubleheaders, which could only be scheduled on the fourth home Sunday. On February 5, 1942, *The Sporting News* announced that Sunday doubleheaders could now be played on any Sunday.[45]

More money for Griffith. Lots more work for the team. A potential quagmire later on.

Griffith knew that just night baseball games and extra doubleheaders would not be the panacea to cure his financial ills. The War would demand more belt tightening and more drastic action.

Perhaps he, too, felt like Landis: that the minor leagues were a form of slavery. Or perhaps he felt that he had too many minor league affiliates on his roster. Whichever was the case, Griffith, unable to get the state of South Carolina to reconsider its Sunday "blue laws" against baseball games, decided to divest himself of his Class B Sally League Greenville Spinners. He had bought the team from Cambria in 1941, when Cambria was forced to sell all his minor league holdings. The team cost him $28,000 in fees and operating losses. Cambria lost his $17,000 stadium and its lighting system. With that move, Washington pared down its farm system to officially include three teams: Class A-1 Chattanooga, Class B Charlotte and Class B Orlando.[46]

Griffith's unloading of his Greenville team was just a part of the iceberg that calved into the ocean of teams lost to the war. Over 500 major leaguers, including present and future stars like Joe and Dom DiMaggio, Bob Feller, Hank Greenberg, Phil Rizzuto,

Hank Bauer, Gil Hodges, Stan Musial, and Yogi Berra, went into wartime service; however, the brunt of the manpower came from the minor leagues. With most of the minor leaguers being young, single and with no dependents, they were prime fodder for the draft. Over 4,000 minor leaguers were called to arms, which significantly affected the entire minor league system.[47]

In 1941, 41 complete leagues (291 teams) started and finished the season. In 1942, 31 leagues started and only 24 finished (207 teams). It grew worse from there. In 1943 (67 teams) and 1944 (70 teams), there were only 10 leagues, with 12 leagues (86 teams) in 1945. Getting an accurate count is hard since many individual teams would play almost halfway through the year and then fold up due to wartime conscription. When the boys came home in 1945, it would all change.[48]

Now was the time for Joe Cambria to earn his keep with the Senators, and the war years made him busier than a woodpecker in a petrified forest.

Clark Griffith had to become creative in order to acquire professional caliber players, and he would need Joe Cambria's expertise more than ever, The Senators lost 13 players to the draft in 1942, more than any other club in the American League.

The biggest losses were All-Stars Buddy Lewis and Cecil Travis. Travis was the sparkplug of the infield; Lewis and George Case controlled the expansive Griffith Stadium outfield. With the exception of catcher Jake Early, first baseman Mickey Vernon and outfielder George Case, the Nats would put an (almost) entirely new team on the field in 1942: Ellis Clary (second base), John Sullivan (SS), Cuban Roberto Estalella (third base), Stan Spence and Bruce Campbell (OF). Dutch Leonard and Ken Chase were gone from their starting pitcher slots. In their place came Bobo Newsom, Early Wynn, Walt Masterson, Alejandro Carrasquel and Bill Zuber.

Cambria would become an integral part of the successes of the Senators between 1942 and 1945. The Nats would finish in the first division twice during those years, in large part due to many of Cambria's American and Cuban acquisitions. In 1942 alone, he was responsible for almost half the team's players: Roberto Ortiz, Chile Gomez, Alejandro Carrasquel, Roberto Estalella, Mickey Vernon, George Case, Early Wynn, Walt Masterson, Bill Kennedy, Eddie Lyons and Alex Kvasnak.

The U.S. government, unwittingly or not, played a major role in Joe Cambria's success during the war years. He was able to bring dozens of Cuban and other Latin ballplayers into the U.S. on a 12-month, non-resident alien status because the government classified them as "entertainers."[49] A provision in the Selective Service act provided that actors, musicians and other entertainers were necessary for the mental health and well-being of the American psyche. Once Joe Cambria got wind of that proviso, it was Katie bar the door.

The slogan "hit .300 and see America" quickly spread throughout the island. Every man or boy who could lift a bat furiously worked on their baseball skills in an attempt to secure a position in either the major or minor leagues. With the tremendous volume of talent on the island, Joe Cambria began spending more time in Cuba than Baltimore.

But Cambria's notoriety became a two-edged sword. It did not take long for the word of the successes of the Latins to spread, and by the end of the decade, Cuba became overrun with baseball scouts. The draft-riddled minor leagues were signing Cubans by the busload, and almost every club had a Latin representative. In the majors, the Chicago Cubs signed Hiram Bithorn (Puerto Rico), Jesse Flores (Mexico), Chico Hernandez,

Jorge Comellas, and Salvador Hernandez (Cuba).[50] The Cincinnati Reds signed Tomas De La Cruz (Cuba) and Chucho Ramos (Venezuela). But by far, the Senators led the recruitment of Latin players.

Yes, Major League baseball was reeling from the number of players who went off to join the war effort, either voluntarily or as draftees. Owners and managers were looking for draft-exempt players, and Joe Cambria was again sitting in the catbird seat. His Latin players were all non-resident aliens from non-belligerent countries and, as mentioned before, would be listed as entertainers for the sake of exemption.

There were, of course, other exemption qualifications at which the owners were looking. The original Selective Service Act of 1940 placed the draft age of men between 18 and 36. Right after the Pearl Harbor attack, the Act was amended to include men 18 to 38. In 1942, it was again amended to include men 18 to 45. Most players were in their prime playing years, between 21 and 35.

Other exceptions, numerically indicated, included:

2 Occupational status
2 A-B-C men in civilian defense, national defense or farm workers
3 A-B married men with dependents
4 D members of the ministry and divinity students
4 F men found to be physically, mentally or morally unfit.

College students who were currently enrolled or had just enrolled were exempted until they finished their course of studies.

The owners scurried about, looking for replacement players, men who could play at the professional level but would relinquish their spots once the service boys came home and fit the exemption criteria. There are several who made the All-Time greatest list of replacements:

Drafted by the Cincinnati Reds in 1944, 15-year-old Joe Nuxhall, unable to shave or to be drafted, became the all-time youngest "man" to play professional baseball when he pitched two-thirds of an inning against the Cardinals in Crosley Field in 1944. The Reds' "milk and cookies squad" also included 16-year-old catcher Ray McLeod. The Phillies drafted 17-year-old Granville Hammer, the White Sox took 18-year-old Casimir Kwietniewski (later to be known as Cass Michaels) as well as 17-year-old Art Houtteman and 18-year-old Billy Pierce. Eddie Yost, found and signed by Cambria out of a Brooklyn semi-pro team, began his long career with the Senators as a 17-year-old.[51]

Joe Cambria got in on the "non-shaving set" by signing 17-year-old Eddie Lyons right out of Reynolds High School in Winston-Salem, North Carolina. Another of his "can't miss" prospects, Lyons played a year in Charlotte/Concord in 1941, hitting .288. Griffith personally invited Lyons to spring training in 1942, but he did not make the club. Lyons' zeal for his country was too great, and he enlisted in the Navy from 1943 to 1945. He got his cup of coffee with the Nats in 1947, playing seven games with 28 at-bats, compiling four hits, two runs, two walks, two strikeouts, and a .143 batting average. Sent down to Chattanooga, Lyons remained in the minors until 1959. He had a long and illustrious career as a coach for the Senators, Reds, and the Cardinals and as a scout for the Cubs until 1995.[52]

Members of the "Geritol Brigade" included famous and, in most cases, just old guys. The Reds drafted two journeyman pitchers, 43-year-old Guy Bush and 46-year-old Hod Lisenbee, who had pitched for the Senators in 1927. Pepper Martin, a member of the Cardinals' World Series "Gas House Gang," made a respectable comeback with the Cards at age 40 in 1944. Future Hall of Famer Jimmie Foxx thought he could hit Major League pitching once again with the Red Sox, but failed miserably in 1942, then tried again with the Phillies in 1944 and 1945.[53]

Even the Senators got in on the Geritol gang. Ossie Bluege, who last saw a ground ball at third base in 1938, strapped on the spikes one more time and worked out with the team at age 41 just in case he was needed. Future Hall of Famer Rick Ferrell (38), who was pretty much draft-exempt by 1941, split time between the St. Louis Browns and the Senators between 1941 and 1947, when he finally ended his baseball career at age 41. Veteran first baseman Joe Kuhel (38), who was the Senators' starting first baseman between 1930 and 1937, took over for Mickey Vernon when Vernon was called into service with the U.S. Navy in 1944 and 1945. Kuhel, acquired from the White Sox, almost evenly split his entire 18-year career between Washington and Chicago.[54] Still desperate for warm bodies in 1944, Clark Griffith hired 37-year-old Eddie Boland off the New York State Sanitation Department team. Boland played 19 games and hit a respectable .271.[55]

Either cookies or Ben-Gay—it did not matter. The leagues needed arms, bats and bodies to put on the field. The above-mentioned are just of few of the many too young or too old who filled up the replacement ranks during the war years.

However, as the war progressed, owners turned their focus to the 4-F player, those who, for medical reasons, were unfit for military service yet healthy enough to play baseball daily. This became one of the more controversial aspects of wartime baseball.

Ailments such as ruptured eardrums, bad backs, flat feet, and significant dental problems were all maladies that could not be addressed in a foxhole. The Service demanded men in superior condition, able to carry heavy backpacks and a rifle, and to be prepared to do hand-to-hand combat if necessary. Concerning the ballplayers, Arthur Daley of the *New York Times* summarized it aptly:

> These lads appear physically fit mainly because their dressings rooms are equipped with whirlpool baths, baking machines, massage tables and adhesive tape. Some of these men have to wear special braces and the majority of them are the most "artificially" physically fit athletes imaginable. They require persistent attention in order to continue for the brief spurts in which they operate. In the Army or Navy, they would get none of that and it was the Army and Navy doctors, it should be remembered, who assigned them his [*sic*] 4F status in the first place.[56]

Resentment towards professional athletes, in both baseball and football, began to grow. People demanded to know: if they could play baseball every day, why couldn't they serve the country in some capacity? The Government suggested that the 4F players be re-evaluated and transitioned into some form of service work. But in 1945, Paul V. McNutt, chairman of the War Manpower Commission, allowed the 4Fs to play out the season.[57]

Every team in both leagues had their share of the too young, too old, waiting to be called, or 4Fs. By 1944, the St. Louis Browns had 18 players classified as 4F, the most famous of which was one-armed outfielder Pete Gray. The Senators were also not bereft of their own misfits:

Ed Butka, first base. Scouted and signed by Clark Griffith himself in 1940, 6-foot 3-inch, 193-pound Butka tried three times to enlist in the service but was denied each time because of a punctured eardrum. Seasoned up in the minors from 1940 to 1943, he earned a late September call-up in 1943. He hit the first pitch he saw for a double in a 15–3 rout by the White Sox. Mickey Vernon was drafted after the end of the 1943 season, and Butka thought he would have a shot at the starting first base job; however, Griffith knew better and quickly signed former Nats first base star Joe Kuhel, and Butka was relegated to the back-up spot. Between 1943 and 1944, Butka got into 18 games with the Nats, with 50 at-bats, 11 hits, two doubles, two RBI, two walks and 14 strikeouts, posting a .220 batting average. He was sent out down to Buffalo in 1945 and stayed in the minors until 1948. After his baseball life was over, Butka became a police officer in his hometown of Canonsburg, Pennsylvania.[58]

Arnold "Jug" Thesenga, pitcher. Nicknamed "Jug" because during the Depression, they said his curveball looked like a jug handle, Arnold Thesenga lived the life of a true baseball gypsy. Endowed with a good fastball and a wicked curve, he bounced around to any minor league or semi-pro team who would pay him to pitch. From his high school years in the mid–1930s through 1944, Thesenga actually made a living, even during the Depression, by pitching. He claimed his fame by becoming the winningest pitcher of the National Baseball Congress World Series, held annually in Wichita, Kansas. It was there in 1944 that he was scouted and signed by Joe Cambria for $2,500. Thesenga was draft-deferred because of his civilian job in an aircraft tool and die factory, and that made him just what the Senators needed. Thesenga made his major league debut against the Yankees on September 1, 1944. He held them scoreless for five solid innings before the Yankees got to him for three runs in the sixth inning. He was used as a reliever for the remainder of the season, with no decisions in five games and a 5.11 ERA in 12⅔ innings. He was not invited back to spring training the following year. He went back to his job at the Cessna plants, continued to pitch semi-pro ball until 1950, and retired into the real estate business.[59]

George Case, Jr., right field. The premiere base stealer of the American League and a Senators front-line starter, Case had separated his shoulder badly in 1944 and 1945, so much so that he was declared 4F by the draft board despite several attempts to join. Case did, however, work in a Trenton, New Jersey, aircraft plant building Avenger bombers during the off-season. Hard sliding and rough play led to many pulled hamstrings, a bad back, and further aggravation to his already hurt shoulder. After a year with the Cleveland Indians in 1946, he ended his stellar 11-year career with the Senators in 1947 at the age of 31.[60]

Alex Kvasnak, outfield. Alex Kvasnak, pronounced ka-WASH-nak, was another of Joe Cambria's "can't miss," two-hit wonder brigade who was signed to the Senators for a barber chair!

Kvasnak, a two-sport star and valedictorian of Sagamore (PA) High School, created such a stir in his hometown press that it was not long before the scouts started knocking on his door. Shirley Povich tells the story this way:

> Kvasnak had enough reputation around Sagamore, Pa., to cause Mike Ryba, Red Sox pitcher, to be interested in signing him for the Boston club. The lad's father, a local barber, listened to the offers of both Cambria and Ryba, and was very much undecided on making a choice for the boy. Cambria finally got the father's signature on a Washington contract on behalf of the boy who was still a minor. He won the father over by delivering a new, streamlined barber chair to the man's shop as a gift from the Washington club.[61]

Kvasnak started his career at Newport, Tennessee, in the Appalachian League in 1941,

hitting a tremendous .341 and stealing a league record 50 bases, earning him the reputation as the next George Case. He was invited to spring training in 1942 and was supposed to be sent back to Charlotte, but manager Bucky Harris felt he saw something in
the boy and kept him around as an extra outfielder, which was a wise move with all of
the players leaving for wartime duties. Kvasnak played in three games for the Nats in
early April, getting two hits in 11 at-bats, three runs, two walks and one strikeout. Seeing the boy needed more playing time than could be afforded in the majors, Kvasnak
was sent down to Charlotte, where he finished the year with 471 at-bats, 121 hits, 12 doubles, and a .257 batting average. He started 1943 at Charlotte but was called up for the
draft and spent his most formative years with Uncle Sam. He came back to the minors
in 1946 and never made it back up to the big leagues.[62] Cambria (who had a difficult time
pronouncing his OWN name), said Kvasnak's name was too hard to pronounce and
referred to him as "Squash Neck" for years.

The wartime pitching squad also relied on an unusual bag of tricks. Four of the
starters—Roger Wolff, Dutch Leonard, Mickey Haefner, and Johnny Niggeling—were
knuckleballers. Instead of the blazing fastballs of traditional aces, their pitches fluttered
and spun in order to confound batters, which in that season of substitute teams proved
effective: The quartet pitched 60 complete games among them and helped the Senators to a league-best 2.92 ERA. The rotation's sole non-knuckleballer, a five-foot-seven,
Italian-born rookie named Marino Pieretti, won 14 games.[63] Rick Ferrell, who was especially adept at catching "the butterfly," was brought back specifically to handle the four
pitchers.

Of course, the greatest number of the draft deferred came from the Cuban contingent. The order from Griffith to Cambria to "lay off the Latins" was still in effect in 1943;
however, it was rescinded when Griffith needed "all hands on deck" in 1944. The Cubans
were exempt under the "entertainer" proviso; however, in 1944, there was a change:
"A Selective Service spokesman today told newsmen that persons in this country on
six-month visa could not be drafted and might remain the full time, return to their
native land and return to the United States without a draft threat. Players from Cuba,
however, must register for the draft in their island home, as must those from Puerto
Rico."[64]

Cambria wasted little time. He brought Cubans to spring training camps by the
busload. Not many stuck with the parent club, but many were offered minor league
contracts. Cambria placed dozens of Cuban players throughout his East Coast operations.

He also resurrected the careers of many of his original finds from the mid–1930s.
In 1942, four Cubans made the Nats roster. In 1943, only two were chosen. However,
1944 was a banner year for the merry rhumba dancers. The United Press reported that
Cambria signed 15 extra Cuban ballplayers. Cambria previously had signed nearly 20
Cubans, some of whom were already in the Washington club's camp.[65]

Cambria was able to place ten Cuban players on the Senators' roster in 1944, the
largest number in any year of the team's history. Unfortunately, it had an opposite effect.
In 1943, with only two Cubans on the squad, the club came in second in the league with
an 84–69 record, the first year of Ossie Bluege's managership. They looked unbeatable
on paper in 1944 but limped to an eighth-place finish with a woeful 64–90 record with
the ten Cubans. But in 1945, they nearly won it all, coming in second on the last day of
the season with an 87–67 record and having six Cubans on the squad.

The reality of the situation in 1942 was that both the majors and the minors were being decimated by wartime conscriptions, and many worried about the demise of the minor leagues. For the D league players, this was a gift from God; for the scouts, this was a kiss from Satan. Mr. J.B. Lemon, Chief Executive of the Florida East Coast League (D League), elucidated the problem to Guy Butler, writing for the 1942 *Miami Daily News*:

> You see, with the services grabbing off big leaguers and minor leaguers left and right, the diamond athlete is going to be in demand pretty soon. Even the Class D leaguers. Point is, the AA and A-1 players have got to move up to plug the ranks of the departed major [league] players; the B's have got to step up to the A-1's and the A's, and that's where we come in. Our players, the better ones, can be sold for pretty good prices for duty in the B and even A or A-1. Already, the earliest I've seen them gumshoeing around, we've had three major scouts in our territory—Johnny Nee of the Yanks, Joe Cambria of the Senators and Bill Pierre of the Giants. (Heine Groh of the Dodgers had also just hit town.)"[66]

No longer could Cambria wave a few hundred bucks under the nose of a low-minor prospect, wrap him up, and tell the others to hold off. Everyone was bidding against each other and themselves for capable players to fill up their B and A league teams. Cambria still worked for the most tight-fisted owner in baseball, and both of them knew: the Cubans were the only way to keep their payroll down during these lean years.

It was boom for the boys and bust for the scouts.

The answer to the manpower shortage was, in reality, right under Griffith's and Cambria's noses: the Negro League Homestead Grays. The greatest of the greats—Josh Gibson, Buck Leonard, Cool Papa Bell, Jud Wilson, and Roy Partlow, just to name a few—were playing in Griffith Stadium regularly and would have made the Senators a championship team throughout the war years and beyond.

But Clark Griffith was not going to rock the boat and begin a controversy in the middle of a great war. Ralph Matthews, writing for the *Baltimore Afro-American,* urged Griffith in 1942 and 1943 to hire colored players, but Griffith was unequivocal in his position. Using the war as a smoke screen, he said:

> The question of the use of colored baseball players in the ranks of organized baseball clubs is no different now than it has been in the last fifty years. Why should propagandists be bringing it up at this time just when we are in a total war and when everyone, both colored and white, should be cemented together in the common cause of winning the war? It is my opinion the colored people should lend all of their efforts to developing their own national following and if properly organized and officered, could eventually take their place in the annals of baseball. It is my belief we should have white baseball leagues and colored baseball leagues."
>
> I have spent much time and lent my aid and use of the ballpark here to the advancement of the National League of colored baseball. Should you ask many of my colored friends who have been instrumental in the development of colored baseball in Washington, I feel sure that they would say that I have been most co-operative, and I know that a lot of other baseball parks have acted likewise."
>
> It is my opinion that organized baseball should lend their assistance to the colored man in helping him to build an organization in which the people would have confidence, and which would eventually put colored baseball on a solid foundation.[67]

Griffith was hopeful that, for the time being, this would put an end to the talk of integration in the major leagues.

The 1942 Washington Senators had ten players who were signed by Cambria. His four Cubans on the team—Roberto Estalella, Alejandro Carrasquel, Chile Gomez, and Roberto Ortiz— helped to keep the Senators competitive throughout the war years (private collection of George Case III).

1943

The War

The tide was turning, and the Allies were winning. The Nazis finally surrendered at Stalingrad in January, and the allies recaptured New Guinea after defeating the Japanese at the Battle of Bismarck Sea. General George S. Patton scored a decisive victory, defeating Field Marshal Rommel at the Battle of El Guettar in Tunisia. General Dwight Eisenhower became the Supreme Allied Commander of the European theater, and America was hopeful again.

"Major Leagues Postpone Opening Until April 21"

Headlines from newspapers from the East Coast to the West shouted out this news in some fashion or another. And big news it was.

In an emergency meeting between Commissioner Landis and the heads of all 16 major league teams, many things were decided, not the least of which was postponing the opening of the season until April 21. This was a compromise between the traditional April 13 start favored by the National League and an April 27 start date favored by the American League. It was further agreed to push back the end of the regular 154-game season to October 3.

The biggest issue addressed at this meeting was the curtailing of travel to remote spring training sites. In an effort to save miles, money and gasoline, Commissioner Landis and the teams agreed to train north of the Potomac and Ohio Rivers and east of the Mississippi, with the exceptions being the Browns and the Cardinals of St. Louis, who would stay in the general Missouri area. Out of bounds would be the South Atlantic states, Florida, Hot Springs, Arkansas, and California.

Landis personally made the announcement concerning the schedule changes and added that "transportation during spring training would be held to a minimum, and after spring training there will be need for utmost cooperation on the part of the various clubs to cut man mileage as much as possible."[68]

For some reason, the Senators did not send a representative to the closed-door meeting; however, Joe Cambria did sit in an anteroom and reported back to Clark Griffith at his office.

At the time of the meeting, only three teams, the Cubs, White Sox and Red Sox, had already secured training sites closer to home. The other teams scurried about, trying to decide where and how. The Senators eventually worked out an agreement to hold spring training on the campus of the University of Maryland in College Park, a mere seven miles from Griffith Stadium.

Even before spring training started, Joe Cambria was a beacon of optimism about this year's Senators and his biggest reason was the new manager, Ossie Bluege.

Ossie Bluege, like pitcher Joe Haynes, was another one of the "Senator for life" brigade. Making the team as a shortstop in 1922, Bluege played his entire 18-year career with the Nats, posting a respectable .272 average. His forte, however, was with the glove, playing every infield position except first base. He transitioned to coach in 1940, then manager in 1943. He became the Director of the Farm system in 1947, then transitioned to the front office in 1955. His biggest claim to fame was signing a 17-year-old, muscular Harmon Killebrew out of Payette High School in Idaho.[69]

Bucky Harris, "The Boy Wonder," had replaced Joe Cronin as manager in 1935 and managed the team until 1942, placing in the first division only in 1936. A dismal seventh-place finish, 39½ games behind the Yankees, led to his replacement by Bluege in 1943.

Both Griffith and Cambria were high on Ossie Bluege; however, Griffith was more measured in his praise: "He has a cold, analytical mind, born perhaps of his younger days as an accountant in the offseason. He is the only manager in baseball history to come out of the accountant's office. He finds out the reason why. This club of ours needed a big dash of discipline. It needed a man who would insist that the players give everything they had. And Ossie can do it."[70]

Cambria, of course, was more effusive, saying "Bluege is a fine leader, a keen student of baseball and one who combines the so-called old and new systems of play. Just keep an eye on this season. It will be a running, colorful team, and the players will hustle for Bluege, one of the finest characters in baseball. Mickey Vernon, George Myatt and George Case stole more than 100 bases last season. Show me a club with a trio like them. Those fellows should burn up the American League."[71]

As we shall see, Bluege brought a disciplined and measured approach to the team which bore fruit in 1943.

Cambria continued to do what he did best: bring in a phalanx of pea-green rookies and hope for the best. He was pulling them off the sandlots from Baltimore to Detroit and throwing them up against the proverbial wall, hoping someone would stick.

His first "can't misser" was 17-year-old Jack Sinnott. Fresh off two Baltimore American Legion championships, Sinnott was touted by Cambria as a fine hitter. Unfortunately, he was a "no glove, no bat" outfielder who did not last a week at camp. He was sent down to Durham and remained in the minors and in semi-pro ball for the rest of his seven-year career.

Next in the parade was another Baltimore sandlotter, big Chester Foreman. Chester also did not have the right stuff, and his only organized baseball record shows him playing for the Seaford Eagles of the Eastern Shore league in 1946, where he went 4–8 on the mound.

Warren Reid was another non-roster invitee plucked by Cambria from the Tallahassee Capitols in 1942, where he went 3–6 on the hill. He had a stint with the Utica Braves in 1943, and from there no record exists.

"I took Bunnell out from under the noses of the Detroit Tigers," claimed Cambria about John Bunnell, 18-year-old whiz kid of the Detroit sandlots. Bunnell had been playing American Legion ball around Detroit and had established a good reputation in the city as a hitter and a pitcher. Unfortunately, he was also unprepared for big league ball. He played one year with Chattanooga with an official record of 0–1. There is no more record of him in organized baseball after that.

Joe Jacobs was an 18-year-old, sure-handed shortstop who flashed some serious leather in spring training camp. Unfortunately, Uncle Sam flashed his enlistment papers sooner than expected, and Jacobs had to return to Wichita to enlist before camp was over.[72]

Joe Cambria's biggest rookie find of the year, literally, was 7-foot-tall Richard Aherns from Oil City, Pennsylvania. As Cambria explained it: "I found him in a grocery store. He was behind the counter reaching for some cans on the top shelf, and when I saw him I thought he was standing on a ladder. But I didn't see any ladder, so I signed him!"[73]

That statement and an accompanying picture went "viral," as they say, hitting papers as far away as California. Alas, Richard Aherns tried his best at camp but was ultimately sent up to the Class A Utica Braves of the Eastern League for the 1943 season. He got another look-see with the Elizabethton Cubs of the Appalachian League in 1945 but was released in May.

Although he had to focus his attention on strictly American acquisitions in 1943, there were two of Joe Cambria's veteran Cubans who played important roles on the team.

Alejandro Carrasquel, originally found by Cambria in 1938, was just too valuable to the pitching staff to be ignored. He pulled double duty under Bucky Harris in 1942. In 35 games, he started 15, finished 13, and saved three. He went 7–7 with a 3.43 ERA in 152⅓ innings pitched. He seemed especially effective against the Yankees, always called in with the bases loaded and someone like DiMaggio or Dickey at the plate. His MVP years in the Cuban winter leagues in the late 1930s had made him an effective and savvy moundsman. Also, Carrasquel was draft-exempt because, as a Venezuelan, he was a non-resident alien and he had already served time in the Venezuelan Army.

Roberto Ortiz was another of Joe Cambria's early finds, coming to the Senators originally as a pitcher in 1938. He was converted to an outfielder and tore up minor league pitchers. He played on the team in both 1941 and 1942 but was sent down mid-season. He was re-acquired from Montreal late in 1943 after he hit .304 with 170 hits, 42 doubles and 10 homers. Ortiz was needed in the expanses of the Griffith Stadium outfield, where he was fast and had a strong arm.[74]

Manager Bluege did bring an air of quiet assurance to the team, even in the uncertain war years. He was aware of Cambria's penchant for green rookies and colorful Cubans. Whereas Bucky Harris would excoriate Cambria for his endless stream of "monkey talk" Cubans and "can't miss" Americans, manager Bluege was more measured in his reaction: "Let him bring 'em in and I'll look 'em over," he said. "This is a year when you can't be too particular. If one of them out of the lot makes good in even a modest way, we'll appreciate it."[75]

Ossie Bluege, in his own way, was just echoing the sentiments shared by many managers around the league. The war had stripped almost every team of their big hitters and slick fielders, and Jimmy Dykes, manager of the White Sox, was famously quoted as saying, "Any team which is able to keep nine men on the field all summer has a chance of winning the pennant this year."[76]

DiMaggio, Greenberg, Feller, Rizzuto, Williams and many other quality players were now in the service; consequently, every team in the league could not afford to be too particular.

Written in 1943 and published in 1944, "I'm Beginning to See the Light" was a top 10 Jazz/Pop hit for Ella Fitzgerald, Harry James, and the song's composer, Duke Ellington. The song's title could be used aptly to describe how many owners and managers around the major leagues felt about Joe Cambria's Cuban experiment, which now seemed to be bearing fruit in 1943.

With the success of Jorge Comellas and Hiram Bithorn (Cubs), Tomas de la Cruz (Reds), Luis Olmo (Dodgers), Roberto Estalella (Athletics), and Alejandro Carrasquel (Senators), almost all the clubs (with the exception of the Phillies, now managed by Bucky Harris) were now "searching through the canebrakes" for capable players. The Giants were trying out Napoleon Reyes at first base and Jesse Flores as a pitcher.[77]

Not only the major leagues but also the minors got in on the Cuban action. Many of Cambria's draftees were scattered throughout the Senators' minor league system. They became hot commodities, sold by Cambria to other teams' high-A affiliates. In some instances, it was for "just in case." In other instances, it was a matter of another great pop standard, "Just in Time."

One of the greatest and most successful War Bond rallies took place on May 24, 1943, when the Washington Senators played host to the team of the Norfolk Naval Air Training Station. The game was the brainchild of celebrated *Washington Post* reporter Shirley Povich, one of the most respected voices in the baseball world. With the backing of the *Post* and the aid of some fantastic stars of the day, Clark Griffith (who personally put down $1,000 for his own seat), raised over $2 million for the war effort.

The United States Navy Band, resplendent in their dress white summer uniforms, marched into Griffith Stadium in front of 29,221 enthusiastic fans and played several ceremonial marches. They were followed by the hilarious antics of former Senators coach Al Schacht. The "Clown Prince of Baseball," Schacht began his baseball clowning routine along with Nick Altrock when both were players for the 1920s Senators.

Fresh from a tour of the troops in North Africa, Schacht went into his famous antics, mimicking the umpires and doing classic imitations of himself, Walter Johnson, and Bob Feller. The biggest surprise of the night came when Schacht went into what had now become a classic: Babe Ruth's "called shot" from the 1932 World Series, signaling to the Cubs' bench and taking his typical Ruthian home run swing. As Schacht trotted down to first base, Master of Ceremonies Arch McDonald exhorted the crowd to look to the right field box seats as the great Babe Ruth himself trotted onto the field and took up the fun at second base. The Bambino went to the microphone at home plate and, with patriotic zeal, urged the crowd to give their all for the boys "fighting in the muck and the mire for us."

The Navy Band followed with a stirring rendition of the National Anthem, sung by Kate Smith. It was the first time the band had ever accompanied a female vocalist. The crowd settled in for what would turn out to be a thrilling game.

The Senators had their first-string team on the field: Sherry Robertson-3B, George Case-RF, Mickey Vernon-1B, Bob Johnson-LF, Stan Spence-CF, Jerry Priddy-2B, Jake Early-C, Johnny Sullivan-SS, and Milo Candini, starting pitcher. However, the Sailors were no slouches. They had a surprising team of current and former major leaguers: Dom DiMaggio (Red Sox)-CF, Phil Rizzuto (Yankees)-SS, Benny McCoy (Tigers)-2B, Ed Robinson (Indians)-1B, Don Padgett (Cardinals)-LF, Jim Carlin (Phillies)-RF/3B, Jack Conway (Cleveland)-3B, Ernie "Hooks" Devaurs (minor leagues)-RF, Vince Smith (Pirates)-C, Charlie Wagner (Red Sox), starting pitcher, and Maxie Wilson (Phillies) relief pitcher.

The Sailors were blanked by the rookie, Candini, for the first three innings. Alejandro Carrasquel took over in the fourth and gave up an unearned run on a rather convoluted play. The Sailors were blanked again until the top of the eighth when they plated three more runs. The Senators, scoreless since the first inning, suddenly came alive in the bottom of the ninth, getting three runs across before reliever Maxie Wilson got Ed Robinson and George Case to fly out and end the contest.

Perhaps even bigger than Babe Ruth's appearance was the seventh-inning stretch entertainment provided by none other than the star of stage, screen, and radio, Bing Crosby. Crosby sang several songs, cracked wise with the Senators, told some uproariously funny jokes, and left the crowd wanting more. Local guitarist Randy Ryan accompanied Crosby's mellifluous offerings and then promptly appeared at his draft board the next day! This special game turned out to the second-highest grossing event in sports history at that time, outdone only by the Jack Dempsey–Gene Tunney fight of 1928.[78]

(Author's note: My father, Dr. Frank Scimonelli, Sr., was the trumpet and Post Horn soloist with the U.S. Navy Band from 1940 to 1966. I remember stories he told of seeing Babe Ruth that day and some of the problems they had accompanying Kate Smith with her rendition of the National Anthem. Due to her low alto voice, the arrangement had to be changed with very little notice. Band members were also a little uncomfortable, in that they had just recently changed over to their summer white uniforms and the evening was unusually cool for late May.)

Joe "the cockeyed optimist" Cambria was at it again, telling the *Washington Post*:

Watch the Senators this year, boys! I want to go on record in predicting Washington will give those Yankees a real battle. They're a cinch to finish in the first division. Bluege has done the fine job I predicted. He has the Senators in second place, and you can't laugh that off. Those Yankees are due for a slump. They have won 13 straight series and many games have been taken by a run. Washington moves into New York next. I expect to see Griff's club give them a lot of trouble Friday, Saturday and Sunday. It wouldn't surprise me if we win the series from the Yanks and maybe a setback will start them on a losing streak. The Senators can still do it and I have my fingers crossed. Washington has a good club and is capable of causing plenty of trouble from here on in.[79]

Cambria could not help but carry water for Griffith and the Senators. He was a dyed in the wool company man who swore allegiance to Griffith. And he was not far off this time. The Senators, in fact, split the September 3–5 series with the Yanks, losing the first two and winning both games of the Sunday doubleheader. The Nats swept the Yanks in their last series, September 17–19.

Predicting the Senators would finish in the first division was a no-brainer for Cambria. The team had been playing well all year. September 10–22, they went on a 10-game winning streak, only to have it broken by the hapless St. Louis Browns. Their last two losses to the Tigers, on October 2 and 3, did them in, however. They lost out on the pennant by 13½ games but did finish in second place with a respectable 84–69 record.

Ossie Bluege's inaugural season turned out to be a boon for all. Attendance was up to an all-time high, and the team chemistry seemed to be there. Everyone was so optimistic that before leaving for their respective homes, the boys all chipped in and presented Cambria with a new wristwatch as a congratulations for the players he had discovered for the team, which included Mickey Vernon, Mickey Haefner, George Case, George Myatt, Alejandro Carrasquel and Roberto Ortiz, among others.[80]

Before closing up shop in Washington and heading south to Cuba for the winter season, Cambria decided to make a little side money. As he had done in decades past, he put together an All-Star conglomerate of major and minor leaguers to pit against one of the strongest teams in the Negro Leagues, his hometown Baltimore Elite Giants. He promoted the doubleheader that was held at the Giants' home field, Bugle Field in Baltimore, on Sunday, October 10.

The Elites (pronounced EE-lites) were having a poor year in 1943, finishing fifth in the Negro National League. But the team possessed some of the most talented players in the league, and many became stars in the Major leagues. Joe Black was just a 19-year-old rookie that year but was polishing up the form that would ultimately bring him 1952 Rookie of the Year honors with the Brooklyn Dodgers. Later in his career, Black became the first black scout for the Washington Senators. Jim "Junior" Gilliam, 1953 National League Rookie of the Year, would also become an integral part of the great Dodgers teams of the 1950s and 1960s, playing his entire 14-year career with the team. Roy Campanella would begin his Hall of Fame journey playing with the Elites. Leadoff hitter extraordinaire Henry Kimbro rounded out the Elites' stellar line-up.

Cambria cajoled many of his major league associates to play in the game and composed a fine team. Early Wynn of the Senators and Joe Haynes of the White Sox were his starters, and Jake Early of the Senators was his catcher. The Nats' Mickey Vernon covered first base, Al Rubeling of the Pirates took second, and Sherry Robertson of the Nats played third. In the outfield were none other than the sensational one-armed Pete Gray of the St. Louis Browns and Cambria's new bonus baby, Jack Sinnott. He rounded out the team with some International League stars, Don Kerr and Marty Tabachek.

The Elites fought bravely but were overmatched by the All-Stars. They dropped both games of the twin bill, 10–1 and 4–1. The Elites made four errors in their first game, which did not help their cause at all. The All-Stars were victorious, the crowd went home happy, the players left for their respective domiciles, and Cambria made a few bucks to tide him over for the winter.[81]

All in all, 1943 turned out to be a banner year for the Senators. The pitching staff, filled with old, new and replacements, turned in a fantastic performance. Young Early Wynn used his fastball for effect and won 18 games. Dutch Leonard's 11–13 record belied his 3.28 ERA and 1.9 walks per nine innings. Rookie Milo Candini sparkled with an 11–7 record and a 2.49 ERA in 28 appearances. Veteran Mickey Haefner fluttered his knuckler to an 11–5 record with a nice 2.29 ERA. Late season acquisition Johnny Niggeling used his butterfly ball to go 4–2 in six starts with an 0.88 ERA. The bats worked, the fielding was smoother than Tennessee whiskey, and the team finished second.[82]

The future looked bright ... for the moment.

But as thunder portends a storm, Shirley Povich's December 27 column foretold what would happen to the 1944 Senators:

> There have been snide cracks at Cambria's penchant for picking up the Spanish-speaking talent and sneers at his attempts to duck the big purchase prices. But Griffith is willing to bear with his scout. Cambria's products who have not made good with the Nats have been assets to the club's farm system.
>
> This year, particularly, the Nats are in no position to turn down any players with ability. The loss of talent to the armed services has made the draft-exempt Cubans a valuable commodity. And no longer is the prejudice against the Latins noticeable. The fan in the stands demands only a good performance.[83]

1944

The War Rages On

The fighting in 1944 grew more bitter, more bloody, and it increasingly favored the Allied nations. In February, the American forces, who had successfully invaded Italy in 1943, were defeated at the battle of Cisterna near Anzio, but the Germans did not dislodge them. Fighting would continue throughout the spring and summer until the eventual liberation of Rome and Florence by the Allies.

Philadelphia A's pitcher Lou Brissie was awarded the Bronze Star for his participation in the Battle of Rome.

The greatest invasion force ever assembled in wartime history came ashore on the beaches of Normandy on June 6, 1944, the beginning of the D-Day offensive. Approximately 2,500 Americans would be lost in that offensive, many of them ballplayers. The Allied push across the Western front resulted in the liberation of Paris in August.

It was the 10-day Battle of the Bulge in December, however, that effectively destroyed any hopes of a German victory in the war, but it came at a huge cost: 20,000 Allied forces died during that fighting.

Boston Red Sox pitcher Earl "Lefty" Johnson was awarded the Silver Star, the third-highest personal decoration for valor in combat, for his participation at the Battle of the Bulge.[84]

These are just a few of the myriad battles fought throughout the bloodiest full year of fighting in World War II, as well as a few of those who were decorated for their valor. By the end of the War, only three major leaguers, Charlie A. Frye, Elmer J. Gedeon, and Harry M. O'Neill, would die in combat, as well as scores of minor league, semi-pro, Negro leagues, college level, amateur, Australian and Japanese ballplayers who also gave their last full measure of devotion.

Baseball would mourn but go on.

Even before the last strains of "Auld Lang Syne" wafted from Guy Lombardo's band at the Roosevelt Hotel on New Year's Eve, Joe Cambria was already preparing for the 1944 season. Something must have changed Clark Griffith's mind about the Cuban ban he placed on Cambria the year before. Maybe it was the loss of Mickey Vernon, Ellis Clary, and more of his front-line players to the service. Maybe it was the draft exemptions for the Latin players. Whatever it was, Griffith lifted his ultimatum. Cambria took the ball and ran with it.

As early as November of 1943, he started scouting and signing almost anything that could move in the Cuban Winter leagues. His three biggest "finds" started with big Roberto Ortiz's younger brother, pitcher/outfielder Oliverio "Baby" Ortiz, followed by outfielder/first baseman Epitacio Torres (voted Cuba's "Player of the Year") and pitcher Santiago Ullrich. As we shall see, these boys were merely the appetizers for the meal that Cambria was going to serve.

But this was not just a slap-dash, "sign anyone with a bat" kind of move. There were several factors involved with all the signings, not the least of which were Frank Lawrence, owner of the Portsmouth, Virginia Cubs, and Earl Mann, president of the Atlanta Crackers ball club, both of whom went down to the Island to sign players.[85] As mentioned earlier, the minor leagues were taking a beating with the loss of wartime manpower. Both major and minor league owners and scouts were turning their attentions more frequently towards Mexico and the Caribbean basin in search of warm bodies to fill their rosters. Cambria was beginning to face some competition for his ivory from the tropics.

Cambria had a plan in place, and it actually started with his brother, John. To sign all the boys he wanted, he would need a place to put them.

"Little Havana on the Susquehanna"[86]

Early in January of 1944, Joe and his brother, John, approached Eastern League president Tommy Richardson to talk business. Richardson was the business manager and publicist for the Williamsport Grays. The Grays had a long-time affiliation with the Philadelphia Athletics; however, the A's were forced to suspend their affiliation with the Grays in 1943 due to the financial crush of the war and the player shortage. The Cambrias came to Richardson because their Springfield Senators franchise was not drawing flies in Massachusetts, and a change was needed. "After a month of negotiations involving the Cambrias, Griffith, Richardson and the Williamsport Community Baseball Association, the Senators signed a working agreement with the Grays on April 7, 1944. Williamsport became the primary baseball haven for Griffith's unique player development programs."[87]

In his seminal history of the Washington Nationals, Morris Bealle stated: "Clark

Griffith had signed so many Cubans that he had to establish a special farm for them in Williamsport."[88]

Ownership of the club would be in elder brother John Cambria's name, since Commissioner Landis had stripped Joe of all his minor league affiliations in 1940. The Williamsport Community Baseball Association agreed to provide the Cambrias financial support to defray the initial costs of outfitting the team and to satisfy some outstanding liens they had accrued in Springfield.[89]

The following table shows the number of players signed by Cambria and Griffith during the winter season of 1943–1944. Assuredly, not a lot of money was expended to acquire their services, and in Cambria's case, he probably signed a majority of them to blank contracts, which of course was taboo. But his overarching goal was talent acquisition with minimal cost. Equitable contracts were one of his flagrant failings.

A few of the names below appear more than once. Throughout 1944, a steady stream of players moved between the Chattanooga Lookouts and the Williamsport Grays as managers deemed necessary, especially during the early spring months when rosters were being prepared.

Senators	Chattanooga	Williamsport
Fermin Guerra	Luis Aloma	Hector Arago
Alberto Leal	Hector Arago	Rene Blanco
Oliverio "Baby" Ortiz	Leonardo Goicoechea	Oscar Calvo
Roberto Ortiz	Jose Lopez	Augustin Delaville
Francisco Quientis	Rene Monteagudo	Mario Diaz
Regelio Rojas	Juan Montero	Aurelio Fernandez
Jose Sanchez	Oliverio Ortiz	Romej "Fred" Fuertes
Luis Suarez	Francisco Quientis	Francisco Gallardo
Epitacio Torres	Armando Roche	Sojo Gallardo
Gilberto Torres	Luis Suarez	Oscar Garmendia
Armando Valdez	Santiago Ullrich	Leonardo Goicoechea
		Chile Gomez
1944 Official Roster		Juan Hernandez
Alejandro Carrasquel		Cheeno Hidalgo
Preston Gomez		Felipe Jimenez
Fermin Guerra		Antonio Martinez
Rene Monteagudo		Daniel Parra
Oliverio Ortiz		Fernando Rodriguez
Roberto Ortiz		Regelio Rojas
Luis Suarez		Pablo Travieso
Gilberto Torres		Rogelio Valdez
Santiago Ullrich		Rene Vega
Rogelio Valdez		Jose Zardon

In the end, these players made the official roster, according to Baseball-reference. com: Rene Monteagudo (P), Preston Gomez (IF), Roberto Ortiz (OF), "Baby" Ortiz (P), Alejandro Carrasquel (P), Fermin Guerra (C), Luis Suarez (3B), Gilberto Torres (IF), Santiago Ullrich (P), and Rogelio Valdez (IF).

Monteagudo and Carrasquel made the starting rotation, caught by starter Guerra.

Others—"Baby" Ortiz (two games), Luis Suarez (two AB), Rogelio Valdez (one AB)—had nothing but a cup of coffee.

The overriding factor in the acquisition of the Cuban players was simple: they were draft exempt. Yes, all the teams, majors and minors, needed players to fill out their rosters. The Senators would have no trouble filling positions in 1944. With the addition of Cubans, Ossie Bluege would take 39 players into spring training camp in mid–March, the largest contingent to date. Shirley Povich of *The Washington Post* said:

> There will be no scarcity of players on the club despite the inroads of the armed services. Five of Bluege's athletes are safely 4-F, and two are over the draft age of 38. There are no less than 14 draft exempt Cubans, Mexican, and South Americans on the squad and the remainder are pre–Pearl Harbor fathers whose induction may be considerably delayed.
>
> President Griffith yesterday declared the personnel of his club will be made up completely of overage, 4-F players and fathers who are subject to military call. "All of our non-exempt players will be holding themselves ready for military duty," he said.[90]

But as with everything else that happens in the Federal Government, contradictions abound.

In May 1944, the United States Selective Service declared the Cubans "non-resident aliens" and issued them six-month visas, in effect granting them immunity from the draft. However, in July, Congress amended the 1940 Selective Service Act by passing the National War Services Act of 1944. In essence, the Act enabled the President to draft essential workers for the war industry and agriculture, "and in other occupations, activities and employments which the President shall from time to time determine to be essential to the effective prosecution of the war, and in order to maintain a proper balance between such workers and persons in the armed forces." It was intended to define a noncombatant work force.

The Act also redefined the Cubans' status as "resident aliens" subject to the draft if they chose to play the entire baseball season. In essence, it was "sign and stay, take your chances, or go home." The specter of the draft forced several Cuban players on the Senators and the Grays to leave before the end of the season, though many cited other reasons for returning to Cuba.[91]

Ah, but a statement like this is too simple to be believed, especially if it is in "Washington-speak." The *New York Times* reported:

> Joe Cambria, baseball scout for the Senators, said today that all Latin American players on the Washington roster entered the United States on six-month visas and were immune to any draft regulations in this country.
>
> A Selective Service spokesman today told newsmen that persons in this country on six-month visas could not be drafted and might remain the [sic] full time, return to their native lands and return to the United States next year without a draft threat. Players from Cuba, however, must register for the draft in their island home, as must those from Puerto Rico.[92]
>
> Griffith knew about the ruling and expected to have a ruling from the Selective Service on the Latin players' eligibility. He was philosophical when he stated it was inevitable, but they were ready to take our chances with the rest of the league.[93]

By July, the situation had become troubling. Of all the Cubans on the team, those affected the most were Fermin Guerra, Roberto Ortiz, and Gilberto Torres. All three were important to the team. Guerra, a sure-handed backstop, was a necessity to spell Rick Ferrell from his duties catching the four knuckleballers. Ortiz's bat was expected to be a hefty item in the middle of the lineup. But Torres was slated to be the everyday third baseman, and his loss would be felt the most. Griffith was able to acquire Harlond Clift from the Browns to play third base, Brooklyn's Joe Vosmik to patrol the outfield, and Nats veteran catcher Al Evans, newly discharged from the Navy, all at the last minute. All three men filled their positions admirably.

In the end, however, only Guerra and Ortiz returned to Cuba. Gilberto Torres decided he had spent too long trying to get into American baseball and chose to stay in the U.S., register and take his chances.

A few of the Cuban players in Williamsport decided to go home for personal rather than draft reasons.

Perhaps no segment of this narrative is as important as the Williamsport experiment. As the old saying goes, "necessity is the mother of invention." The war necessitated a reevaluation of scouting and signing techniques. Cambria had already established that by his continuous forays into Cuba starting in 1934. With a majority of the front-line players off to the war effort, players had to be found quickly to fill their slots. With his shackles loosed by Griffith, Cambria had free rein to find all the Cuban ivory he could. He invented the "Cuban pipeline" to shuttle players back and forth between the U.S. and Havana as necessary, and he considered Williamsport to be a major part of that conduit.

Moving the Springfield franchise to Williamsport was the next invention. He was betting on the fact that he would get tremendous support from the Williamsport populace (which he did), and they would be enthusiastic about seeing the new brand of baseball played by the Cubans.

In April 1944, the Grays assembled for spring training in College Park, Maryland. Of the 23 men assembled, 16 were Cuban. By the time the season started, and players were shuttled between the parent club and their high minor league affiliate, the Chattanooga Lookouts, the Grays would have a cast of 12 Cubans and six Americans. With only three weeks to prepare for opening day, poor Grays manager Ray Kolp had to take the "12 Week Berlitz Easy Spanish Course" in a quarter of the time!

Kolp, a seasoned veteran of 12 Major League seasons pitching for the Browns and the Reds, had the unenviable task of trying to mesh a team of Latins and Americans. He was lucky in that his Cubans were not a bunch of pea-green rookies. Most of them made their living playing in the Cuban winter leagues, as well as barnstorming, exhibitions and tournaments. They had their own brand of "go-go" baseball that would make anyone envious. Because of their diminutive stature (most of the players averaged about 5 foot 6 inches), they had no legitimate power hitter. Theirs was a brand of gap hitting, bunting, multiple steals, and hustling play, peppered liberally with a great deal of spirited chatter on the diamond. Their style of play was usually referred to as "inside baseball," where the home run is eschewed for the sake of the strategic bunt. For these boys, stealing home was a badge of honor.

> Williamsport's fans had never seen anything like the Cubans before. League beat writers dubbed them "The Rumba Rascals," "The Laughing Latins," or simply "The Williamsport Canebrakes," indicative of the stereotyping of Latin Americans prevalent among sportswriters of the era and the public at large.[94] Al Decker, former sports editor for *The Grit,* noted that their "constant chatter, blazing speed, and defensive athleticism set them apart from the other [Eastern League] teams."[95]

The ugly truth of this whole experiment was the lack of acculturation and isolation of the players and the racial attitudes of their opponents. The players faced the constant language barrier and a colder physical climate than what they were used to. They were housed as a group five miles outside of the city at the Haleeka campgrounds. It is not clear if management's decision to house the Cubans at Haleeka was designed to prevent the isolation of individual players or to sequester the team as a whole from contact with the public. The Grays did hire an interpreter/trainer to assist the Cubans with the language and to ease their transition to life in Williamsport.[96]

However, if the Cubans thought the Pennsylvania climate was cold, the climate on the ball field was a mix of the Antarctic and the Sahara:

> They get bean balls thrown at their heads by closed-shop (and closed brained) rivals. They face pitchers who willingly throw away their arms bearing down on them in an effort to escape the "ignominy" of yielding a hit to them. They get a measure of grass-singeing abuse from the "jockeys" on the enemy bench. From their own team they get rock-bottom pay, and from many of their own teammates they get a wintry ostracism. Those who want to befriend then are halted by the difference in languages.[97]

This type of hatred unnerved the young Cubans. Because of their strong winter schedule in Cuba, they got off to a very fast start and had a brief stay in first place in 1944. But the constant barrage of insults, coupled with a tedious schedule of make-up doubleheaders, surely precipitated their decline into the second division. But if they thought 1944 was rough, as they said in Brooklyn, wait till next year.

The 1945 Grays started their season without the services of their speedster, Antonio Zardon, and catcher Rogelio Valdez, both sent to Chattanooga and then to the Senators. "Papa Joe" Cambria quickly replaced them and signed several others to more than compensate for any other losses. However, in spite of this new talent, the Grays just did not gel like the previous season, sank to the bottom of the league by June, and stayed there for the season. It is almost certain that this decline was precipitated by the increasing amount of racial hatred and physical violence they experienced from the other Eastern League teams. The most serious of these came from their rivalry with the Utica Blue Sox.[98]

Led by a tobacco-spewing redneck by the name of Cecil "Turkey" Tyson, the Blue Sox led the league in "bases on brawls." Tyson and his teammates delighted in race-baiting epithets and downright insults directed at the Grays. They continued this throughout the season, much to the consternation of the Cubans. The *denouement* occurred on July 8 when the Grays played the Blue Sox at their home field.

> Pitcher Leonardo Goicochea sent Tyson sprawling to the ground with a deliberate brush-back pitch. Whipped into frenzy, Williamsport fans serenaded Tyson with the "Turkey Call," a derisive cacophony of gobbling that reverberated from the stands. This goaded Tyson to take menacing steps toward the mound with a bat in hand before the plate umpire intervened to prevent the bludgeoning of Goicochea. Surprisingly, neither player was immediately ejected. Play resumed with Goicochea striking out Tyson to end the inning. Tyson, however, went directly for the Cuban pitcher, setting off a bench-clearing donnybrook that also involved Williamsport fans pouring out of the stands before city police quelled the "riot." Eastern League president Tommy Richardson levied fifty-dollar fines and three-day suspensions on Tyson and Goicochea and lesser punishment to their teammates.[99]

Unreported but not unnoticed was a private fight that also occurred on July 8 between reserve infielder Hector Arago and first baseman Bill Schaedler. The fight did not last long; however, it continued on July 11 when Arago accused Schaedler of "doggin' it" (malinger, slow down, not put in full effort) at practices. This resulted in Schaedler punching Arago in the nose, and Arago responding with a baseball bat. Schaedler was eventually released from the team, but the damage was done; the team was fractured along racial lines both in and out of the dugout.[100]

One last fight occurred between the Blue Sox and the Grays on July 16. Tyson again went after the Grays' pitcher, Daniel Parra, but Parra refused to back down physically or verbally. Fisticuffs again ensued, order was restored, and Tyson was slapped with a tremendous 15-day suspension, but the damage was done. Psychologically defeated by abusive fans and internal fighting, the Grays whimpered to a dismal 52–85 record to end the season.

Tired of the hostility and resentment shown by the Eastern League in general and by the lack of control exhibited by the league officials, Griffith and the Cambria brothers did not renew their affiliation with the Grays for 1946.

But the experiment was not a total failure.

It is my belief that the Williamsport experiment was the inception of Joe Cambria's dream of making baseball an international sport. He had played in the Canadian leagues as a young man and knew of its prowess. (The Montreal Royals would play host to such Hall of Famers as Jackie Robinson and Tommy Lasorda.) Joe Cambria had owned and managed a Negro Leagues team in 1933 and knew of their prowess as well. His dream was to have baseball played all over the world, of course with him supplying as much talent as he could find for all entities!

Griffith had intimated that there should be a three-way World Series between the Negro and Major Leagues: Cambria envisioned one with all four leagues; Canadian, American, Negro and Latin all competing in a huge round-robin style World Series. He would begin that international dream by bringing the Havana Cubans to Florida in 1945.

Cambria also believed in the power that baseball had to shape the lives of young men and knew that his dreams would never be realized without building up the talent pool from which Major League baseball could choose. In his earliest days in the Baltimore sandlots and into his first forays of team ownership in Hagerstown and Albany, he ran baseball camps and academies designed to sharpen youngsters' baseball skills. Talking to the *Tallahassee Democrat* in 1944 about the influx of young talent from Cuba, he said, "And someday I hope to open a baseball school in Havana to train youngsters."[101]

A March 3, 1944, Associated Press article in the *Tallahassee Democrat* datelined Havana reported:

> Joe Cambria, scout for the Washington Senators of the American League, visited president Fulgencio Batista yesterday before starting his return journey to the United States. Cambria pointed out to the Cuban leader that at least twelve island players had been signed by the Washington team and added that "my highest hope is that one of them will be a star."[102]

This is but one example of the influence Joe Cambria had with the movers and shakers of the island. Cambria's proclivity for signing mass numbers of young ballplayers from Cuba made him, in the words of the 1965 hit by the Kinks, "a well respected man." Cambria enjoyed good relations with the heads of Cuba's government even after Castro's takeover, and he was granted free access to the country even up to the time of his passing.

I wonder what would have happened if Batista had a good curve ball?

Cambria may have had the most altruistic of intentions when it came to the young ballplayers on the island, but there was one person who was not buying it: his vexatious nemesis, Jess Losada.

Losada was the sports editor of Havana's *Prensa Libre*, contributing writer for *Carteles* magazine, and chief of the Cuban Bureau of Public Relations and Sports. One of the most respected voices in Cuban baseball, Losada was an outspoken critic of Cambria ever since Cambria's stunt of "stealing" four Cuban amateur players from under the noses of Losada and the Cincinnati Reds, a deal Losada worked hard to complete. Cambria was permanently ensconced in Losada's doghouse, and Losada took him to task on a regular basis. It was Losada who called him the "Christopher Columbus of baseball" for plundering the island of its baseball riches.

In 1944, it was Cambria's affection for a young star pitcher in the Cuban amateurs, Julio "El Jiqui" Moreno, that once again brought forth Losada's ire. The young hurler was legitimately compared with a young Bob Feller for his blazing fastball. Said Losada about Cambria:

> The other factor's name is Joe Cambria. This Italian American is a scout by profession. A savvy man in "baseball human material," he has a clinical eye and an anemic wallet. A baseball talent sniffer for the Washington Senators, one of the teams of the big leagues that pays the worst salaries, Joe has successfully signed the best Cuban players to date. A few have escaped but very few. Cambria, regularly, offers two hundred dollars and even less to sign a Cuban player. And if this scout of a meager payroll has offered three thousand dollars as royalty and seven hundred dollars as a monthly salary to Moreno, it's because Moreno is worth three times this amount! Moreno will not go with Washington. He wants to remain in Cuba until the war is over.[103]

One must imagine how fantastic Moreno must have been for Cambria to offer him $3,000 to sign. For Cambria, that was a fortune since his normal signings were closer to $200 or $300.

Moreno made good on his promise. He stayed in Cuba, pitched his San Antonio de los Banos team to a championship, and got married. *Then* he signed with Cambria and the Senators in 1947 and was placed with the Havana Cubans in the Florida International League. Morena came up to the Senators in 1950 and became a part of the starting rotation.

However, Losada was unapologetic.

> Cambria again is trying to sign every Cuban amateur of note, and I am trying to get the government to pass some sort of law to stop indiscriminate recruiting of our young players. A Cuban who is not ready for league ball in the United States signs. He is thrown back. He no longer is an amateur and he is not good enough for our pro league. What happens? His career is ruined. I want that sort of thing prevented from now on.[104]

This proviso in the Cuban baseball rules was no small thing. It effectively became a two-edged sword for a lot of Joe Cambria's Cuban draftees, especially many of those who played in Williamsport. After two years of playing Class A ball in the U.S., they could not go home to Cuba to play ball anymore. If they wanted to stay in organized ball, they were relegated to the American or Mexican minors. For some, it was an opportunity to stay in America, play ball for as long as they could, and make a better life than in Cuba. For others, it was tantamount to exile.

Jess Losada was not the only voice crying out in the wilderness against Griffith and Cambria. Sam Lacy, noted writer for the *Baltimore Afro-American*, had no qualms about taking Griffith, along with Cambria, to task about the lack of black players on the Senators. He was particularly acerbic about the 1944 season when he wrote, "I just threw a rock at Clark Griffith for his latest trick of scouting Cuban bush leaguers to make up his quota of 'ballplayers' for the coming season. He had Joe Cambria wash the mud out of the ears of a lot of unknowns and guide their hands across the dotted line of Washington Senators contracts so that we wouldn't have to face the dilemma of using colored players or no players at all."[105]

Lacy's objections were thrown at Griffith mostly, and Cambria was more guilty by association. Lacy's major point was Griffith's refusal to use the Negro Leagues players who were right under his nose: "It's Clark Griffith and Connie Mack, you know, together with one or two other 'old beards' who stand in the way of baseball's acceptance of qualified colored players."[106] (There will be more discussion on this in a later chapter.)

If it had been up to Cambria, he would have brought Griffith a host of outstanding Negro Leagues players, but Griffith was not a boat-rocker. So Cambria set about doing what he did best: beating the bushes both here and abroad. This did not come without sacrifices, as told by *The Pantagraph* of Bloomington, Illinois:

> He has fought the transportation problems in Cuba and Mexico as well as the good old USA and knows all there is to know about young mothers with crying babies, trains that are carrying several hundred more persons than capacity, etc., but he is "hanging in there," loyal to his boss, for whom he has toiled for more than a quarter of a century. He rode a boxcar all the way from Jacksonville, Fla., to Washington with four Cubans last winter. He has gone for 24 hours without a bite to eat on trains. He has suffered almost every known torture to keep pace with competitors, but he is still hale and hearty, and going stronger than ever.[107]

All of Joe Cambria's hard work paid off in the end, however. In December, *The Sporting News* voted Joe Cambria as its minor league "Man of the Year," "whose pioneering in the Cuban field opened up a source of talent that helped both the majors and minors to tide over the manpower shortage."[108] Joe Cambria shared the stage with such greats as St. Louis GM William DeWitt, Sr., St. Louis Browns manager Luke Sewell, Cardinals great Marty Marion, Baltimore International League manager Alphonse Thomas, Albany manager/first baseman Rip Collins, Cardinals manager Billy Southworth, and 29 game winner "Prince" Hal Newhouser among others.

Of course, this was not the first time in 1944 that Cambria would make the news. In October, he was the subject of a great five-page retrospective in the prestigious *Esquire* magazine. Written by noted sports writer Jake Wade, the article chronicled his rise to the majors, the controversies surrounding his signing of "Alabama" Pitts and the bearded Alan Benson, his affinity for Cuban ballplayers, and his run-ins with Commissioner Landis and minor league president W.G. Bramham. His good friend Clark Griffith was quoted as saying: "Joe is a mighty good baseball man. He has a flair for showmanship that helps make the game. It's too bad he's always getting in jams. He never does anything wrong intentionally."[109]

The article went on to tell of his tete-a-tetes with Landis, his minor league ownership, and his successes and failures with his many Cubans. However, one quote summed up Joe Cambria's love and respect for his boss: "Cambria thinks there's no one quite like Clark Griffith. 'He's the greatest man in baseball. There never was a finer judge of baseball material. When those wise old eyes stamp approval on one of my kids, I know I've got something.'"[110]

Cambria was sincere, of course. His loyalty to Griffith was steadfast and unwavering, as he expressed to Frank "Buck" O'Neill of *The Sporting News*: "I would rather work

The 1944 Washington Senators boasted ten draft-exempt Cuban players and five American players directly signed by Joe Cambria. Unfortunately, the "Cuban experiment" did not work in 1944, with the Senators languishing in last place for the season (private collection of George Case III).

for Mr. Griffith for nothing than work for any other man I've ever known for a higher salary."[111]

For Joe Cambria and baseball, 1944 would end on one future high and several lows.

Wartime sports were thrown a vicious curveball in December when the Federal Government, specifically War Mobilization Director James F. Byrnes, ordered all flat, harness and dog racing tracks around the country to shut down by January 3 and called upon all draft boards to "review immediately the classification of men engaged in professional athletics."[112]

Once again, officials were questioning how able-bodied young men were competing on the baseball diamond and the football gridiron yet were physically unfit to serve their country during the war. Baseball responded by citing the words of the late Commissioner Landis when he said, "the game would ask no favors and would continue as long as nine men could be put on a field." Abe Green of the National Boxing Association asserted that "if sacrifices are needed boxing will and should not be found wanting." Elmer Layden of the National Pro Football league responded, "anytime anyone is fit for military duty there is no question in our minds that he serve." The National Hockey League was deeply affected since the majority of their players (at that time) were Canadians and were subject to strict supervision by the Dominion government even before being permitted to play.[113]

Officials in the track racing community from California to Florida to New York responded promptly that they would cooperate to the utmost. Colonel Matt Winn, head of Churchill Downs in Kentucky, summed up the feelings of owners around the country by saying, "There is only one thing to do and that is to obey the boss. Things must be pretty serious for the Government to take such action, and we should follow every instruction."[114]

In the end, racing shut down for a little while but reopened in enough time for the Triple Crown to be run. Baseball went on with the same wartime travel restrictions in place. The War in Europe was over in May of 1945, so football and hockey went on unabated.

The second low of the year was the performance of the Senators. Tagged by everyone including manager Ossie Bluege, boss Clark Griffith, and scout Joe Cambria as a World Series contender, the 1944 Senators kamikazed all the way to the cellar, finishing 25 games out of first place with a vomitous 64–90 record. The four "butterfly" pitchers fluttered by, posting a lackluster 40–52 record. Dutch Leonard went a respectable 14–14 with a 3.06 ERA. Mickey Haefner went 12–15 with a 3.04 ERA. Johnny Niggeling posted a 10–8 record and a good 2.32 ERA. "Wild" Roger Wolff went a dismal 4–15 with a 4.99 ERA and walked 3.5 batters per nine innings. Even fireballer Early Wynn fizzled to an 8–17 record and a 3.36 ERA. Venezuelan Alex Carrasquel went a very respectable 8–7 with a 3.43 ERA. The pitching staff combined for a 3.49 ERA, placing them fifth in the league.

The loss of Mickey Vernon and Jerry Priddy to the service proved to be the team's undoing. Hitting and run production once again eluded the Nats. "Father Time" for the older players (Rick Ferrell, Joe Kuhel, both 38) and "baseball rust" for the returning players (Al Evans, Hillis Layne) made for a long season indeed. Stan Spence turned out to be the heavy hitter for the team, bringing in 100 RBI and belting 18 homers, only two of which were hit in Griffith "Yellowstone" Stadium. Cuban Gilberto Torres proved Joe Cambria to be a genius. Playing mostly third base, Torres flashed an astounding .953 fielding percentage to go along with a very respectable .267 batting average. Roberto Ortiz (.253 BA, 35 RBI) and Mike Guerra (.281 BA, 29 RBI) also produced at the plate; however, the remaining six Cubans were mostly underutilized. It would most definitely be "wait till next year" again for the Nats.

The real bright spot in the Senators' season came unexpectedly from a 17-year-old, two-sport New York University standout,

"Stolen" from the Boston Red Sox and the Philadelphia Athletics, 17-year-old Eddie Yost, through hard work and discipline, became the Senators' starting third baseman for a dozen seasons. His formidable batting eye made him one of the greatest leadoff hitters in baseball (National Baseball Hall of Fame Library, Cooperstown, New York).

Eddie Yost. Yost played shortstop on the baseball team and point guard on the basketball team, alongside other fine future major leaguers Ralph Branca and Sam Mele. After his freshman year, Yost got a weekend-long tryout with the Boston Red Sox, fine hotel and meals included. Manager Joe Cronin liked the young ball hawk and thought that general manager Eddie Collins had signed him. He had not. Joe Cambria somehow found out about the youngster and signed him for $500. The Phillies apparently offered him twice as much but showed up at the training site a day late and a dollar shorter than Cambria.

Yost only played seven games in 1944 at the end of the season. In October, he turned 18 and joined the Navy. After 18 months in service, he returned to the Senators, guaranteed of his old job. However, both he and Griffith wanted him to go down to Chattanooga to sharpen his skills. Commissioner Happy Chandler, afraid to set a precedent with the National Defense Service act, refused to send him down. Yost instead received some great on the job training from manager Ossie Bluege, a former standout third baseman himself. Yost took over the job for the next 12 seasons with the Senators and turned into the most productive leadoff man in franchise history.[115]

1945

The War

On May 8, bluebirds flew over the white cliffs of Dover. A jubilant sailor passionately kissed a white-clad nurse in the middle of Times Square, "and everywhere there was song and a celebration." The War was over in Europe. The Axis had been defeated in Europe, but it would take several months for Japan to fall as well.

And through it all, the one constant was baseball.

In January nobody knew anything: how long the war would last, how many more young men would die in battle, how many of the ballplayers who were involved in the fighting would return, how baseball would survive another year.

Survive it did.

Attendance was tremendous in 1944. Fans supported their teams and the various War Bond games and rallies that occurred. The St. Louis Browns cobbled together a team of misfits, old men and 4Fs, and pulled off the impossible: they won the American League pennant and faced the mighty St. Louis Cardinals is a six-game "trolley" series won by the Cardinals.

History was made.

Despite the Senators' dismal last-place finish in 1944, the utilization of the Cuban players had proven to be a success. They played with speed, heart, and gusto, and they brought in the fans. In fact, two of Griffith's minor league clubs, Chattanooga and Williamsport, had successful seasons at the turnstiles, thanks to the all-out style of play exhibited by the Cubans. The Senators did not fare too badly at the gates, but the fans were coming to see the team more out of hope and loyalty. Clark Griffith needed to put nine good men on the field in 1945, and he needed Joe Cambria's help to do so.

So, Joe Cambria went crazy.

Starting in the late fall, Cambria did not scout just the Cuban winter leagues. He scoured the back lots, sandlots and semi-pro teams throughout Cuba, Venezuela, Puerto Rico, and Mexico in search of usable talent, and he signed almost anyone who moved. The newspapers announced that more than 50 Cubans would be taken to spring camps and, as the chart shows, Cambria brought more than 30 players to camp in Washington, Williamsport, and Chattanooga. Several of his older Cubans wound up with other clubs. Scouts from both leagues were hot on the tracks of Latin players, and Cambria's singular grip on the Caribbean basin was slowly loosening.

Here again certain names appear more than once, as many players were sent to different teams throughout the year, and several were promoted to the Senators late in the season.

New Senator Invitees	Chattanooga	Williamsport	1945 Senators Roster
Armando Abreu	Luis Aloma	Hector Arago	Alejandro Carrasquel
Manuel Alegre	Angel Fleitas	Lazaro Bernal	Fermin Guerra
Augustin Delaville	Armando Gallart	Augustin Delaville	Armando Roche
Roberto Del Mazo	Leonardo Goicoechea	Gaspar Del Monte	Gilberto Torres
Angel Fleitas	Joaquin Gutierrez	Mario Diaz	Santiago Ullrich
Armando Gallart	Armando Roche	Valeriano Fano	Jose Zardon
Pedro Gomez	Jorge Torres	Aurelio Fernandez	
Manuel "Chino" Hildalgo	Armando Valdez	Francisco Gallardo	
Miguel Lastra	Jose Zardon	Leonardo Goicoechea	
Delio Martinez		Manuel "Chino" Hidalgo	**Other Latins on Teams**
Agapito Mayor		Felipe Jimeniz	Tomas de la Cruz—Reds
Ernesto Morales		Daniel Parra	Napoleon Reyes—Giants
Jose Luis Redondo		Fernando Rodriguez	Rene Monteagudo–Phillies
Armando Roche		Jose Traspuesto	Reggie Otero—Cubs
Alberto Rodriguez		Cecilio Torres	Jorge Comellas—Cubs
Fernando Rodriguez		Rogelio Valdez	Roberto Estalella—A's
Manuel Salgado			Isidoro Leon—Phillies
Jose Sanchez			Adrian Zabala—Giants
Isaac Sedane			Luis Olmo—Dodgers
Fernando Solis			
Luis Suarez			
Armando Traspuesto			
Jose Traspuesto			
Armando Valdez			
Rogelio Valdez			

Of course, Joe Cambria brought all these Cuban players into the U.S. under the assumption that they were draft-exempt. But the Selective Service was cracking down on non-resident aliens and subjecting them to the same regulations that applied to any other American. As explained: "Any alien gainfully employed in this country is considered a resident and subject to the draft. This is true for War plant workers as well as baseball players."[116]

Every person under this proviso was allowed 90 days to file residency papers, and the Selective Service was cracking down on that as well. Trying to outsmart those who would try to circumvent the filing, the SS further announced that aliens could not spend 88 days or so in this country, leave for a bit, then return and claim they had 88 more days.[117] The Senators had a lot to lose with this deal. Three of their finest, Gilberto Torres, Roberto Ortiz and Fermin Guerra, had registered and were hoping Uncle Sam would forget they were there.

Cambria took a little time off from his ivory hunting to accept a few accolades. In between games of a doubleheader at Havana's Tropical Park, he received a gold watch from one of his first signees, Tomas de la Cruz, who presented it to him on behalf of the many players he had signed over the years. Eladio Secades, sports editor of *Diario de la Marina*, the island's longest running newspaper, presented him with a bronze plaque. Dr. Rogelio Valdes Jorge, president of Cuba's professional baseball league, and Cambria's friend and one-time old Washington Senator Merito Acosta spoke briefly.[118]

The Senators, with all their Cubans, got off to a decent start in 1945. They had a record of 40–34 for the first three months of the season and things were looking good. The snake in the woodpile this year, however, was a wealthy Mexican businessman named Jorge Pasquel.

The Pasquel family was one of the most wealthy and well-connected families in Mexico. Their dealings in oil, shipping, import-export, finance, tobacco, publishing, real estate, cattle ranching and contracting tallied into the tens of millions of dollars. At one point a cousin, Manuel Avila Camacho, was the President of Mexico.

Pasquel loved all things baseball and became one of Mexican baseball's wealthiest patrons. In 1940, he bought the Azules de Veracruz team, and he and his brothers became minority owners in several other teams. By 1946, he was named president of the Mexican Leagues. However, as early as 1937, he singlehandedly integrated a baseball league by recommending the signing the immortal Martin Dihigo to the Aguilas, also in Veracruz. Through his connections with Alex Pompez, the black–Cuban owner of the American New York Cuban Giants, he was able to convince Satchel Paige to jump from the Negro Leagues down to Mexico. Paige, in turn, convinced other great Negro Leagues stars like "Cool Papa" Bell, Josh Gibson, Ray Dandridge, "Wild Bill" Wright, and Willie Wells to go jumping as well.

American Major League players jumping leagues began in 1945, and it affected Cambria and the Senators. Roberto Ortiz and his brother, Oliverio, decided to play in Mexico and jumped their Senators contracts early in the spring of 1945. They were followed by fellow Cambria signees Tomas de la Cruz of the Reds, Chile Gomez from Williamsport, Chico Hernandez (Cubs), and Antonio Ordenana (Pirates). The worst and most celebrated of the jumping began in the 1946 season. Pasquel and his brothers were flying into New York with suitcases literally filled with money and personally enticing players to jump to the Mexican league. Most notable among them were Danny Gardella (Dodgers), Sal Maglie (Giants) and Vern Stephens (Browns). The Pasquels, however, were hungry for a legitimate superstar. They offered exorbitant sums of money to Joe DiMaggio, Hank Greenberg, and Ted Williams, who turned them down. They offered Stan Musial $75,000 plus a $7,000 signing bonus to jump his Cardinals contract, which offered him $13,000. He thought about it and eventually turned it down. Pasquel went so far as to invite the great Babe Ruth down to Mexico, all expenses paid of course, and offered him a managing position of any team he desired or to be named Commissioner of the league. The Babe eventually passed on that offer.[119]

Former Senator and Governor of Kentucky Albert Benjamin "Happy" Chandler, who succeeded Commissioner Landis after his passing in 1944, was swift in his retribution with the league jumpers. He imposed a stiff five-year suspension on any players who did not live up to their contracts. In 1945, he also used that threat on several Senators players, Gilberto Torres and Fermin Guerra in particular, who were playing Cuban winter league ball along with the Ortiz brothers, who had been suspended for jumping at the beginning of the 1945 season.[120]

Through it all, Jorge Pasquel was unapologetic and called out Cambria by name:

I am surprised at Branch Rickey and others in organized baseball who are now complaining. For many years, while our Mexican League was struggling to get along, major league scouts in general and Joe Cambria in particular, visited our cities and, right under our noses and over our protests, stole our players who were signed to Mexican League contracts. Any number of Mexican league players, including a lot of Cubans we are now luring back, jumped our contracts and went north to play in organized baseball. Why? Because organized baseball offered them more money than we could afford. Yes, it hurt us a lot in those days, but those days are gone forever. Now, it's every man for himself and players looking for bigger salaries will come to the Mexican League, instead of shunning us for attractive major league offers of the past.[121]

But the die was cast. Ballplayers everywhere were aware of the huge salaries the Pasquel brothers were offering, and many used that knowledge to renegotiate their paltry pre–War salaries. By the time all the boys came back home from the war, they were not afraid to tell the club owners: I just risked my life for this country. Surely you can do better than this.

One Cuban who did not bite on Jorge Pasquel's bait was a young speedster from Havana named Jose Antonio Zardon. Zardon was part of the huge Cuban contingent Joe Cambria rounded up in 1944. His only experience at that time was playing on his high school team and for the Loma Tennis Club.[122] "The Senators signed me for $6,000. I bought a model year Buick for $800. It had leather seats. It was a real head turner."[123] Zardon was assigned to the Williamsport Grays,where he batted .292 and stole 38 bases.

"Tony," as he was called by the press, got his chance to play when three of his contemporaries, Gilberto Torres, Roberto Ortiz, and Fermin Guerra, returned home to Cuba instead of registering for the U.S. draft. (Zardon had obtained a non-resident alien visa and was draft-exempt.) He so impressed manager Ossie Bluege in the 1945 training camp with his blazing speed and running catches that he got the shot as the left fielder on Opening Day.

Zardon got a seven-day trial with the team and then, for some inexplicable reason, he was sent down to Chattanooga in May. There, he hit .300 and became a standout. He was recalled to the Senators in mid–July after injuries to George Case and Jake Powell and the weak hitting of George Binks. Zardon played 45 more games , hitting a cool .290 to help the Nats to a second-place finish.[124]

Nineteen forty-five would be Tony Zardon's only year in the Majors. He was sent down to Chattanooga, then Charlotte in 1946, then became a star for the Havana Cubans in the Florida International League from 1947 through 1952. Zardon remained in the American and Mexican minors until 1955 and never regretted a day he played the game he loved.

It would seem that with his multitudinous signing of Cuban baseball talent between 1943 and 1945, our Mr. Cambria had almost single-handedly pulled off a major

Cuban-American good will coup. The Cubans considered any of their countrymen who reached the majors to be heroes, and their prestige, and that of Joe Cambria, grew exponentially.

In 1945, Vice President Henry A. Wallace personally received many of the young players. Clark Griffith extended invitations to Cuban Ambassador Aurelio F. Concheso, Minister Counselor Dr. Jose T. Baron, Special Attaché Captain Efrain Hernandez, and several other members of the Cuban official family to greet the young ballplayers and attend Senators home games.

The American press sent special wire stories to all the Latin American countries, touting the skills and triumphs of the youngsters. The young Cubans, with their infectious smiles and their willingness to co-operate, went a long way to compensate for their lack of English-language skills.[125]

Griffith and Cambria became known as unofficial goodwill ambassadors to the island. It was a huge win-win situation for all parties involved, and this became a steppingstone for Joe Cambria's next big vision.

Baseball with an International Beat

Joe Cambria finally realized his dream of making baseball an international sport in the fall of 1946, when he and his friend Pedro "Merito" Acosta became the founding members of the Florida International League. They, along with seven other impresarios, put up money to field baseball teams to play in both Florida and Havana, Cuba.

Cambria probably decided to take this route after seeing and hearing about the amount of racial abuse his Cuban boys had to endure in Williamsport. In 1946, he, his brother John, and Griffith all gave up their interests in the Grays to Michigan businessman Earl E. Halstead, who affiliated the Grays with the Detroit Tigers.[126] The amount of good will emanating from Cuba was enough to convince Griffith to terminate his working agreement with the Grays and move it to Cambria's new club, the Havana Cubans, or *Cubanos* as they were often referred.

Griffith had a great fondness for family and treated his baseball franchise the same way. Up until the time of his passing in 1955, Griffith's managers and front office executives were populated almost exclusively by former Senators players. The same was to be said for this latest venture.

Pedro "Merito" Acosta became president and part-owner of the Cubans, and Joe Cambria became the General Manager. Acosta, former outfielder with the Senators from 1913 through 1916, also had a distinguished career in the Cuban professional leagues from 1912 through 1923. Acosta brought with him firm Spanish-language skills as well as an intuitive knowledge of the inner workings of the Cuban professional baseball system.

The FIL began as a Class C league with six teams in 1946: Havana, Tampa, Miami Beach, West Palm Beach, Lakeland, and Miami. By 1947, two more teams, Ft. Lauderdale and St. Petersburg, joined the league. The league remained in the C category until 1949, when they were raised to the B Class.[127]

With more than a decade of scouting and connections under his belt, Cambria was able to secure some of the finest talent from the entire island, including from the Cuban professional teams. Every person in Cuba was baseball crazy, and every ball player would be crazy *not* to want to play with the Cubans. Scouts would be all over the FIL, and it was a sure-fire way to big league baseball. Consequently, the Havana team dominated the league, winning five consecutive regular season titles from 1946 to 1950, and dominated at the turnstiles, drawing over 200,000 fans from 1947 through 1949. Two of their most dominating pitchers, Sandalio Consuegra and Conrado Marrero, went on to become part of the starting rotation for the early 1950s Senators, and a third, Miguel Fornieles, became a regular with the White Sox and the Red Sox.

Cambria wasted little time in expanding his worldview. No sooner had the ink dried on the FIL deal than Cambria, in conjunction with Cuban sports director Luis Orlando Rodriguez, the Landis of Cuban baseball, arranged for three major league teams to travel to Cuba to play games there. The Red Sox would play March 10 and the St. Louis Cardinals agreed to play games on March 16 and 17. The Senators would also venture to the island to play some games with the Cuban players. Cambria gushed to the *Baltimore Sun*: "Rodriguez and his associates will pay homage to Griff when the Red Sox play the Senators. It will be known as Clark Griffith day and quite a ceremony will be arranged. It is fitting that Cuba honor Griff. He is the smartest baseball man in the majors."[128]

With the help of the four knuckleballers who found the plate with greater accuracy, six Cubans who filled in admirably, and several key veterans, the Senators fought the whole year. In a close race, they finished in second place, only a game and a half behind the Tigers for the pennant.

George Case and George Myatt stole 30 bases apiece, batted .296 and .294, and drove in 72 and 81 runs respectively. George "Bingo" Binks (62 runs) and the ageless, 39-year-old Joe Kuhel (73 runs) teamed up with Harlond Clift (49 runs) and Gilberto Torres (39 runs) to help the team put runs on the board.

The "butterfly brigade," with the savvy help of veteran catcher Rick Ferrell, posted a much better year, winning 60 games and losing 43, and keeping their strikeout to walk ratio much higher than the previous year. The surprise of the year, however, was a 5-foot, 7-inch *piasano* named Marino Pieretti. The 23-year-old Rule 5 draftee was also 4F draft-deferred. Pieretti had a career year his first year in Washington. He pitched in 44 games, with 27 starts, 14 complete games, three shutouts, and a commendable 14–13 record. His 3.34 ERA would be his lowest in his six-year professional career.

The Cuban veterans on the staff provided some good relief for the four knucklers. Alejandro Carrasquel pitched in 35 games, went 7–5 with a 2.71 ERA and two shutouts. Santiago Ullrich threw 28 games with a 3–3 record and a 3.34 ERA.

When the ballplayers-turned-soldiers came back, they were greeted as the heroes they were. Hillis Layne, in his first full year back, played in 61 games at his old third base slot, hit .299 and brought in 22 important runs. Buddy Lewis earned a Distinguished Flying Cross for his multitudinous missions, "flying the hump" across the rugged China-Burma-Indian border region. Lewis, enjoying having his feet firmly on the outfield grass of Griffith Stadium, got into 69 games, scored 42 runs, and posted a magnificent .333 batting average in 258 at-bats.

Three-time All-Star Cecil Travis returned from the Battle of the Bulge with a Bronze Star, four battle stars, and two badly frostbitten feet, which he almost lost. In his short, 15-game return to third base, he had 54 at-bats, with 10 RBI and a .241 batting average. The damage to his feet was severe enough that he had to retire after the 1947 season.[129]

The true inspiration of the year occurred on August 4 when Bert Shepard took the mound for the Senators in a 14–2 blowout by the Boston Red Sox.

Shepard was a minor league pitcher when he got drafted in 1942. He signed up for the Army Air Corp, went to flight school at Daniel Field in Georgia, and earned his wings and a commission as a 2nd Lieutenant. Flying a mission over Berlin in his P-38 Lightning, he was shot down. A doctor in a German POW camp amputated his leg 11 inches below his knee. In February of 1945, he was involved in a prisoner exchange and returned to his Clinton, Indiana, home. While there, he determined to teach himself how to pitch again using his leg prothesis. He was eventually sent to Walter Reed Hospital in Washington, D.C., to be fitted for a new artificial leg. While there, he was visited by Undersecretary of War Robert Patterson, who presented him with a commendation for his gallantry. When Patterson asked Shepard if he had one wish, Shepard replied he wanted to pitch in a major league ball game. Patterson immediately contacted his old friend Clark Griffith, who arranged for Shepard to have a tryout at spring training camp. Shepard showed that he could handle the mechanics of the mound, and Griffith offered him a contract as a coach until he was able to gain more command and control of his pitches. On July 10, after General Omar Bradley pinned the Airman's Medal on his uniform, Shepard started, went four innings, and won an exhibition game against the Dodgers. Impressed by his fortitude, Griffith activated him to pitch in the second game of the August 4 doubleheader. Entering in the fourth inning in relief, Shepard struck out the first batter he saw. He stayed in for the remainder of the game, giving up only one run on three hits in 5⅓ innings.

On August 31, Bert Shepard was awarded the Distinguished Flying Cross in between games of a doubleheader. He was released by the club on September 1.[130]

His wish fulfilled, Bert Shepard never again appeared in a major league game.

CHAPTER 6

1946–1949:
When the Boys Came Back

The War

Japan finally surrendered on August 15, 1945, six days after the U.S. dropped its last atomic bomb on Nagasaki. Surrenders continued throughout the Asian and Pacific theaters for the remainder of the year, and troops began to mobilize for the slow return home.

As the soldiers returned, factories that had turned out tanks and jeeps and military housing instead turned out automobiles, and new homes were built, all to meet the demand of new families. American infrastructure, which had taken a back seat since the war began, now needed manpower to make roads, bridges, and cities. The peacetime economy boomed like a Howitzer.

All with the exception of a ballplayer's salary, as we shall see.

Ossie Bluege had had enough of Cambria's Cuban dreamers. In 1945, he put up with the 30 that came to training camp and the 10 that stayed. Less pejorative than his successor, Bucky Harris, he still found that the two Cubans who were the most productive on the field, Gilberto Torres and Fermin Guerra, spent more time interpreting for the pitching staff than actually playing, although Bluege was prone to hyperbole. Torres and Guerra lost their jobs to returnees Cecil Travis and Al Evans, but they were productive reserve players.

Bluege's pitching rotation got a much-needed shot in the arm with the return of Sid Hudson, Bill Kennedy, Max Wilson, Vern Curtis, Ray Scarborough and Early Wynn, to go along with his four knuckleballers and the well-traveled Bobo Newsom, fresh off stints with the Browns and the A's. His defense was shored up admirably with the return of Cecil Travis at shortstop, Jerry Priddy at second base, and Mickey Vernon at first. Vernon won the first of his two batting crowns in 1946 with a highly respectable .355 batting average and also made his first All-Star team.

With practically a whole team of wartime players returning, all of whom were guaranteed their jobs back, Ossie Bluege made it known that his Spanish skills were nil and he needed to focus on putting his best nine on the field. Although Cambria brought in several players for a look-see at the 1946 camp, only Guerra and Torres stuck with the parent club.

Two important issues would take up the bulk of the newspaper ink in 1946: the Pasquel brothers and the outlaw Mexican League raid on American baseball, and a tense but important labor dispute between all the American ballplayers and Organized Baseball itself.

In between games of a Boston–Washington doubleheader at Tropical Stadium in Havana in early March, Colonel Luis Orlando Rodriguez, Director-General of Sports for Cuba, presented Clark Griffith with a gold medal for his contributions to the advancement of baseball in Cuba and for being the leader in Cuban player advancement in the major leagues.

Cuban government officials, as well as Commissioner Chandler and American League President Will Harridge, were on hand to praise him. Griffith, in turn, praised his Cuban signees: "I took these boys because I not only liked them personally, but I have always appreciated their sincere efforts and their gentlemanly conduct. Their actions on and off the field have been a credit not only to them, but to their country as well."[1]

Griffith could not pass up the opportunity to take a shot at Jorge Pasquel and the outlaw Mexican league raiders:

> He pointed out the "menace" of the Mexican leagues' raids on Cuban playing talent and likened organized ball's position in Cuba with the early struggles of organized ball in the United States. "We of America had this same battle, but we fought it through, cleaning out all crooked and shady elements. Baseball cannot harbor contract jumpers and unreliables. You of Cuba unfortunately have a thorn in your side in the presence of the outlaw Mexican league, which persuade your boys and our boys to jump contracts and obligations they owe to Organized Ball. The menace must be and can be done away with."[2]

The Mexican threat actually started quietly in the mid–1940s and reached its zenith in 1946, when the Pasquel brothers succeeded in stealing dozens of players from the American, Negro and Cuban leagues.

A war of words soon erupted. Commissioner Chandler reiterated his five-year ban on any players who jumped their legitimate contract and extended it to include other players, in this case in the Cuban leagues, who played with any jumpers. A conference was held in Havana where it was agreed that support (spearheaded by Branch Rickey and Clark Griffith) should be given to the "legitimate" Mexican National League. Consisting of teams from Chihuahua, El Paso, Juarez, Mexico City, Saltillo, and Torreon, this Class-B league was recognized as a subsidiary of Organized Baseball. Major league teams could send their players there for more seasoning but, as in all other minor league affiliates in Major League Baseball, Blacks were not allowed to play. Clark Griffith was quick to rally to their cause, saying the league could be organized quickly and even suggesting that Organized Baseball could provide "overflow free-agent players to help develop their youth in baseball."[3]

Unfortunately, two teams were forced to fold in April, and the league itself folded in May, leaving only Jorge Pasquel's outlaw Mexican league to continue.

To legitimize his claim, Pasquel charged that Organized Baseball was acting "like a slave market." Through the Spanish language paper *Esto,* Pasquel charged that American baseball was a monopoly and that its originators "established their own rules, decided the salaries, created the system of being the proprietors of men, like of any object … the players who enrich the proprietors can do nothing but accept the best offer available."[4]

Again, Pasquel reiterated that he was only doing what Major League Baseball had been doing for decades: raiding the Mexican leagues of all its good players and offering them a pittance. He was at least offering plenty.

More accusations flew, this time between Joe Cambria and Mexican baseball officials. Don Aurelio Ferrara, executive of the Monterey club and vice-president of the Mexican League, told the *Sporting News*: "When the Washington Senators sent their scout Joe Cambria into Mexico to look over our players, I took Cambria into my home and had him as my guest at the ballpark. I told him I didn't want him to take any of my players and he promised me he wouldn't. Yet, he rounded up two of my boys, Hec Leal and Lamalla Torres, at midnight and tried to spirit them out of town!"[5]

Cambria's version of the story was, of course, completely the opposite and perhaps a bit more hyperbolic. Writing from Havana, Cambria said:

> I never was in Ferrara's home in my life. I was forced to pay to get into the ballpark and then chased out at the point of a gun. We never took a player from his league. He had [Fermin] Guerra and [Roberto] Rodriguez and [Agapito] Mayor, who belonged to us. I signed Leal and Torres in the Cuban Winter Leagues. I talked with Ferrara over the phone about Torres and he said it was fine to go ahead and sign him. I took the Springfield club to train there, and they tried to steal all the players. Ask Johnny Marion about this. No, Mexico was not nice to me.[6]

Being run out of town at gunpoint was probably a little over the top, but it was soon picked up by sports scribes around the country. It was Joe Cambria just being Joe, and it made for good copy.

If ever there was a skunk at a garden party, it happened on March 16, 1946, to our own Clark Griffith, when he was rudely and unsuccessfully forced into a meeting with his arch-rival, Bernardo Pasquel, part-owner of the outlaw Mexican League. Pasquel had been openly critical of Griffith in both the American and Mexican papers after Griffith inexplicably canceled a meeting they were to have in Havana on March 9 and 10.

Griffith was to be feted at a goodwill luncheon hosted by Cuban sports writers to celebrate Griffith and the Washington sports writers for all of their efforts on behalf of Cuban baseball. After a 90-minute delay caused by the tardiness of Colonel Luis Orlando Rodriguez, Cuban sports minister, Pasquel walked in together with Rodriguez, much to Griffith's amazement. After embarrassed pleasantries, it was announced that there was to be a meeting the following day with Griffith representing American baseball interests, Pasquel Mexican interests, and Rodriguez the Cuban interests.

It was an obvious attempt to put Griffith on the spot and try to force a tete-a-tete concerning the Mexican League situation. Griffith, however, nimbly sidestepped the proceedings, saying he had no authority to act on behalf of American baseball or for Commissioner Happy Chandler. Apparently, Rodriguez had been appointed by Chandler to act as an intermediary between the two warring interests, and he took it upon himself to set things in motion unilaterally.

Pasquel's presence was more embarrassing than productive. There were pleasant speeches and conciliatory handshaking, but the atmosphere was awkward. Everyone put on a happy face, photos were taken with all involved, including with Cambria, but the atmosphere was as friendly as a pride of lions at a wildebeest convention.[7]

The Mexican situation did not go away anytime soon. In 1946 alone, Pasquel and his associates were able to lure away over 30 American, Cuban, and Negro Leagues players. Many of them were some of Cambria's best signees like Alejandro Carrasquel, Rene Monteagudo, and Roberto Estalella. However, the best-laid plans of mice and men, as they say.

Pasquel lost $400,000 in 1946, over four million in today's dollars. That was the price, almost to the penny, of the salaries of all the white players he had signed. Costs obviously needed to be cut. He scrapped the building of a 50,000-seat stadium in Mexico City, as well as other stadiums scheduled to be built inside the country. He sat down with the major leaguers and told them the cruel facts: their salaries were being reduced, in some instances by as much as 50 percent.[8]

Pasquel finally called it quits in 1948 after spending too much money in salaries and not enough in supporting the league's administration, infrastructure, and stadiums. By 1948, most of the American players, tired of the bad food, harsh living conditions (by their standards), and pay cuts, surreptitiously made their way back to their parent clubs. Commissioner Chandler dropped his five-year ban two years early when lawsuits brought by Pasquel and Danny Gardella threatened Major League Baseball's hated "reserve clause," which gave the average player absolutely no control over his own baseball life or future. Gardella's lawyer threatened to challenge the reserve clause on the basis of the Sherman Anti-Trust Act of 1922, which would have proved Major League Baseball to be a monopoly. Rather than fight, they settled out of court, dropped the players' ban, and all was forgiven.[9]

However, this would not be the last time that the reserve clause was attacked in the 1940s.

The boys came back home, and the last thing they were expecting or would tolerate was the status quo. Many of them had put their lives on the line, and in some cases had taken a bullet for their country. They were told to take this or that town or hill and do whatever was needed to secure it. They were not about to come back to their home lives to be told blithely to show up for your job at the same time for the same pay. For some of the ballplayers, it was just that: you are chattel for the Boston Red Sox; show up for spring training or stay home. The new G.I. Bill may have guaranteed them their old jobs back upon their return; however, the employers reasoned, same job, same pay. Consequently, many of the boys simply held out rather than sign their contracts and demanded more money, stating they could make more money playing semi-pro ball around their hometowns. The Mexican League specter was always in the shadows.

War always seems to turn out profitably for the winners, and the returning G.I.s felt entitled to some of that largess. Major league ballplayers certainly felt that way. But as they say in the music business, it is never "what have you done for me lately, it is what have you done for me *now*."

Major league owners, in their infinite wisdom and parsimony, just sent their returning service players their same contracts with the same salaries they got before the war. Their reasoning? Since these guys had been away, in some cases for three years, they certainly were not worth now what they were worth before they went into the service. This arrogant, insouciant attitude by the club owners naturally angered many of the returning G.I.s, who felt their wartime sacrifices had been blatantly disregarded:

> The problem of rising expectations, though, was much bigger and more serious than that of GI rights, which was, after all, short term. With the return of the players from the War there was a growing feeling within the baseball world that in the emerging postwar economic climate players were being crudely exploited at current salary levels. The players had no real way to push for higher wages. They were bound to their clubs by the so called "reserve clause" in their contracts, which [neither] a world war [nor] an atom bomb could break. Section 10 (a) of the Uniformed Player's Contract bound a player to his club until such time as the club either released him, sold him or traded him away.[10]

Enter Robert Francis Murphy, a Boston attorney who organized the American Baseball Guild two days before the start of the 1946 season. A former examiner for the National Labor Relations Board, Murphy set out to unionize baseball. This was, of course, not a new idea, as baseball had attempted unionization as far back as John Montgomery Ward's Brotherhood of Base Ball Players in 1890. Other attempts started and failed in 1900 and 1912. All of these unionization attempts, however, centered around one particular *leitmotif:* the reserve clause. This fourth instance at unionization, however, was also fueled by the Mexican League threat.

All the players were aware of the enormous amounts of money being thrown at some of the marquee players by the Pasquel brothers, and many of them had also been approached. They were also aware of the booming post-war economy. They were just not buying the "same pay" doctrine espoused by the owners, and they definitely did not believe the cries of poverty falling from the club owners' mouths. Having been familiar with the inner workings of the NLRB, Murphy struck hard at the 1922 Supreme Court decision and the reserve clause, as well as the poor pay and working conditions. By reminding the players of their rights under Federal law to bargain collectively, Murphy hoped to build some momentum within the rank and file. The Guild sought to organize players by teams, with an elected spokesman for each team.

Many of the players thought they could get some support from Washington Senators owner Clark Griffith. He had been the main catalyst for the formation of the Ball Players Protective Association in 1900. It was not successful in helping formulate ballplayers' rights but was successful in the formation of the new American League in 1901. However, the old "wild-eyed arch conservative" would have none of it and proclaimed loudly that a players' union would mean the end of baseball.

Many players joined the Guild, but an abortive test case in Pittsburgh failed to carry off a strike threat. However, owners got the message and were fearful of the Guild's possible success, the Mexican threats to the reserve clause, and to debates in Congress about post–war economic factors. In August of 1946, they met with player representatives and conceded to the following: a $5,500 minimum salary, severance pay, expense money, and contractual adjustments, mainly, that a player on a major league contract who was sent down to the minors would receive his major league salary.

The players' expense money became known as "Murphy Money" for years following the negotiations. A player got his cap and uniform from the team on the first day of spring training. Nothing else. If he needed a shave, haircut, shoeshine, or a meal outside of camp, it came out of his own pocket, as well as the expense of bringing his family down to training camp. The expense money became a major incentive for the players.

The issue that was tiptoed around by the players was the reserve clause. Yankees owner Larry MacPhail had made it known in July that the topic was sacrosanct. Although Murphy tried unsuccessfully to institute changes to the Uniform Players Agreement in other ways, the great Pirates slugger Ralph Kiner, who became active as a player representative later in his career, said, "We never, *never* thought we had a chance of getting rid of it."

On August 20, the Guild was defeated in another Pirates team vote, and it was essentially dead. The players and Murphy held a hand stronger than they knew, and if properly played, they could have had the whole orchard. Instead, they settled for an apple.[11]

As always, Joe Cambria was still busy with many fingers in many pies. In February, he was named to a 16-member "All America" Board of the National Baseball Congress. He was to pick the Nation's top sandlot players from a group of 500 semi-pros to compete in the national tournaments in August.[12]

Joe Cambria's "baby" was his Havana Cubans team in the new Florida International League. Newspapers from Havana to New York were all atwitter with the prospects of this auspicious international undertaking, and the Miami papers were writing reams about the players. Cambria and his friend, team President Merito Acosta, were sitting in "the high cotton" of good players. Manager Oscar Rodriguez was a legend in Cuban baseball and had managed in the Cuban leagues for decades. Pedro Gomez at shortstop and Hector Arago at second had had some playing time with the Senators, so they were bona fine big leaguers. The most wonderful thing in all of this was the rest of the players on the team. Almost all of them had played together in the Cuban juvenile or professional ranks or with the Williamsport Grays in the old New York-Penn League. Their language, customs, traditions and in some instances their hometowns were the same, and it made for a very homogeneous group from the very start.[13]

Senators boss Clark Griffith felt so good about this venture that he put up his own money to buy 20,000 shares of the team and become a majority stockholder. "Havana someday will be in one of the bigger minor leagues," he gushed.[14] Griffith entered into a working agreement with the club, sat back, and hoped for the best.

The 1946 Senators

Despite being *persona non grata* in Mexico (*la pistola* in the ribs notwithstanding), Cambria had other places from which to find his talent for the Senators, and he set about scouring the Caribbean, finding players for them and for his new Havana team. However, with the return of so many boys from the war, especially Mickey Vernon, Jerry Priddy, and the pitchers, Cambria's Cuban talent became expendable. Almost everyone he sent to Griffith was sent elsewhere.

Jose Zardon, who had played so admirably as a replacement player in 1945, was sent to Chattanooga as partial payment for Griffith's new slugger, Gil Coan. Pedro Gomez, Francisco Gallardo, and Emanuel Hidalgo were sent to the Cubans. Alejandro Carrasquel was sold to the White Sox. Santiago Ullrich decided to play ball in Mexico and Cuba, and Angel Fleitas was sent to Chattanooga.

Two "Gaspars," Del Monte and Del Toro, were a curious case. Gaspar Del Monte, another of Cambria's "can't miss" brigade, originally played in Williamsport in 1945. In 1946, he was sent to the Charlotte Hornets and never made it up to the majors in his 11-year career. Gaspar Del Toro suffered the same unfortunate fate as Roberto Estalella. With his complete lack of English language skills, Del Toro was sent to Washington with a note pinned to his jacket and was promptly sent to the Welsh Miners of the Appalachian League where, once again, some kind soul had to play charades with him to find out what position he played.

The only Cubans to make the Senators' roster in 1946 were Ossie Bluege's favorites, Gilberto Torres and Fermin Guerra. Torres was a good-field, small-hit infielder who could spell a lot of the old-timers, and Guerra had proved to be a competent back-up catcher, a real "unicorn" in baseball parlance.

With the return of his front-line players and Mickey Vernon's league-leading batting average, the Senators put together a respectable 76–78 season and a solid fourth place finish in the standings.

Nineteen forty-six and 1968 would be the last times that both the original and expansion Senators would place in the first division for the remainder of their years in Washington, D.C.

1947

The beginning of the year marked a paradigm shift for the Senators. With all his regulars back on the squad, Clark Griffith was sure he could win with American talent and told Cambria once again to lay off his heavy scouting of Latin players.[15]

Cambria did as he was told. There was not one Latin player at the Senators' spring training camp in 1947. He continued to scout the island for boys for his Havana team and for the Nats' Chattanooga and Charlotte clubs.

Cambria's Havana team was doing land office business, however, and he was fixing his attention there. He had put up lights for night games for the first time in Tropical Stadium, and the team drew 225,000 people at home and 35,000 people on the road. The Cubans came in first in their league in 1946 but just like Salisbury in 1937, the team had to forfeit 17 games for using too many "class" men. Cambria was determined to make the Cubans into the powerhouse of the Florida International League.[16]

Losing a Step

For Cambria, with the advent of the outlaw Mexican league, the shake-up about salaries in the major leagues, the changing face of the post–war economy, and the relative stability of the Cuban professional leagues, the scouting landscape had changed. Ballplayers were less naive and more aggressive about signing contracts for better money. Gone were the days of waving a $100 bill under a boy's nose and getting his name on the dotted line. Everyone knew what the money was like everywhere, and both the scouts and the owners were now placed in a more competitive situation.

One case in point was the hunt for Roberto Avila. Bobby Avila was a Mexican National League standout with the Angeles de Puebla team. He was in Havana in the winter of 1947, playing with the Marianao Tigres and winning the batting championship. Cambria had talked with him and had his Senators contract all ready to go; however, much to his chagrin, Avila said he liked to play "rough" ball and preferred to play for the Dodgers. Whatever it was, Avila shocked both clubs by playing with Puebla again in 1947 and then signing a contract with the Cleveland Indians in 1948. He had a fine 11-year major league career with the Indians, amassing 1,296 hits, with seven seasons of 100+ hits, a .281 batting average, .359 on-base percentage, and .388 slugging percentage. He won the American League batting championship with a .341 average in 1954.[17]

Finding another Mickey Vernon was getting harder and harder.

Cambria just could not resist one more prospect! He convinced manager Ossie Bluege to take a look at a youngster from Havana, *Doctor* Hiram Gonzalez. Yes, that is correct. Hiram Gonzalez graduated from the University of Havana with a Doctor of Medicine degree, not too long after the great Dr. Bobby Brown got his degree from

Tulane University and roomed with Yogi Berra. Gonzalez was a swift first baseman who had some pop in his bat, unfortunately not enough to please manager Bluege. Gonzalez washed out of camp on his second try, so Cambria took him over. Gonzalez played from 1947 to 1950 with Cambria's Havana Cubans and then for nine years in the American and Mexican minors.

Nothing ventured, nothing gained.

Different Commissioner, Same Carpet

Once again, Cambria managed to get himself into trouble, this time with officials of the Florida International League, in the summer of 1947. Being one of the most high-profile members of the FIL, it is unfathomable to explain how Cambria could do what he did and still get away with it.

In fair Havana, where we lay our scene, Cambria announced in April that he had signed a blockbuster deal with Branch Rickey and the Brooklyn Dodgers. So enamored were they by his scouting prowess in Cuba, the Dodgers agreed to pay him $20,000 (approximately $236,000 in today's money) for the services of three players, sight unseen. It was the highest price to date for any Class-C ballplayers.[18]

The three players eventually named were pitchers Rafael Rivas and Rogelio Martinez and catcher Mario Diaz. Diaz was the sure-handed backstop for Cambria's 1944 and 1945 Williamsport Grays and went on to have a good 13-year minor league career. Rivas played for the Cubans in 1946 and 1947 and spent 15 years in the minors. The only one with a modicum of success, if it can be called that, was Rogelio Martinez. Martinez played for the Cubans from 1947 to 1949 and made a very brief trip up to the Senators in 1950. Pitching in two games in relief, in 1⅓ innings pitched, he faced 10 batters and gave up four hits, four earned runs, and two walks, for an 0–1 record and a 27.00 ERA. He was promptly sent back down to the minors.

This background is given to elucidate two things: first, these players were more of an exercise in futility for all parties concerned since they obviously did not have the stuff to be major league ballplayers, and second, in spite of the brouhaha yet to come, all three wound up playing for Cambria in the end.

Our little drama opens with charges filed by Branch Rickey and Mel Jones of the Dodgers, alleging that the three players, who were assigned to play for their Montreal farm club, refused to report for the specified $250 salary. When asked why, they boasted that they could make more money playing "under the table" for Havana, which of course was against FIL rules. Rickey and Jones complained to George L. Trautman, president of the Minor League Baseball association, who initiated the primary investigation.

Compounding the initial situation was Cambria. He was politely asked by FIL president Wayne Allen to "appear or be expelled from the league" in order to explain his $9,000 in "scouting expenses," which smelled like three-day-old fish. A meeting was held on August 4 in Ft. Lauderdale, where Cubans team president Merito Acosta emphatically stated that he had nothing to do with financial transactions of any kind. He was totally vindicated of any wrongdoing, and Cambria began his explanation. The next day, President Allen announced that he was delaying the investigation a few days on behalf of Senators owner Clark Griffith. Griffith advised Allen that he was sending Eddie Eynon, the Senators' business manager, to make a full and complete investigation of the allegations. The Senators were the principal stockholders of the team, and Clark Griffith wanted no part in any impropriety.

It took Eynon a week to get there, but he went straight to Havana to investigate. The three ballplayers, under oath, denied making the statements. In Florida, Cambria successfully explained his scouting expenses; however, blame was eventually assigned. "After a thorough investigation," said Wayne Allen:

> It has been decided that there have been salary violations by that club [Havana]. It has been admitted that these were caused a great deal because of solicitations made by the Mexican outlaw league which had a representative in Havana soliciting baseball players. The Havana baseball club through its officers has assured the president of the league that there will be no further violations of the salary limit and that in the future they will be kept in the salary limits as set by the league and the national association. The president of the league is hereby imposing a fine of $500 upon the Havana club because of such violations. The case is closed as far as I'm concerned. I probably will make a report to Trautman. I don't know exactly when.[19]

Cambria emphatically maintained that his financial negotiations were above board and with his vest pocket administrative system must have showed President Allen enough proof of his innocence. Once again alluding to his boss, he said: "I'm very happy to be cleared. You may say I'll be in baseball a long, long time with the aid of my very good friend Clark Griffith."[20]

What Griffith said to Allen is, of course, lost to the ages. Obviously, it was enough to assuage any misgivings Allen may have had concerning Cambria's shoddy expense report. Once matters in Florida were settled, Joe Cambria headed to Texas to do some scouting. He needed something to go right for him in 1947, and it came in the most unlikely of places.

As mentioned earlier, Cambria found 17-year-old Eddie Yost and signed him after seeing him only three times at a Boston Red Sox tryout camp. Yost played only seven games for the Nats in 1944 at the end of the year. Enlisting in the Coast Guard during the off-season, Yost was gone from 1945 through 1946. Upon his return, he was guaranteed his job back under government rulings. But both Yost and Griffith knew he was not ready for big league ball, having had no previous experience to speak of, and they petitioned Commissioner Chandler to let him be sent down to Chattanooga for more seasoning. Chandler refused to buck the precedent and denied their request.

So, in 1947, Eddie Yost showed his mettle. He was the first on the field and the last off. He took extra-long mentoring sessions at third base with manager Bluege, who patiently showed him the ropes a step at a time. He was a squirrel around the batting cages, always eager for advice. His hard work paid off. In 115 games, his .238 batting average and 102 hits were solid enough. He also inherited the very hard leadoff spot in the batting order, a role he was to play for almost his entire Senators career. His 45 walks that year would only be a precursor to his amazing 1,614 lifetime walks, placing him at number 11 all-time. Yost would be a fan favorite during his entire 14 years with the club.[21]

The Buzz Dozier Saga

When he was asked if his latest phenom, six-foot, five-inch, bespectacled Buzz Dozier could pitch, Cambria replied: "If he can't, we'll paint him white, stretch him out and use him for the left-field foul line!"[22]

Buzz Dozier, scouted off the Baylor University baseball team, was an 18-year-old fireballer, another of Cambria's "can't miss" troupe. What Dozier was really, was a very young man who was rushed up to the major leagues without enough experience or expertise. Baseball-reference.com has him with no minor league experience in 1947. Debuting on September 12, Dozier pitched two games in relief for the Nats, 4⅔ innings pitched, with two hits, one walk and two strikeouts. That little toe dip got him a ticket to Charlotte in 1948, where he showed respectable ability. In 39 games, he went 8–8 in 167 innings pitched, giving up 198 hits, 115 earned runs and 115 walks for a 6.20 ERA. He won a trip back up to the Nats in 1949. This time, it would not go smoothly. He pitched two games in relief again, this time with 6⅓ innings pitched. He gave up 12 hits, eight runs, and six walks to go with one lone strikeout. His 11.37 ERA won him a quick ticket to Chattanooga, where he did not fare well, and he was sent down to Charlotte again, never to return to the majors. He ended his career in 1951 with short stints in his home state at Port Arthur, Texarkana, and Sherman-Denison.[23]

At least, Joe Cambria was keeping his scouting in this country.

Cambria may not have been embarrassed by Buzz Dozier, but he got a taste of red face from the Yankees. In June of 1947, right before the end of the trading deadline. Griffith sent Cambria to New York to talk manager Bucky Harris into letting go of right-handed-hitting outfielder Johnny Lindell. Lindell would become an important cog in the world champion Yankees' wheel in 1947, which ran roughshod over the Brooklyn Dodgers in one of their many World Series appearances.

Bucky Harris, who knew Joe Cambria well and hated all his Cubans, maybe was exacting a bit of revenge upon our Italian laundry man. He said, "sure, you can have Lindell. In fact, I'll even throw in Bill Bevens. You just give me Early Wynn and Sid Hudson in return!"[24]

Bevens (3.82 ERA, 7–13) was the *only* pitcher on the Yankees' staff with a losing record that year. Wynn and Hudson were, of course, the heart of the Senators' rotation. Lindell would have hated Griffith Stadium, with its 407-foot left field line, as opposed to the 318-foot line in Yankee Stadium. In any event, Cambria beat a hasty retreat back to D.C., no doubt with the echoes of Bucky Harris' laughter in his ears.

The 1947 Senators

With not one Latin on the squad, the Senators ended up in seventh place with a dismal 64–90 record. Despite good showings at the plate from several of Cambria's finds (Vernon, 159 hits, Yost, 102 hits, Buddy Lewis, 141 hits), the team only scored 496 runs for the year. Early Wynn was the only pitcher with a winning record (17–15), and the team ERA ended at 3.97.

It was time for a change, and Griffith was quick to action. Instead of asking him to manage the team for another year, Griffith asked Ossie Bluege to become the director of the farm system. Bluege took the job since he had been lobbying for some sort of shake-up in the farms for the last five years. "I spoke to Griffith so often about his haphazard farm system that I guess I talked myself into the job!" Griffith told the *Washington Post*:

[This is] the most important job in the baseball organization. It's even more important than my job as president. Our team can only go as far as our players from the farm can take us.

The day when you could buy or trade for good players is over. There are no clubs that need money. It used to be that teams could make big profits selling players, but now they know that the most profit is to be made at the gates, on attendance. About 12 years ago, we came up with Cecil Travis and Buddy Lewis from our Chattanooga farm team. They were great players and for 10 years we didn't have to worry about two positions on our team. We lost hundreds of thousands of dollars operating Chattanooga, but Travis and Lewis compensated us. We've been letting our farm clubs rock along without smart supervision. It's a big job we're giving Bluege.[25]

This announcement would have a significant impact on the entire organization of the team. With a bona fide farm director, gone were the days of dealing with independent operators like Joe Cambria and Joe Engle. Now there would be accountability at all the class levels and one person to whom everyone would answer. Within a year, Ossie Bluege would double the number of teams in the farm system from six to 12 to bring it in line with the majority of the major league teams. He did so by increasing the number of B league teams from one to four, C league from one to three, and D league from three to four.

Chattanooga was the AA mainstay of the organization, along with Charlotte (B), Havana (C), and Orlando (D). Ossie Bluege kept those in his stable and branched out to include a much larger portion of the country. He got teams in the Big State (Texas), Colonial (CT, NY, NJ), Kitty (KY, IL, TN), Virginia, Southeastern, Longhorn and Mid-Atlantic leagues. By expanding the farms, Bluege and Griffith would have a better look at talent from across the country, not just the East Coast. Of course, no one was going to outdo the Yankees with their 17 teams or the Cardinals with their 21-team farm system. Griffith went about signing working agreements with all of the new clubs.

Just as with night baseball, Griffith had to see for himself that something worked before he would commit to doing it, and if it made money. To convert so quickly to a farm system was typical behavior for Griffith: he had to see it work for the Yankees and the Cardinals first before making his commitment. As mentioned before, being an arch-conservative in baseball matters, he sided with Commissioner Landis in the 1930s and decried the farm system as a form of slavery; however, his Senators were sinking into oblivion, and a modern farm system was the only way he had to ensure a good stream of talent from which to pick rising starts. Griffith desperately needed to have one star gate attraction to get people into the stands. "From quantity comes quality" still rang true but snake-bit as he was, Griffith never found a Feller or a DiMaggio among all his teams. Cambria had brought him a gross of Cuban ballplayers. Very few made their way into the major leagues.

To ever optimistic Joe Cambria, a farm system was a godsend. All it meant was more teams for him to fill up with talented youngsters, Anglo or Latin. His Havana team was doing great, winning the championship decidedly in 1947. At the minor league winter meetings, tempers flared when only five out of the eight teams in the FIL voted to expand to the B league and thus were denied. The FIL would eventually enter the B level in 1949. But that did not stop Cambria from predicting that Havana would be sought to become a major league city very soon. He never gave up on his dream of making baseball an international sport when he suggested to the *Tampa Times* that "a real International League right now would be to get seven Canadian and American Class AAA teams into a league with Havana. The records show that Havana has made more progress in the last five years than any city in organized baseball."[26]

1948

Raymond "Hap" Dumont would play an important role in Joe Cambria realizing his dream of international baseball. Dumont was the organizer and founder the first National Semi-Pro Baseball Congress and Tournament in Wichita, Kansas, in 1931. The tournament, the first to be held on a national level, was intended to showcase talented ballplayers from all non-professional levels; that is, no one signed to an organized baseball contract. This included sandlot, semi-pro, town teams, industrial, manufacturing, and business teams. It also included Negro Leagues teams, American Indian teams, Catholic league teams and later, Armed Services teams.

Dumont's success started from the very beginning, when he was shrewd enough to hire the great Satchel Paige and his barnstorming team to participate in the true first tournament in 1935. Dumont, absolutely penniless, promised Paige $1,000 (approximately $18,000 today) if he would pitch. Paige pitched in four games and set tournament records for wins and strikeouts which still stand today. Dumont made enough money to pay Paige and show a profit.

The participation of Paige at the inaugural tournament drew the attention of Commissioner Landis and J.G. Taylor Spink, the mighty publisher of *The Sporting News*. Dumont bought advertising with the paper, and Spink brought full attention about the Congress to the public. It was Dumont, however, who first hatched the plan to take the tournament internationally. He lined up teams from 19 nations to participate in a tournament to be held in September of 1945. However, when he suggested inviting a Japanese All-Star team to play in the tournament, the outcry from the press and the public was deafening. The Japanese had not fully surrendered by the time the tournament was to be held, and the times being what they were, the invitation was rescinded.[27]

In January 1948, Joe Cambria was named Commissioner of non-professional baseball in Cuba. J.G. Taylor Spink, who had been named National Baseball Congress Global Commissioner, confirmed that Cambria would represent Cuba at the NBC meetings in New York in February. Four nations, Canada, Mexico, Cuba, and the United States, would make up this Congress. Baseball, at least at the semi-pro level, was truly going world-wide.[28]

It was a new season and time to put a team on the field. Griffith wasted little time in finding a new skipper for the helm of the ship, and as was his yen, he liked to stay with family. The new old face at Senators training camp in 1948 was none other than Joe Kuhel. He had been Washington's first baseman from 1930 to 1937, replacing the venerable Joe Judge. Injuries and sagging production sent him to the White Sox in 1938. Kuhel played well for the Sox from 1938 through 1943, then came back to his Senators roots as a replacement player for Mickey Vernon from 1944 to 1946. When Vernon came back from the war, expendable Joe Kuhel was sent back to the White Sox for two years, then managed the Sox's Class-C Hot Springs Bathers in 1947.[29]

Griffith also went all-in with the farm system. He signed the knowledgeable Jack Rossiter to join the newly expanded scouting system. Rossiter ran a highly successful baseball school in Cocoa, Florida, and the deal was that Washington would have first pick from his stable of hot prospects. The scouting team was now Rossiter, Mike Martin, and Spencer Abbott, with Joe Cambria as chief scout.[30]

Ossie Bluege was swift to take action with the new expanded farm system, and the place that needed it the most was in Texas. With his knowledge of the Mexican and Cuban players and the proximity to Mexico, Cambria was sent to Sherman, Texas, just north of Dallas, on the first of March, to take over all the clubs in their southern division. This included Class-B Sherman-Denison and the Bridgeport Colonial clubs of the Big State League, the Class-C Henderson Oilers of the Lone Star League, and Big Springs of the Longhorn League. On March 15, as Joe Cambria always did since his Hagerstown days, he immediately set up a baseball school in Sherman with managers Joe Rodriguez of Sherman, Guy Sturdy of Henderson, and Pat Stassey of Big Springs as his instructors.

Joe Cambria had just concluded a tour of South America with his Havana club, which had won the FIL league championship in 1947. Still plugging his international initiative, he could not help but wax profound to *The Sporting News* when he said, "baseball and all other sports is the answer to true peace. We invaded the countries that supposedly bred revolutionists and we were acclaimed as heroes."[31]

Joe Kuhel came up to the Senators with only one year of minor league managerial experience but a lifetime of interacting with players. Unfortunately, it was now his turn to deal with Joe Cambria and his army of "can't miss" recruits.

Cambria brought to the Nats' spring camp outfielder Dean Stafford, shortstop Larry Drake, and pitchers Buzz Dozier and Earl Davis, as well as two Cubans, Ramon Garcia and Angel Fleitas. As always, Cambria was over-optimistic and ebullient with his praises about his new recruits. There was one who did show the right stuff. Larry Drake, a slick-fielding, hard-hitting shortstop, came out of the Big State League to Chattanooga, where he put together a 37-game hitting streak. He spent 1941 through 1944 in the high minors and was sold to Philadelphia in 1945, where he had a one-game cup of coffee and was promptly sent down to Toronto, then Baltimore. He was bought back by the Senators and played 1946 and 1947 in Sherman, then got a four-game trial with the Nats. He was sent back to Chattanooga and never returned to the majors.

Dean Stafford was short and sweet: he never made it through training camp and spent the majority of his minor league career with Chattanooga or in the Big State League.

Eighteen-year-old pitcher Earl Davis spent 1947 through 1951 in the minors and never set foot in a major league park.

The aforementioned Buzz Davis pitched in Charlotte in 1948, came up to Washington for a two-game cup of coffee which he promptly spilled all over himself, and spent the rest of his career in the minors from 1949 through 1951.

Cambria signed Ramon Garcia to a Senators contract, not a minor league contract, after seeing him pitch for the Havana telephone company team. Not the pros, not the winter leagues, the telephone company. Garcia, of course, had no English language skills but evidently could throw pretty hard, enough to impress Joe Kuhel, who kept him on the roster. Garcia pitched four games in relief, finishing two. In 3⅔ innings, he gave up seven runs on 11 hits for an astounding 17.18 ERA. He spent the remainder of his baseball life in the minors and the Cuban winter leagues.

Angel Fleitas was another of the myriad short Cuban infielders of the "good field, no hit" type. He spent three years with Chattanooga from 1945 through 1947 and got his cup of coffee with the Nats in 1948. He had 13 at-bats in 16 games, with one hit and one

RBI. He was sent back to Chattanooga in the middle of the season and remained in the Senators' minor league system until 1952.

It was a hot August 30 night game between the Senators and the Indians. Over 28,000 fans came out to see the Nats throw their ace, Ray Scarborough, against the Indians' indefatigable Satchel Paige. Ol' Satch had the stuff to quiet the Nats' bats, and they were in front of the Senators, 8–0, by the eighth inning.

It was probably frustration that made center fielder Ed "Bud" Stewart do what he did when batting second in the inning, Paige threw Stewart an "eephus" pitch, a very slow, very high-arching pitch which is baffling to most hitters because it is so slow and so high. Stewart swung through it and slammed his bat down in disgust. Determined to not be fooled again, he got under the next pitch and popped up a weak foul ball to the third baseman. He walked back to his bench through the pitcher's box and called Paige "a black S.O.B." Paige, who was no stranger to such epithets, simply walked over and picked up the rosin bag to get on with the game. Umpire Bill Summers, witness to the whole thing, walked up to Paige and asked what Stewart had said. "He called me a black S.O.B." Paige said, "Why?" "Because I want to make a report of it," replied Summers.

It seems no report was filed; however, when questioned about the incident, American League President Will Harridge replied:

> Our umpires have no orders to this effect. Summers may have wanted background information for a detailed report in case something further developed of a more serious nature. Paige is the same in this office as Bob Feller. He is just a Cleveland pitcher and his race doesn't count. The Cleveland club and Paige, I'm sure, want it this way. There's one thing I can tell you. Paige has handled himself very well since he has been in the American League.[32]

Evidently, this was not the only time Paige was disrespected by a Senators batter. In a July series in Washington, catcher Al Evans repeatedly stepped out of the batter's box at the height of Paige's windup, something that is usually done in Little League and sandlot baseball.[33]

The 1948 Senators

Nineteen forty-eight turned out to be a bust for the Senators but a boon for Joe Cambria. The Nats, in Joe Kuhel's inaugural season, limped to a dismal 56–97 record for a firm grasp on seventh place, two games ahead of the White Sox and 40 games behind the World Champion Cleveland Indians. Ray Scarborough was the only Senators starter to post a winning record of 15–8. Wynn, Masterson, Hudson and Haefner were all in the loss column. Al Kozar, Mickey Vernon, and Eddie Yost were the team leaders in hits that, unfortunately, did not yield many runs batted in. Another season of "wait till next year."

Cambria, however, was living the high life. His Big Springs Broncs of the Class-D Longhorn league came in first with a team consisting completely of 21 Latins, and his Sherman-Denison Twins, filled with 15 Latin players, won the Big State League championship with a stellar 94–51 record and showed a profit of $11,362.92, almost unheard-of in minor league ball. Joe Cambria liked the team so much he started making arrangements to have them train in Havana for the upcoming season.[34]

Meanwhile, his Havana Cubans were a juggernaut. Pitcher Antonio Lorenzo was almost unhittable, leading the league in wins (23) and strikeouts (275), while the ageless Connie Marrero pitched to an infinitesimal 1.67 ERA. They would repeat in 1949 (95–57, Marrero 25 wins, 167 strikeouts) and would win the league championship in 1950 (101–49) but lose the championship to Miami, four games to one.[35]

Unfortunately, Havana was *too* good, and rumblings abounded in the FIL. Cambria had showed everyone what top-flight professionals the Cubans were, and the competition and the other club owners were complaining. Cambria was ecstatic about the possibility of the league being raised to the Class-B level, but Merito Acosta was circumspect. He told the *Tampa Tribune*:

> I don't know whether moving the classification from our present C rating to B will help improve the caliber of play in the league and boost wanning attendance in all the loop's cities. The club owners have to stop their petty jealousies and start thinking for the betterment of the FIL or it may collapse. To get the benefit of the drawing power offered by Havana, the other seven clubs in the league must be stronger than they have been up to the present times. Havana baseball fans want close competition. The best things for the FIL would be for the Cubans to lose a lot of games to Tampa, St. Petersburg and Miami over the season at Gran Stadium [in Havana]. Then the attendance would be greatly increased.[36]

Acosta created a firestorm of controversy by suggesting the possibility of a new manager for the team. Immediately, the Havana populace were up in arms. By December, Cambria made it known: "There has never been the slightest of doubt about Oscar Rodriguez managing the team next year. I don't know who started speculation on Oscar's departure. He is a great manager and we are sticking by him. How could we drop a man who has won three pennants for us?"[37]

The biggest buzz of the December meetings was Cambria pushing the idea for his Havana team to become a AAA team, taking over the Newark team's classification. He had the entire city of Havana in a tizzy over the possibility: "It's just that Havana has everything to make it a Triple A or even a major league city. We have two good ball parks, we have the players, communication facilities, plenty of money and what's more we've got attendance. Why, the Havana Cubans with their 225,000 attendance not only outdrew the rest of the clubs in the Class C league, but also such Triple-A clubs as Baltimore, Toledo, Newark, Jersey City, Syracuse, Louisville and Columbus."[38]

Joe Cambria's international dreams were becoming closer to reality.

1949

This would be a pivotal year for Joe Cambria and Clark Griffith. Some things in their world would go smoothly; others would not. Like all years in the baseball world, it began with hope. For Griffith, it would end in disaster. For Cambria, it would be a year of change.

For several years, it had been an embarrassment of riches for Joe Cambria and his partner in the Havana club, Merito Acosta. The Havana Cubans were spectacular and were making a shambles out of the other seven teams in the league. Pitchers Connie Marrero, Julio Gonzalez, and Antonio Lorenzo led the league in everything and the style of play by the Cubans left their rivals shaking their heads. This obviously stuck in the craw of the other team owners, who felt that (1) they could not get a fair shot at league championship because Havana was too good; and (2) they could not draw flies in attendance unless it was a game against Havana. Ill will slowly showed its ugly face.

The year started ominously for Cambria and Acosta, and controversies continued throughout the year. In February, in a fit of pique, Acosta threatened to resign as president of the Havana operations, citing other business interests that were taking up his time. Cambria, as business manager, was expected to take over.[39]

This may have been a smoke screen to cover the real problems. The first of them was the broadcast rights with the Cubans and the other teams in the league. Acosta claimed that all the clubs had been paid a flat rate for the broadcasts, and the other owners were trying to boost the rates. At a meeting in Tampa on March 6, Acosta made two proposals: (1) pay the league a flat rate of $7,000 for distribution to the seven other clubs; or, (2) offer each club a flat rate guarantee of $500 plus expenses, regardless of the number of games they played. Under league rules, clubs visiting Havana had the right to take 25 percent of the gate receipts or 10 percent plus expenses, whichever the visiting team chose. Acosta said the owners had been given a certain sum each year for the rights to have the games sent to Cuba, and each year they had tried to raise the ante. Western Union carried a direct wire account of all the Cubans' games played in the U.S. to Havana, where the games were broadcast over a Havana station. The station paid the ball club for the rights to those broadcasts, and a similar set-up existed in all the Florida cities in the league. Acosta thought the practice unfair and once again told the *Tampa Tribune*:

> I don't see why the Havana Cubans have to divide their radio money with the other FIL clubs. I certainly don't ask the Florida owners to give me part of the money they receive for the broadcasting in their cities. Havana is a real baseball city, and the people there want to know at all times what the Cubans are doing. That is why the rebroadcasting of the games from the Florida cities is important. It only helps the other club owners if they would only see it. If a club gives the Cubans a tough series and even beats them and the series is broadcast, think of how many more fans will come out to the series at Gran Stadium when that team visits the Cuban baseball city. I don't think the club owners have been fair in their dealings with the Havana station on the radio broadcasting and I hope that something fair can be worked out at the FIL meetings.[40]

Morris McLemore, one of the more caustic writers for the *Miami News*, took the opposite view: "The feeling of some mainland club officials is expressed by one who [said:] 'Havana has been screaming for competition. The Cubans have been saying competition will make [for] bigger crowds in Havana. Well, they're getting competition this year and what happens? Attendance there falls off. That's the rub. In fact, for my money, that's the only real rub.'"[41] Of course, the person behind the statement was not mentioned, and no figures were given.

The second stink bug on the porch light was the question of gate revenue sharing. Both Cambria and Acosta cried foul at the "gouging" practices of the league. Havana's attendance was up from the 1948 season, and the league seemed to be taking it out on them. Cambria said, "Sure it's a good gate, but with the financial arrangement we have with the U.S. teams coming here, we'll soon be going into the red. We just can't continue on the current basis." Acosta stated, "we'll be forced out of the league if this keeps up. Did you know we're paying U.S. clubs so much to come here that we're actually paying their ballplayers' salaries for more than a month?"[42]

What they were complaining about was twofold. First, under the present arrangement, installed in 1949, Havana paid visiting teams $750 plus expenses during each series in the Cuban capital. The Havana club kept all revenues from radio broadcasting rights, a questionably lucrative source of incomes. Second, when Havana visited U.S. teams, the Cubans received only their expenses. "And these are split up among the clubs we play," said Acosta. In 1948, U.S. teams were given a choice of either 10 percent of the gate plus expenses or 35 percent of the gate and no expenses. Cambria and Acosta contended that they needed to return to the same basis as last year.[43]

Acosta stated: "it will cost us $39,000 to bring U.S. teams here this season under the present set-up. At $750 per series, that's $3,000 per club for its seven trips here—or $21,000 for all seven teams. Expenses run about $18,000 for all clubs or a total of $39,000." Breaking it down further, Acosta, the "facts and figures" man, said, "it costs a club approximately $131 per day in salaries for its players. Since we pay each club about $5,500 during the season, that means we will be, in essence, paying the salaries of every club in the league for more than a month. And don't forget we still attract the biggest crowds wherever we go."[44]

Cambria revealed the unfortunate truth behind the situation with the Havana radio stations to the Florida papers. He explained that there were four stations. One quit broadcasting the Cubans' home games, and one refused to pay them. They were not getting the income from radio that they expected. "You can't get blood from a stone," said Cambria.[45]

Incensed over this gouging, Cambria and Acosta asked FIL president Phil O'Connell to take a mail vote on returning to the former system of guarantees on trips to Havana. Research indicates that the other club owners declined to change the rule. Still angry over the ruling, Acosta met with H.B. Taber, Jr., president of the Miami Sun Sox, to discuss the possibility of making a joint bid for franchises in the Class-AA Southern League. Acosta was prepared to leave the FIL and move the Cubans to the spot occupied by Joe Engle's Chattanooga club. "I discussed the matter with Engle when he was in Havana this spring and he is favorable to making the change," said Acosta. "I am going to discuss the matter with Taber and I am hopeful that Miami and Havana can make their bid together."[46]

In the end, everyone stayed put, but a deep divide began between Acosta and Cambria.

Clark Griffith had a team to put together, and changes were being made. With Griffith, it was always about the money, which is the only possible reason why he would trade his most productive hitter and league leader, Mickey Vernon, to the Cleveland Indians for the very capable and solid journeyman Eddie Robinson. Robinson, a fine defensive first baseman, did stints with every team in the American League except the Red Sox. He was a solid contributor for the Nats in 1949, posting a .294 batting average to go with 18 homers, 155 hits, and 78 RBI.

On the Cuban side, Cambria brought a few Latins to camp but none of them stayed. Ramon Garcia, a pitcher from Chattanooga, was the only one to turn Griffith's head. Garcia pitched four games in relief for the Nats in 1948 before being sent down. In Chattanooga, Garcia posted an 8–7 record, but more importantly, his command of his curve ball improved significantly. Garcia was another one of Joe Cambria's inexplicable signings. He found him playing for the Havana Electric Company sandlot team. In May, the telephone company promoted him to a foreman, and he was hesitant to leave his job, so he held out on Griffith. He was offered more money, which he took.

He did not make the club. Instead, Cambria sold Griffith on Julio Gonzalez. Gonzalez had been one of the aces of his Havana club, pitching to a fine 15–13 record and a minuscule 2.18 ERA. Another wicked Cuban curveballer, Gonzalez pitched in 13 games for the 1949 Senators but had no decisions. In 34⅓ innings, he posted a 4.72 ERA before he was sent back to the Cubans.

Having had enough of the Mexican leagues, Roberto Ortiz returned to the Senators in 1949. In 40 games, he recorded 36 hits, four doubles, one homer, 11 RBI, and a .279 batting average before he was dealt to the Athletics mid-season.

Paul Calvert, a bespectacled journeyman pitcher from Canada, was recommended by Cambria to Griffith after Cambria saw him pitching in the Cuban winter leagues. Calvert, a rare free agent, having purchased his own release from the Toronto Maple Leafs, quickly came to terms with Griffith. Originally slated as a reliever, Calvert brought the team up to the first division with several key victories as a starter. The Nats were in second place, only 5½ games behind the Yankees by mid–June, before the wheels came off the bus. Calvert ended the year going 6–17 and leading the league in losses. Ray Scarborough (13–11) was the only winning pitcher on the club that year.[47]

"Clark Griffith Sees the Light," shouted the *Baltimore Afro-American*. Sam Lacy, one of Griffith's principal detractors on the race issue, was beside himself with glee when Griffith told him personally that he had instructed his scouts, Joe Cambria and Joe Engle, to keep an eye out for "the right kind of boy." Just as with night baseball and the farm system, Griffith had to see it work first before committing to it. Griffith explained:

> Yes, I've been convinced we may have overlooked an opportunity here and there to strengthen the Senators. And you can say I'm definitely interested in signing a good young colored player. He must be good, though, and he must be young. He's got to be good because we don't have the kind of farm system that will permit us to ship him for seasoning. We're not as rich as the Dodgers and Indians, consequently, we're not in a position to send a youngster to one of several farm clubs. The only farm teams we have are in the south, and we'll have to wait a while before anything can be done about that phase of it. That's why the boy we sign, when we do sign, has got to be good. In addition, I said I want a young fellow. And there's a reason for that too. I could probably find an older player like these other fellows are getting [Veeck and Rickey] and I guess he might help us some at the gate. But I've opposed this thing from the beginning because I've been opposed to exploitation. If we can locate a youngster who looks fairly good, we'll go after him. We'll even be willing to go along with him for a season, maybe two, to await his development. But he's got to show us something to look forward to.[48]

Griffith's allusion in this entire statement was they were looking for a good, smart, young player who, like Eddie Yost, they could season while he was on the team. Griffith was afraid, and rightly so, of the Jackie Robinson–like suffering a young player would receive playing for any team in the Jim Crow South. A noble gesture on his part to be sure, but the reality was that he would have received bad treatment wherever he played.

It would take five years for Griffith to make good on his promise.

Cambria was not bringing that many Cubans to the Senators' spring training because he was too busy developing "The Cambria System" in Texas. Just as at Williamsport, Cambria was using all his Texas-affiliated clubs as training grounds for his Havana Cubans. Big Springs and Sherman-Denison, both with a preponderance of Cuban players, won their respective league championships in 1948, and Big Springs repeated in 1949. (At Big Springs, the only Anglo on the squad was the manager!) Both teams fed his Havana club with seasoned rookies who could plug in at a moment's notice.

Cambria's enterprise was getting bigger and more well-known, so there was only one thing left to do: get more teams. He took on the Ardmore Indians of the Sooner State League, the Del Rio Cowboys of the Rio Grande Valley League, and the Abilene Blue Sox of the West Texas-New Mexico League. Cambria furnished each club with a complete or partial roster without signed agreements and received no compensation for his troubles. His only goal was to help the boys.

Cambria filled up these teams with the prototypical Cuban player: fast, good arm, plenty of defensive finesse, and popular with the fans; however, they were all small in stature and lacked the power of a big-league player. These boys made a decent living playing in the many Texas state leagues and the Mexican Leagues, but their chances of making a Major League team were slim and none. Still, they were doing what they loved to do: playing a children's game for as long as they could.[49]

Perhaps it was all the time he was spending tending to his Texas teams, or perhaps it was his problems with his Havana team. Whatever the reasons, Cambria's control over the baseball talent on the Cuban island was slowly on the wane. Many teams, the Dodgers and the Pirates in particular, saw the successes the Washington club had with their low-priced players during the war years, and now that Cambria had constructed another pipeline for his talent in Texas, other teams with deeper pockets were invading his territory. Gone were the days when he could boast that he could sign a kid for the price of a Panama hat. He was simply being outbid by the other teams, and he was hard-pressed to compete.

Such was the case with Rene Solis and Vincente Lopez. Both pitchers had been involved in Cuban amateur and professional baseball on the island and somehow were snatched up by the Dodgers. Playing for the Miami Sun Sox in 1949, they accounted for 32 of their 69 victories, leading them to the playoffs; however, they did not do well there. They lost to Tampa in the playoffs, who in turn beat Havana for the championship. Solis spent nine years in the American minors, splitting his time between Brooklyn-affiliated clubs and the Florida International League. Lopez spent 16 seasons in the minors, split between Brooklyn-affiliated clubs and the official Mexican leagues.[50] Cambria, with his fingers in so many pies, was bound to let someone fall through the cracks.

Back in Havana, though, Cambria was taking the good with the bad. In September, he had to fine and suspend one of his favorites, Tony Zardon, for deserting the Havana team to play exhibition games in Venezuela. Zardon left the club with only 11 men to play the Miami Beach Flamingos in the deciding game of the playoff series. Havana would eliminate the Flamingos but lose the championship.[51]

On the other hand, Cambria and his partner, Acosta, made a little money. Clark Griffith opened up his wallet and bought some much-needed help. Connie Marrero and Sandy Consuegra went to the Senators, and Gumersindo Elba and Rogelio Martinez went to the Chattanooga Lookouts. Consuegra and Marrero became part of the 1950 Senators' starting rotation.[52]

Whatever they made on these pitchers, it was peanuts compared to what they lost during the season. At the October FIL league meetings, discussions about revenue sharing became so heated the topic was tabled until the minor league convention in Baltimore in December. Lou Ordway, sole owner of the West Palm Beach club, angrily stated: "All the FIL clubs but Miami lost money last year. I lost money, and I hear that the aggregate for all the FIL teams in the red was $90,000."[53]

The 1949 Senators

Ending up in seventh place in 1948, manager Joe Kuhel felt there was nowhere to go but up in 1949. He would be wrong.

The Senators ended up dismally in last place with a horrific 50–104 record, three games behind the hapless St. Louis Browns and 47 games behind the World Series champion Yankees. It was their worst won-lost record in 40 years. They were last in the league in almost every statistical category. As previously mentioned, Ray Scarborough was the only winning pitcher on the team (13–11), and that included all the relievers as well. Eddie Robinson led the team with 155 hits, 78 RBI, and a fine .294 batting average. Gil Coan, the young slugger who hit 22 homers for Chattanooga in 1947, was cursed with the 30-foot high "black monster" right field wall in Griffith Stadium. He hit only three home runs to go along with his anemic .218 batting average. The team made 1,330 hits and scored 584 runs, as compared to the Yankees, who had 1,396 hits and scored 829 runs.[54]

The season ended on October 2. By October 4, the papers announced that Griffith was in the market for a new manager. "It's just baseball," said Griffith. "I found no fault with Joe's managing. It was just the breaks that ruined Joe. Joe's a fine boy and in the two years with us, things just didn't break for him. It's time for the Senators to try something different."[55]

They did not. Griffith went back to his tried and true: hiring someone he already knew. By the end of October, he hired Bucky Harris to pilot the club. Harris had won pennants with Washington in 1924 and 1925, then had come back to manage from 1935 to 1942. In 1947, he managed the Yankees to a Championship against the Dodgers. This would be his third stint with the club.

Griffith could only hope.

CHAPTER 7

1950–1954:
Keeping Them Competitive

The Senators of the 1950s were a veritable vegetable soup of adjectives, mostly unflattering. They were, at times, professionally adept, at times, unbelievably inept. They were fast, they were slow, they were highly error prone. They did not have peaks and valleys; they had mountains and canyons. They would vacillate from great arms and poor bats to just the opposite. Like the famous television wrestler Bruno Sammartino, they would put a stranglehold on the second division for the entire decade.

By the end of the decade, however, new president Calvin Griffith would put together an arsenal of bats that would envy the fabled "Murderers' Row" of the 1927 Yankees, yet still come up short in the end. They just never seemed to gel.

The biggest constant within the decade would be change, culminating with one of the biggest changes to all of baseball in 1960: league expansion.

Change would be a major part of Joe Cambria's life as well. His teams would rise and fall. His scouting eye would get sharper, especially in Cuba. He would branch out into different endeavors. He would travel even more extensively than before. He would have his fingers in so many pies he could have opened a bakery.

Joe Cambria had a long way to go and a short time to get there.

The biggest story concerning Cambria in 1950 was his row with his friend Merito Acosta and his ownership of the Havana Cubans. Evidently, ill-will had been festering for some time between the two, with Acosta claiming that corruption in Havana and Cambria's shoddy business practices led to the Cubans becoming a loser at the gate while being league champions since their inception in 1946. The feud disrupted the whole Florida International League. They were unsure if the Cubans would resolve this issue in time to start the regular season in April and threatened the success of the league as a whole. The timeline of the fracas goes something like this, giving or taking a day or two:

3/6/50: Acosta held a stockholders meeting, allegedly with ten people, most of them his relations. The stockholders named a new board of directors and anointed Acosta president for 1950. Those attending represented approximately 11 of the 50 club shares.

3/16/50: Joe Cambria, representing majority stockholder Clark Griffith, held his own meeting where 32 shares of club stock were represented. At that time, he stated that "some stockholders holding less than one-third of the capital stock pretended to elect, against the will of holders of more than two-thirds of the shares, a board of directors." His published notice was a warning that a "true" board of directors would be chosen. They were chosen at a subsequent meeting, and Dr. Antonio Casuso, prominent Havana attorney and former amateur league star pitcher, was named president of the Cubans.[1]

3/18/50: Cambria announced that Dr. Jose Martinez, secretary of the Griffith group, sent legal proof of their status to FIL president Phil O'Connell.[2]

3/21/50: Cambria and Senators minor league director Ossie Bluege were sent to Havana by Griffith to talk with Acosta. Griffith was perplexed at how his eighth-place Senators could still make money while a team that had won a flag for three years straight was losing money. Meetings with Acosta proved futile. He was in favor, naturally, of his own nine-member board. Cambria and Bluege met with lawyer Martinez, who suggested they hold a meeting of all the stockholders to hash out the problem. Acosta was livid in his dissent, but the meeting was held nonetheless. At the meeting the next day, Acosta arrived with a phalanx of police and tried to have Bluege and Cambria arrested for "disturbing the peace and an illegal meeting." Martinez intervened and explained to the police that the meeting was indeed legal, whereupon Acosta stormed out. The stockholders approved Dr. Casuso as president and Calvin Griffith and Ossie Bluege as first and second vice-presidents. Enraged, Acosta went to Gran Stadium and padlocked all the offices of the Cuban club, which included the equipment. It hampered them for a day or two, until the Cambria faction supplied them with new equipment. Concerned for his safety, Bluege asked for and received a police escort to the airport for the return journey.[3]

3/24/50: George Trautman, president of the minor leagues, recognized Griffith as chief owner of the Havana Cubans, with 70 percent of the club's stock.[4]

3/29/50: FIL president O'Connell met with Acosta, Cambria and Bluege to determine if a team would be on the field for the opener the following week. Despite court actions instituted by Acosta in Cuba, both factions assured O'Connell that their team would be there for the opener.[5]

7/29/50: Acosta won his appeal with the Cuban courts. "In a decision dated July 29, 1950, Cuban courts direct administration of Havana Cubans baseball club be reverted and restored to directorate elected March 6, 1950. Court enjoins illegal directorate headed by Casuso, et al., to return all equipment, personal records, contracts, and material and further desist representing themselves as legal administration of this club. Official confirmation follows by mail." Manager Oscar Rodriguez, who sided with the Cambria-Griffith faction, was replaced by former Washington Senator Gilberto Torres.[6]

Evidently, Acosta had stacked the deck at the March 6 meeting. Acosta, who owned only 11 shares of club stock, parceled the shares out to 10 of his friends and relatives, claiming them as executives of the team, thereby giving them one vote apiece, according to an old Cuban law. The votes in the opposing faction were controlled by Griffith, Cambria, Bluege and Calvin Griffith, Clark's nephew, which counted as only four votes; consequently, the previous ruling was voided, and Acosta was reinstated as president. (Their corporate by-laws forbade the passing around of stocks to create more votes.) Griffith vowed to carry his case to the Cuban Supreme Court and oust Acosta once and for all.[7]

8/13/50: In a lengthy interview with the *Miami News*, Cambria stated emphatically:

I am going to stay here and do my job and I am going to run the ball club—under Griff's supervision, of course. Merito Acosta has not attempted to take control of our ball club and we are still operating it. Insofar as I'm concerned, we will continue to operate it. We will make all the decisions. And I can tell you now Oscar Rodriguez is still the manager and as long as he can win pennants—he's won four in a row—he will remain with us. I have not seen, nor have I heard anything from Acosta. Dr. Antonio Casuso is still president, and I am still treasurer.[8]

In the same interview, Frank Arias, the Cuban business manager of the Havana club, explained to the *News* that, as he understood it, the Primera Instancia court, which ruled for Acosta in this matter, was only a small circuit court in Marianao. It ruled that Acosta and his group owned the belongings in a small house from whence they were doing business in Marianao, that Acosta had locked them out of the business offices at Gran Stadium, and the ruling had nothing to do with anything in Havana and nothing to do with Acosta being president of the club.[9]

Cambria then went on to say:

> I don't know much about what's happened but I do know this and you can quote me: I have my hard earned cash in this ball club. So has Griff, my friend of many, many years. I'm representing both Griff and myself in this investment and between the two we own 75 percent of the stock, or $33,000 out of a possible $50,000 worth. I am certain that Commissioner Chandler and George Trautman know who owns the ball club, who put up the money and who is rightfully entitled to operate it. Personally, I have worked like a dog trying to round up players for Havana, signing players for Griff, trying to run things and I don't intend to get out and see somebody else take charge. You can say for me, I'm here to stay as long as my work is satisfactory to my boss, [Mr. Griffith.] I have no intention of leaving.[10]

FIL president Phil O'Connell, one of many who sided with the Cambria-Griffith faction, told the *Miami News*, "I received some communications from Merito Acosta, but it seems to me that anybody who owns $33,000 out of $50,000 worth of stock [Griffith-Cambria] would be entitled to run the operations, whatever it might be. I'm afraid Merito, if he gets back in control for a time, will eventually lose out. I can't see it any other way."[11]

Cambria did, in fact, continue to run the ball club, reinstating manager Oscar Rodriguez. Acosta wound up in Cuban parts unknown. It was reported that he was waiting until he could get an official translation and approval from the U.S. Consulate there before coming back to the U.S. and presenting his case to FIL president O'Connell, Happy Chandler, and George Trautman.

All of the pugilism between the two factions was almost for naught, for there were bigger fish to fry. The American FIL club owners were fed up with the Havana Cubans for a variety of reasons (not the least of which was the internal wrangling) and were making noises about throwing them out of the league. As previously mentioned, the *Cubanos* were an embarrassment of riches. Although Cambria had sent his two star moundsmen, Marrero and Consuegra, to the Senators, he had ample back-up with Antonio Lorenzo (18–10), Julio Moreno (16–14), and Santiago Ullrich (17–10). With great hitting from Jose Zardon, Gilberto Torres, Francisco Gallardo and Manuel Hidalgo, the team was a powerhouse, leaving the others in the league red-faced with shame and singing the old "let's break up the Yankees" song. The Cubans posted an astounding 101–49 record and would win the league title again in 1950, but inexplicably lose the championship to Miami four games to one.

The FIL team owners were dead serious about ousting the Cubans from the league. In a preliminary meeting in June, the owners aired their grievances to President O'Connell, who grudgingly admitted to the Miami press: "The Havana situation is now under discussion; it is to be discussed and settled at our October meetings." When pressured by the media about whether that meant getting rid of the team altogether, he replied, "Well, we discussed not having Havana in the league."[12]

The club owners' reasons for ousting the Cubans were as such:

   1. More economical operation of the league. It was pointed out that the FIL treasury would save $1500 in travel expenses for the umpires if the plane flights to Havana were eliminated, among other expenses.

   2. They wanted "saner" baseball. The Cubans were too good for the league and the other teams were forced to exceed the Class-B salary limit in order to keep up with the Cubans.

   3. A tighter, closer league. The owners wanted to replace Havana with a Jacksonville team, keeping competitions in-state.

   4. Elimination of the constant worry over the Cubans and their adherence to rules. Havana had been fined $500 and had 23 victories taken away for violations in the past four years and wanted no more part in that; consequently, they ran strictly "by the book."[13]

Some of the club owners further muddied the waters, stating that they would like to see a second Havana club in the FIL, possibly one of the weaker teams in the current league, in an effort to strengthen the league. The other club owners, Griffith included, wondered why they just did not build up their own clubs through scouting and trades.

Cambria and Griffith decided to do an end run around the dissident FIL club owners. In late September, the Senators bought the Sherman-Denison Twins club in the Class-B Big State (Texas) League. Up until then, Sherman had only a working agreement with Griffith. In buying the club outright, two things could occur: 1. Cambria would be free to move some of his Havana players to Texas and shore up that club; 2. If the FIL ousted him from the league, he could move the entire team to Texas. Sherman also provided a place for Cambria to mix his Cuban players with players from the Mexican leagues that Cambria scouted still.[14]

In actuality, 1950 was the beginning of the end for the Havana Cubans. The team had a fantastic record, although they lost the championship to the Miami Sun Sox. Cambria was confident he could repeat in 1951.

In 1951, Griffith was successful in his court battle, and Merito Acosta was ousted from the presidency and replaced by Cambria. This did not work out well for Griffith or Cambria. Acosta, a pleasant and affable person, was liked on the island, and his ouster did not sit well with the rabid baseball populace of the island.

Joe Cambria wanted to shake things up on the team. Possibly caving in to the pressures of the other owners, Cambria intimated he was putting his veterans Jose Zardon, Gilberto Torres, Francisco Gallardo and Manuel Hidalgo on the trading block and was going to field a younger, faster team. In another inexplicable move, he fired his immensely popular manager, Oscar Rodriguez, and, hoping to attract more paying customers at the gate, hired the Cuban legend Adolfo "Dolf" Luque to skipper the team. Rodriguez had been a vocal opponent of Merito Acosta and a loyal friend to Griffith and Cambria. He was also well loved and respected by both the Havana and Florida populace.

That did not work. The 1951 Cubans sank to fifth place with a 68–71 record, their first losing season since their inception. Luque resigned after the 1951 season and was replaced by former Washington Senators backstop Fermin "Mike" Guerra for 1952.

That did not work. The 1952 Cubans once again lay claim to fifth place with a 76–77 record. Cambria again changed managers, this time choosing another Cuban baseball legend, Armando Marsans, Clark Griffith's first Cuban ball player in 1911.

That did not work. Nineteen fifty-three was the nadir for the Havana Cubans. The team had been so strong for so long that interest for the team in Florida waned. Added to that was the fact that the Cuban winter league teams played far superior baseball on the island and Cambria's team was considered just a minor league club, so interest on the island waned as well. Cambria was also not in good financial straits and complained that the team had a lot of two-game series, which cost him a significant amount of money to travel back and forth to the island. Added to that was the problem that he could not secure an adequate lease on Gran Stadium, now owned by Roberto Maduro. The Cubans actually started their season in Key West, and Cambria intimated that he might transfer the club there if he could not obtain a good lease on the Stadium; however, a suitable lease was eventually secured, and Cambria announced that the Cubans would stay in Havana. The team fared only somewhat better, posting a 63–69 record to place fourth in the league; however, Griffith and Cambria saw the writing on the wall. In May of 1953, they sold their interests in the Cubans to Roberto Maduro, a Cuban insurance millionaire, for $40,000. Cambria stayed on for the rest of the year as a scout, and the working agreement with the Senators remained.[15]

In 1954, Maduro moved the team to the AAA International League, where they became the Havana Sugar Kings. The team lasted until 1960.

Clark Griffith had a ball team to put on the field. He had seen how effective the Cuban players had been during the war years and he saw how strong Cambria's Havana Cubans ball club had been for five years. He knew Cambria could supply him with prodigious Latin talent, despite new manager Bucky Harris's grousing to the contrary. Harris could not afford to grouse too much about anything. He had the Herculean task of trying to rebuild Joe Kuhel's dead-last club, and he was going to need all the help he could get.

Harris brought with him a $70,000 trio of prospects from the Pacific Coast League, led by slick-fielding, hard-hitting Irv Noren. Noren, the Hollywood Stars' batting star, powered the team to the league pennant and playoff championship with 224 hits, 29 homers, 130 RBI and a tremendous .330 batting average. He would now have to contend with Griffith Stadium's shortened 386-foot left-field power alley. Two other draftees were Stars shortstop George Genovese, who brought a great glove and a modest bat (65 hits, 35 runs, 25 RBI, .259 average in 102 games played,) and Steve Nagy, who went 15–14 for the 1949 San Francisco Seals. He was slated to be in the Nats' starting rotation.

The real catch was catcher Mickey Grasso. Grasso, who had a seven-game cup of coffee with the 1946 Giants, proved his durability behind the plate with the 1949 Seattle Rainiers, playing in 109 games and posting a modest .251 batting average to go along with 75 hits, 31 RBI and seven homers.

Harris would find some luck with two of the finest veterans, in every sense of the word, Mickey Vernon and Eddie Yost. Vernon, who had been inexplicably traded to the Indians in 1949, was re-acquired from the Tribe when first baseman Eddie Robinson was sent to the White Sox and pitcher Dick Weik was sent to Cleveland. Vernon would do what he did best: hit! In his 90 games and 327 at bats with the 1950 Senators, he would post 100 hits, 65 RBI, 17 doubles, nine homers, an .836 OPS, and a team-leading .306 batting average to go along with his stellar play at first base. Eddie Yost would do what he did best: walk! He played all 154 games at third base. With 573 at bats, he would post 160 hits, 27 doubles, 11 homers, 58 RBI, a strong .295 average and a great .440 on-base percentage because of his 141 walks. His keen batting eye and impeccable play at third base made him one of the few indispensable players on the team.

Bucky Harris would get good support from Irv Noren (160 hits, 14 homers, .295 average) and from another veteran, Gil Coan, who was named *The Sporting News* Minor League Player of the Year in 1945. Coan appeared in 104 games in the cavernous Griffith Stadium outfield and hit a very respectable .303, with 111 hits, seven homers and 50 RBI.[16]

Every warrior needs a sword, and every ball club needs a pitcher to do battle. Make no mistake: Bucky Harris had neither. He declared to Shirley Povich of the *Washington Post*:

> As badly as we need the right kind of second baseman, we need pitching more. Look over our list. Ray Scarborough is the only solid man on it. We're gambling too heavily on comebacks by other veterans and hoping, in too many cases perhaps, that our rookies will come through. We're so thin in our pitching I'd be lying if I said I wasn't worried. You're darned right I'm worried and I don't like the situation. A club counts itself lucky if one rookie pitcher comes through in a season. We don't have any right to hope for more than that.[17]

Harris was optimistic that rookies Dick Weik, Lloyd Hittle and Steve Nagy would blossom into reliable starters. He also held out hope that Griffith could make a deal for the Tigers' Dizzy Trout, who was said to be dissatisfied with his position in Detroit.

The Trout trade never materialized. Weik went 2–5 in 54⅓ innings for a 6.58 ERA and was traded to Cleveland. Hittle would go 2–4 in 43⅓ innings for a 4.98 ERA and was sent down to Chattanooga. Nagy would go 1–3 in 44 innings for a 4.30 ERA and was sent back to San Francisco in the PCL.

Here is where our Mr. Cambria stepped in.

Clark Griffith must have called Joe Cambria and said something like, "Send me some arms!" and Cambria must have said "No sooner said than done, boss!"

Cambria's Havana Cubans had made an embarrassment out of the Florida International League, winning the league title five years in a row and the championship twice. This was due in large measure to a battery of tremendous pitchers. Since the FIL was grousing about how unfair it was to have the Cubans in the league, Cambria may have thought now was the time to break up the team a bit.

As was his custom, Cambria sent a brigade of players to Bucky Harris during the spring in hopes that a few of them would stick with the parent club. In this case, most of them did.

The big buzz around camp was the coming of **Carlos "Patato" Pascual**. Pascual could have been the Shohei Ohtani of his day, had he been handled properly. Playing third base for the Big Springs Broncs of the Longhorn league in 1949, Pascual had 458 at-bats, 158 hits, 33 doubles, 16 homers and put up a fantastic .345 batting average. Struggling for a pitcher one day, his manager asked him to pitch the first game of a doubleheader against Odessa. He shut them out, 8–0. The manager asked him to pitch the second game as well. He shut them out again, 4–0, striking out 10 in both games and pitching a hitless stretch of 10⅓ innings.

Cambria kept an eye on Pascual by keeping him in Havana for most of the 1950 season. He was, after all, only 19 years old. When he was called up for his cup of coffee with the Senators later in the year, he did as well as could be expected for a teenager with no experience. He started and completed two games, with a 1–1 record in 17 innings, giving up five runs, 12 hits, eight walks, striking out three, and posting a 2.12 ERA. He was sent back to Havana and remained in the Cuban and American minors until 1962.

Also back again was **Roberto Ortiz**. Roberto had been a mainstay with the Senators throughout the war years; however, he was one of the original jumpers to the

Mexican leagues in 1945. Once the ban on jumping players was rescinded by Commissioner Chandler, Ortiz found his way back to his Washington family. The 35-year-old Ortiz was used primarily as a utility outfielder and interpreter, appearing in 39 games, with 75 at-bats, 17 hits, four runs, two doubles, and a .227 average. He finished out the year with the Athletics, then disappeared into the minors until 1956.

Julio Moreno was a *Cubano* starter. In 1947, he was 19–4. Injured in 1948, he went 3–2. In 1949, he roared back with a fine 12–6 record for the Cubans. Unfortunately, his luck did not transfer to the Senators. In four games for the Nats, including three starts, he was officially 1–1 in 21⅓ innings pitched, with 12 walks, seven strikeouts and a 4.64 ERA. Moreno was sent back to Havana, where he went 16–4 in 1950. He found his stride, was brought back up in 1951, and remained a starter with the Nats until 1953.

Thirty-two-year-old veteran **Rogelio Martinez** was another of Cambria's mound aces. He went 19–9 in 1949 and looked like he had the goods to stick with the Nats. He did not. His was a whiff of the coffee as it went by. Officially having a 0–1 record, he appeared in only two games, pitched 1⅓ innings, gave up four hits, four earned runs, two walks, and no strikeouts, and posted a dismal 27.00 ERA. He was sent back to Havana, where he went 10–4 and remained in the minors until 1955.

Sandalio "Sandy" Consuegra was a 29-year-old veteran of the Cuban semi-pro leagues before coming to the Havana Cubans in 1949, where he went 6–5 for the champs. For the 1950 Senators, Consuegra went 7–8. In 124⅔ innings, he posted a 4.40 ERA, with 57 walks, 38 strikeouts and two shutouts. Consuegra was an integral part of the Nats' starting rotation for four years. In 1954, he had his best year with the White Sox, going 16–3 and earning a berth on the American League All-Star team.[18]

The cream of the Cuban's pitching crop and undoubtedly one of the best of Cambria's Cuban signees was the legendary **Conrado "Connie" Marrero.** Short and stubby, he looked more like a baker than a pitcher. His delivery was most poetically described by Dominican Felipe Alou, eldest of the famous Alou brothers, as a "windup that looked like a cross between a windmill gone berserk and a mallard duck trying to fly backwards."[19]

Connie *"El Curveador"* (The Curveballer) Marrero, born in 1911, was already a very seasoned professional before he made his "rookie" debut, at 39 years old, with the Senators in 1950. Marrero had pitched and won several Cuban Amateur World Series championships, and had played in the Cuban professional leagues and, of course, with the Havana Cubans in American organized baseball. With his huge Cuban cigars, his fractured English, and his herky-jerky wind-up, Marrero fast became one of the most popular players in Senators history. He had the most fun, however, with the many journalists, especially around the mystery of his age:

In August 1952, journalist Collie Small stoked controversy by reporting that the wily hurler had at various times reported that he was "positively thirty-five, absolutely thirty-seven, indisputably forty-three, and definitely forty-two"—yet when pressed for details, he always coyly admitted (with appropriate amounts of journalistically jumbled foreign idiom) only that "Me old enough, but me not too old."[20]

Marrero's legend preceded him in 1950 even before the season got fully underway. Arriving at camp on March 7, Bucky Harris slated him to pitch an exhibition game against the Athletics on March 8, saying, "None of our other pitchers is really ready and Marrero has been pitching in Cuba all winter and ought to be in shape."[21] He was, and he won.

Marrero was unquestionably the most dominant pitcher in the Florida International League throughout the late 1940s. In 1947, he led the Cubans to the championship with a league-leading 25 wins, 251 strikeouts and a microscopic 1.66 ERA. In 1948, he went 20–11 with another minuscule 1.67 ERA. Marrero's pitching prowess was instrumental in elevating the whole FIL into the Class B classification in 1949. That year, he once again led his team to the championship with another league-leading performance of 25 wins, 167 strikeouts and a tiny 1.53 ERA, which surprisingly did not lead the league. That honor went to Chet Covington's infinitesimal 1.46 ERA.[22]

Connie Marrero became a workhorse in the Senators' rotation from 1950 through 1954, posting three winning seasons from 1952 to 1954, and was an All-Star selection in 1951, although he did not play. Marrero, whom Bucky Harris considered his most valuable "stopper," posted a 39–40 record for a team that flirted with the cellar throughout his tenure with the club. In 1955, the 44-year-old Marrero went back to his homeland and pitched another three years with Bobby Maduro's Sugar Kings, finishing his stellar career in 1957.

Connie Marrero would have one last, great moment in the sun, though. In March of 1999, he was selected to throw out the ceremonial first pitch in an exhibition game between the Baltimore Orioles and the Cuban National Team, the first time an American team had been allowed to play in Havana's *Estadio Latinoamericano* since Castro's shutdown of Cuban baseball in 1960. American baseball commissioner Bud Selig, Orioles owner Peter Angelos, and Cuban president Fidel Castro were all in attendance to see Marrero stride out to the mound. But instead of just tossing out a normal slow, high-arching "softball," the 88-year-old Marrero motioned Orioles batter Brady Anderson to dig in and proceeded to toss him a series of pitches with all the "mustard he could muster." Always a true patriot, Marrero wanted to show Fidel Castro and the world that he had not lost a step. Marrero died April 23, 2014, just two days short of his 103rd birthday. At the time of his death, he was the third-longest-living veteran of any professional baseball league.[23]

Clark Griffith and Joe Cambria had been praised and rewarded by the governments of both the U.S. and Cuba for their goodwill towards Cuba, its people and its ballplayers. In 1950, they were once again recognized by official Cuban state channels for their unwavering support of Cuban baseball and its players, only this time it was sort of a reverse situation.

In July of 1950, Señor Luis Machado, Cuban Ambassador to the United States, hosted a lavish State luncheon for Griffith, Cambria, and other team officials, to honor Conrado Marrero, Sandalio Consuegra and Roberto Ortiz, three of the leading Cuban players in America at the time. Marrero and Consuegra had "double handedly" kept the Senators out of the cellar with several notable pitching performances, and Ortiz was known as Bucky Harris's go-to pinch-hitter and Cuban interpreter.

In a statement to the American press, Señor Machado said, "I believe this is a wonderful demonstration of Point Four and the foreign-aid plan in reverse. We are pleased that our baseball players have helped your team. Cuba is glad to render this technical assistance to America." To which Griffith replied, "If this is the sort of mutual assistance guaranteed by Point Four, I would like to congratulate our Congress for considering the Bill."[24]

The point to which they were referring was the Point Four Program, so-named because it was the fourth point in President Harry Truman's 1949 inaugural address.

The program was a policy of technical assistance and economic aid to underdeveloped countries around the world, in an effort to ward off the ever-increasing threat of Communism. The program focused on agriculture, public health, and education. It was the first U.S. plan for international economic development.[25]

The good will engendered by this type of mutual aid would be tremendously beneficial to Griffith and cement relations between Cambria and the island for the entire decade of the 1950s, until Castro's takeover in 1959.

The 1950 Senators

With winning records by Sid Hudson (14–14), Bob Kuzava (8–7), and Joe Haynes (7–5), and good hitting by Mickey Vernon (.306, 9 HR, 100 H), Gil Coan (.303, 7 HR, 111 H), Ed Yost (.295, 11 HR, 169 H) and Irv Noren (.295, 14 HR, 160 H), the 1950 Senators came in fifth in the

The colorful Conrado "Connie" Morrero, with his fractured English and huge Cuban cigars, was a ten-year veteran of the Cuban semi-pro leagues and a three year veteran of the Florida International League before his debut with the Senators in 1950, at the age of 39 (National Baseball Hall of Fame Library, Cooperstown, New York).

American League with a 67–87 record. In the league, the team was seventh in batting average (.260), eighth in homers (76), sixth in hits (1,365) and fifth in runs (690). The pitching staff posted a fifth-best ERA (4.66) and finished third in most hits allowed (1,479), third in most runs allowed (813), and first in fewest homers allowed (99). The 385-foot left field line was a nemesis for all.

Marrero went 6–10 in 27 games, and Consuegra was 7–8 in 21 games. Considering the talent he had to work with, Bucky Harris was significantly more accommodating to the Cubans than in his previous iteration as manager. He did a lot less grousing.

On June 25, 1950, 75,000 troops of the North Korean People's Army streamed across the 38th parallel, the line of demarcation between Communist North Korea and the Democracy of South Korea, in an effort to establish a stronghold in the south of the peninsula. Once again, America was thrust into a conflict that had global ramifications. Once again, American baseball men worried: would they postpone baseball? Would there be another conscription? Would there be blackouts? Would the minor leagues wither and nearly die as they did during World War II?

Once again, what would happen to foreign-born ballplayers playing in the U.S.?

1951

Even before the season started, Bucky Harris was in trouble. Roberto Ortiz was traded late in the 1950 season to Philadelphia, leaving him to rely on relief pitcher Gene Bearden, whose command of a curve ball and the Spanish language was only a bit less pathetic than Harris'. Bearden, who had picked up his Spanish in the Mexican leagues and some "California Spanish" from the West Coast, tried his best to act as an interpreter for the three Cuban pitchers, although he was not completely sure they understood what he was saying.

Harris prodded Griffith to acquire the services of veteran catcher Fermin "Mike" Guerra from the Red Sox. During his war years with the Senators, the good field, light hit Guerra had always impressed Harris with both his hustle behind the plate and his linguistic skills, which Harris coveted even more than his bat. Guerra, one of Cambria's earliest signees with the 1936 Albany Senators, had a masterful way of handling the somewhat temperamental Cuban pitchers. Harris was also hopeful that Guerra could help the young Carlos Pascual find his footing in the big leagues, as well as communicate with the other Cuban veterans, who respected Guerra greatly. The deal was made, and Harris slept soundly for a while.[26]

The first headache that Clark Griffith had to address was, once again, the draft eligibility of his players. The Korean War was a different kettle of fish but a war nonetheless, bringing its own concomitant rules and procedures. Shirley Povich summed it up in his own inimitable way:

> On the well-grounded suspicion that there will be no interruption of baseball, Clark Griffith is being very fore-handed about his 1951 ball club, with draft-proof veterans in every position except two which are now inhabited by lawfully wedded 4-F's with dependents. And just in case, he has gone in for Cubans wholesale with eight on his roster. No draft-bait, they.
> The good-looking, 19-year-old rookie, once the goal of every club owner, has now been devalued. He's under the gun of Selective Service. The ball player the owners want now is the 29-year-old, married, with children, and a war record. That covers most of the Nats' pitchers, all of their catchers, three of their four regular infielders, and two of their three top outfielders.[27]

Griffith and Harris were confident that with this strategy, the other teams would get hurt more than they, should the Selective Service come sniffing around major league clubhouses. They were confident that, as in 1945, they would move up in the standings due to war-time attrition.

They would be wrong.

Thursday, March 1 dawned sunny and bit cool in Orlando. It was the start of Senators spring training and the start of Joe Cambria's headaches. By Saturday, almost all of his Cuban signees were three days late for camp, and Bucky Harris and Clark Griffith were not pleased.

Sandalio Consuegra was the only one who made it in on time. The diminutive right-hander posted a respectable 7–8 record in 1950 and was anxious to improve his record. Conrado Marrero had received a dispensation from Griffith for a week to tend to his huge cattle ranch outside of Havana. Julio Moreno, Carlos Pascual, and rookie

Roberto Fernandez were all in the process of packing up and were supposedly on the next flight out. Santiago Ullrich, who was playing winter ball in Venezuela, was on his way to Havana. He was hit in the eye during a game and was having it looked after. The only one left was shortstop Willie Miranda, who was simply holding out for more money from Griffith. Bucky Harris was more interested in his English language skills than his fielding and wanted him around just in case.[28]

Cambria's two biggest headaches were Cirilo Ramos and Roberto Fernandez. Ramos, a 140-pound, left-handed pitcher, had made a big shout in the Class-D Texas League, winning 10 games in a row. He refused to report to camp because, as reported by Sandy Consuegra, Ramos felt he was not ready for the big leagues. He never made it up to the big leagues. Something to be said for prescience.[29]

Roberto Fernandez Tapanes was another of Cambria's "can't miss" anomalies. Whereas the prototypical Cuban was usually a five-foot, six-inch shortstop type, Fernandez was a strapping six-foot, 180-pound outfielder who looked more like Roberto *"El Gigante"* Ortiz. Fernandez had whacked the Big State League at a .385 rate in 1949. When Cambria signed him up for his Havana Cubans in 1950, he powered the batting order. With 562 at-bats, he had 168 hits, 26 doubles, 11 triples, five homers and a .299 average. Bucky Harris liked him because he needed a right-handed bat in his outfield. Fernandez impressed Griffith when he reported to Chattanooga. As Griffith described him: "He can fly in the outfield and what I saw about his throwing arm I liked, but what struck me best was his batting stroke. It's a fine level stroke and he stands up there with his feet wide apart like Joe DiMaggio and takes that small stride like DiMag. He must have been studying DiMaggio intently to come up with that kind of style and you'd have to say he picked out a fine model."[30]

Fernandez played 12 years, predominantly in the Texas, Cuban and Mexican Leagues. He never made it to the big leagues. His major contribution to baseball, however, was his suggestion that Cambria go to see a young Pedro "Tony" Oliva play for his hometown Pino del Rio ball club. The rest is history, as they say.

Eventually, Cambria did, however, find all of his Cubans and got them to camp about a week late.

When Jackie Robinson broke the color line in Major League baseball in 1947, Cambria was quick to see the writing on the wall. He scouted the Cuban winter leagues every year and knew of the great Black players, both Cuban and American, who played there regularly. He told Griffith about them at great length; however, being the arch-conservative that he was, Griffith was not about to rock the proverbial boat. In 1951, Cambria decided to do something about it.

Cambria was losing money with his FIL Cuban team because the Cuban people knew great talent when they saw it. And they were not seeing it on the Havana Cubans ball club. Even though the team was comprised of mostly tan players, they were considered to be a white team, and the fans in Havana were losing interest in them. The Cuban winter leagues showcased some of the greatest Black players of all time: Sam Jethroe, Monte Irvin, Hank Thompson, Roy Campanella, Ray Dandridge, Ray Noble, and "The Cuban Comet," Orestes "Minnie" Minoso. The level of play was faster and better, more akin to Major League baseball, and considerably more interesting to the rabid Cuban baseball fans.

Cambria found several Black Cuban players and invited them to work out with his Cubans during spring training. Everything was going well until he decided to inquire how some of the other FIL owners felt about having Black players in the league.

They were not pleased, especially the owners in Tampa and Miami. They made it abundantly clear to Cambria that Black players would not be welcomed in their cities.

Cambria knew he had been gut-punched, but he was not down for the count. Cambria sent those players, along with a few more, to the Big Springs Broncs, the Senators' affiliate in the Class D–Texas Longhorn league.[31]

One Black Cuban player Cambria had his eye on was shortstop/third baseman Hector Rodriguez. However, in a true case of "turnabout is fair play," Rodriguez was stolen from him by the Brooklyn Dodgers. As Clark Griffith reported to the *Baltimore Afro-American*:

> Cambria, as you know, handles the Washington club's Havana interests and does our scouting in Latin America. He saw this fellow playing in the Cuban leagues and offered him a job with Havana. They agreed to terms and Rodriguez made the trip to Venezuela with the team with the understanding he would sign his contract on their return to Havana. After playing in four games for Cambria, Rodriguez said he was sick and wanted to go home. The club gave him $145 and permission to leave. But when Rodriguez got back from this trip, Cambria discovered that the fellow had joined the Brooklyn outfit.

The *Afro-American* began to speculate that the Dodgers had talked with Rodriguez while he was down in Venezuela. This, however, was denied by Harold Parrott, road secretary and public relations chief of the Dodgers. "We don't know anything about Washington's dealings with Rodriguez," said Parrott.

> All we know is that the guy showed up one day at Vero Beach where the farm clubs have been training since March 10th. He said he wanted a tryout and, since it's our policy to look at any ball player, we let him work with Montreal. He came to us voluntarily, without any promises from us and without any previous talks. My latest information is that our men at Vero Beach aren't so high on him. Apparently, he hasn't made much of an impression and besides he's 31 years old. It may develop that Washington will get him after all—if they really want him.[32]

Hector Rodriguez played the 1951 season with Montreal, then was dealt to the White Sox in 1952. He won the starting third base job for a team populated with All-Stars like Sherm Lollar, Minnie Minoso, Eddie Robinson, Nelson Fox, and Chico Carrasquel. Playing almost every day, he had 407 at bats, drove in 55 runs with 108 hits, and posted a very respectable .265 batting average; however, not respectable enough compared to the power numbers of Lollar, Robinson, Minoso and Sam Mele. Rodriguez put up a solid .959 fielding percentage for the season. Had he stayed with Washington, he would have been hard-pressed to unseat the very dependable Eddie Yost for the third base job and would have been relegated to the bench. Rodriguez, who had played primarily in the Mexican leagues from 1943 to 1951, had his one good year in the sun with the White Sox. He was sent down to AAA Syracuse in 1953 and remained in the high minors until 1964.[33]

With the Nats slipping in the standings in June, Harris was looking around for a new arm or two to help stem the tide. Cambria, as usual, seemed to have the answer in the form of a 25-year-old, six-foot fireballer he had signed to his Havana club named Fernando "*Trampoloco*" (Crazy Top) Rodriguez. Said Rodriguez to the *Washington Post*, "I got my name *Trampoloco* because I was pretty wild at the start of my career. Sometimes I was good on control and other times [bad.]"[34]

Cambria, of course, was high on his young prospect: "He has a fine fast ball, a good curve, nice control and a good baseball sense. He ought to go well in the big time. Why, in a game here recently he pitched nine balls and struck out three batters. This surely set some kind of record, at least in Cuba."[35]

In today's parlance, that is known as an "immaculate inning," a feat that is hard enough to accomplish in any league. Rodriguez occupies the ranks of such notables as Robin Roberts, Jim Bunning and Sandy Koufax.

Despite Rodriguez's strikeout proclivities, Griffith and Harris did not see enough in him to warrant a trip to the Majors. Rodriguez stayed with the Cubans in the FIL, where he led the league with 62 strikeouts in 62 innings. "Freddy" Rodriguez got his cup of coffee with the Cubs in 1958 (seven games, 7⅓ innings pitched, eight hits, five walks, 7.36 ERA) and the Phillies in 1959 (one game, two innings, four hits, three runs, one home run, 13.50 ERA). He was sent down to Buffalo, then ended his career in the Mexican leagues in 1962.[36]

It may have been a blessing in disguise for Cambria that "*Trampoloco*" did not make it with the Senators. Cambria needed at least one good arm to supplant the three he sent away. He was facing a trainload of heat from both the Florida and the Havana fans for the second division performance of the Cubans. Fans were vocal in their denunciation of Cambria for sending Marrero, Consuegra and Moreno, the three strongest arms in the FIL, to the Senators: "Look," said one fan, "Even with Marrero and the others, Washington isn't going anywhere in the American League, but the Cubans could certainly use some pitching help. There's going to be trouble."[37]

The "trouble" was aimed at Joe Cambria, of course. He had always made his money by selling off his good players to Major League teams. In this case, he may have thought he was doing the other FIL owners a favor by leveling the playing field. Unfortunately, it came back to bite him in the posterior.

Cambria tried to rationalize his situation by purporting that Havana wanted a higher class of baseball.

> It's because we're not giving Havana the summer baseball it wants. We had a team that won the pennant five years [in a row] since we started in 1946. Florida clubs in our Florida International League yapped their heads off that we were too good. They threatened to kick us out of the league for that. Truth is, Havana wanted even better baseball. We need Class AA or AAA baseball in Havana. We are only Class B now and Havana will not go for this. If we can't get into a better league, I think the FIL, now Class B, ought to be moved up to Class A, with say five of Florida's top cities. Or put it AA with two teams in Havana and four in Florida. Or why not a real International League, with Montreal, Toronto, Baltimore, Rochester, Miami, Syracuse and Havana?[38]

Joe Cambria put forth this proposal time and time again to the FIL owners. At the winter meetings in December, it was defeated once again.

The real truth of the matter was that attendance at Cubans games was tanking, due in large part to: 1. Poor performance on the part of the team; 2. The firing of Oscar Rodriguez and his replacement by Dolf Luque; and 3. The ousting of the very popular Merito Acosta. By breaking up his pitching staff and selling off his good hitters, like the FIL owners wanted, Cambria left himself open to criticism from all sides.

All of this left a bitter taste in the mouth of the Havana fans and a smile on the lips of the vengeful FIL owners.

Joe Cambria was a businessman, first and foremost. As mentioned earlier, he knew that part of the reason for the poor attendance at his Havana Cubans games was the lack of superior talent in the form of the many excellent Black ballplayers that were still banned from playing in the minor leagues, even after the majors had broken that barrier in 1947. The "gentlemen's agreement" was still in effect in the deep South, and Joe Cambria had had enough of it.

In the winter of 1951, Cambria announced that he was signing several Black players for his Cubans team. He sent contracts to the league president, asked for and received permission to do so, and as far as he was concerned, that was that. He had "gone along to get along" with the unwritten racial rules of the FIL. "But this year it will be different," said Cambria.

> They can't invoke a rule that doesn't exist, and I have great hopes that the colored players will be acceptable to the whole league. Baseball's thinking in the South has changed. Jackie Robinson was permitted to play in Atlanta and other southern cities where there were supposed to be racial barriers and there were no incidents. And those teams of [barnstorming] colored players which Robinson and Roy Campanella led through the South this fall were given warm receptions.[39]

As far as his boss, Clark Griffith, was concerned, Cambria received no push-back on the idea. Griffith had never been one to upset the status quo. Just like night baseball, he had to see something work before he would commit to doing it himself. Once he saw the success of Jackie Robinson, he gave Cambria the go-ahead to find "the right boy" for the Senators. Griffith had always had a plethora of excuses for not signing a Black player: "the time is not right" or "I won't sign a colored boy simply for the sake of exploiting him" or "I don't want to break up the Negro Leagues." This time, however, it was, "I want the boy who can make good for us, and I hope Cambria can turn one up."[40]

The first two Black players Cambria signed were outfielder Angel Scull (pronounced SCHOOL) and shortstop Juan Delis (pronounced de-LIZE). Cambria bought Scull from the Wellsville, NY, Pony League off waivers and signed Delis out of the Havana semi-pro leagues. Scull hit .328 with Wellsville and stole 51 bases. Cambria and Griffith both were highly impressed by the fact that Scull had twice beaten Orestes Minoso, "The Cuban Comet," in challenge races in Havana during the winter season. Delis was said by Cambria "to have more range than Chico Carrasquel of the White Sox and will be a better hitter."[41]

In December, the *Pittsburgh Courier* reported that Cambria was going to break the FIL color barrier by signing Silvio Garcia from the Cienfuegos *Elefantes* of the Cuban professional leagues. The 37-year-old Garcia was by no means a boy. With 20 years' worth of playing experience, he had become one of the most respected players in the Caribbean basin.

Garcia started his career in 1931 as an 18-year-old, playing for the Habana Leons in the Cuban amateur leagues. He started his professional career with Veracruz in the Mexican Leagues in 1938 and had become a legend playing with the New York Cubans of the Negro Leagues for two years. The quintessential Cuban player, Garcia played every position and had a brilliant pitching record early in his career before his arm finally gave out. In 1947, he hit .324 for the New York Cubans and helped them win the Negro World Series. Playing in 114 games for the Havana Cubans in 1952, he had 121 hits, 22 doubles, and three homers and posted a respectable .283 batting average. By the time his career ended in 1954, he had played in Mexico, Venezuela, the Dominican Republic, Puerto Rico, Cuba and the Negro Leagues. Unfortunately, he did not spend a day in the Major Leagues.

1951 Washington Senators Cuban players. Marrero (11–9) would be the only winning pitcher on the team, which boasted ten players signed by Joe Cambria (private collection of George Case III).

This was not the first time, however, that Silvio Garcia had been picked to integrate a white league. He, along with Monte Irvin, Satchel Paige, Buck Leonard and Jackie Robinson, were on the short list of players wanted by Branch Rickey to be the first Black player in the Major Leagues. It was actually Irvin whom Rickey wanted; however, he passed his induction physical and was drafted in 1943 before he could sign with Rickey. Rickey then turned to Garcia. As the story goes:

> In the 1940s, when the president of the Brooklyn Dodgers, Branch Rickey, started thinking about bringing a black player to the major leagues, he initially considered the star Cuban shortstop of the day, Silvio García. According to Edel Casas, the noted Cuban baseball historian, Rickey met with García in Havana in 1945 to explore the possibility of bringing the excellent right-handed hitter to the Dodgers. In the course of the interview, Rickey asked García, "What would you do if a white American slapped your face?" García's response was simple and sincere. "I kill him," he said.[42]

This, of course, ended the conversation for Rickey.

The 1951 Senators

Despite the good play of all of Cambria's Cubans (Consuegra, Marrero, Moreno, Guerra, Miranda, Campos) and his American players (Vernon, Yost, Pete Runnels), the

1951 Senators seesawed through the second division and managed to limp into seventh place with a disappointing 62–92 record. The team's batting average improved slightly from 1950 (.263), as did their hit total (1,399). But they still were seventh in runs scored (672) and homers (76). The pitching staff seesawed but not in a good way. They were seventh again in team ERA (4.66), were worse in hits allowed (1,429) as well as runs allowed (764) and they gave up 110 long balls, second-most in the league.

In an amazing display of loyalty, 750,000 fans crowded through the Griffith Stadium turnstiles despite the team's mediocre efforts. In September, Shirley Povich reported in *The Sporting News*, "Griff to Swing Big Broom on Senators." Griffith and Harris made it known that everyone, with the exception of Irv Noren, Gil Coan, Eddie Yost and Pete Runnels, was on the trading block. This included Mickey Vernon, Cass Michaels and Mickey Grasso. As Povich explained:

> The only department which could retain its status quo is the pitching. Harris feels that his hurlers deserve a better fate than what has been theirs this season, for lack of run-getting on their behalf and defensive play that too often has been shoddy. He visualized a staff of Bob Porterfield, Sid Hudson, Conrado Marrero, Don Johnson, Dick Starr, Mickey Harris, Sandalio Consuegra and Julio Moreno as adequate if not brilliant. Griffith, the old baseball man, holds Bucky blameless for the failures of the Senators. The pair of them will plot the new make up of the Washington club.[43]

Of course, the intimation that Vernon was trade bait was all talk. Harris could ill afford to lose one of the most brilliant bats in baseball. The only two sure things Harris had on his team (courtesy of Joe Cambria) were Ed Yost and Mickey Vernon. Yost, with his impeccable batting eye, had a marked proclivity for getting on base and scoring runs. Vernon was already a major league batting champ. He had all the grace and power of a Ted Williams but was hampered by the 30-foot-high wall that occupied almost all of Griffith Stadium's right field, made even higher with a huge National Bohemian beer sign on top of it. Both Yost and Vernon would anchor the corners of the Senators infield and be the nucleus of the team throughout the decade.

Clark Griffith, with all of his baseball savvy, had made a mistake. He let his heart win out.

Griffith, who always liked to "keep it in the family," took a chance on rookie manager Joe Kuhel to get his Senators out of the second division. Kuhel had spent his entire career with the Nats, and Griffith always rewarded those who were loyal to him.

This time he was wrong.

After two disastrous years in the cellar in 1948 and 1949, Griffith knew he needed an experienced man at the helm and once again tapped Bucky Harris to lead the Nats out of the second division. Harris knew the only way to do this was to shore up the Senators' farm system, which was a disaster, and to try and trade up from within the division. The needy Nats were the last in all the majors in farm teams (seven) and second to last in terms of scouts (11). They had no AAA affiliate. Joe Engle was concerned more with running the AA Chattanooga team. Joe Cambria, who focused his scouting on Latin players almost exclusively, had provided the Senators with reliable, albeit cheap, ballplayers; however, in all his years scouting in the tropics, he had not supplied the team with one bone fide superstar, with the exception (in Bucky Harris's mind) of Conrado Marrero. Harris, however, was hopeful that rookie Francisco "Frank" Campos would become a fixture in the Nats' outfield after he hit productively in his eight-game cup of coffee with the team in 1951.

Bucky Harris was the manager of the team on the field. He left the futures market up to Griffith. Harris knew were all the good players were, as described by Shirley Povich in his biography of the Senators:

> Their deals were mostly with the Yankees, and for good reason. The Yankees had all the ball players. Harris, after three seasons with the Yanks, was painfully aware of the inadequacies of the Senators' farm system and yearned for some of the talent he knew with the Yankees. "Let's not kid ourselves," he told Griffith. "The Yankees have the best scouts and they come up with the best players. Let's go after some."[44]

Bucky Harris, through shrewd maneuvering, was able to acquire the services of Bob Porterfield, Frank "Spec" Shea and Jackie Jensen from the Yankees, as well as Mickey McDermott from the Red Sox and Chuck Stobbs from the White Sox. Jensen had one good year in right field for the 1953 Nats, then was traded to Boston for McDermott and Tom Umphlett. Porterfield had a career year in 1953 with a monstrous 22–10 season, and Harris got solid performance from the other pitchers as well.

1952

On April 9, 1952, Joe Cambria joined three of his fellow FIL owners in doing something that had never been done in Jim Crow Florida before. They integrated the Florida minor leagues. Silvio Garcia, along with teammate Angel Scull and George Handy of the Miami Beach Flamingos, took the field and ushered in the change of mind that had been so long overdue.

Unfortunately, it did not help the Cubans.

The Cubans struggled at the plate all year and finished next to last in team batting average with a paltry .228 average. The averaged only three runs a game and were shut out 27 times. Garcia, however, was the team's leading hitter, with a .283 batting average to go along with 121 hits, 22 doubles, three homers and 40 RBI. Angel Scull posted a .274 average, with 149 hits, 15 doubles and 14 triples. The *Cubanos* ended fourth in the league and were never really in contention for the whole season.[45]

But the change had come, and Cambria was there to make it happen. He was adamant that it was all too little too late. He told the *Washington Post*:

> They say they want a colored ball player. Now they tell me! I could have had them a million dollars' worth of colored players a few years back. I owned the park where the Baltimore Black Sox played. They all came there. I told them about Larry Doby and Roy Campanella and all I got was a black look. It was the same thing a couple of years ago in Cuba. I begged them to sign my boy Orestes Minoso. They could get him for peanuts. Bill Veeck took him to Cleveland and then traded him to the White Sox. You couldn't get him away from the White Sox for $200,000. Now, they tell me to watch out for good colored players.[46]

Maybe it was because Cambria decided to break the color barrier in the FIL. Maybe it was because the Cubans always seemed to be the better team. Whatever it was, the FIL owners, tired of Cambria playing fast and loose, were always looking for some way to catch him in a conundrum. By April of 1952, the owners had taken both notice and umbrage of the fact that Cambria, whenever a Cuban player was hurt or sold, always seemed to have two others waiting in the wings just as good, if not better. It seemed as if his tap on Cuban talent was always turned on.

They decided that, in order the catch Cambria at his game, each team should present to the umpire the names of all players on their list instead of just the starting nine. It did not work. Not once throughout the season did Cambria turn in the wrong list. The owners demurred and went back to presenting only the list of starters.[47]

Next came the case of Carlos *"Patato"* Pascual.

Joe Cambria always seemed to be cash-strapped and hounded by creditors. Whenever this happened, his favorite thing to do was to pick up the phone and sell a player. And it seemed his first phone call always went to the St. Petersburg Saints President, Vernon Eckert.

In May of 1952, Cambria offered to sell Eckert pitcher Carlos Pascual and agreed to Eckert's cash bid. Then Pascual refused to report to St. Petersburg. Eckert and the media asked Cambria why. In frustration, he explained:

> I have Pascual's papers with me now—in my valise—but I don't know. I just don't know! Pascual might not report. I wouldn't want to sell Eckert a player who wouldn't report. And my manager [Mike Guerra] doesn't like it. He wants to win. You know how these managers are. I tell you. You ask Patato himself. He want to come to the Saints, he come. He don't want to come, he don't come. You go to Havana with the Saints Monday and you ask him then. He says yes, you get him like that (snaps fingers). I hope he says yes. We need the money.[48]

Eckert was just as perplexed. He reported that he discussed the possibility of Pascual coming to the Saints with Pascual himself and that Pascual was willing to come to the team. When asked by Eckert about that scenario, Cambria replied, "I tell you, these Cubans change their minds like that. Maybe when you come to Havana, he'll change his mind again, huh? You ask him!"[49]

Unfortunately, it ended there. Cambria said come to Havana. Eckert said he could not make the trip. Cambria said he would let Eckert know. Eckert angrily replied, "That's what you always say, Joe—you'll let me know. You never let anybody know!"[50]

Pascual remained with the Cubans. To add insult to injury, when Cambria first called Eckert to offer him the deal, he called collect!

Nope. Cambria was not done yet. He had more shenanigans to pull.

He was once again embroiled in a controversy with a player. In May, Lakeland Pilots president Bob Doty filed a formal complaint with league president Henry S. Bayard, accusing Cambria of tampering with former St. Petersburg Saints outfielder Roberto Fernandez Tapanes. Tapanes had been with St. Petersburg at the start of the season and was sold to Lakeland the first week of May. The gist of the story goes as such.

1. Shortly after being traded to Lakeland, Tapanes stated he was dissatisfied with the conditions there, just a short time after Cambria had offered the team $500 for him and was turned down.

2. Tapanes' excuses closely resembled the ones proffered by Cambria, that his wife and family members were dissatisfied. His wife complained she had no one to talk to in Lakeland and wanted to go back to Havana.

3. Tapanes requested his release. Doty said no because of the $1,500 they had invested in him.

4. Tapanes offered to buy himself out of his contract, knowing he could get the money from Cambria. He offered $1,300 and Doty agreed.

5. Cambria, however, had sold Tapanes to St. Petersburg in the winter of 1951 for $2,000. When the time was ripe, he attempted to regain Tapanes for $500, thus making a cool $1,500 on the transaction.

6. Doty accused Cambria of "tampering" with Tapanes by influencing him to secure himself for $1,300, thus making a profit for Cambria nonetheless.

7. Cambria, of course, denied the tampering charges; however, he sent a check to Lakeland for Tapanes, Doty was happy, Cambria was happy, Tapanes went back to the *Cubanos*, and he and his wife were happy.

The Curious Case of "Bitsy" Mott

Although his career was substantially more productive than "Moonlight" Graham of *Field of Dreams* fame, Elisha Matthew "Bitsy" Mott is one of thousands of minor league players who would be forever forgotten had it not been for Joe Cambria, Elvis Presley and one of the most convoluted cases of "reverse discrimination" in the history of minor league baseball.

Bitsy Mott was born June 12, 1918, in Arcadia, Florida, and spent the bulk of his career in the Sunshine State. He started his professional journey in 1939 with the Americus Pioneers of the Class-D Georgia-Florida League. He bounced around the league through 1941. Between 1942 and 1943 he was involved in the war effort. He wound up with the Utica Blue Sox of the Eastern League in 1944, a Class-A affiliate of the Phillies. He did well there, slashing a .282/.380/.340.

Bitsy Mott was rewarded with his one good year in the sun with the Phillies in 1945. Playing 90 games at shortstop, Mott had 289 at bats, 64 hits, eight doubles, 22 RBI, and a modest .221 average. Alas, the baseball gods smiled not upon his performance, and he was relegated back to the Florida International League Tampa Smokers in 1946. Mott bounced around the FIL and the Florida State league until bumping into Cambria in 1952.[51]

For once in his life, Joe Cambria did something for purely altruistic reasons. He saw a good player and offered him a contract to show his skills to the world. Unfortunately, it was for the Havana Cubans. He played in one game in Havana, pulled a muscle in his leg in the first inning, left the game, and was sent back to Florida the next day with his unconditional release.

It seems the Cuban media and the fans as well would have nothing to do with a "White American" playing with the Cubans. "I couldn't read their newspapers," said Bitsy Mott, "but Charlie Cuellar translated them for me. In just so many words, the papers were asking why the Havana club had to sign an American player with so many Cuban ball players around. Joe just told me that he guessed that it just wouldn't work out and gave me my release. But that's ok. I'm going to land another job and make a go of it. I feel like I still have a lot of good baseball left in me and I intend to play out the string."[52]

Mott's friend Charlie Cuellar also received flak from the Havana media because, although Spanish by parentage, he was born and raised in the United States. Mott was the first white, non–Spanish speaking ball player ever hired by Cambria for the Havana club.

Mott was signed by the Tampa Smokers upon his return to Florida and remained in the minors until he hung up his cleats in 1957. But the story does not end there.

From 1955 through 1973, Bitsy Mott became the personal security manager for Elvis Presley. Mott, who was a brother-in-law of Elvis's manager, Colonel Tom Parker, arranged travel between small, close road venues and provided Elvis with the much-needed security from his rabid fans. Bitsy Mott appeared in four of Elvis's films and was one of the select few who attended Elvis's funeral in 1977. Mott died in 2001 in Brandon, Florida. He was 82 years old.[53]

If anything could be said about Joe Cambria, it was that he was unconventional and a little bit of a gambler.

In need of a big bat in his Havana lineup, Joe Cambria heard that his old friend, Roberto Ortiz, was looking to relocate. Ortiz had spent a year with the Phillies in 1950, then was sold to the Red Sox, who sent him down to play with the Southern Association Birmingham Barons. Roberto Ortiz wanted to play in his native Havana, and the Sox were willing to sell. Bob Addie reported in the *Washington Times-Herald* that the deal went something like this: "They were haggling over the price, with Cambria offering $3,000 and Joe Cronin, GM of the Red Sox holding out for $8,000. 'Tell you what I'll do,' said Cambria. 'I'll toss a coin and if I win, I'll give you $3,000. If I lose, you get $8,000.' Cambria won the toss."[54]

Joe Cambria tried many changes with his Havana Cubans in 1952. He hired the first Black players for his club. He hired the first White player for his club. He changed managers, pinning his hopes on Fermin "Mike" Guerra, veteran Senators back-up catcher, to manage the team to the first division. "Guerra's fine experience in the big leagues, his ability to hustle and get the team to do likewise ought to make him a fine playing manager," said Cambria, "He's such a fine catcher that I may have trouble keeping him around, as I've already had some big league nibbles, although he is not, what you might say, on the market. But of course, if he got a real chance, we wouldn't stand in his way."[55]

Unfortunately, although he tried many changes, his fortunes got no better. Despite a wealth of talent, most of which found its way to the Senators within a few years, the Cubans could only manage a fourth-place finish with a 76–77 record, which was still better than their fifth-place finish the previous year.

In the spring of 1952, Bucky Harris was busy prognosticating about the year at hand. He was satisfied with what he saw with his hitters. But, as always, his pitching was a mystery. "Right now, I'd have to go along with the complaint that we have only one solid pitcher—Bob Porterfield," said Harris to the *Washington Post*. "The others have to come through for us or we could be sunk."[56]

Harris was hopeful that Sid Hudson's sore arm was not as sore as imagined. He had high hopes for several others: Mickey Harris, Don Johnson, rookie Glenn Elliott from the Pacific Coast League, Harley Grossman from Charlotte, and Sonny Dixon from Chattanooga. He had some true veterans upon which to rely like Walt Masterson, Spec Shea, Randy Gumpert, Joe Haynes, and Lou Sleater. Much to his surprise, after the season started, Clark Griffith traded for the ancient Bobo Newsom. At 44 years old, Newsom was senior to the other "ancient mariner" on the team, 41-year-old Connie Marrero. Newsom was on his fourth and final tour of duty with the Nats. He remains famous for being the only pitcher after the Deadball Era to win 20 games and lose 20 games three times in a career.

Then there were the Cubans. Bucky Harris had his stalwarts: Connie Marrero, Julio Moreno, and Sandy Consuegra. Santiago Ullrich was hung up in Havana because he had lost his passport, and as always, Cambria was always ready with more. He sent up Raul

Sanchez and Jose Narango from his Havana Cubans team, bringing the grand total of pitchers working out to 22, the largest in Nats history.[57]

Sanchez and late-season call-up Miguel "Mike" Fornieles proved blessings in disguise for Bucky Harris. Both of them pitched shutouts in their Major League debuts.

Fornieles was a grocery store clerk before Cambria saw him pitch in the amateur leagues, signed him up in 1950, and sent him to the Big Springs Broncs in the Texas League to get a taste of big-league pitching. After Fornieles went 17–6 in Texas, Cambria brought him back to the Cubans in 1951, where he went 14–12 with a 2.66 ERA. Cambria kept yelling to the Nats brass that he had the best kid in the minors just waiting for his shot, but Calvin Griffith was less than convinced. "We can't ever believe Cambria," said Calvin. "He yells wolf so often we never know when the real thing comes along."[58]

Not known for his tolerance for Cambria's Cuban contingent, Bucky Harris surprised everyone and became a big fan of Fornieles. He liked particularly the way the kid pitched himself out of trouble in the early innings and broke off both his fast ball and his curve with the same flick of the wrist. "He may be a flash in the pan, but a manager can dream, can't he? [Besides,] what he doesn't know about pitching maybe we can teach him."[59]

Fornieles was certainly no flash in the pan. He went 2–2 with a stellar 1.37 ERA for the Nats in 1952, pitching brilliantly in relief. In desperate need for left-handed pitching, the Nats dealt him to the White Sox in 1953. Fornieles went on to have very respectable 12-year career with the White Sox, Orioles, Red Sox and Twins. He went 63–64 lifetime with a 3.96 ERA.[60]

Bucky Harris also became a big fan of another Cambria protégé, Francisco "Frank" Campos. Signed by Cambria out of the Cuban amateur leagues, Campos spent time with the Portsmouth Cubs of the Piedmont League from 1944 to 1948. Cambria picked him up for his Havana Cubans team in 1949, then sent him to Charlotte in 1950. In 1951, Campos murdered the Tri-State League with a .368 batting average and 171 hits, which earned him a September call-up to Washington. He doubled in his first at-bat in the majors and continued his hot hand by having four multi-hit games in his next seven appearances. Bucky Harris loved his numbers: 26 at-bats, 11 hits and a .423 batting average. "He's my fourth outfielder," Harris said, "and the minute Gil Coan or Sam Mele or Irv Noren let me down, Campos is my third outfielder and that won't make me mad."[61]

Campos made 53 appearances in 1952, 29 as a pinch-hitter, and hit .259 in 112 at-bats. In 1953, he only played in 10 games, with nine at-bats, one hit and two RBI, before he was sent to Toronto, then Charlotte. His career ended with the Chattanooga Lookouts in 1954.[62]

In the eight years that Bucky Harris piloted the Senators from 1935 to 1942, he had little respect for Cambria or his multitudinous Cubans. He decried their "monkey talk." He hired players for their bilingual abilities rather than their bats. He berated Cambria to the press for the headaches he caused him. He couched his prejudices in measured rhetoric to the press, but it was prejudice all the same. And he was downright nasty to them.

But the tune changed a bit in 1952, and Harris could not help but respect Cambria and his scouting proclivities. Cambria had provided him with Francisco Campos, Miguel Fornieles, Raul Sanchez, and four out of his seven starting pitchers, Sandalio Consuegra, Conrado Marrero, Julio Moreno and Walt Masterson. There were others like Fernando Rodrigues, Santiago Ullrich and Orlando Echeverria, powerhouses from

Cambria's Havana Cubans roster, who turned some heads in the Senators' camp but did not make the final roster. Add to that list Mickey Vernon and Ed Yost, and you had the makings of a very good team. All products of Joe Cambria.

The 1952 Senators ended the year back in fifth place with a winning 78–76 record and a .506 winning percentage, thanks in large part to the combined pitching staff. Consuegra (6–0), Fornieles (2–2), Moreno (9–9), and Marrero (11–8) all had a good year. The offense posted the lowest average in the league, .239. Though the pitching staff allowed the fewest homers in the league (78), they were fifth in runs allowed (608) and first in hits (1,405).

Mickey Vernon and Eddie Yost, along with Pete Runnels and Jackie Jensen, provided timely hitting and had tremendous on-base percentages. Their individual performances notwithstanding, the rest of the team was weak. The team was last in home runs (50, that darn fence!) and seventh in hits (1,282) and runs scored (598).

All in all, it was a solid performance for the team, due in large part to the crafty acquisitions of Joe Cambria. "Cuba is now more thoroughly scouted for talent by major league bird dogs than any section of the United States," reported Ossie Bluege, the Nats' farm director, who added, "And the other clubs used to laugh at Joe Cambria's operations there."[63]

Cambria obviously had enough headaches with which to deal. Surely, he did not need to have more added, but added they were.

In June of 1952, the U.S. Congress passed the Immigration and Nationality Act, H.R. 5678, otherwise known as the McCarren-Walter Act. The Act upheld the national origins quota system established by the Immigration Act of 1924, reinforcing this controversial system of immigrant selection. It also revised the laws relating to immigration, naturalization and nationality.

Just as in the 1940 Draft act, where ballplayers were classified as "entertainers," the McCarren Act also reclassified the term "immigrant."

Sec. 101-(15) (15) The term "immigrant" means every alien except those within one of the following classes of nonimmigrant aliens:

> (H) an alien having a residence in a foreign country which he has no intention of abandoning (i) who is of *distinguished merit and ability* and who is coming temporarily to the United States to perform temporary services of an exceptional nature requiring such merit and ability; or (ii) who is coming temporarily to the United States to perform temporary services or labor, if unemployed persons capable of performing such services or labor cannot be found in this country; or (iii) who is coming temporarily to the United States as an industrial trainee.[64]

In an op-ed piece in the *St. Petersburg Times*, sports editor Bill Beck delineated all of the hoops through which Joe Cambria would need to jump in order to get his Cuban ballplayers into the country.

He pointed out that aliens "of distinguished merit and ability" needed to do the following to receive non-immigrant alien work visas:

1. Get somebody in this country to go to the Immigration Bureau and petition for permission to "import" them.
2. Get somebody to prove they DO have distinguished merit and ability.
3. Produce birth certificates and affidavits as to former residence and habits.
4. Get somebody from their native land to testify as to their good character.
5. Get this wealth of information into the hands of immigration authorities along with a $10 petition fee.

He also asked a rather important question, one the miserly Mr. Cambria must have pondered: "When this torturous process has been undergone once, is it good for all season, or must it be done over and over for as many times as a baseball player enters the country DURING the season?"[65]

With 20 men, a business manager, trainer, and manager, it would have cost Cambria a whopping $2,800 for the entire season to shuttle his Cubans back and forth from Havana to Florida. Beck asked the Miami District Officer in charge, Joseph Savoretti, what the official ruling might be, to which he responded, "My opinion is that once entry privilege has been extended it would be good for all season."[66]

That was, of course, Savoretti's opinion. Mr. A.J. Mixon, officer in charge of Immigration and Naturalization in Tampa, said he was in no position to render a decision on the subject but "it certainly was a good question." Research has found no evidence that the question was ever answered to anyone's satisfaction.

Not all changes are good. This one certainly was not, and it left Joe Cambria ending 1952 on a decidedly low note.

On December 9 of 1952, Joe Cambria lost his brother, John, following a long illness. They were partners in at least a dozen of Joe's minor league teams, including Joe's two big teams, the Albany Senators and the Williamsport Grays. It was John who acted as Joe's squire when Joe was forced to divest himself of all his minor league holdings in 1945. John was 66 years old.[67]

1953

The Eisenhower Years

Joe Cambria was livid. "The McCarran Act! How can a Senator from Nebraska [he was actually from Nevada] know what's good for ballplayers in Cuba!"[68]

As reported by Shirley Povich in the *Washington Post*, Cambria had been hounding the U.S. consulate, the embassy, and the IRS every day since the beginning of March, only to be bogged deeper in the quicksand of the immigration law's red tape. At issue that March was the release of seven of his players from Cuba; pitchers Conrado Marrero, Julio Moreno, Raul Sanchez, Sandalio Consuegra, and outfielders Francisco Campos, Angel Scull and Luis Vistuer.

"I've been there so often, they think I'm one of the clerks," said Cambria.

The other day the guard checked me in and said, "Late again. You must have some pull around here." There must be Yankee or Cleveland rooters in this embassy. Orestes Minoso of the White Sox, they cleared him quick. Willy Miranda of the Browns got his visa with no trouble. My Washington players get nothing but troubles from the embassy. All we get from them is *mañana*, and *mañana* never comes! I thought Eisenhower was going to straighten the country out. If he could forget Korea for five minutes and think of Cuba and me, that's all it would take.[69]

In reality, Bucky Harris was primarily concerned about his two starters, Marrero and Moreno. The other players would not figure as prominently as the pitchers. Scull and Vistuer, however, were a different matter.

Angel Scull and Juan Vistuer were two Black ballplayers, both were in the Senators' farm system, and both were Clark Griffith's promises to keep. Griffith told the *Washington Post*, "I will sign a negro ball player just as soon as we can find one who can play in the big leagues. We welcome the opportunity to look over these colored boys and the opportunity to make themselves a job with us is wide open. All they have to show us is that they can play big league ball and they'll be signed to Washington contracts."[70]

Scull, reputed to be the fastest man in Cuba, hit .278 and stole 51 bases in the FIL in 1952. Pittsburgh offered the Nats $8,000 for him during the winter. Six-foot-tall lefty Juan Vistuer hit .321 with 12 homers with the Big Spring Broncs in 1952.

However, Harris and Griffith were equally impressed, if not more so, with the hitting prowess of another of Cambria's stars in waiting, Juan Delis. He was hitting .400 with the Danville Dans of the Mississippi-Ohio Valley League before a broken ankle sidelined him for the season. While working out with the team in Orlando, he hit eight straight balls over the Tinker Field left field fence. "We like his speed," said Griffith, "and when we asked him how fast he could run, he said if we would let him take his shoes off, he'd really show us some speed."[71]

Also caught up in the ongoing bureaucratic boondoggle was another of Cambria's "can't miss" prospects, a young Venezuelan infielder named Pompeyo "Yo-Yo" Davalillo. Cambria called Davalillo an "all purpose" player, meaning he could play second base, shortstop or third base. Officially listed as five-foot, seven-inches tall, "Yo-Yo" was more accurately measured once he came into camp as five-feet three and ¼ inches in his bare feet. Griffith purported that Davalillo was the smallest person to ever play professional baseball outside of Eddie Gaedel, the three-foot, seven-inch pinch-hitter used by Bill Veeck in St. Louis in 1951.[72]

The *Washington Evening Star* reported on March 3 that only Sandy Consuegra and Davalillo had been cleared by all of the myriad branches of government and were expected into camp momentarily. Connie Marrero had been cleared to leave but was granted permission by Griffith to finish out his stint with the Cuban winter leagues and report by March 12. All the rest of the Cubans, Campos, Scull, Vistuer, Moreno and Sanchez, were delayed indefinitely.[73] "We started working on visas for those fellows in January," said Griffith. "As I understand it, the McCarran Act requires that they be cleared by the State Department, then screened by Internal Revenue and finally passed on by the consulate in Havana."[74]

By March 14, Marrero, Moreno, and Frank Campos reported to camp. All the rest of the Cubans did report a few days later. As with all new bureaucratic things in Washington, it took a while for everyone to know where everything was and where it was supposed to go. There were no further incidences of visa problems in the following years.

While Bucky Harris was dealing with the McCarran-delayed Cubans, he received some welcome news from the South. Cal Ermer, pennant-winning manager of the Nats' Chattanooga affiliate, came into camp expounding the virtues of his four best arms: Sonny Dixon (19–14), Al Sima (24–9), Jim Pearce (12–5), and Bunky Stewart (6–9). Ermer told Harris:

> Sima, with a bit better luck, could have won 30 games for us. He has come up with a better fast ball to go with his curve. Dixon has a slider to go with the speed and if he didn't have to pitch relief for us, he'd have won more than 19. That 12–5 record of Pearce's is better than it seems. Big Jim didn't get away well and had only a 5–5 record, but in those last weeks when we were trying to hold our league lead, he won seven in a row for us. You've got to like him.[75]

Bucky Harris liked them all, took all four of them, and they all made the roster. Dixon went 5–8 with a 3.75 ERA in 120 innings with 31 walks and 40 strikeouts. Sima went 2–3 in 68.1 innings with 31 walks, 25 strikeouts, and a 3.42 ERA. Pearce, used mostly in relief, went 0–1 in 9⅓ innings with six walks and a 7.71 ERA. Stewart started two games and lost both with a 4.70 ERA. All four men had short but solid major league careers. Bunky Stewart, in particular, had a good five years with the Nats before ending his career in the minors in 1962.

Bucky Harris may have been comfortable about his new pitchers, but he had a problem at second base. "Anybody who can play second base is a welcome addition to our team," he said. "Cambria is high on Davalillo. We don't take Joe's recommendations lightly anymore. He has come up with too many good ballplayers for us. The second base job is wide open, and I want to take a good look at Davalillo."[76]

Obviously from the statement above, Harris came into the 1953 season with two things; a renewed respect for Joe Cambria and a real need to find a good second baseman. Harris had six warm bodies to choose from: Floyd Baker, Mel Hoderlein, Leroy Dietzel, Wayne Terwilliger, Jerry Snyder and, of course, "Yo-Yo" Davalillo.

Harris gave them all a thorough going over and settled on sure-handed Wayne Terwilliger for the position; however, there was a steady parade going back and forth between second base and shortstop, mainly due to the fact that no one could hit!

Mel Hoderlein played 11 games at second and two at short, recording a .191 average and nine hits. Jerry Snyder played four games at second and 17 at short, for a .339 average with 62 at-bats and 21 hits. Pete Runnels, a soon-to-be AL batting champ, was the regular shortstop, playing 121 games there but also 11 games at second. Tony Roig, a career minor leaguer, got in three games at second before being sent back to Chattanooga.[77]

The biggest disappointment was Davalillo. Terwilliger was the most sure-handed of the lot, so with him ensconced at second, Davalillo was relegated to shortstop. Bucky Harris was counting heavily on his bat for power to go along with Vernon, Yost, Jim Busby, and Jackie Jensen. Unfortunately, Davalillo got a case of what is called "the yips." Usually, it happens to catchers who cannot throw the ball back to the pitcher. With pitchers, it is usually a case of extreme wildness. With Davalillo, the ball just could not find his mitt. Davalillo, usually a vacuum cleaner in the infield, committed six errors in the short span of 17 games; however, he did turn 10 double plays. In 58 at-bats, he managed 17 hits, with two RBI, scored 10 runs, stole one base, and had a .293 batting average. He was sent back to Charlotte, then played with the Havana Sugar Kings and in the Mexican Leagues before his career ended in 1965.

After a 19-year career in both the major and minor leagues, Wayne Terwilliger, "Twig" as he was called, retired from playing in 1968 to become a coach for the expansion Senators under Ted Williams. He was a long-time coach and scout for the Texas Rangers and the Minnesota Twins. He then went into coaching in the minor leagues. At the age of 80, he managed the Ft. Worth Cats of the independent Central League to the 2005 league championship, then remained a coach for them until he retired at age 85. "Twig" spent 62 years in professional baseball. He passed away in February of 2021 at the age of 95.[78]

By April, another feud erupted, this time between Cambria and Roberto Maduro, owner of the Gran Stadium in Havana. This time, Cambria would not prevail.

The same problems that had plagued Cambria last year persisted this year: disinterest in the team by the Cuban fans in Havana and the difficulty in securing a lease from Roberto Maduro to use the stadium. Asked what caused the decline in interest [in the Cubans], Roberto Maduro said: "Many things. At first the Cuban [fans] tired of their team winning the pennant every year [they won the first five straight]. It did not help when Merito Acosta was ousted as president by Cambria and Clark Griffith. And in recent years, the fans have revolted against the use of older Cuban players instead of youngsters."[79]

It also had not helped that Cambria had sold off a host of very well-liked players like Napoleon "Nap" Reyes, Roberto Ortiz, Carlos Pascual, Connie Marrero, Julio Moreno, and Sandy Consuegra, only to replace them with less than adequate players.

Maduro was also a good friend of Merito Acosta, and not renewing his lease at the Stadium may have been his way of getting back at Cambria, "Reports from Havana say that operators of Gran Stadium don't want any part of Cambria and will refuse to let any team he is connected with use the park. If this is true, it will be necessary for him to find a new home, and Key West is the logical spot."[80]

The reference to Key West was as it was the previous year. Cambria complained that he had too many two-game series to play in Havana, and the travel costs of flying the mainland teams into Cuba were prohibitive. Cambria insisted that he would play his 24 Havana games in Key West as his home site if he could not either get the costs reduced or get a reasonable lease from Maduro to use Gran Stadium.

Phil O'Connell, FIL president, said changing the schedule in that way would require approval by the league presidents and the FIL board of directors, which surely would not happen. It would be all right for two teams on the mainland to switch playing dates between them, but a large-scale schedule change as proposed by Cambria would mean a change in arrangements for all the umpires, which would need league approval.[81]

Joe Cambria was, in essence, getting the "Bill Veeck treatment" from both the FIL owners and Maduro. Bill Veeck, owner of the St. Louis Browns and a notorious "rule stretcher," had earned the ire of the other Major League owners with his, as they termed it, "silly" promotions. He became even more cash-strapped than Cambria. By the end of the 1953 season, his management was asking the fans to give back their foul balls because they did not have enough stock to play the games. Veeck wanted to move the team to a bigger fan base but was refused by the other owners. He had no recourse but to sell the team to a Baltimore business conglomerate, who moved the team to Baltimore where it became the Orioles.

With the FIL owners refusing to allow him to play his Havana games in Key West and with Maduro being obdurate about the stadium lease, Cambria was being forced to "fish or cut bait." By late April, he announced that he "expected to reach an agreement with Maduro to play at least 60 percent of our games in Havana."[82]

The deal must not have transpired to Cambria's liking because on May 3, Roberto Maduro bought the Cubans from Cambria and Griffith for $40,000. Cambria stayed on as a scout for the remainder of the season, and the affiliation with the Senators remained in place as well. The FIL owners approved the sale and, most likely, were happy to be rid of Cambria and his grousing. Now they could concentrate on other problems.

With the sale of the Cubans, the Nats' farm system went down to a paltry six teams: Chattanooga (AA), Scranton (A), Charlotte (B), Bluefield, Orlando and Fulton (D). Without the burden of running a baseball team full-time, Cambria had the opportunity to wax profound (or profane) on the state of baseball and the farm system. From the sound of his rhetoric, I am sure he had Griffith and himself in mind.

The independent owner of a baseball team has only a 10-percent chance. You can take it either way—to come out financially or to win a pennant which usually is the same thing. Clubs like Brooklyn, the two St. Louis teams, the White Sox and the Giants, for example, control from 300 to 700 players. This of course includes their farms. An independent owner controls 30 or 35. If his club is in a pretty good spot to finish at or near the top, the big league club can transfer more power to its farm team. The independent guy will wind up maybe fifth. The little guy likewise has a poor chance to sign up a boy in his own hometown. If the player shows anything, one of the big leagues can give him maybe $50,000 just to put a cap on. Something must be done to get the independent owner in a better position. Baseball can't be the game it is without him. Baseball ought to get its cost down, speed up play and keep the uniforms clean. It should stick to baseball, cut out all the side-shows such as weddings, queens, midgets and all that stuff![83]

Obviously, he was taking a pot-shot at Bill Veeck, as well as the big-money clubs like the Dodgers, Yankees and Giants. Baseball was changing because the times were a-changin'.

The Korean War ended in July of 1953. America was in a peace-time economy for the first time in a long time. Jobs, especially in the technologies, were plentiful and in demand. This led to new cars, suburban houses, and plentiful consumer goods. Kids had disposable income for the first time. The transistor radio brought baseball and Rock 'n' Roll right into their ears.

The Yankees, Giants and Dodgers dominated baseball, until everyone started to go away to greener pastures in Milwaukee, Kansas City and California. Televisions brought baseball's "Game of the Week" into living rooms across the country. Big money was dominating baseball.

Joe Cambria was yearning for the good 'ol days when he could sign a ballplayer for travel money.

They were long gone.

Although their relationship was often marked by tension, Roberto "Bobby" Maduro and Joe Cambria are shown here in a collegial moment. Maduro would buy the Havana Cubans from Cambria in 1953 and rename them the Sugar Kings (private collection of Paul Scimonelli).

The 1953 Senators

The 1953 Senators would play solid ball throughout the year, ending up in fifth place again with a 76–76 record, an even .500, 23½ games behind the Yankees. The team batting average would improve to fifth place (.262), and they would place fifth in runs scored (687), sixth in hits (1,354) and last in home runs (50). The pitching staff would once again go up and down. The team ERA improved to 3.66, they allowed fewer hits than last year (1,313) and gave up a few more runs (614) and more homers (112).

Of all the Cubans on the team, Connie Marrero was the only one who lasted through the season. Frank Campos, Sandy Consuegra, Pompeo Davalillo, and Julio Moreno were all sent back to the minors.

Marrero had another winning year, going 8–7. In 145⅔ innings, he surrendered 130 hits and 48 walks, struck out 60 batters, and posted a fine 3.03 ERA. With the exceptions of Walt Masterson and Johnny Schmitz, all of the starting pitchers had a winning record. Bob Porterfield had a career year. He went 22–10 with 24 complete games, led the majors with nine shutouts, and was named *The Sporting News* Pitcher of the Year. Just a few more wins would have put the Senators in the first division, someplace they had not been since 1945.

The brightest spot in the baseball firmament in 1953 was Mickey Vernon. Locked in a tight battle with Al Rosen throughout the year, Vernon narrowly edged out Rosen for the batting championship with a .337 batting average to Rosen's .336. Eddie Yost led the league with 123 walks.

So there were a few very positive things happening for the Senators in 1953. However, Senators Vice-President Calvin Griffith said, "We need a change of faces."[84]

As always, changes would come.

1954

The Greek philosopher Heraclitus said, "Nothing is permanent except change." Ralph Waldo Emerson said, "We change, whether we like it or not."

Like it or not, the Senators had to change if they were ever going to see the first division again. They, and the rest of both leagues, were facing perhaps the most dominant Yankees team of the century. The Yankees of the 1950s (eight AL pennants, six World Series wins) eclipsed the Yankees of the 1920s (six pennants, three World Series wins). They were so dominant that perennial bottom-dwellers like the Senators, Athletics and the Pirates would start their seasons eschewing a World Series ring and just hoping to make the first division.

And every spring in baseball, the optimum words are hope and change. The biggest change the Senators would make for spring training in 1954 would also be the source of some of their biggest trouble.

Cambria had received the word from Clark Griffith to "find the right boy," meaning the right Black player, to bring into the Senators' fold. Cambria, as usual, sent another army of boys for tryouts. Some were Black and some were not. Some, like Connie Marrero, Frank Campos and Yo-Yo Davalillo, had been there before.

New to camp this year were Jose Valdivielso (ss), Carlos Paula (of), Roberto Zapata (1B), Julio Becquer (1B), Humberto Bernal, Evelio Hernandez, Roland Bacardi, Camilo Pascual, Raul Sanchez, and Gonzalo Naranjo (p), Juan Delis (of), and Angel Scull (of).

Unfortunately, the appearance of so many dark-skinned players at the Senators' camp was a cause of consternation for someone.

On Thursday, March 18, the FBI was called into Winter Garden, Florida, to investigate reports that Zinn Beck, the general manager of the Nats' Chattanooga Lookouts, was ordered "by somebody supposed to be the chief of police" to get the seven Negro players out of town by sundown. Acting at the direction of Attorney General Herbert Brownell, FBI agents questioned officials of the Senators to make sure "civil liberties will be protected."[85] Both Chief of Police Maynard Mann and city clerk E.M. Tanner admitted that they visited the training facility during practice and told Beck there was opposition to having colored players practicing in the park, but both denied making any such statements about getting them out of town.

Joe Engel, owner of the Lookouts, said he received an anonymous phone call on Thursday night, telling him to "get those niggers out of town right away."[86] All seven of the players, for their own safety, were sent to the Senators' home field in Orlando, but returned shortly thereafter. The seven were Juan Delis, Jose Valdivielso, Roberto Zapata, Rolando Bacardi, Camilo Pascual, Evelio Hernandez, and Humberto Bernal.

It made no difference to the caller who was what; he just saw dark-skinned players and assumed they were all Negro. Pascual and Valdivielso were both of Spanish heritage. Zapata was actually an Indian from Barranquilla, Colombia, in the Colombian Professional Baseball League. Delis, Bacardi, Hernandez, and Bernal all identified as Black. Saying "there's no point in provoking any trouble," Pete Appleton, manager of the Charlotte Hornets, another Senators-affiliated team who actually owned the seven players in question, sent two of them to the Class-D league in Big Springs, Texas, while the other five stayed and worked out with the Orlando Senators of the Florida State League.[87]

The Senators were not going to cave in to any pressures from "anonymous sources." When asked if the Nats would train their Negro players in Winter Garden in the future, executive vice-president Calvin Griffith, Clark's nephew, stated, "There is no reason why we shouldn't—if we get any prospects who look good. We have a ten-year contract with Winter Garden and we asked the city officials cold turkey if they wanted us to continue. They assured us they did and that nobody would be barred in the future. They said it was all a misunderstanding and that an irresponsible party had made the threats on his own."[88]

The situation was still tense, however. The Cubans involved refused to go back to the Winter Garden training site and preferred to stay in Orlando, "We don't bother nobody," said one player through an interpreter. "All we want to do is play ball. There has never been an incident where one of us has stepped out of line. I think that as a group we're the best behaved in the game. We want only the same kind of treatment that we give the visiting players in our winter league in Cuba. That isn't too much to ask."[89]

The situation was made all the more poignant by the fact that Clark Griffith had promises to keep. Griffith, anxious to get the whole integration thing out of the way, vowed to break the Senators' color barrier once he found "the right boy." He had signed Angel Scull, Juan Delis and Carlos Paula from Cambria and was hopeful one of them would play in the Nats' outfield that year. "Maybe the right one has come along," said Griffith after watching Paula hit and Scull field. "I always said we'd have a colored boy on this ball team when the right one showed up. They've been saying I didn't want any Negro players on my team and I've been saying that I do. I've been telling them when they showed me the colored boy who could make it, I'd have him in a Washington uniform."[90]

In the end, the investigation turned up nothing. It seemed it was the actions of one unreasonable person. Spring training went on as usual, and the Senators prepared for another campaign.

There would be another change in the Senators' outfield for 1954. Gil Coan, who sustained a fractured skull, a chipped wrist, and a broken ankle in 1953, never seemed to live up to the potential he showed in Chattanooga, where he hit .372 with 16 homers and 201 hits in 1945. Griffith and his managers kept him going along for eight years, and they must have felt their investment was not paying off. Coan was sold to the newly minted Baltimore Orioles for veteran outfielder/first baseman Roy Sievers.

Sievers, who was voted the first American League Rookie of the Year in 1949, was similar to Coan in many ways. Sievers hit .309 with 19 homers and 106 hits for Springfield in 1948 and was a sure-handed outfielder but also prone to injury. After hitting .306 with 16 homers and 222 total bases in 1949, Sievers slumped badly in 1950. By midseason in 1951, he was sent down to the Texas League for more seasoning, where he suffered a severely dislocated shoulder. He dislocated it again in spring training of 1952, underwent an experimental surgery, and limped back to hit .270 in 92 games in 1953. "When I come to the Senators in '54, I asked Bucky Harris, my manager, where'm I gonna play? I told him I still couldn't throw too good so's I couldn't play the outfield. He just said, 'You get rid of the ball fast as you can. I need your bat in the lineup.' So, he put me in left field. I would just kinda loop the ball to the shortstop best as I could."[91]

Roy Sievers played 133 games in left field and 8 games at first base. He had one of his best years at the plate, hitting 24 home runs and besting Zeke Bonura's franchise-record 22 homers. Sievers became a major gate attraction for the Senators for the rest of the decade.[92]

"That's my boy!" exclaimed Joe Cambria when he was asked about his new "can't miss" phenom. Gonzalo "Cholly" Naranjo was only 16 years old when Cambria first saw him. As he explained, "I was still in school when I was chosen to play in Mexico for my country in the Amateur World Series. Joe first see me there and he sign me the next year."[93]

Signed by Cambria in 1952, Naranjo was assigned to the Chattanooga Lookouts and then to Richmond, where he went 6–6 with a 3.26 ERA in his first year of professional baseball. In the spring of 1953, he appeared in several exhibition games. Once, he held the Pittsburgh Pirates, then owned by Branch Rickey, to seven hits and struck out seven to beat the Bucs, 4–1. As Cambria explained: "Naranjo will make them forget about Fornieles [in Washington]. Before the season is over, he's going up to the Washington club. The Pirates would grab him right now for $50,000."[94]

Joe Cambria had Naranjo on his 1953 Havana Cubans team, then brought him back to Chattanooga in 1954. True to his word, he brought Naranjo up to spring training that year. The journalists were having a hard time pronouncing his name and asked him if he had a nickname. He answered, "Cholly," a diminutive form of the Cuban word "Cholito," describing the shape of his head.

Cholly Naranjo did well in pre-season games, beating the Yankees once, and was slated to make the team. His claim to fame, however, rests in the fact that he played catch with President Eisenhower. On Opening Day, the Chief Executive traditionally throws out the first pitch of the season. In 1954, Eisenhower threw a high hard one that sailed past everyone. One of the photographers asked if he would be kind enough to do it again. He spotted Naranjo by the Nats' dugout and motioned him over, whereupon he threw a perfect strike to him. He then motioned for Naranjo to toss it back, whereupon a quick game of catch ensued.

Because of his English language skills, Cholly Naranjo was asked by manager Harris to go sit with the President and protect him from errant foul balls.

Naranjo spent the next 30 minutes having a very pleasant conversation with the president. As Naranjo explained in an interview, "The President had a very regular conversation with me. It was about my life, my parents, you know, family stuff. He never talked [to me] about baseball, just about my father and where he went to school. After about a half-hour, he told me, 'I won't need any more protection, I think I'll be all right.'"[95]

Cholly Naranjo went back to the bench and was told after the game to pack up his things, he was being sent to Chattanooga. But! Not before he was put on a train for New York City, where he appeared on the television show *I've Got a Secret* that evening. Naranjo remained with the Senators' organization until he was sold to Pittsburgh in 1956. He had his one good year in the sun with Pittsburgh in 1956, pitching in 17 games and going 1–2. In 34⅓ innings, he gave up 39 hits and seven homers, struck out 26 and walked 17, for a 4.46 ERA. Naranjo was with both Pittsburgh and Cincinnati between 1955 and 1961, and continued to play winter ball in Cuba, where he was greeted as a true major leaguer for the rest of his career.

Clark Griffith's directive to "find the right boy" notwithstanding, the specter of racial prejudice still reared its ugly head within the Senators' organization. Maybe it was because Cambria broke the color barrier with the Florida International League in 1952, or maybe because he was going to bring Black Cubans to Senators spring training in 1954: no can be really sure what prompted the following incident.

In 2017, a huge exhibit entitled *Chasing Dreams: Baseball and Becoming American* was organized by the National Museum of American Jewish History in Philadelphia. The exhibit featured writings, memorabilia, pictures, and correspondence related to how America's immigrant population—Irish, Italian, Jewish, Latin, Asian, and others—used baseball to assimilate into American life.

Researchers of the exhibit unearthed correspondence typed on official Washington Senators letterhead, between farm director Ossie Bluege, Chattanooga Lookouts president Joe Engle, Joe Cambria, and Mrs. Davis Sandlin, assistant to Joe Engle. The letter, written in December 1952, concerned a young pitcher, Raul Lago, signed by Cambria to the Charlotte Hornets, who was applying to attend the Winter Garden players baseball camp. The text of the first letter is as follows:

> December 9, 1953
>
> Mrs. Davis Sandlin
> Chattanooga Baseball Club
> Chattanooga, Tenn.

Dear Mrs. Sandlin:

I am enclosing an application card in behalf of a Cuban player…. RAUL (PUIG) LAGO, whom Cambria signed to a Charlotte contract with the understanding that he would be given the opportunity of attending the School.

I don't know whether he is colored or not, have written Joe that in the event he is that we cannot have [him] in the school and for him to govern himself accordingly….

So, as a matter of record, please file this with your other applications. If he's white all go and well, if not, he stays home….

> Regards,
> Ossie Bluege

There were handwritten notes on the bottom of the letter, this one among them: "If any colored blood want to know now."

On December 15, Joe Engel himself wrote to the Senators' Cambria (who was also referenced in the letter), saying, "Dear Joe: If Raul Lago has any colored blood at all, I do not want him to come to Winter Haven, for the Baseball School or for spring training. Sincerely, Joe."

Typed in capital letters below Engel's signature: "NO COLORED BLOOD AT ALL, POSITIVELY WHITE, AS SNOWBALL."

Handwritten below that is what seems likely to have been Cambria's response: "Dear Joe—Snow White. White OK. No Worry. Joe."

Three days letter, Ossie Bluege sent an inter-organization memo to Mrs. Sandlin of the Chattanooga team.

Subject: Winter Garden School Player Raul (Puig) Lago

Dear Mrs. Sandlin,

I just heard from Cambria in regard to the above player and he informs me that the boy is "Snow White." So, all is in order for him to make his appearance.

Ossie[96]

Ossie Bluege was part of the Senators' family, having served the organization as a player, coach, and manager since 1922. As such, he was extremely loyal to Mr. Griffith; however, research cannot prove, and no one can ascertain with any certainty, that Bluege was instructed by or acting at the behest of Mr. Griffith in this correspondence. Bluege may have been being cautious. He had been in Winter Garden for years and knew about the living conditions and racial tenor of the city. If Lago was a Black man, Bluege knew what he would face. He may have been sincerely concerned for Lago's safety. It would be unfair to castigate Bluege and paint him with the sole racist brush. Bluege could have just been stating the obviousness of the times; if he is Black, he stays home. It was, after all, as deep into the Jim Crow South as one could get.

Two of Bluege's daughters, Wilor Bluege and Lynn Bluege-Rust, wrote a biography of their father. They were very disconcerted when the letters were brought to light during the exhibit.

"I've seen the letter and I was shocked," said Lynn Bluege-Rust, his daughter, from Grand Rapids, Minn. "All I can say is he never spoke ill of Cuban or black players, and they were often guests in our home."[97]

All of the furor about the letters may have been much ado about nothing. Newspaper records indicate Lago was a limited service pitcher who played in the Sooner State League in 1951. In 1952, he played two months with the Class C Vernon Dusters of the Longhorn League and was released outright on May 27.[98] There are no further newspaper records of him playing after 1952, and there is no data on Lago at Baseball-Reference.com. It was just a product of the times.

Cambria was, as always, very high on all of his Cuban players, Scull and Paula in particular. In a 1954 interview with Senators radio announcer Bob Wolff, he was effusive and down to earth about them both.

BOB WOLFF: "Well, I'm talking now with Joe Cambria, scout for the Nationals. Joe, I hear you have a few players to bring to the club. What can you tell us about Angel Scull?"

JOE CAMBRIA: "Hustler! Full of pep and colorful in the game!"

BW: "Will Scull make the team?"

JC: "Well, he has everything to make it with. All he has to do is play! That's it!"

BW: "So you think he will?"

JC: "Yes sir, he ought to make a splendid lead-off man for Griff."

BW: "Next to Scull, who would you rate as the next most prominent player?"

JC: "I would say Paula. Big outfielder, 6'2". Lots of power, runs like the wind and a great arm. Just a question, he may have to go to AAA to get his establishment at the plate a little better. But Bucky's got his eye on him and I understand they're gonna take him to St. Petersburg, so that's a good sign."[99]

Bucky Harris had famously little patience with the Cuban ballplayers, however, and with Joe Cambria. He still hated what he termed their "monkey talk" on the base paths, and he had little tolerance with their tardiness in reporting to camp. "I never know where Cambria's Cubans are until I see them in uniform. Reporting dates mean nothing to those fellows. All they have to do is claim passport troubles and who can argue with them? When they feel like coming to camp there is never any passport trouble"[100]

With Cambria, he grew more and more skeptical each day. Talking about Angel Scull, he said, "I'd be more impressed if Scull were not Cambria's ball player. He goes off the deep end on every Cuban he sends up to us. The fact remains that down through the years since Cambria has been shipping us Latins, Connie Marrero is the only one who has made good."[101]

He was just as skeptical about Carlos Paula. "Cambria was telling me last fall about his other Cuban outfielder named Carlos Paula. He was telling me about Paula's size, his 6–3 and 195 pounds and how he could gallop and go get the ball and how he couldn't miss being a great major leaguer. I had only one question for Joe. How come if Paula is such a wizz-bang, he hit only .309 with Paris, Texas, in the Big State League last year. He didn't have a handy answer."[102]

Though .309 would be a respectable batting average in any league, for Harris it was not enough. One can only

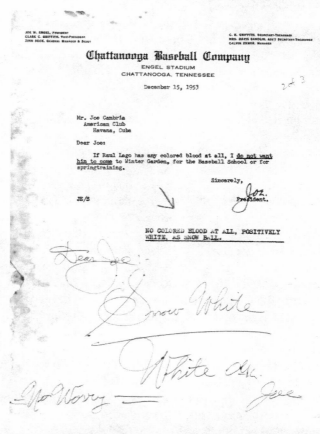

The notorious "white as a snowball" letter from Joe Engle, president of the Chattanooga Lookouts, to Joe Cambria concerning the racial identity of Raul Lago, a dark-skinned Cuban pitcher. The Senators were still apprehensive about signing a Negro player in 1953, although they would relent the following year (private collection of LTC (R) Dave Grob).

believe that because of Harris' prejudices, Paula should have been hitting .399, which would have been more than Mickey Mantle ever did.

Harris had another "embarrassment of riches" with which to deal. Besides Paula and Scull, Cambria had also sent him a sterling young first baseman, Julio Becquer.

Becquer (pronounced bek-CAIR and turned into "Baker" by the press) was wowing Harris not only with his glove work but also with his prodigious hitting prowess. As Harris observed, "He's a definite pull hitter and wants to hit everything to rightfield, but I have no objections to pull hitters."[103]

Becquer, however, was laboring under a misconception. There was no way anyone was going to unseat Mickey Vernon, the reigning batting champion, from his customary position at first base. Becquer was a rookie and unproven. At best, he could have been kept around for bench strength or possibly to take over if Vernon ever decided to hang them up. Plus, there was also Roy Sievers, who was very adept at covering that bag as well.

What was he going to do with Delis, Paula, Becquer and Scull? Bucky Harris had a double-whammy with which to contend: not only were they Cuban with limited English-speaking skills, they were also Black. They were not light-skinned or tan with straight or wavy hair. These were *mulatto* Black Cubans who identified as such. The "Castilian Identity" would not work in their cases. Cambria had told the press they were Black, and everyone knew it.

Bucky Harris probably did not like it.

Harris had 46 "Whiz Kids" in the 1954 camp, most of them 25 years old or younger, and he needed someone in right field. At first, he seemed to set on playing Jim Busby in center and Tom Umphlett in left, letting Scull and Paula battle it out for right field. Because of his outfield hustle and his timely hitting, Scull was named Charleston's Most Valuable Player in 1953.

Scull's quest to fill the coveted right field slot was aided by the ringing endorsement he received from Griffith's nephew and assistant director of the Nats' farm system, Sherrard "Sherry" Robertson. After a scouting trip to see the Nats' recent signees and after observing Schull, he had this to report. "Scull could be our right fielder," said Robertson to manager Harris. "He's showing the experience he gained with Charleston W. Va., in the Triple A American Association, and if we ever get a Busby-Umphlett-Scull outfield together, nothing in either league can match the speed of that trio. Scull is the fastest thing in shoes. He beats Minnie Minoso of the White Sox in all those match races in Havana." Shirley Povich asked Robertson if Scull wasn't a bit too small at 5'8" and 162 pounds. "I know that," said Robertson, "but Scull isn't small either. I'd call him a big little man. He has arms like a washerwoman, and he can whip that bat like a 180-pounder. He won't knock down any fences but the outfielders will have to respect him for the distances he can get."[104]

However, as the spring season went along, Roy Sievers started to show his 1949 Rookie of the Year brilliance and won the starting left field spot. Busby was moved to center, and Umphlett was moved to right. Harris told the papers:

> Sievers tones up our attack and so far I haven't seen where he's going to damage us too much defensively. His arm will get stronger as he plays more and even though he can't throw overhand I don't believe there will be too many occasions when we'll be hurt by having him in the outfield. There will be times, of course, when the opposition will have a runner on third who will score as the result of a long fly to Sievers. But how many times do you see a runner

thrown out at the plate on a long fly. Not many. On the other hand, Scull has a good arm, he's speedy and he'll give us maneuverability. When we're leading in the late innings he'll replace Sievers. I want to have Scull around, too, as a pinch runner.[105]

By the end of the spring season, as they broke camp in early April, the reality of the situation was completely different. Delis, who was embroiled in a lawsuit in Havana, never reported for spring training. He and Julio Becquer were sold to the Havana Sugar Kings for a modest amount of money. Scull, on the other hand, cost Bobby Maduro $20,000. Carlos Paula was sent down to the Charlotte Hornets.

In the official spring training roster posted in February of 1954 by Calvin Griffith, these Cubans were listed: Conrado Marrero, Gonzalo Naranjo, Camilo Pascual, Raul Sanchez, Julio Becquer, Yo-Yo Davalillo, Francisco Campos, Juan Delis, Carlos Paula, and Angel Scull.[106]

When the official team roster was published in April, only Marrero and Pascual made the team. There would be no Black ballplayer coming to Washington in April.

However, when Charlotte's season ended, Paula, along with teammate Jim Lemon, would be September call-ups. Lemon, who eventually teamed up with Sievers to become a solid 1–2 punch in the middle of the lineup, told the Washington scribes, "If that Paula ever gets hot, Washington fans are going to love him. He's big, fast and strong. He has a wonderful arm too."[107]

So, seven years after Jackie Robinson broke the color line in Major League baseball, Carlos Paula was penciled in the lineup for a doubleheader on September 6, 1954, making him the first Black man to play for the Washington Senators. In his nine September games, Paula would have 24 at-bats with four hits, two RBI, two walks and four strikeouts for a .167 batting average. Paula would play two more years with the Nats, until he was sent down to Miami in the International League in 1956.

Meanwhile, down in Florida, Cambria made this prediction: "Higher class ball is coming. It is just a matter of time. And I am sure that will be the solution to [the] attendance troubles. There is no question but that you will have higher ball. Havana is going fine in

Breaking the color barrier. Carlos Paula, Washington's first black ballplayer. Paula debuted in September of 1954, seven years after Jackie Robinson's historic appearance in 1947 (National Baseball Hall of Fame Library, Cooperstown, New York).

the Triple A International League, and Miami should be up there with Havana. Maybe the jump will come next year."[108]

It seemed that Cambria had been preaching this gospel since the Florida International League began in 1946. Due to his successes with his Havana Cubans, he was able to raise the FIL from a Class-C to a Class-B rating in 1949. But there it would stall. The Cubans kept winning, and Cambria kept going to the winter meetings, begging and cajoling the league officers to raise the league up to an A league rating.

Because of those many championships, the 1954 season opened with the Cubans, now owned by the much-beloved Bobby Maduro, elevated to the AAA International League. Joe Cambria was beside himself with joy, of course, and told anyone who would listen that the FIL would be raised up shortly.

Such would not be the case. The attendance problems mentioned by Cambria in the quote above alluded to the fact that the FIL had shrunk to six teams in 1953 and attendance, which had lagged all over the minor leagues, was down to disappointing levels. The 1953 season was the first season in which at least one FIL team failed to draw at least 100,000 fans. Havana, with most of its stars playing for the Washington Senators or their affiliated minor league teams, drew only 20,000 fans for the season.[109]

The FIL tried to cull some teams from the Florida State League in an effort to keep the FIL afloat. Clark Griffith agreed to sign a working agreement with the Orlando team in the Florida State League, and Cambria said he would try to get a franchise in Ft. Lauderdale if that team moved back to its original home in Miami Beach.[110]

Miami and Tampa folded on May 5, leaving only six teams. Attendance dropped so badly that the league ceased operations on July 27, 1954, and the FIL, the brainchild of Joe Cambria and Merito Acosta, faded into obscurity.

The 1954 Senators

Bucky Harris showed the baseball world that he was a winning manager. He had astounded the critics as a 27-year-old player/manager, piloting the 1924 Washington Senators to their first World Series championship and nearly repeating it in 1925. He would again win a World Series ring with the 1947 New York Yankees. He managed the Nats on three separate occasions, from 1924 to 1928, 1935 to 1942, and 1950 through 1954.

The 1954 season would, however, be Harris's swan song with the Senators. The team posted a 66–68 record, putting them in sixth place in the American League. It would be his fifth straight year in the second division, and Clark Griffith knew it was time for a change. Bucky Harris was let go at the end of the season and replaced by former Brooklyn Dodgers manager Charles "Chuck" Dressen.

The 1954 Senators worked hard but always seemed to come up short. The good news was Roy Sievers' emergence as the team's first legitimate power hitter. Sievers blasted 24 homers that year, 14 on the road and eight at home. He seemed to feast on the White Sox in particular, hitting five homers in friendly Comiskey Park (352 feet down the left-field line) and hitting three more against them at Griffith Stadium (388 feet down the left-field line). He had 102 RBI but a dismal .232 batting average, one of the lowest in his career.

Bucky Harris got good hitting from Mickey Vernon (.290, 97 RBI), Eddie Yost (.256, 101 runs). and Jim Busby (.298, 83 runs). He also got respectable hitting from reserve players Tom Wright, Jerry Snyder, Clyde Vollmer, ancient Johnny Pesky, and newcomer

Jim Lemon. However, the team came in seventh in the league in batting average (.246), seventh in homers (81), seventh in hits (1,292) and fifth in runs scored per game (4.08).

The pitching staff came up a little short again in 1954. Staff aces Bob Porterfield (13–15, 3.32 ERA) and Mickey McDermott (7–15, 3.44 ERA) struggled to keep their strikeouts more than their walks; Porterfield succeeded. Johnny Schmitz (11–8), Chuck Stobbs (11–11) and Dean Stone (12–10) all posted solid records and respectable ERAs. The staff was fifth in the league in ERA (3.84) third-highest in hits allowed (1,396), third-highest in runs allowed (680), and second-fewest in home runs allowed (79).

The other good news came in the form of another Joe Cambria acquisition, Camilo *"Patato Pequeño"* (known colloquially as "Little Shorty") Pascual. In a phone interview, Camilo Pascual, in his own words, told the story of Joe Cambria and his good fortune.

> He was a beautiful man, beautiful guy. You know what, I got something to tell you about Joe Cambria. He was the guy that give me the opportunity, he give me two opportunities! In 1951, I sign with Joe Cambria and he send me to Big Spring, Texas. I was only 17 years old. In those days, those leagues were full of veteran players. I was real young and I was not strong enough. My fast ball was real weak. He give me the opportunity but they release me. So, I went back to Cuba in 1951 and he signed me again in 1952 and he give me the opportunity to pitch in a league which at that time was a very strong league, the Havana Cubans. In those days they played in the Class B league in Florida International League. He give me a break and sign me again and he give me a chance and that was all that I was needing. I was doing very well at that time and everything was great. I play two years for Havana, 1952 and 1953. Then the Senators invited me to spring training in 1954 and I was very lucky, I made the team. And I stayed with the team until 1960, we moved to Minnesota. In 1961 until 1966. I come back to the Senators in 1967-8-9. Then it was down the hill from there!![111]

Younger brother of Carlos, who pitched for the Nats in 1950, Camilo Pascual became the workhorse in the bullpen. In 119⅓ innings in 48 games, primarily in relief, he posted a 4–7 record, a 4.22 ERA, 60 strikeouts and 61 walks. He started four games and finished 27. His devastating three-quarter sidearm curve ball, taught to him by Cuban legend Dolf Luque, was described by Roy Sievers as "the nastiest curve I ever saw." Camilo Pascual would become an ace of both the Senators' and the Twins' pitching staffs.

Joe Cambria had only three Cubans on the team that year: Connie Marrero, Camilo Pascual, and Carlos Paula. Paula was the only Black man on the team, and his was a grudging nine-game cup of coffee in September.

There would be major changes in store for 1955.

CHAPTER 8

1955–1959:
The Making of a Champion

"Keep it close, boys, and I'll think of something," was one of Chuck Dressen's favorite sayings.

Labeled as brash, arrogant, and cocky by the prevailing press, Chuck Dressen was a five-foot, six-inch powder keg of energy. Dressen was a disciple of Leo "The Lip" Durocher, himself a product of the spikes high, no-holds-barred old school of baseball. At times affable, at times truculent, Dressen was not shy about using profanity for full effect, to umpires and his players alike.

Like Durocher, Dressen loved to talk, mostly about himself and baseball. Whereas the colorful Casey Stengel, with his brand of "Stengeleese," could wax poetic for hours at a time and in the end say practically nothing, Dressen used the media to show off his encyclopedic and statistical knowledge of the game. His knowledge of situational baseball became legendary. He had been blessed with supremely talented teams, especially with the pennant-winning Brooklyn Dodgers of the early 1950s, so his knowledge and expertise seemed to flow naturally.

Such would not be the case in Washington.

In late December of 1954, Dressen inherited pretty much the same club that Bucky Harris left, and he immediately announced that the Senators would end the 1955 season in the first division.

Unfortunately, he would be wrong. "We don't have a bad ball team," said Dressen to the Washington press. "We played 50 games that were decided by a one-run margin, and we won only 20 of them. That sort of indicates that with a little bit of application here and there and perhaps a few corrective measures, we can win a lot more of these one-run affairs next season."[1]

The "corrective measures" to which he alluded would, of course, be trades, and all of the trades were now being handled by Clark Griffith's adopted nephew, Calvin Griffith.

Calvin Griffith was born Calvin Robertson in Quebec, Canada in 1911. His father, James Robertson, was a minor leaguer who unfortunately succumbed to alcoholism, leaving a wife and seven children. James's sister, Addie, married a brash young ballplayer named Clark Griffith. Upon the news of James's death, Addie and Clark visited the family, agreed to take Calvin (age 11) and his sister Thelma (age seven) to live with them, and raised them as their own. Although never formally adopted, Thelma and Calvin both changed their names to Griffith.

Calvin was almost immediately pressed into service as a bat boy for the championship Senators teams of 1924 and 1925. After military school and college, Calvin went into the family business. Between 1935 and 1941, Calvin learned the business with the Chattanooga Lookouts and the Charlotte Hornets. In 1941, he was given a job in the Senators' front office. For the next 14 years, he took over more and more of his uncle's responsibilities until he was named vice-president of the team, eventually taking over the team in 1955.[2]

When it came to trading, Calvin despised being "stampeded," as he called it. "We had plenty of opportunities to make trades but we're not so desperate that we have to make any of those 'Baltimore' deals. We won't give up one of our solid players unless we get one in return; these first division clubs try to overwhelm you with volume."[3]

The "Baltimore deal" which he mentioned was a 17-player mega-swap between the Yankees and the Orioles in November of 1954. The Yanks gave up 10 players for seven Orioles.

The Indians, Yankees, White Sox, and Red Sox all made offers for Eddie Yost, Pete Runnels and Jim Busby. Griffith said:

> All they offered us were numbers. It was the same old story of trying to smear a lot of their old-timers and unproven rookies on a second-division club and get a good ball player in return. We'd rather gamble on some of our own rookies and keep our solid players. The Indians made a pitch for all three of those players and when I mentioned Doby, Avila and Rosen, they swooned. They expect you to give up a good player and take a chance on their rejects. It was a waste of time talking.[4]

Calvin Griffith, however, was not above trying the same tactics with other second division clubs as well. At one time during the winter, he tried to trade for the speedy Cuban outfield phenom, Victor Pellot Power, by offering the Kansas City A's 44-year-old Connie Marrero, 2–9 reliever Spec Shea, and backup catcher Joe Tipton. Obviously, that deal did not make it.

If Calvin Griffith was going to be so recalcitrant about talent acquisition, he would have to rely heavily on his scouts in-house to supply him with better arms, legs, and bats.

Whereas Bucky Harris had been openly contemptuous about Cambria and his dark Cubans, Dressen had a much more conciliatory tone. He had piloted the Dodgers with the likes of Jackie Robinson, Roy Campanella, Sandy Amoros, Don Newcombe, and Joe Black, so he was well aware of the prowess of the Black ballplayers. He was also not averse to the Cuban players, who by now had learned enough English to be fairly conversant and understood. He would look at Cambria's prospects but was looking for more quality and seasoning.

For the 1955 season, Chuck Dressen kept the perennial Connie Marrero and newbie Camilo Pascual, who had proven themselves in 1954 to be adequate relievers. He also brought in three of Joe Cambria's Black Cubans, Juan Delis, Carlos Paula and Julio Becquer, who had showed great potential before being unceremoniously demoted to the minors by Harris.

Cambria also brought up several new Cubans who would go on to have a major impact on the team.

Most important would be Pedro Ramos. Ramos was signed by Cambria as a 17-year-old. As Ramos explained in an interview, "I first meet Joe in 1952–53. I was just a kid. I was throwing batting practice for some teams in Cuba and he saw me. Then he go to my home town and that's where he sign me."

Pedro Ramos was pitching for the Corojo Village club in his Pinal Del Rio provincial *Liga Libre* (Free League), and Joe Cambria got his father's permission to sign him.

> He was a very nice guy, I believe he was the first guy to put Cubans in the U.S. The first year 1953 I go to Morristown, Tennessee. I feel safe there. I don't speak English at all, I just wanted to play baseball, so I adjust very well to that little town. I have no problems at all. So the second year I go back to Morristown, but Morristown went out of the league, so then they send me to Kingsport [TN], which was in the same league. Then the whole league fell apart, so they send me to Hagerstown [MD], class B. and I completed my second year there. And the next year, Washington send me a contract to Charlotte NC, class A, with an invitation to go to spring training in Orlando FL, and then I made the team.[5]

Pedro Ramos made the parent club in 1955. Although he had a marked proclivity for giving up the long ball, he and Camilo Pascual would become the two most durable pitchers on the team, averaging approximately 1,050 innings pitched in their Senators years in Washington.

Jose Valdivielso was another of Joe Cambria's juvenile signees. A friend and teammate of Pedro Ramos on the Charlotte Hornets, 16-year-old Valdivielso was playing for the *Pueblo Nuevo* team in his home province of Matanzas. Cambria saw him playing in the junior baseball championship in Havana in 1951 and drove to his home, 90 miles away, to get his mother's permission to sign a Senators contract. Valdivielso would play second base, shortstop and third base in the 1955 and 1956 seasons, was sent down to the minors to improve his hitting, and returned to the team from 1959 through 1961 in Minnesota.[6]

Vibert "Webbo" Clarke was a 27-year-old Panamanian signed by Cambria and sent to training camp in 1955. Clarke had played three years with the Cleveland Buckeyes of the Negro Leagues before getting his shot with the Senators. He tried hard but just could not cut it in the big leagues. He appeared in seven games for the Nats, starting two games and finishing five. He was 0–0 with a 4.64 ERA in 21⅓ innings. He gave up 17 hits, 11 runs, and 14 walks, with nine strikeouts. He was sent back to Charlotte and stayed in the minors until 1957.

Vincente Gonzales was a Mexican League standout but, unfortunately, a Major League fall-out for the Nats. Another of Cambria's "rookie" acquisitions, Gonzales spent 1951 through 1954 playing for Juarez and the Mexico City Reds. He pitched in exactly one game for the Senators, the second game of the season, against the Yankees. Losing 13–1, Gonzales was called in to mop up in the seventh inning. In his two innings, he faced 15 batters, gave up six hits, six runs, and three walks, and managed to strike out just one batter. Gonzales and his astounding 27.00 ERA were quickly ticketed back to Juarez. He remained in the Mexican leagues until 1969.

Julio Becquer should be mentioned here in a bit more detail. He was a solid 5'11" and 180 pounds, with a good pop in his bat. Cambria signed him as a free agent when he saw him playing for a road construction company team in Havana. Becquer was first sent by Cambria to play for Drummondville in the Canadian Provincial League. He felt that Becquer, who was Black, would have an easier time acclimating to baseball life by playing in Canada. In 1953, Becquer played with Cambria's Havana Cubans, and again in 1954 when they became the Sugar Kings. He was invited to training camp in 1954 and did not make the team, but was called up in late 1955 for a nice 10-game cup of coffee. He returned to the club and played between 1957 to 1960, then was taken by the Los Angeles Angels in the expansion draft. A natural left-hander, Becquer played primarily first base and was used extensively as a pinch-hitter from 1957 through 1960. He is forever remembered in Minnesota for his pinch-hit, walk-off grand slam on the 4th of July in 1961 off Warren Hacker of the White Sox.[7]

Alex Crespo was a beneficiary of Cambria's philosophy, which might be described as "Young? Old? Doesn't matter! Can he play?" Crespo debuted in the Cuban winter leagues in 1939–1940, where he led his team in RBI and hits. His first trip to the States was with the New York Cubans in 1940. In 1941, he left for the Mexican leagues, where he became a perennial standout at the plate and on the field. He continued to shuttle back and forth between the U.S., Mexico, Venezuela, and Cuba throughout his 19-year career.

The 39-year-old Crespo was finally convinced by Cambria to come to Washington for a tryout in 1955. In his own words, Crespo explained:

> I play with the New York Cubans in 1940 and 1945. I no like much, I get homesick. Besides, no money. Joe Cambria keep after me to come to the states. He say come here, they pay big money. They no pay big money! I get $1,000 a week playing in Venezuela and can play all year round. [I come to the States] because I getting old now. I no like the long bus rides in Mexican league. I 39 years old. No good for 24–30 hours riding bus over mountains. So I decide, okey I try it here for awhile. Cambria wrong about money, but I try anyway. I got wife, 4 kids in Havana, and remember, I 39 years old![8]

Crespo saw action with the Senators in several exhibition and spring training games; however, he was cut by Dressen when the team broke camp to go north. He was sent down to Charlotte, where he remained until he hung up his spikes for good.

Things change. Maybe not quickly, but they change.

By 1955, Joe Cambria had become an anachronism in the Caribbean. The *loco americano* in the guayabera shirt was dealing with a new mindset that did not play to his advantage. "His Island" was now literally crawling with big league scouts, looking for the best Cuban and Negro players they could find. The Dodgers, Cincinnati Reds, Pittsburgh Pirates, and the New York Giants in particular were actively seeking new blood. Howie Haak, protégé of Branch Rickey, donned his own guayabera shirt and practically owned the Dominican Republic, beating out Cambria for many players during that time. He famously recommended that Rickey, then president of the Pittsburgh Pirates, sign a young Roberto Clemente from the Dodgers organization in 1954.

Gone were the days where Cambria could wave a $100 bill under a youngster's nose and sign him for nearly nothing. Most of the good players were, by now, well seasoned by many years playing in the Cuban winter leagues or in the Mexican leagues. Ever since the days of Jorge Pasquel's outlaw Mexican League in the late–1940s, the boys of the 1950s had been well aware of what kind of salaries players were making in the U.S., and they certainly were not going to settle for just a "C-Note" as bonus money.

"Papa Joe" and "Uncle Clark" would have to delve a little deeper into the old wallet, and Cambria would have to go the extra mile to find new, if not somewhat gullible talent. With so many scouts in Cuba during the mid–1950s, Cambria had to search for talent in many different places. The older, established players in the Cuban winter leagues wanted too much money, so he started raiding the juvenile leagues. It was from there that he signed Pedro Ramos, Camilo Pascual, and Jose Valdivielso when they were teenagers. He searched the Mexican, Venezuelan, and Dominican leagues. He had "bird dogs" working for him on two continents.

In one instance, he signed Leonardo Umberbatch and Humberto Rosales to contracts to play for the Hagerstown Packets. He found the two young infielders playing in the Panama Canal Zone league. He, of course, touted them as more "can't miss" prospects. Unfortunately, they did not play a day in Major League ball.

Always on the prowl for the next big thing, Cambria continued his trek across Central America. In July, he signed a working agreement with the Yucatan Lions of the Yucatan Provincial League to affiliate with the Senators organization in 1956. He promised to send them Max Garcia, a pitcher from the AA Chattanooga club.[9]

One of the biggest things to change was Major League Baseball's attitude towards winter league play in Cuba. At first, they expressed concern that constant play, especially with pitchers, would do more harm than good. However, after reviewing the results of year-round competition, they were convinced otherwise. They considered winter league play, especially with younger players, almost equivalent to an extra year's worth of experience. The National League, in particular, was the recipient of the successes of many of the new rookie players. Beginning in 1949, when the Rookie of the Year was awarded in both leagues, five of the first six recipients all cut their teeth playing winter ball in Cuba: Don Newcombe (1949), Sam Jethroe (1950), Joe Black (1952), Jim Gilliam (1953), and Wally Moon (1954). Both Newcombe and Black said they really learned how to pitch in the winter leagues.

It was by no means a coincidence that four prominent Rookies of the Year were Brooklyn Dodgers: Robinson, Newcombe, Gilliam and Black. Branch Rickey had been poking around in the Cuban leagues since the 1940s and was well aware of the talent that lay within. He finally got wise and hired the multi-lingual Al Campanis as a full-time Caribbean scout. Campanis had been scouting around the island since 1949. The handsome Campanis quickly learned the *patois* and the customs of the island, which endeared him to the native Cubans. Dodgers fans everywhere thank Campanis for signing Sandy Amoros out of the Cuban leagues in 1952. Amoros' famous running catch of Yogi Berra's long drive to left field in the 1955 World Series preserved a 2–0 Dodgers lead and led to them eventually winning Game Seven of the 1955 Fall Classic.

(Newcombe, Robinson, Gilliam and Black were rookies only in the sense they were in their rookie season of Major League ball. All had been well seasoned by years of play in the Negro Leagues and the Cuban winter leagues before their foray into the majors.)

In December of 1954, the Cincinnati Redlegs, the team from whom Cambria famously stole four players in 1940, went all-in and signed a working agreement with Cambria's old team, the Havana Cubans. Gabe Paul, General Manager of the Redlegs, was highly optimistic about this new venture. He stated: "We entered into the working agreement with Havana because we felt for the first time in quite a few years that our farm system had developed to the point where we can work satisfactorily with a Triple-A club."[10]

This was obviously good news for Cambria's rival, Bobby Maduro, and it put the Redlegs onto the fast track of corralling Latin talent. For the remainder of the decade and well into the future, the Redlegs would mine the Caribbean basin for the best arms and bats they could find. These included Lou Cardenas, Pat Scantlebury, Vicente Amor, Danny Morejon and Orlando Pena, to name but a few.

The 1955 Senators

Cambria kept bringing in young Latin players throughout training camp. In the end, manager Dressen saw what he wanted to see. Dressen kept Julio Becquer, Webbo

Clarke, Juan Delis, Vince Gonzales, Camilo Pascual, Pedro Ramos, Jose Valdivielso and Carlos Paula. The "ancient one," Connie Marrero, passed his baseball mantle over to the 20-something youths on the team and quietly slipped back to the AAA Havana Sugar Kings to play out his life's drama. The Latin contingent made up 20 percent of the team and brought a new surge of hope and enjoyment to the long-suffering Washington fans.

Suffer they would, however. Despite the good hitting of Mickey Vernon (162 hits, 14 homers), Pete Runnels (143 hits), Roy Sievers (138 hits, 25 homers), and Carlos Paula (105 hits, six homers), not one of the pitchers on the team posted a winning record, the closest being Mickey McDermott with a 10–10 record. The Senators ended up in last place (53–101), behind the hapless Baltimore Orioles (57–97), in only their second year of existence. The team was seventh in team batting average (.248), hits, runs, and homers. The pitching staff was seventh in team ERA (4.62), second in hits allowed (1,450), and second in runs allowed (789). It is important to note that, with the left field fence still at 388 feet, the team surrendered only 99 total homers and only 45 at home.

One bright, shining ray of hope that twinkled in the firmament was the play of a young teenager named Harmon Killebrew from Payette, Idaho. Upon the incessant urging of Idaho State Senator Herman Welker, Clark Griffith dispatched Ossie Bluege to go see the boy play. Driving through a torrential rainstorm, Bluege and the young Killebrew sat in his car and talked until the storm passed. When the game started, Killebrew did not disappoint, clubbing a tremendous, 400+-foot homer out of the park. Killebrew made his debut with the Senators in 1954 in a limited capacity. As a "bonus baby," major league rules stated that he had to be put on the Senators' roster for two years rather than go to the minors for seasoning. It was obviously a bit much for a 17-year-old to fathom. Said Killebrew: "I had never even seen a major league stadium, and all of a sudden I am playing in them with and against major league players I had read about. So everything was strange."[11]

In 80 at-bats in 1955, Killebrew had 16 hits, four home runs, and 12 runs, but struck out a whopping 31 times for a .200 batting average. Obviously in need of more seasoning, Killebrew began his trek through the Nats' farm system until getting his chance to start at third base after the trade of Eddie Yost in the winter of 1958. Killebrew had tremendous years in 1959 (42 homers) and 1960 (31 homers) and would continue to murder the ball when the team moved to Minnesota in 1961 (46 homers), earning the nickname "Killer" for the rest of his career.

Down in Cuba, attitudes about Joe Cambria were changing. Although Jess Losada and others had been openly critical of Cambria and his scouting practices, others were more effusive with their praise for "Papa Joe." Cuco Conde, writing in the 1955 October edition of *Carteles* magazine, practically sent up Cambria for beatification with his article.

This article was translated by researcher Nicholas Sheets, who in 2020 was working on his doctorate in Spanish literary, cultural and linguistic studies. There is a marked difference between grammar and syntax in the English and Cuban languages that may seem odd to American ears and eyes.

Camilo Pascual, Pedro Ramos, Carlos Paula and José Valdivielso, with their brilliant performances in the American League, and now in contending for the Cuban League, have again put the name of the aged talent seeker, Joe Cambria, in the mouth of our fans. Throughout the years, since 1934 when he visited us for the first time, Cambria has been one of the most discussed persons of Cuban baseball, for reasons, precisely, of his work: looking for elemental youth for Washington and their subsidiaries.

Some have accused Cambria of "exploiting" our material for the benefit of the organization of [the] old Clark Griffith for whom he works and who, without any doubt, is one of his principal masterminds, even though here, in our environment, he passes as just another scout; but what is for certain is that for Griffith and his associates, he is much more than a scout. A man that has produced beneficial results to Washington and who is a slave to the friendship toward the aged Clark, demonstrated in more than one occasion. {Let's remember that five years ago, when Griffith was almost at a point of losing the presidency for Washington for not accounting for the majority of stocks. Under the hood, Cambria took out his, giving them over to his owner, and that's how the veteran of so many years could continue the fight in baseball, at the front of the club's destiny of the North American capital.}

According to our judgement, Cambria has been an extremely important factor in Cuban baseball for years. And year after year, he has maintained that rhythm of opening the doors to North American baseball to Creole baseball players.

Cuban baseball has seen great figures, who, if it hadn't been for Cambria, would never have come to figure in our professional contending, and much less in the Big Leagues. It suffices to mention a few names: Fermín Guerra, Roberto Ortiz, René Monteagudo, Gilberto Torres, Tomás De la Cruz, Jorge Comellas and Manolo Fortes. This group that abandoned La Habana in March of 1937, who surged months before in the amateur ranks, found in Cambria the man that opened to them the path that would later take them to stardom. In those days, no one here worried about the amateur players with class to jump to the professionals, reach for which, without hesitating, they accepted the contracts, some which were advantageous and others sometimes with reduced salaries; but it was the first step, and they had to take it.

Now we have the case of Pedro Ramos, Pascual, Paula and Valdivielso. The same story. No one saw in them any prospects. When "Patato" [Carlos] Pascual was praised, old Joe discovered the faculties of the smallest of the family [Camilo]. And he signed him. While two years ago it was debated over who was better between Humberto Fernández and Willie Miranda, in the press box he showed a contract and said: "The best within a few years I have signed here." He was referring to Joey Valdivielso.

Cambria, with his thousands of defects, has been a great help for Cuban baseball, even though some of our magnates don't esteem him as such; but it's sufficient to take a look at the values that they themselves have had in their hands since 1934, and will have to give to the old man the credit that some try to deny him. Here we are going to mention a few names of Cuban baseball players that have gone, and some who are still in the Major Leagues, taken by Joe Cambria: Fermín Guerra, Regino Otero, Tomás De la Cruz, Adrián Zabala, Roberto and Oliverio Ortiz, "Mulo" Morales, Roberto Estalella, René Monteagudo, Willie Miranda, Conrado Marrero, Gilberto Torres, Sandalío Consuegra, Angel Fleitas, Miguel Fornieles, the "Patato" [Carlos] and Camilo Pascual brothers, Witto Alomá, Limonar Martínez, Carlos Paula, José Antonio Zardón, Preston Gómez, Jorge Comellas, Luis Suárez, Enrique González, Joey Valdivielso, Raúl Sánchez, "Jiqui" Moreno, Juan Delís, and Pedro Ramos.

At the time of sentencing [as of this writing], if he has or [has not been] beneficial to Cuban baseball, it suffices to remember names ... and those who are still headlining. Four of the stars of the current contending [Cuban leagues] belong to this headliner [Cambria], who continues being producer of good material for our championships.[12]

The section in braces refers to a hostile takeover of the Senators that was attempted by John James Jachym (pronounced Yo-kum) in January of 1950. Griffith was able to fight off the takeover with the help of Cambria's 150 shares of stock, as well as those of the Richardson family, part of the original ownership group.[13]

This article and others like it were part of a positive sway of opinion in Cambria's favor that occurred throughout the late 1950s. The Cuban people and the baseball writers were beginning to lionize Cambria for all of the good players he had given the tremendous opportunity to play in Major League baseball. His unswerving loyalty to "The Pearl of the Antilles" was without question.

Clark Griffith was blessed with remarkable health well into his 70s. He drank very little but did smoke the occasional cigar. His only major surgical procedure was an appendectomy in 1929. However, his health started a precipitous nosedive once he turned 80. In December of 1950, he had a hernia operation and spent a month in bed. He collapsed twice during the 1951 season but bounced back both times.

In September of 1955, Griffith developed neuritis in his lower back to go along with his constant lumbago and was bedridden through September and October. On the 19th of October, he checked into Georgetown University Hospital "for complete rest" as prescribed by team doctor George Resta. In the afternoon of October 22, Griffith had a massive stomach hemorrhage. Placed on the critical list, he was given blood transfusions. Griffith seemed to rally and was getting progressively stronger but was still listed as critical. Dr. Resta remained guarded. On the 24th, he developed congestion in his right lung and was placed on oxygen. Again, he seemed to rally and was getting progressively better. He fell asleep around 7:30 p.m. on the 27th, suffered a sudden relapse around 8:00, and died around 8:40 p.m. that evening, about a week shy of his 86th birthday. He had spent 67 of those years in baseball.

Condolences poured in from presidents, congressmen, foreign dignitaries, movie stars, and of course, a plethora of baseball people. The viewing and the funeral were reported to be the largest gathering of baseball people since the passing of Babe Ruth in 1948.[14]

Clark Griffith holds the distinction of being the only man in major league history to serve as a player, manager, and owner for at least 20 years each. Above all else, he wanted to be the owner of a baseball team. He sold the family ranch, bought the Washington Senators, and achieved his dream. He was fortunate enough to win a World Series and three pennants in his lifetime. He remained passionately loyal to his team and the city of Washington for his whole life.

The Changing of the Guard

Calvin Griffith had been effectively running the ball club for the last two years of Clark's life. On November 1, 1955, Calvin was officially elected president of the Senators at age 43. Although vowing to the press that he would never leave the city, he had been secretly planning to move the franchise since 1954.

But in a show of solidarity, Calvin quickly announced, "we are not going to stand still." On November 8, he announced a bold nine-player deal with the Boston Red Sox. "Let's face it," said Griffith. "We don't have anything in our farm system of the caliber of the young fellows we are getting from the Red Sox, whose average age is 23, while we are giving up one 37-year-old first baseman and a 31-year-old pitcher. We are trying to stock up without denying that we are giving up two fine ball players."[15]

Supposedly, Calvin received the imprimatur to do this deal from his Uncle Clark while he was still in the hospital. "This is the deal you ought to try and make," said the elder Griffith and ticked off most of the names in question.[16]

Calvin was determined to build a younger, faster team, and the trade reflected that thinking. He went ahead with the transaction once he got the recommendations of both Ossie Bluege and Joe Cambria about the Red Sox players.

Gone to the Red Sox were Mickey Vernon (37), Bob Porterfield (31), Johnny Schmitz (34), and Tom Umphlett (24). Coming from the Red Sox were Karl Olson (25), Neil Chrisley (22), Dick Brodowski (23), Truman "Tex" Clevenger (23) and Al Curtis (25).

When notified about the trade at his West Virginia home, Bob Porterfield said, "I'm tickled pink! I can't put my finger on it but I didn't like the way he ran the club or handled me. I don't want to create any friction along the line. So I had better not say any more, but I'm real happy about the deal."[17]

Porterfield was not the only one who was at odds with Dressen. Johnny Schmitz and Mickey McDermott were also critical of some of their skipper's heavy-handed tactics. Porterfield, in particular, complained that Dressen would pull him abruptly for relievers, and Dressen complained that Porterfield had lost his fastball.[18]

Dressen, of course, deflected the accusations. "I always got along well with McDermott, and I doubt if there are many better pitchers in our league. That doesn't sound as if we didn't hit it off, does it?" asked Dressen. "As far as Porterfield is concerned, I never had words with him at any time."[19]

Personality wars notwithstanding, the fact of the matter was that the Washington farm system was an embarrassment. They simply did not have enough teams, enough scouts to find good talent, or, frankly, the money to keep it all going. Cambria had done what he could to find low-cost talent in the Caribbean, but he had provided no bona fide stars … yet. He tried his best to fill up his minor league affiliates with good players, but so far, all he had were minor leaguers.

"I have to be realistic," said Calvin Griffith. "Our farm system doesn't yet have the talent a major league team can lean on so we want to stock up with young players from other farm systems. When you think along those lines, you automatically think of the Yankees and the Red Sox."[20]

When he was managing the Senators, Bucky Harris echoed those same sentiments. "There's no sense in deluding ourselves." Said Harris. "We don't have the scouts or the organization to bring in good young players. You have to do business with teams like the Red Sox and the Yankees."[21]

Things change. And with Calvin Griffith, they would change quickly.

1956

One thing was certain: Calvin Griffith was not his uncle.

Whereas Clark Griffith was definitely a "glass half-full" kind of owner, Calvin was exceedingly blunt. As he told Shirley Povich of the *Washington Post*, "this team of ours is, on paper, the worst looking Washington team I have ever known. We have to face some facts and I want to face them along with the Washington fans. I want to tell them that I still find reason to be encouraged even though we look unimpressive on paper. I think there are many hidden factors from which we can take heart. Before the season is over, I think they will like this young team of ours."[22]

This kind of frankness was unheard-of from an owner; however, Calvin made it abundantly clear that it would be a new dawn under his administration. Things were going to change, and quickly. Everything he attempted to do was for the betterment of the Washington Senators.

Making good on his promise that there would be "new faces on this club," Griffith did what he said he was going to do and worked out another big trade, this time with the Yankees. The linchpin in this transaction was Mickey McDermott. McDermott, who went 10–10 with a 3.75 ERA for the Nats in 1955, was one of the team's front-line starters and was highly coveted by the Yankees. He and Bobby Kline were dealt for five Yankees, two veterans and two rookies. Coming to D.C. would be southpaw Bob Wiesler and catcher Lou Berberet. Wiesler had been in the New York system since 1949 and was used almost exclusively in relief. Berberet had been in the Yankees' system since 1950 and had the ignominious task of being Yogi Berra's third backup.

Calvin Griffith needed outfield help immediately and seemed to find it in Dick Tettlebach. A Yale graduate, Tettlebach had five years' experience in the Yankees' minor league system. He had great range and a good bat. Infielder Herb Plews received gushing praise from none other than Philadelphia A's great Mickey Cochrane. "He's the best infielder I saw in the minors last season. Plews not only made all the plays, he was the hustlingest kid I ever saw. He has the same kind of energy Enos Slaughter shows a team. Plews never walks anywhere he can gallop. He's a dugout pacer and a big morale booster on a club."[23]

Hopefully he would answer the big question: who is going to play second base? Once again, Joe Cambria and Ossie Bluege scouted all of the players before giving their approval to their new boss.[24]

Calvin Griffith vowed that he was going to be "more progressive." He of course wanted the team to make money, but he also wanted to give the fans a better experience at the park, and home runs seemed to please the crowds a lot. Much to his Uncle Clark's chagrin I am sure, he decided to pull in the left field fence to give his power hitters an easier time of it. The monstrous 388-foot left field line now became a more manageable 350 feet, and left-center became 380 feet instead of 391 feet.[25]

Calvin Griffith waxed optimistic about this change. "Sievers, Yost, Olson and Paula are going to be shooting for those closer fences. So will young Harmon Killebrew who will run Yost out of his third base job if Eddie doesn't hit. There are some exciting possibilities on this young ball team, and the fans will be aware of them, I'm sure. At first glance, it may not be much, but I have the strong feeling we'll come up with the kind of a team that will be easy to root for."[26]

The boys would not disappoint. Eddie Yost found the seats 11 times during the season. Paula, Olson and Killebrew, used sparingly throughout the year, combined for 13 homers. The power-hitting duo of Roy Sievers and Jim Lemon, however, found great delight in the shorter left field distances. Lemon hit 21 of his 27 homers at home, while Sievers hit 11 taters at home and 18 away. Together they combined for 56 wallops, the most in the team's history up to that date.

Of course, "What's good for the goose is good for the gander." The other American League teams combined to put the long ball over the short fences 85 times for the year. The Yankees, naturally, feasted on the short porch, dumping 17 dingers into the stands. From the time the Stadium was built in 1911 until 1955, there never were 100 home runs hit in Griffith Stadium. That total jumped from 45 in 1955 to 139 in 1956. Fence busting had begun![27]

In another attempt to please the Washington fans, Calvin Griffith decided to sell beer in Griffith Stadium for the first time. Reporting in the *Post*, Shirley Povich said, "The sale of beer in Griffith Stadium, now being planned in a departure from precedent, was always vetoed by the late Clark Griffith, who repeatedly said, 'beer and baseball don't go together.' However, beer was sold at the park in Griffith's Chattanooga farm club for 12 years before he was aware of the fact."[28]

To this end, Calvin Griffith hired attorney John E. Powell to handle the "Suds for Nats fans" plan. Powell received a letter in March from the Alcoholic Beverage Commission, stating that they could not grant a Class F license, which would allow sale to fans seated in the rows. They would only grant a Class D license which would require patrons to be seated in a designated area. ABC rules also prohibited patrons from standing up or walking to another site with a beer in their hand.

Phone calls and letters followed until the Senators won their Class D beer-selling license. On August 10, the Beer Garden was officially open in the left field stands. At first it only accommodated 170 patrons but was soon expanded to a 500-seat capacity. Beer was sold in paper cups only, lest some disgruntled fans decide to toss a glass bottle at an opposing player. At that time, it left Philadelphia and Pittsburgh as the only two parks not selling beer.[29]

If the Senators stank, well, at least they could cry in their beer.

Underlining his pledge to be more progressive, Calvin Griffith vowed to improve the farm system. One of the first things he did was to set up a working agreement with the Triple A Louisville Colonels franchise of the American Association. The franchise, controlled by the Boston Red Sox, had been vacated by them for San Francisco of the Pacific Coast League. This was the first time the Senators ever had an agreement with a AAA club. Although Cambria had the AAA Albany Senators back in the 1930s, his agreement with Clark Griffith was an informal handshake, with no real financial obligations.

This time, Cambria became Calvin Griffith's "angel." With his decades-long connections in Havana, Cambria convinced a group of wealthy Cuban businessmen to fund the cost of the team. The principal of the group was Victor G. Menocal, a wealthy sugar broker in Havana. Victor's late father had served in the Cuban House of Representatives and was the nephew of former Cuban president Mario Menocal. Included in the group were Louis G. Mendoza, a sugar planter who was also in stocks and bonds; his associate Gonzalo Vega; Arthur Rankin, a native Kentuckian who was vice-president of a shipping and cattle-raising concern in Cuba; Edward Wheeler, superintendent of Western Union for Cuba; and Cambria, who would be listed as vice-president and working in a player advisory and procurement position.[30]

The Colonels also indicated that, for the first time in their history, the team would be integrated, and Parkway Stadium, their home field, would become integrated as well.[31]

Menocal was especially enthusiastic about working with Cambria, saying, "He was the only one to give a CHANCE! We didn't have a CHANCE to buy a club in Havana." He explained to the local newspapers in Louisville that ownership of clubs in the Cuban winter league and the International League were all sewn up, and they were excited to own an American franchise.[32]

Washington's farm system now expanded to include Louisville (AAA, working agreement), Chattanooga (AA, owned outright), Charlotte (A, owned outright), Hagerstown, MD and Hobbs, NM (B, working agreement), and Erie, PA, and Ft. Walton Beach, FL (D, working agreement). Calvin Griffith further increased the number of full-time scouts from 13 to 20.[33]

Cambria did what he did best: he filled the Colonels club with Latins. Of the 51 men on the roster, more than 30 percent were Latins: 14 Cubans, one Venezuelan and one Panamanian. Cambria shuttled the majority of them between Washington, Charlotte and Havana. The Colonels also became the holding ground for several players who wound up on the Senators' roster that year: Ted Abernathy, Dick Brodowski, Bud Byerly, Truman "Tex" Clevenger, Carlos Paula, Tony Roig and Jose Valdivielso.

Manager Red Marion, brother of the great St. Louis Cardinals shortstop Marty Marion, had a tough time trying to work with all the Latin players, but he handled it with aplomb. When asked about the situation, his good friend, Brooklyn Dodgers great Eddie Stanky, told Francis Stann of the *Evening Star*, "not very many of them speak English. A manager with a low boiling point would not have much hope."[34]

Red Marion also had to put up with Cambria's incessant shuffling of players in and out of camp. On one occasion, Marion's good humor helped to defuse an awkward situation.

> Just the other week, two more Cubans, sent to the club by Joe Cambria, showed up in Louisville uniforms. When one of the newcomers, Louis Morales, was inserted at third base May 5, a writer asked Marion for more information on the infielder. "I couldn't say," the Colonels skipper responded. "He just came in this afternoon. You had better ask Oscar Rodriguez [the club's Cuban coach]. You know, I believe some of the Cubans don't know who I am. They probably think I'm trying to make the ball club!" he laughed.[35]

But it did not stop there. By July, the situation became more convoluted. Ray Holton, the club's primary catcher, was sold to Miami. Jack Parks became the sole catcher for the team, so Cambria wired Marion that help was on the way from Cuba in the form of young Raphael Enoa. Days passed and the new Cuban was a no-show. Parks got injured July 4, and shortstop Yo-Yo Davalillo had to don the "tools of ignorance." Davalillo did his best, but no catcher was he. Cambria and Marion were ready to call out the National Guard until they received a phone call from an airline official in Charleston, South Carolina, alerting them to the fact that Mr. Enoa, who spoke no English, had found his way to Charleston, South Carolina, when he was supposed to meet the team in Charleston, West Virginia.[36] Maybe Joe Cambria should have pinned a note to Enoa's jacket!

All of this *mishegoss* helped little. By the end of the season, the team stank and sank into the abyss of the cellar with a 60–93 record, dead last in almost every team category. In terms of attendance, the team could not draw flies. Cambria resorted to one of his old tricks, giving away a new car to some lucky fan. On the day in question, fewer than 1,300 people showed up for the game.[37]

On average, the team drew fewer than 1,000 fans per game, not even 80,000 for the year. Consequently, Cambria, who had somehow become the head of the owners' syndicate, lost $50,000 for the season and $100,000 for the year.[38] The team ultimately went into receivership. On September 23, Cambria sold the team to Phil O'Hara, a Tampa public relations man, for the price of the debts.[39]

Herewith begins a saga that can only be described as "Cambria-esque."

For some inexplicable reason, in July of 1956, Cambria negotiated the sale of the Orlando Sertomans of the Florida State League to the Louisville club. The Sertoma Club

"Papa Joe" Cambria surrounded by his adoring Cuban Senators circa 1956. From left to right are Cambria, Pedro Ramos (p), Carlos Paula (of), Julio Becquer (1B), Camillo Pascual (p), Gilberto Hooker (p), Jose Valdivielso (ss), Webbo Clarks (p), Yo-Yo Davalillo (ss).

originally bought the team in an effort to keep professional baseball in Orlando; however, they did not have the infrastructure to run it successfully. Cambria whimsically renamed the team the Colonels and, unfortunately, they stank just as bad at the Louisville Colonels. Maybe he thought he could do what he had done so many times before. He would buy a failing club (Hagerstown, Albany, Harrisburg, Salisbury), fix up the stadium, bring in some flashy Cubans, and try to please the fans.

It did not work this time. By the time Joe Cambria got to Orlando, there were only about 30 days left in the season. Trying to procure decent talent was next to impossible in that short space of time: "I realize that the Colonels are losing, but I'm unable to get any new talent at this late date. No ball player is going to sign for just 30 days."[40] So Cambria resorted to his old tried and true practices. Unfortunately, the other team owners and the fans were unhappy with those practices.

He sold off his top players (who were the most popular) in order to make his expense money and brought in a raft of Cubans from the amateur leagues (for *very* little money), who were as unhappy to be in Orlando as Orlando was to have them. Baseball-Reference.com's minor league encyclopedia indicates that, on average, fewer than 400 people came to see a game on any given day. Just like in Albany, Cambria tried booster nights, ladies' nights, friends' night (each paying customer brings in a friend for free), and other promotions to lure in the fans.

Nothing worked. In desperation, Cambria threw open the gates for free admission for the final 14 games the Colonels played, putting up baskets at the turnstiles to encourage donations. "I told 'em to let everyone in free and left the gates open," said Cambria. "There was a basket to toss change in if they felt guilty."[41]

In late July, Cambria was talking big as he always had. He intimated that he would try to bring the Orlando team up to Class-B ball and would organize a new league with St. Petersburg, Tampa, West Palm Beach, and Daytona Beach as members.[42]

In the end, Joe Cambria spent $1,600 to acquire the franchise and lost another $5,500 on the season. It is important to note that Cambria did, in fact, pay off all of the debts incurred by the team. Despite his usually roseate attitude, he began to cool to the idea of either keeping the club or staying in Orlando in 1957. As Cambria explained:

> I will have a full working agreement with Washington and a much better club than this year's. But I feel as though the city should fix up the park before I'd put a team in there. I'm not talking about a new park but just a little paint and some minor repairs. And I would have to have assurances from the fans that they want baseball. If they indicate during the next few months they're willing to support baseball, I'd be willing to return. Otherwise, I'll probably put the franchise in some other city.[43]

By October, Cambria announced publicly that he was pulling out of Orlando. He talked with officials in Clearwater and Lakeland but finally settled on an offer to move the club to Key West.

Paralleling the Orlando Colonels' troubles was the disposition of the Louisville Colonels. Phil O'Hara and Cambria still had controlling interests in the Louisville club and were looking to relocate that team as well. Talks began in earnest in September and by October, it looked as though Tampa was the odds-on favorite to gain the team. As reported in the *Tampa Tribune*, "Phil O'Hara, Tampa publicity man, who says he has been given power of attorney by the 20 stockholders in the Louisville club, said the stockholders have agreed to move the club to Tampa and all he needs is permission of the league officials. Also, a small sum of $100,000 must be paid off to the Colonels' creditors before the club can be moved."[44]

On October 28, the Florida State League directors approved the Louisville move to Tampa, but John Krider, league president, declared Orlando's franchise forfeit under Cambria's management and canceled Orlando's membership. Noting that Cambria's involvement in the Orlando Colonels was never sanctioned, he urged the other directors to act against Cambria, saying he did not like Cambria's methods of operation and declared, "if a club operated in a league like Cambria's, I wouldn't want it. And I'd say the same thing to Joe if he were here."[45]

Cambria was, of course, incensed by the decision. In Havana at the time, he was represented by Phil O'Hara at these meetings. O'Hara said Cambria would protest to Minor League President George Trautman and would sue for damages unless he was compensated for the loss of the franchise and the players.[46] "This cannot be done under baseball law," said Cambria. "I have retained a Miami attorney who will see that justice is done in the courts of baseball. All I did was help the Florida State league finish the season with its full eight teams. I did not leave any debts unpaid at the end of the season."[47]

Cambria then lashed out at the *Miami News* for their previous day's article.

Gentlemen:

In a column in yesterday's newspaper there was an article about me which I will thank you to clarify because I know you will be glad to do so when the truth of the situation is made known to you.

I purchased the Orlando baseball franchise about six weeks prior to the close of the 1956 season when the club was in last place and when the attendance was at its lowest ebb. I naturally continued with the General manager and put him in charge of operations and it was too late in the season to acquire new players and get the team out of the cellar. I did the best I could with a bad situation and I certainly have paid all debts of all kind and character in the Orlando territory, and closed the season with a clean bill of health but with a bad ball club. I continued with the same general manager when I took over the franchise and he is responsible for the operation of the club and all that I did was to pay the bills. I made a tentative working agreement with the Washington Senators and fifteen players already have been allotted or placed on the reserve list of the Orlando club.

I regret the unfavorable publicity given to me and will appreciate your retracting same in such manner as you see fit with the above facts which are true.

Sincerely,
Joe Cambria[48]

In a subsequent telephone conversation on October 30, Cambria was advised by president Krider that the 21 players, with whom Cambria planned to build a team next season on option from the Senators, would not be seized by the league. and that Cambria could thresh out the franchise forfeiture at the December league meetings.[49]

By November, in a magnanimous display of support, Calvin Griffith announced that the Senators, hoping that Cambria would retain ownership, would have a new working agreement with whoever Orlando deemed fit to own the franchise. At the same time, he broke his ties with the Louisville Colonels because of the team's shaky financial situation.[50]

Meanwhile, back in Louisville, Joe Cambria had another fire to stomp out. The Louisville Colonels had been placed in receivership because of the $100,000 debt the team had accrued. New owner Phil O'Hara and Cambria both stated that the amount of the debt was grossly inaccurate and maintained it was a much lower figure. O'Hara and the other stockholders, headed by Cambria, were "ready, willing and able to re-finance their Louisville operation but have been prevented from doing so by the interference of other members of the league's directorship."[51] American Association president Ed Doherty, however, ordered the league's attorney to go to the receiver and make a bid for the club's assets.[52]

Doherty then decided he would give the franchise away free to the city's mayor or a group of citizens who could raise sufficient funds to operate the club. Cambria and his other stockholders were vehemently opposed to any move of the club. "How can he give something away [that] he doesn't even own? The Havana stockholders are confident the mayor and the citizens will not co-operate with Doherty, who tried to take the club to Des Moines and who was up for contempt of court for trying to move the franchise."[53]

After a December audit, a Kentucky court found that the debt was in actuality $166,000 and could be settled for $25,000. O'Hara said his clients were prepared to pay the $25,000 and would also agree to pay off the balance of the $166,000 from the following year's club profits.

The league refused to accept the proposal.

Doherty said the court on December 15 would award the franchise to a bidder the court deemed satisfactory. He further stated that the American Association had already appropriated the $25,000 from its treasury in anticipation of the court's verdict in their favor. In order for the Cuban ownership group to regain the franchise, they would have to have approval of three-fourths of the other seven clubs. Playing hardball, Doherty had already secured six votes in opposition to the Cubans in favor of a new syndicate from

Louisville. "I have no ax to grind with these people [the Cuban syndicate]," Doherty said. "Under baseball law if a club fails to meet its debts it loses its franchise. If they are so anxious to pay their debts now why didn't they do it before?"[54]

As predicted, the Kentucky courts found in favor of Doherty and the American Association. They accepted their bid of $25,000 to take the team out of receivership and, in turn, handed the club over to Falls Cities Professional Baseball Foundation, a non-profit civic organization, which in turn began a massive fund-raising campaign to solidify the team.[55]

Why the Cuban syndicate did not just pay the $25,000 fee is a mystery for the ages. The Colonels stayed in the American Association, affiliated with the Orioles in 1958, then with Milwaukee Braves from 1959 until the American Association ceased operations in 1962.

Ping-ponging back to Orlando, Joe Cambria officially lost his bid to run the Orlando Colonels when Minor League President George Trautman upheld the league's actions against Cambria.

However. Cambria appealed that decision, and at the December meetings, the directors voted to restore Orlando's franchise to him. He said he wanted the opportunity to recoup at least part of his losses. Cambria was given a week to post the FSL entry fee or sell the franchise to another buyer and was not permitted to move the franchise to another city.[56]

Cambria sold the team. On December 23, the *Orlando Sentinel* announced that stock car racing and rodeo promoter Larry Sunbrock had purchased the Orlando Colonels from Joe Cambria for "$1 and other considerations" and received the approval of league president John Krider.[57]

However. In February, Sunbrock announced he was pulling out of the ownership, citing that he had too much on his plate with his other business interests. John Krider tried to persuade Washington to take over interest in the team. They refused, and Krider said the team was definitely kaput for 1957.

On March 17, a new owner, Arthur Shapiro, said he would take over the club with the same working agreement with Washington. On March 21, he backed out of the deal and Sunbrock returned. On March 25, Sunbrock said he had jumped the gun and backed out of ownership … again.

In April, officials of the FSL found a new owner, Robert M. Feemster, a business executive in New York City, named a new manager, and the Orlando Colonels lived to fight another day.[58]

Thus ended the ballad of the Dueling Colonels. If ever a sadder song were sung, I cannot imagine which one. Now, back to Washington.

Managing the Cincinnati Reds in 1911, Clark Griffith signed Armando Marsans and Rafael Almeida as the first two Cuban ballplayers in the 20th century. Managing the Washington Senators in 1913, he signed the first Cuban Senator, Merito Acosta. From that time forward, Griffith believed in the possibilities of the Cuban players and forged a bond between the two countries made even stronger by the work of Joe Cambria.

It was only fitting, then, that for the first time in history, a foreign nation's Independence Day was celebrated in a Major League baseball park on May 13, 1956. The Cuban flag was raised over Griffith Stadium, and their red-white-and-blue bunting was draped over the Presidential box, this time occupied by Dr. Miguel Angel Campa, Ambassador of Cuba. Ambassador Campa presented Calvin Griffith with a memorial scroll and tossed out the ceremonial first pitch as native Cubans Camilo Pascual, Pedro Ramos and Jose Valdivielso participated in the ceremony. The game was scheduled for the 13th because on their actual Independence Day, May 20, the Senators would be playing out of town.

Speaking in English, Ambassador Campa addressed Calvin Griffith and the crowd of 10,415 appreciative fans: "The Washington Baseball club, under the wise and inspired guidance of the late Clark Griffith and now under your direction, has done outstanding work in the progress of the relations of the many baseball fans of Cuba and those of the United States."

After more congratulations from the Ambassador, Master of Ceremonies Bob Wolff read cables of congratulations from Arturo Bengochea, president of the Cuban Winter league, Cuche Rodriguez of the Cienfuegos club, and a heartfelt message from Joe Cambria.[59]

Rumors were beginning to swirl. Responding to a statement from California Congressman Patrick Hillings urging Los Angeles Mayor Norris Poulson to explore the possibility of buying the Senators' franchise due to a "serious lack of interest in baseball here," Calvin Griffith issued this statement to the *Washington Post*:

> The Washington Baseball Club has never considered and does not contemplate transferring its franchise to Los Angeles or any other city. Reports to the contrary are baseless. These careless rumors are based on the false premise that the Washington Baseball Club is facing a serious crisis and attendance is very poor. The facts are the Washington Club faces no crisis whatsoever, and that attendance is above what it was a year ago.
>
> The Washington Baseball Club is now undertaking a thorough rebuilding program which will ultimately bring this city a contending team. We have found more interest this year among the citizens of this community than ever before. We feel that when the weather improves, the fans will support us in increasing numbers. Washington is a great baseball city. We point out that for 18 home games this season, we have drawn 123,295 paying spectators in contrast to 118,330 over a similar period a year ago. This is in spite of declining attendance elsewhere in baseball.
>
> We are not opposed to Major League baseball on the West Coast. We simply urge those interested in looking elsewhere and not Washington for the franchise.[60]

Congressman Hillings, an active campaigner for Major League Baseball's expansion, was obviously shilling for California in general and Los Angeles in particular to draw a major league team to the West Coast. Los Angeles lost out on attracting the St. Louis Browns in 1953 because they could not guarantee them a new stadium.[61]

Please note the above statement for future reference.

The 1956 Senators

The Senators of 1956 actually improved ... to seventh place, with a 59–95 record, thanks to the Athletics' woeful 102 losses. The team hit well, as noted below:

Pete Runnels—179 hits/ 8 homers/ .310 average
Jim Lemon—146 hits/ 27 homers/ .271 average
Roy Sievers—139 hits/ 29 homers/ .253 average
Eddie Yost—119 hits/ 11 homers/ .231 average
Clint Courtney—85 hits/ 5 homers/ .300 average

The most that could be said about the team was it was just average. The team on-base percentage was .341, which was the league average. They just did not score many runs. They were sixth in the league in runs scored with a 4.21 average. They hit a lot of home runs for Griffith Stadium, but their overall home run average was seventh in the league, 112 as compared with the Yankees' 190.

The biggest culprit, however, was the pitching. Chuck Stobbs went 15–15 with a 3.60 ERA and gave up 29 homers. Pedro Ramos went 12–10 with a 5.27 ERA and surrendered 23 homers. Stobbs and Ramos were the only winning pitchers on the staff. Camilo Pascual had a terrible year, going 6–18 with a 5.87 ERA and throwing 33 long balls. However, Pascual struck out 162 batters, a feat that had not been done by a Washington pitcher since the great Walter Johnson did it in 1918. Pascual explained his long ball performance thusly: "I was young back then. They would hit home run off me and I get very angry. Then, I try to throw harder and they hit me even more. That very bad. But I learn to control myself later."[62]

Pascual played Winter League ball in Cuba and used the time there to work on his control. Cambria sent back a glowing report to manager Dressen when he watched Pascual strike out 15 batters in a 14-inning shutout victory. "Pascual now makes every pitch count, and he gets his good stuff over the plate."[63]

Of the entire staff, Stobbs was the only pitcher with an ERA in the 3.00 range. They were the highest in the league in ERA (5.33), highest in hits allowed (1,539) and runs allowed (924), and second in home runs allowed (171). They also had the highest ERA in Griffith Stadium (5.55). As stated before, the team gave up only 99 homers in 1955. The shortened left-field fence would prove to be their nemesis for the remainder of the decade.

In deference to the pitching staff, a quick perusal of the team's schedule at Baseball-Reference.com shows that, despite a few real blowout games, the majority of the Senators' losses were 2 or 3 run ball games. They were just lacking run support, runners getting on base or timely hitting. Two players, Clint Courtney and Pete Runnels, hit over .300. They had losing records against every team except Boston.

If you could say anything positive about the 1956 team, it would have to be, "at least they didn't finish last!"

1957

There is an old saying: "It ain't the dog in the fight. It's the fight in the dog."

This was Joe Cambria. Like a dog with a bone, he just would not let anything go. He fought to get his FSL Orlando franchise back, was successful, then eventually sold the team. Such was the case with the Louisville Colonels. In January, Cambria filed a lawsuit with the Kentucky Supreme Court, appealing the sale of the Colonels to the Falls Cities Professional Baseball Foundation, which was sanctioned by the American Association and President Ed Doherty. Kentucky Appeals Court records were inconclusive as to the outcome of the case, unfortunately. However, it would be safe to say that Cambria's appeal fell on deaf ears. The Colonels remained with the Fall Cities group and affiliated with the Orioles in 1958, and with the Milwaukee Braves from 1959 to 1962.[64]

In reality, Cambria only had himself to blame. As he was wont to do, he would sell off any player with a modicum of talent in an effort to keep the team afloat, often to the detriment of the remaining team. The Colonels were a case in point. By the end of the season, manager Max Carey turned around and realized he had only 14 men in the dugout. Riffing like a jazz pianist, he quickly converted two pitchers into outfielders and a third pitcher into a first baseman. Then he converted his regular first baseman, Julio Becquer, into a third baseman.

Only one problem. Becquer was left-handed. Left-handed third basemen are as rare as dodo birds and left-handed catchers. But Becquer did his best. Writing in the highly non-politically correct verbiage of the day, Morris Segal quoted Becquer in the *Washington Daily News*, "I think maybe the manager ee ees loco when he tell me to play No. 3 base! The only time before I ever been on theese base is when I running home. But the manager he geeve me a glove and say play. I say 'caramba' many times but I play. Not gude, but I play. I think all the time she ees better to play the No. 3 base than no to play nothing."[65]

The experience certainly did not hurt Becquer. He made it up to the Senators from 1958 through 1960.

Hope springs eternal when it is time for pitchers and catchers to report, and 1957 loomed large in the minds of Chuck Dressen and Calvin Griffith. They were scurrying like proverbial church mice, talking deals with anyone who would listen. But as Calvin Griffith told the *Washington Post*, teams were offering mostly "garbage." Again, the big boys like the Yankees and White Sox were after the likes of Roy Sievers and Clint Courtney, and he was not going to give up his stars for "scrubs" as he called them. And nobody was going to offer much more to a last-place club. So they began to scour their farm system in search of their diamonds in the rough. Some made an impact, others did not. (Griffith was going for youth and speed this year, with only three players, Yost, Sievers and Courtney, over the age of 30.)

Although it took a little while, **Jimmie Hall** became an impactful player for the newly minted Minnesota Twins. Jimmie (his real name) spent eight years toiling in the Washington farm system before making the jump to the Twins in 1963. He got a good look-see at the Nats' 1957 spring camp, but manager Dressen was not impressed at the time. Illness, injury, and Uncle Sam extended his minor league career until he finally made a good impression at the 1963 Twins' spring camp. He made a big noise in his rookie year by hitting 33 home runs, which beat out Ted Williams' rookie record. He had a respectable career with the Twins but became trade bait for several teams between 1967 and 1972.[66]

Bob Allison surprised all the critics and blossomed into one of the most feared hitters in the American League once he made the team! He spent all of his 16 baseball seasons in the Senators/Twins system. Allison was six foot three inches tall, 220 pounds with movie-star good looks and the body of an underwear model. He actually got his look-see at the spring camp of 1956 but was horribly overmatched at the time. Sent down to Charlotte, he roomed with a young Harmon Killebrew, and they became life-long friends. Allison worked hard at Charlotte and Chattanooga in 1956 and 1957 and earned an 11-game September call-up in 1958. After honing his skills in the Cuban Winter league, he exploded on the Washington scene in 1959. He hit 30 home runs and batted .261, was named an All-Star and won the Rookie of the Year Award. Allison remained with the Twins until he retired in 1970.[67]

Dan Dobbek was a big, strong kid signed by the Senators out of Western Michigan University in 1955. He tore up the B leagues with the Hobbs Sports, batting .340 with 23 home runs in 1956. He was all set to go to spring camp until Uncle Sam took him away for 1957 and 1958. He reported for duty with the Chattanooga Lookouts in 1959 and earned a 16-game call-up with the Nats in September. His left-handed bat and rifle arm made a lot of noise, and both *Sport* magazine and *The Sporting News* named him a rookie sensation in 1959 and 1960. Unfortunately, he showed poorly when the Senators moved to Minnesota in 1961. With only 21 hits and four homers in 141 at-bats and an anemic .168 batting average, he was sent down to the minors and remained there until he hung them up in 1963.[68]

Nineteen fifty-four bonus baby **Harmon Killebrew** got another look during spring camp, was deemed not ready by manager Dressen, and went choo-choo-ing back to Chattanooga. He did earn a nine-game September call up in 1957. In 33 plate appearances, he hit two homers and got nine hits.[69]

Ted Abernathy posted a respectable 12–16 record with Joe Cambria's horribly pathetic, last-place Louisville Colonels in 1956, which earned him a modicum of respect and a brief call-up with the Nats. He posted a 1–3 record with two complete games. Chuck Dressen liked what he saw in Abernathy at the 1957 camp, and he made the team. He went 2–10 in 26 games, for a 6.78 ERA in 1957. Abernathy had a successful 14-year career in the majors.[70]

Dick Hyde got his first look-see with the 1954 Senators. His unique submarine style of pitching was explained thusly.

> I didn't start that submarine style until 1954, although I'd been pitching since 1949. After getting out of the service, Cal Griffith was watching me in spring training in 1954. He saw my sidearm and told me to get down lower. That's how my submarine pitch developed. Every spring I got to work at that sort of delivery again. As I get along in spring training I dip farther and farther down util I'm almost scraping the ground with my knuckles. It became natural after awhile.

Dick Hyde pitched in three games for the Nats in 1955, did not do well, and was sent back to Chattanooga. He showed up very well at the 1957 spring camp and won a spot on the roster.[71]

There were fewer Cubans in spring camp this year, but Cambria still found a few hurlers for manager Dressen to look at. At one time during training camp, Cambria told him of a Cuban pitcher he had seen who could throw hard but could not speak English. Dressen roared to Cambria, "Sign him! I know plenty of guys who can speak perfect English and can't get their mother out!"[72]

Oscar Chinique and **Waldo Gonzalez** both spent seven years in the Washington minors but never had the stuff to make the parent club.

Lazaro Rivero was a well-respected pitcher in his native Cuba, but while playing in Nicaragua, he was forced to flee the country after the assassination of President Anastasio Somoza in 1956. Joe Cambria saw him pitch in the Cuban Winter Leagues and signed him pronto. His fast ball was great, but his English skills were not. He spent 1957 with the Midland/Lamesa Indians in Texas, where he struck out 151 batters but allowed 154 hits and walked 79. He spent two years in the Mexican Leagues, then returned to Cuba after the revolution to work as a coach and manager. He became very successful coaching the Pinar del Rio team (1967–1973) and the Cuban national team of the 1967 Pan American games, in Nicaragua in 1983, and in Italy in 1993.[73]

Evelio Hernandez, however, did have enough stuff to impress Dressen, who picked him to go north with the team. He did his best, but in 14 games, he posted a 4.25 ERA with 17 earned runs, 15 strikeouts and 20 walks. He was sent down and remained in the Mexican league primarily until 1967.

The biggest buzz in the 1957 spring camp was the appearance of **Sam Hill,** the first American Negro player ever to be invited to a spring camp in the Senators' history. Carlos Paula, of course, was the first Black man to play with the Nats, but he was Cuban. Signed by Cambria to the Louisville team, Sam Hill told the *Baltimore Afro-American:* "You know, I keep trying to figure out how that Cambria heard about me. I'll bet it was Ray Perez, our Cuban catcher last season who told him about me. They say that Cambria has contacts everywhere. I hope I make good for him and me. I understand that's there's a big colored community in Washington. I hope I can make them proud of me too."[74]

Hill was by no means a novice. As a teenager, he played with the Chicago American Giants of the Negro American League from 1946 through 1948. In 1954, he made the Eastern League All-Star team. In their mid-season All-Star Game, he drove in two runs and scored the other run in a 3–1 victory.[75]

Sam Hill had a good, long look by manager Dressen, but just did not have enough for Dressen's liking. He was assigned to the Charlotte team and remained in the minors until 1958.

Always believing in the power of family, Calvin Griffith invited young **Richard "Dickie" Harris,** son of the Senators' three-time manager, Bucky Harris, for spring camp in 1957. The 23-year-old Harris, a second baseman like his dad, showed off the leather but not so the wood. Dressen was pleased but not impressed. As Dickie Harris told the *Washington Evening Star*:

> I guess I'm dead here but I'm not complaining. Mr. Dressen gave me a good shot at it. Funny thing, for the first week I was scared stiff. Now I know I can make it in the majors. I never wanted anything so much in my life as I want to stick with this club. I learned a lot. For one thing, Mr. Dressen taught me to be more aggressive at the plate. I guess I have always been too lax up there. And that Cookie [Lavagetto]—he's wonderful. If you want to talk baseball he'll talk it anytime!

Dickie Harris was sent down and remained with Charlotte and Chattanooga for the remainder of 1957 through 1959.[76]

Manager Dressen and his coach, Cookie Lavagetto, also believed in family, Dodgers family. On August 1, the Senators finally broke their color line by hiring their first American-born Black player, former Dodgers ace **Joe Black.** Another veteran of the Negro Leagues and the 1952 Rookie of the Year, Black helped the Dodgers win the National League pennant in 1952 and 1953. By 1957, however, he was arm sore and mound weary. Suffering from torn muscles in his throwing shoulder, Black pitched in only seven games, giving up 22 hits, 11 runs and four homers, with a 7.11 ERA in 12⅔ innings pitched. The Senators released him in November but hired him as a roving scout, making him the first Negro scout in the team's history.[77]

Dressen saw what he saw, liked what he liked, and took who he wanted up north to Washington for the home opener on April 15. Shirley Povich gave his fair and honest assessment to *The Sporting News.*

> Pitching—Chuck Stobbs, Camilo Pascual and Pedro Ramos to carry the load.
>   Depth is lacking.

Catching—Solid

Infield—Bolstered by Jerry Snyder's return to shortstop. Solid at third base with
Eddie Yost, good at second with Herb Plews. Pete Runnels, on first, only
established hitter.

Outfield—Lemon and Sievers provide long-ball power. Center field open, could be
filled by Schoonmaker.

Summation—No first division threat. Any position higher than sixth would be an
upset.[78]

The expectant crowd of 37,223 watched President Eisenhower toss his first two pitches
high and outside. The first one was caught by Orioles reliever Don Ferrarese and the
other by the Nats outfielder Neil Chrisley. Dressen sent Bob Chakales out to face the
Orioles' Hal "Skinny" Brown, and the season began. The Senators, however, continued
their losing streak of home openers. With the game tied 6–6 going into extra innings,
Camilo Pascual, pitching in relief, gave up doubles to Dick Williams and Gus Triandos
in the top of the 11th inning to give the O's a 7–6 victory.[79]

This would unfortunately portend the outcome of the whole 1957 season. The pitching staff just did not gel. Besides great hitting by Roy Sievers, the rest of the hitting was
Jell-O. By May 6, the team was mired again in last place with a 5–16 record.

Calvin Griffith always said he was not his uncle, and he would do what he wanted to
do. He certainly did something that had not been done in the history of Clark Griffith's
franchise. He fired Chuck Dressen even before mid-season and promoted Cookie Lavagetto to manager.

Lavagetto, whose pinch-hit double in Game 4 of the 1947 Yankees-Dodgers World
Series broke up Bill Bevens' bid for a no-hitter, was regarded as a baseball icon. Lavagetto was Dressen's man, giving up his career in 1951 to hire on as a coach with Dressen.
Lavagetto was much more of a "players' manager," preferring to room with someone
rather than stay alone. He was more comfortable shuffling cards with the boys than
shuffling the lineup card.

At first, Lavagetto refused to take the manager's job, wanting to remain loyal to his
friend. "It's sickening," he said. "They want me to take the job and I won't. I'm still with
Chuck wherever he goes." It was Dressen who convinced him to stay in D.C. saying,
"Look, Cookie, this is your big chance. This is the way it happens in baseball. I got my
first job as a manager when one of my best friends was fired. Nobody is a better friend
of mine than Bucky Harris, but I also took his job in Washington when he was fired."[80]

It took a little while, but Cookie Lavagetto got used to the manager's solitary existence. He did his best to right the ship but, in the end, it was for naught. The pitchers
could not close, and the hitters could not hit, and the team continued on a downward
spiral until the end of the season.

There was one bright star in the firmament that year that gave both Lavagetto and
the long-suffering Washington fans something to cheer. That was the tremendous hitting of Roy Sievers. Since coming to the Senators in 1954, Sievers had bested the team's
home run record each year, hitting 24 in 1954, 25 in 1955, and 29 in 1956. When he went
to Calvin Griffith for a raise at the end of the 1956 season, he was famously told "we
wound up in last place with all your home runs, we could have wound up there without them."[81] Trying for a bigger salary, Sievers held out at the start of the season but was
forced to settle for a very paltry $500 raise. "Calvin was a tight old bastard," said Sievers.
"Negotiating with him was tough."

Determined to make Griffith eat his words, Sievers set a torrid home run pace from the beginning of the season. He hit four in April, six in May, and seven in June. But it was July when he really heated up. Staring in the second game of a doubleheader on July 28, Sievers homered in six consecutive games, tying a record held by Ken Williams of the 1922 Browns and Lou Gehrig of the 1931 Yankees. He homered in the Saturday game of July 27, making his total seven homers in eight games.

Sievers also got into a home run-hitting race with Ted Williams and Mickey Mantle which made the Washington newspapers as prominently as Joe DiMaggio's 56-game hit streak. In the end, Sievers outslugged them both. He led the league with 42 homers, 114 RBI, and 331 total bases. He was named an AL All-Star and placed third in the MVP voting behind, you guessed it, Mickey Mantle and Ted Williams. His .301 batting average was also his highest since his 1949 Rookie of the Year .306. Sievers would go on to set the franchise record for home runs hit in Griffith Stadium with 91.[82]

Needless to say, Roy Sievers's salary was nearly doubled the following year.

Cambria was not immune from the losing drama occurring in D.C. He was just occupied with other things. By 1957, he had lost his signatory claim as the only Latin talent scout in the Caribbean. All of the Caribbean Islands and Central America were overrun by scouts from every team from both leagues. As Bob Addie of the *Washington Post* expounded, "There was a time when Cambria had the Cuban and Mexican territories all to himself. But the Senators had so much success with their Latin-American imports that the other scouts began to scour Cuba and Mexico. Like everything else, the field is [now] overcrowded."[83]

Only four teams, the Yankees and the Tigers in the AL, and the Cardinals and the Cubs in the NL were without a Latin player. With the successes of the likes of Connie Marrero, Sandy Amoros, Vic Power, Minnie Minoso and Roberto Clemente, other teams besides the Senators knew it was foolish *not* to find great talent in the Caribbean basin.

Six teams in each league had Latins on their rosters: 14 played in the AL and 14 in the NL. Of those 28 players, Cambria had signed 10. Both the Negro and the Latin players were proving themselves to be indispensable. By the end of the decade, the number of Latin players in the majors rose from 28 to 51.[84]

Of course, the greatest thing to happen to Cambria and the other scouts was the Cuban Winter League. For the thousands of Cubans who could not get off the island to see American baseball, it was their Major Leagues, and they treated it as such. It was the best amateur baseball they had, and every kid on the island dreamed of playing in that league.

The winter leagues allowed for marginal players to hone their skills, and for many underpaid Latin major league players, a chance to make extra money during the winter months. What also made it so competitive was the plethora of Negro League players and young American rookies. Their rule was that no American could play if he had more than 45 days of play in the big leagues. Young players who had signed minor league contracts and those who had just a few weeks' cup of coffee in the majors were always eligible.

The Cubans loved the American and Negro players, but they were both rabid and extremely vocal about the level of play. The Senators' pinch-hitter and utility man extraordinaire, Julio Becquer, explained to Bob Addie:

I think American fans have the wrong idea of the Cuban league. The Americans think a lot of ballplayers go down to loaf and pick up some easy money. But you've got to put out or those fans really get on you. And when they do, it isn't like the States where they just boo. Those Cuban fans can get violent! The thing is that you get practically 100-percent big-league personnel, so it's good ball. Cubans, like everybody else, want to see only the best—which may be the reason Triple-A ball hasn't done too well.[85]

By now, Cambria was living full-time in Cuba and was sort of in a state of semi-retirement. His travels took him all over Central America, the Caribbean and Venezuela. His suite in the American Club was now a daily hang-out for dozens of young boys who by now knew that one word from Joe Cambria could send them to America, the land where dreams could come true.

With no ball team to manage or run, he had some time on his hands. So he decided to become a scribe!

The *Times of Havana* hired Joe Cambria to write a (mostly) bi-weekly column entitled "Don't Die on Third, Every Knock is a Boost." The column was predominantly a collection of opinions, factoids, helpful hints, and a lot of "graybeard stories" about the glories of baseball days past. Stories of Babe Ruth, Walter Johnson, Pie Traynor and Rogers Hornsby abounded. For example:

> All this talk about bonus babies reminds me that Babe Ruth signed up with the Orioles for $125 a month when he came out of the Maryland Industrial School. In an exhibition game Ruth (then a pitcher) of course shut out Connie Mack's powerful A's with only two hits.
> Manager Jack Dunn of the Orioles was so impressed that as a bonus he offered to buy Ruth anything he wanted. Well, Ruth wanted a bicycle. Nothing else would do. And he ran all around Fayetteville on that bike. It was a familiar sight in those days to see young Babe Ruth pedaling around to his heart's content.
> Ruth was never very good on names. One day after he had been sharing a room with the same teammate for a couple of months, a reporter for the *Baltimore News* asked him who he roomed with. "I don't know his name," said Ruth, "But he plays centerfield!"[86]

Cambria waxed philosophic as he explained the meaning of the article's title "Don't Die on Third":

> All the world's a baseball diamond—you are one of the players. Perhaps you have reached first base by your own efforts. It may be the sacrifices of your parents or friends have enabled you to reach second. Then someone's long fly into the business world, a fly that was not long enough to prevent his going out or someone's fluke on the rules of simple morality and square dealing have advanced you to third. The opposition against you on third is stronger than at either first or second. At third, you are to be reckoned with: your opponents concentrate all their attention on you, pitcher and catchers, coaches and opposing fans are watching to tip off your plans and frustrate them. From third you either become a splendid success or a dismal failure. Don't die on third.[87]

He wrote articles advocating for State subsidies for ballparks and 25-cent ticket prices, so everyone could go to the games affordably. Always the true Senators man, Cambria would predict the Nats would never end in last place, and he would always be wrong!

Cambria always had a soft spot for young boys just learning to play ball. He used this "bully pulpit" to dispense his own wisdom of the game. Here are his "Do's and Dont's" of the game.

1. If you want to make baseball your career study the fundamentals in this column—they are correct and used by all the great stars of the past and present.

2. You cannot learn too much about baseball and the sportsmanship it teaches—how to be humble in both victory and defeat.

3. Concentrate on your work. HUSTLE both mentally and physically.

4. You are hustling when you learn to say "No" to excessive smoking and drinking. "Gimme a Coke" sounds better from a ball player than "Gimme a highball."

5. You can make yourself a good hitter by learning to overcome your weaknesses.

6. Your physical ability is the biggest asset you have in baseball—don't do anything to harm it.

7. Protect your eyes—read after the game—be sharp at game time.

8. Don't take the third strike and yell at the umpire—remember—"If they are close enough to call, they are close enough to hit."[88]

Cambria also signed a contract with the Remington Rand corporation of Cuba that

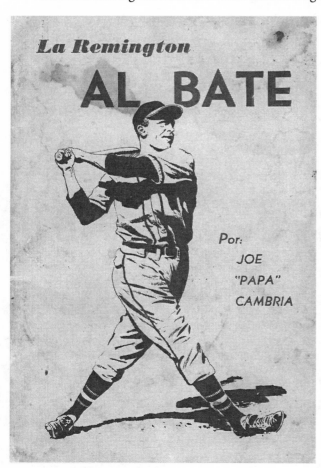

A rare copy of the *Al Bate* baseball primer written by Joe Cambria. Written in Spanish, the book was meant to be a beginner's guide to the intricacies of playing baseball (private collection of Paul Scimonelli).

year.[89] They agreed to publish two books written by him. Both pocket-size editions written in Spanish, one focused on batting (*Al Bate*) and the other on base running (*Las Bases*). In *Al Bate*, Cambria described the grip, the swing, pivoting, bunting, the position of the feet, hitting the curve, high balls and low balls, and all of the basics of the swing. He talked about the swings of DiMaggio, Babe Ruth, Pie Traynor, Ty Cobb and Stan Musial among others. They were very basic books. Each description is about one page in length, about 30 pages in total, and with drawings instead of pictures.

By way of example, Joe Cambria wrote one chapter on Turning the Body. In today's parlance, he would be talking about "clearing the hips."

Turn the Body

Turning the body, the shoulders and the hip is definitely necessary to finish "the swing." It is not possible to finish the "swing" without turning the body and turning the wrists. The front hip, the closest to the pitcher/thrower, must be

EL GIRO DEL CUERPO

Voltear el cuerpo, los hombros y la cadera, es definitivamente necesario al terminar el "swing". No es posible completar el "swing" sin el giro del cuerpo y el giro de muñecas. La cadera delantera, la más cercana al lanzador, debe empezar a moverse con el "swing". Uniendo la cadera delantera y el costado desviarán por completo el "swing".

En lanzamientos hacia dentro, el bateador debe mover la cadera delantera fuera del medio un poco adelantado y comenzar el giro del cuerpo un instante antes de hacer contacto con la pelota.

Esta acción para abrir camino facilita al bateador hacer contacto con la pelota antes de llegar el cuerpo al punto normal para los buenos batazos.

AGACHARSE

Agacharse es una falta común entre los malos bateadores. La frase vieja, "los buenos bateadores nacen, no se hacen, ha sido desaprobada muchísimas veces. No debe de haber ningún secreto para ser un buen bateador.

Conectar la pelota sólidamente, viene del conocimiento básico de las reglas fundamentales. Miles de peloteros han aprendido cómo batear después de adquirir conocimientos, tras estudios, imitando buenos bateadores y experimentando.

El bateador dibujado podrá aprender el estilo propio y tendrá mejor éxito al bate cuando elimine el agacharse. Es realidad probada que uno no puede ver bien cuando los ojos están moviéndose.

"Turning the Hips" section of the *Al Bate* book. Here, Cambria is explaining the proper technique for "clearing the hips" through the swing, along with the upper body follow-through (private collection of Paul Scimonelli).

moved together with the swing. Moving together the front hip and the side of the body will completely misdirect.

During the inside throw, the batter must move the front hip away from the middle, a bit forward and start turning the body right before making contact with the ball.

This action to open makes it easier for the batter to make contact with the ball before the body returns to its normal position, resulting in good hits.

Joe Cambria was not a Shakespeare by any means! His language was extremely simple and direct. Both "how-to" books were meant as primers for the young player to study and apply to their own batting and running style. Cambria had always started training camps for young rookies in his early team ownership days and believed teaching should start early, when boys were in their early teens. He may have been thinking ahead to when he would become his own instructional camp counselor, as he explained to the *Miami News.*

"They used to laugh when I kept sending all those Cubans to the big leagues. Now, I can't move down there for all the other scouts from all the other clubs. The only thing I can do is get the kids when they're real young and teach 'em myself. Why, it's gotten so bad down there, we even have bonus players!"[90]

He continued his literary endeavors with the *Times,* albeit less and less frequently, until 1959.

The 1957 Senators

Nineteen fifty-seven was a volatile year for the Senators. Whenever you have a managerial change, even early in the season, it disrupts the team chemistry. Both the team and the new manager need to get used to each other, especially the pitching staff. Lavagetto had a more hands-off style than Chuck Dressen, and knowing how to handle your pitching staff is a major factor to a team's success. The team finished dead last with a 55–99 record.

"We had a good team and some fine ballplayers," said Roy Sievers. "Problem was, we just couldn't hit!"[91] This was unfortunately true. Besides Sievers' career year of 42 homers, 114 RBI and 331 total bases, the rest of the team faltered. Jim Lemon hit a respectable 17 home runs with 147 hits but struck out 94 times, highest on the team. The rest of the team's hitting was mediocre at best.

The pitching staff was just as dismal. Not one of the starters posted a winning record. Chuck Stobbs, the Nats' most dependable starter, went 8–20 in 211⅔ innings but struck out 114. Camilo Pascual went 8–17 in 175⅔ innings but struck out 113. Pedro Ramos was the workhorse on the staff, going 12–16 in 231 innings. Tex Clevenger (7–6), Dick Hyde (4–3) and Bud Byerly (6–6) were effective in relief, but they had to be. The starters were knocked out so frequently that Clevenger, Hyde and Byerly combined to pitch in 151 games, and only George Zuverink of the Orioles pitched in more.

Collectively, the team was just bad. Their .244 batting average was the lowest in the league. They were seventh in hits (1,274) and sixth in home runs (111) and in runs scored (603), thanks in large part to Mr. Sievers. Pitching was sad. The team had the highest ERA in the league (4.85) and gave up the most hits (1.482), runs (808) and home runs (149), second only to the woeful Athletics' 156 homers.

Calvin Griffith was muttering to his toast and talking to Minnesota.

1958

"I had a great year in 1957," said Roy Sievers. "I was gonna make 'em pay for it!"

Roy Sievers' multitudinous home runs and the classic battle waged with Mickey Mantle and Ted Williams were the stuff of legend for 1957. It put Washington on the sports map in a positive light for the first time in many years. Sievers became the Senators' biggest gate attraction since Walter Johnson. Noted baseball writers Shirley Povich and Bob Addie both alluded to the fact that there was never a good reason to go to a Senators game in the 1950s other than to watch the play of Roy Sievers. His prodigious home run hitting was the only thing that kept the fans coming to the cavernous and dreary Griffith Stadium, increasing attendance by 45 percent between 1955 and 1959. During those years, Senators attendance (as well as their division standing) was either seventh or eighth in the league, yet Griffith still was able to run the team in the black.

Consequently, Roy Sievers's contract hold-out in 1958 became more stuff of legend. He was absolutely adamant that he wanted his salary doubled from $18,000 to $36,000. Griffith countered with only $30,000, and Sievers refused to sign. Griffith tried the old dodge of dangling Sievers as trade bait. He had talks with Frank Lane of the Tigers, but Lane would not part with pitcher Frank Lary or shortstop Reno Bertoia. Griffith talked with the Yankees, but Casey Stengel would not part with Gil McDougald, nor the $100,000 Griffith was asking for. Sievers had hit homers in every American League ballpark and had proven himself to be a bona fide star. Griffith was definitely not going to trade him for "scrubs or second line players."

But Roy Sievers was smart. He knew he was not going to get $36,000 out of the notably parsimonious Griffith, so he started high and settled for what he wanted, which was $33,000. It made him the highest paid player in Senators history to date. Sievers rewarded Griffith by having another productive year.

If Griffith could have gotten $100,000 from the Yankees for Sievers, he probably would have taken it because he was taking a bath with the television revenues. The Senators' T.V. sponsors, who had spent $25,000 for four games in 1957, dropped the team for the 1958 season. The "first in war, first in peace and last in the American League" Senators were just not attracting fans in the seats or viewers on the screen, Roy Sievers' home runs notwithstanding. The African American population of the District of Columbia, disappointed with the lack of Black faces on the team, also decided to water their flower gardens rather than attend Senators games. Griffith was stuck between a rock and a hard place. Besides Sievers, Pascual and Ramos, Griffith had little else with which to deal. He was not going to give up his three most effective players unless he got equal or better in return, none of the top-tier teams wanted to be seen trading with the AL doormats, and none of the players wanted to be traded to the D.C. graveyard.[92]

Griffith was truly damned if he did and damned if he didn't.

Spring training dawned bright and hopeful yet again in 1958, even though almost everyone knew there would not be any more hope than last year. Many of the club owners, Griffith included, complained about the lack of depth in their lineups, mainly because the Yankees had all the depth in the world. If a Gil McDougald went down, Casey Stengel could plug in a Bobby Richardson and never miss a beat. They had Bob Turley, Whitey Ford, Don Larsen, Tom Sturdivant, Bobby Shantz, Johnny Kucks, and Art Ditmar, not a loser in the bunch. Seven top-line pitchers could make up three teams' worth of quality starters. No one was going to unseat them from the throne.

So, Calvin Griffith wheeled and dealed as best he could. In January, he sent the "underperforming" Pete Runnels to the Red Sox for first baseman "Big Norm" Zauchin (6'4", 220 lbs.) and rookie outfielder "Little Albie" Pearson (5'5", 149 lbs.). Both of them would be referred to by their monikers throughout the season. Zauchin, Julio Becquer and Roy Sievers would platoon duties at first base for the year. Pearson would patrol center field and earn Rookie of the Year honors for 1958.

For Runnels, it was the breath of new life. Without the 320 foot "cavern" down Griffith Stadium's right field line, and mentored by the aging Ted Williams, Runnels quickly became a hitting machine. In his five years in Beantown, he collected 805 hits, hit 137 doubles, was a three-time All-Star, and was a two-time batting champion.

Joe Cambria still had a little juice left in the tank and sent up a few of his charges to Orlando for tryouts. He sent 20-year-old Orlando Valdes up to Phil Howser, manager of the Nats' Charlotte Hornets team, who took him into training camp. The six-foot, 170-pound fireballer was highly regarded by both Cambria and Howser, who remarked, "Papa Joe says he's got everything—speed, curve, control and the changeup. But the thing that makes me believe that Valdes might be a good boy is the fact that Joe gave him a coupla thousand to sign. Cambria doesn't believe in bonuses beyond an old baseball or a used glove."[93]

Valdes got his look but the Senators did not like him. He did not even make it to the B league Hornets. He spent two years in D league ball and finished up with a year with Veracruz in the Mexican Leagues.

Cambria did send up one supposed superstar, Ossie Alvarez. Alvarez and Camilo Pascual were two of the leading stars of the Cuban league champion Cienfuegos *Elefantes*. Alvarez had been in the Senators' farm system since Cambria signed him to Big Springs in the Texas League in 1954. Alvarez, a spectacular second baseman, made good in 1958, sticking with the parent club. He played in 87 games and posted a .209 batting average in 196 at-bats. He landed with Detroit in 1959, then finished his career in the Mexican Leagues from 1960 through 1966.

Also sent up from Charlotte was pitcher Angel Oliva, another Cambria Cuban. Oliva had been signed by Cambria to the Roswell Rockets in the Longhorn League in 1954. His best year was a 16–10 season with Charlotte in 1957, which got him his look-see at the 1958 camp. Lavagetto and Griffith did not see enough to promote him to the parent club. He toiled in the Senators' minor league system until 1962, making it up to AAA ball in 1959. He also played with Marianao in the Cuban Winter Leagues and ended his career with Poza Rica in the Mexican Leagues in 1962. He never made it to the Show.

David Cameron, Bob Saban, Richard Shutz, Gary Mitchell and Tom McAvoy were also escapees from the Charlotte hinterlands. Cameron, Saban, Shutz and Mitchell never made it out of the Nats' farm system. Tom McAvoy got his "Moonlight Graham" moment when he pitched 2⅔ innings for the Senators in 1959.[94]

One Hornet who did stick with the 1958 Nats was scrappy infielder John Schaive, who had been toiling in the White Sox's and Senators' farms since 1952. He got cups of coffee in 1958 (eight games), 1959 (16 games) and 1960 (six games). His best year was 1962 with the expansion Senators. In 82 games, he had 225 at-bats, 57 hits, 20 runs, 29 RBI, and a respectable .253 batting average. He lasted only three games in 1963, then was relegated to the Mexican Leagues from 1964 to 1966, when he ended his 14-year career.[95]

Also back for another perusal were rookies Bob Allison, Harmon Killebrew and Jim Kaat. Both Allison and Killebrew showed well, but neither was ready to unseat the regulars. Killebrew hit 29 homers and drove in 101 runs for Chattanooga but struck out an amazing 123 times. Eddie Yost still had one of the most productive on-base percentages in both leagues, and outfielders Roy Sievers and Jim Lemon were the team's big 1–2 punch. Kaat looked good but not enough for Lavagetto. He went 16–9 for Missoula in 1958. All three would make it up to the Show in 1959.

The "egg on his face" award went to the Senators' new farm director, Sherry Robertson. Brother of Calvin Griffith, Robertson signed up a promising Black infielder, six-foot, two-inch, 195-pound Navarro Ramon Davis, and promptly declared him to be "the shortstop of our future." Davis, who had hit .393 on a Detroit sandlot team in 1957, was recommended by Nats scout Jack Rossiter, who ran a famous baseball school in Cocoa, Florida. "I have been trying to sign him for two years," said Robertson, "but I wanted a figure that would put him in the bonus class. I call him the finest young infield prospect I've ever seen. He is a right-handed hitter with a lot of power."[96]

In 1958, Davis batted .098 for Fox Cities in the 3-I League, .170 for Gainesville in the Florida State League, and .000 for Elmira in the New York-Penn League in his only year in organized baseball.

"Senators' Rookie Crop Slim," assessed Joe Reichler, sports reporter for the *Orlando Evening Star*. And unfortunately, he was right. Reichler went on to tick off the names of some new and old faces who were coming to camp with renewed hope. Although they all had big league experience, not many were big-league worthy.

Don Minnick: 17–6 with Chattanooga, he pitched 9⅓ innings with the 1957 Nats, lost his only decision, and posted a 4.82 ERA. He did not make it back up.

Neil Chrisley: Everybody needs left-handed hitters, and Chrisley was effective. He hit .298 with 24 homers in Louisville in 1956. With the Nats in 1958, he smacked five homers, drove in 26 runs, and posted a .215 average. He was sold to Detroit in 1959.

Carlos Paula: Washington's first Black player hit .288 in Minneapolis in 1957. He did not make it through training camp and went back to the Cuban and the Mexican Leagues.

Whitey Herzog: Aptly nicknamed "Wild Child" by the great Satchel Paige, Herzog made the team in 1958, played eight games, and was promptly sold to the Athletics.

Bob Malkmus: Formerly with the Braves organization, Malkmus made the team as a backup for starting second baseman Ken Aspromonte.

Hal Griggs: Hal Griggs went 1–6 for the Nats in 1956 and was used as a reliever in 1957. He made the squad but posted an unfortunate 3–11 record and a 5.52 ERA for 1958. He spent one more year with the Senators, then finished his career in the minors in 1966.

Jim Heise: Heise went 0–3 for the Nats in 1957. He did not make the team in 1958 and played out his career in the minors until 1961.

Ralph Lumenti: A bonus baby with a good fastball, Lumenti had little success with the Nats. He went 0–1 in 1957, 1–3 in 1958 and 0–0 in 1959. He stayed in the Washington system until 1962.

Bert Guenther: A $20,000 bonus baby from Cincinnati, he did not have enough to make the team in 1958. He spent 1958 through 1961 in the Nats' minors and never made it to the Show.

Steve Korcheck: Originally drafted by the San Francisco 49ers as a center/fullback, Korcheck chose baseball instead, signing with the Senators in 1954. He was a backup catcher in 1954–1955, did two years in the Army, and came back to the Senators for 1958 and 1959 as Clint Courtney's number 2 man. After baseball, he earned a doctorate in education from George Washington University and rose to become the president of the State College of Florida, Sarasota-Manatee from 1980 to 1997.

Jose Valdivielso: He was originally signed by Joe Cambria to play in Lubbock in 1953. He played in 184 games for the Nats in 1955–1956, then was sent back down to the minors. He resurfaced with the club in 1959 and had his most productive year in 1960, playing full time at shortstop. In an interview, he revealed that he had a serious problem. He was falling asleep on the buses, trains, planes and occasionally in the dugout and was thought to be a carouser by his managers. He was actually suffering from a serious case of undiagnosed sleep apnea, which caused him to wake up between 40 and 60 times a night. Once diagnosed, he was prescribed medications which allowed him to get the rest he needed, but he said it almost ruined his baseball career and could have cost him his life.[97]

Cookie Lavagetto and Calvin Griffith saw everyone above, and there was not a Mantle, Berra or Ford in the bunch … yet. They broke camp and headed north with almost the same team as the year before. Their hopes were higher this year upon the news about Camilo Pascual received from Joe Cambria down in Cuba. Cambria wrote to Griffith to say that Pascual never looked better, that his color was good, and he had gained some valuable weight. Griffith reported to the *Washington Post,* "We had Pascual examined again this winter and Cambria reports the boy never felt better. We think he can come into his own this season because he won't get so tired halfway through the season."[98]

What Calvin Griffith was alluding to was that the team had insisted that Pascual quit playing winter ball in Cuba, citing a little-known rule which stated that if a member of a major league club is physically unfit, he can be kept out of playing winter ball. Griffith claimed that Pascual's right shoulder, injured by an Al Cicotte line drive in May of 1957, needed rest because Pascual was of little help for the rest of that season. He did not pitch for six weeks after the injury and was ineffective after that. Griffith was pinning his hopes on his two Cuban starters, Pascual and Ramos. They had finished 1–2 in the 1956–1957 Cuban Winter League Series. Truth be told, if he could have, Calvin Griffith would have stopped them both from playing Cuban winter ball, but Ramos would have none of it. The Cubans could be funny that way.[99]

But, as the old saying goes, insanity is doing the same thing over and over again and expecting different results.

As things began to change in Cuba, Cambria waxed reminiscent in a lengthy interview with Bob Addie of the *Washington Post.* He lamented the fact that he lost a young Stan Musial when Branch Rickey, then owner of the St. Louis Cardinals, convinced Clark Griffith that the skinny kid would never make it in the majors. He lost Minnie Minoso much the same way to Cleveland.

He was proud, however, of the many good players he was successful in snaring for the Senators, from Eddie Yost and Mickey Vernon down to Pascual and Ramos. And he stuck to his philosophy he had adhered to throughout his scouting career. "I never paid a nickel for a ballplayer," said Cambria. "I don't believe in giving a boy financial success before he earns it. That's the trouble with the Cuban kids today. They are like Americans now and want a bonus. Imagine giving a Cuban kid $4,000. That's what some big-league scouts are offering now!"[100]

But that was not the trouble. Fidel Castro had been fomenting insurrection in Cuba since 1953. Up until now, it was confined to the outer regions of the island. But in March of 1957, a large group of insurrectionists, led by students, launched an attack on the Presidential palace. Many were killed in the unsuccessful coup. By August, President Fulgencio Batista suspended many of Cuba's constitutional guarantees. Attacks continued in earnest throughout 1958, culminating with the final overthrow of the Batista regime on New Year's Day, 1959.

Consequently, Cambria's freedom of movement around the island was severely limited. Armed military now patrolled Gran Stadium lest an insurrection begin at the ballpark. The island, which had once been Cambria's exclusive provenance, was now crawling with American scouts.

"I try to interest the kids in baseball, but now everybody is playing Cowboys and Indians in the streets. I've got to get the ballplayers when they're still young kids, about 14 or 15. I can't wait for them to develop because some other scout is going to outbid me."[101]

Cambria's latest batch of talent, Pascual, Ramos, Julio Becquer, Jose Valdivielso and the up-and-coming Zoilo Versalles, were plucked from the island as teenagers in the mid–1950s. With the revolutionary fervor gripping the country, fewer and fewer people, kids included, were interested in baseball. By 1961, Castro would shut down the island and ban the trade of players from the island permanently.

So Cambria busied himself with a new venture. He, along with a Mr. W.A. Chiara, started a new club, the Havana Cuban Giants, and petitioned to get them into the Pioneer league. Cambria set up an ambitious 120-game exhibition schedule and toured with the team throughout Montana, Idaho, Utah, Colorado, Iowa and Indiana. He was proposing to enter the league as an eighth team as a "road club" without official headquarters or a home park. However, with the demise of Twin Falls, the league contracted to six teams and decided to remain in that configuration for 1959.[102]

Joe being Joe, he sold some of his best players to the Missoula Timberjacks, most notably Bert Cueto, Minnie Mendoza, and Sandy Valdespino, all of whom played for the Twins. Unfortunately for Joe Cambria, his world would come falling down. On September 18, 1958, his beloved wife, Charlotte, died at St. Joseph's Hospital in Baltimore. She had been an invalid for over 20 years and had been hospitalized shortly before her passing. Charlotte had been the glue that kept the Bugle laundry business together while Joe was off with his many baseball adventures in the 1920s and 1930s. Joe returned home to attend to her needs and to accompany the body to Roxbury, Massachusetts, for burial. She was approximately 74 years old.[103]

The mystery of Charlotte Kane Cambria is most intriguing. Throughout the research for this book, there was precious little information to be found on her. Two newspaper articles in the *Boston Globe*, dated November 7, 1912, and September 7, 1915, briefly mention a Miss Charlotte Kane working on labor committees for the Boston Central Labor Union. In his reason for deferment in World War II, Joe Cambria listed his wife as "sickly." Aside from those mentions and one other previously mentioned from the *Baltimore Sun*, Charlotte Cambria lived and toiled almost in obscurity. Their marriage, unfortunately, produced no children.

The 1958 Senators

Well, you guessed it already. The Senators finished in last place once again, although they posted a better record (61–93) than in 1957 (55–99). The Yankees ran away with it all for another year, but they had to come back from a 3–1 deficit, and it took them seven games to down the Braves, who just could not tame Hank Bauer's hot bat.

Once again, the Nats just could not hit in the clutch. Roy Sievers had another career year, with 39 home runs, 108 RBI, and a .295 average. Jim Lemon smacked 26 taters, plated 75 RBI, and had a .246 average but struck out an enormous 120 times in 555 plate appearances. "Big" Norm Zauchin hit 15 homers, but with only 37 RBI and a lowly .228 average. "Little" Albie Pearson had 146 hits but scored only 63 runs and had a .275 average. Courtney, Aspromonte, Bridges and Yost all contributed, but just not enough. Not many got on base, and when they did, nobody could bring them home.

The pitching staff toiled hard but once again came up short due to lack of timely hitting. Ramos, the workhorse, went 14–18 with 132 strikeouts but a 4.23 ERA. Pascual showed better than last year. He went 8–12 but led the staff with 146 strikeouts and a 3.15 ERA. Russ Kemmerer went 6–15 with 111 strikeouts and a bloated 4.61 ERA. The two main relievers, Dick Hyde (10–3, 53 games) and Tex Clevenger (9–9, 55 games), helped the Nats to more wins but had to work hard to do so.

They were once again at or near the bottom of the league in batting average (.240), hits (1,240) and runs scored (553), but were a respectable fifth in home runs (111) thanks in large measure to Messrs. Sievers, Lemon and Zauchin. The pitching staff ignominiously led the league in all the wrong categories: hits (1,443), runs (747), home runs (156), and ERA (4.53).[104]

Changes once again needed to be made, and in December, Calvin Griffith traded two of his more productive hitters, Rocky Bridges and Eddie Yost, along with reserve outfielder Neil Chrisley, to Detroit for slick-fielding Reno Bertoia, journeyman Ron Samford, and veteran Jim Delsing.[105]

New farm director Sherry Robertson finally convinced Griffith to expand the farm by adding nine new scouts. That put the count at 29 full-time scouts, second only to the Orioles' 32 in the field. Sherry Robertson also hired Harry Reid and Joe Black, the first two Black scouts in the team's history. The farm system was expanded to eight teams: Chattanooga Lookouts (AA), Charlotte Hornets (A), Fox Cities Foxes (B), Missoula Timberjacks (C), and four D league teams, the Fort Walton Beach Jets, Gainesville G-Men, Superior Senators, and Elmira Pioneers.[106]

Once the season ended, Calvin Griffith worked harder than before. Trades were talked about almost constantly. Griffith liked the idea of the new District of Columbia Stadium that was being talked about but continued to entertain talks and offers from cities other than Washington. Concerning his ongoing talks with the Minnesota consortium, Bob Considine, never at a loss for an opinion, published a scathing commentary about Griffith and his family:

> What the good burghers of Minneapolis should know, as they entice the Washington Nats to that fair city, is that the club will remain a non-descript bargain-basement outfit as long as it is in the hands of the people now running it.
>
> The Griffith family, all nice folks to be sure, inherited none of "Uncle Clark's" baseball savvy, trading skills, ability to gamble money now and then, or gall. Calvin Griffith is a fine young fellow, and his brothers, sister Thelma and brother-in-law Joe Haynes couldn't be finer, but their attitude towards the property which old Clark Griffith left to them has been: "It's a living."
>
> There has been only wishful thinking about improving the club. A last-place Washington team is sufficient to satisfy the family's modest needs. Attendances has been meager, but so are the salaries of the players and staff and the retainer fees of what passes for a scouting system. Besides, there is always radio and TV to fall back on for revenue.[107]

Everything that Considine said was true. Clark and Addie Griffith had no children of their own, so, through Christian charity born of their 19th century mindset, they "adopted" and raised Addie's niece and nephew, Calvin and Thelma Robertson, as their own, and later, the rest of Robertson siblings. Clark strongly believed in family and ran his ball club like an extended family. He hired all of the Robertsons to serve the team in some capacity. It was truly a "mom and pop store," and the Griffiths lived modestly.

Altruistic as it was, it was not a good business model. Other major league teams were run by seasoned businessmen who ran their teams as commercial enterprises. They had the necessary monies available to buy and train the greatest players in the game. Although Joe Cambria had supplied Griffith with some good talent (Case, Welaj, Yost, Vernon, Pascual, Ramos), they were not great.

But things were about to change, again. Some said not for the better, however.

1959

A new year could not have dawned in a more dramatic fashion.

In the wee small hours of Thursday, January 1, 1959, Cuban president Fulgencio Batista abdicated his position in the government. A military *junta*, led by Chief Judge Carlos Manuel Piedra as provisional president, was named by Batista, and he fled the country for the Dominican Republic, as Fidel Castro's "26th of July" rebel forces overtook the city. By the end of the day, American warships arrived in Cuban waters, prepared to evacuate American citizens. Castro's lieutenant, Che Guevara, rode into Havana unopposed on Saturday, January 3. Castro himself did not arrive in Havana until January 8, refused to work with the *junta*, and began his own provisional government with himself as Prime Minister and Manuel Urrutia as president.[108]

The impact this had and is still having upon Latin America has reverberated for a half-century. The impact it had on American baseball in general and on the Washington Senators was immediate.

The Cuban Winter Leagues were in the midst of their playing season when the revolution occurred in Havana. Forty American players were on the four Cuban teams, and nine of them were on the Senators' roster: Americans Jim Constable, Johnny Romonosky, Albie Pearson and Bob Allison and Cubans Pedro Ramos, Camilo Pascual, Angel Oliva, Jose Valdivielso and Julio Becquer.

After talking with Commissioner Ford Frick and Minor League President George Trautman, as well as the State Department, Nats president Calvin Griffith did not immediately withdraw his players from the Cuban teams.

> I was told by Frick and Trautman that it was up to me to withdraw my players and that I'd be justified under a "peril clause" in the agreement between the Caribbean Baseball Federation and major league baseball. I talked to the State Department and was told that none of the ballplayers should be in danger unless they took an active part in the rebellion. The American players are quartered about 20 blocks from the center of Havana and should be in no immediate danger. I understand from the Associated Press that all ball games have been canceled [this was on January 2nd] but that play would be resumed Sunday. I debated whether to recall my American players, but on the assurance of the State Department, I decided to let things ride for a while. If the situation gets worse, I shall certainly give orders for the four Americans to return home or at least quit playing.[109]

Seemingly untroubled by it all, Joe Cambria sent Griffith a rather "business as usual" letter. Griffith told the *Post,* "The letter was dated Monday and Joe sent me a clipping, in Spanish, telling of a great two-hitter that Ramos threw on Monday. Pascual was scheduled to pitch on Tuesday when the revolution broke out in full force. Pascual was supposed to have pitched against Romonosky."[110]

In a telephone interview, I asked Camilo Pascual if it was an especially scary time for him and the others. He responded, "No, it wasn't that difficult. At that time, the beginning of the revolution, I mean it was a problem for those guys who got involved in politics. But we not have any problem really."[111]

Things were tremulous on the island for a while, but they eventually returned to a semblance of normalcy and baseball went on.

"I'm going to shake up the bottle and maybe the cream will come to the top," said manager Cookie Lavagetto to the *Washington Post*.[112]

This was basically a polite and positive way of saying what every mercurial manager in every spring training camp says in February: I am on my knees rolling dice, trying to piece together a lineup that will win a few ball games. It was also Lavagetto's polite way of saying that everyone's job was up for grabs, a statement that does little or nothing to promote structure and continuity in a ball team. "The only exception," said Lavagetto, "is Roy Sievers. Let's face it. Roy is a good ballplayer. He's a star. He'll do a good job wherever you put him. But the rest of them are going to have to hustle."[113]

And a star he was. Already a two-time All-Star, Sievers was coming off monstrous back-to-back seasons of 42 homers, 114 RBI in 1957 and 39 homers, 108 RBI in 1958. A notorious holdout, Sievers demanded $40,000 to sign for 1959 and Griffith, of course, refused. In a taped interview, Sievers said that Griffith's dodge about his salary was that "he didn't lead the league in any categories." Roy Sievers sat home in St. Louis with his wife, Joan, and the kids, Shawn and Robin, and worked out with Bob Bauman, trainer for the Cardinals, until Griffith eventually came around to a $36,000 offer.

But not before Griffith paraded Sievers around the league like a show pony, trying to see who would offer what and for whom. Chicago offered Billy Goodman, Ray Boone, Ron Jackson, Bubba Phillips and two minor leaguers for Sievers and Yost, which Griffith found less than attractive. Lavagetto discussed deals with Casey Stengel for Sievers and reliever Dick Hyde, but the Yankees would not give up any of their front-line players.[114] The Indians offered a blockbuster deal: Minnie Minoso, Woody Held and pitcher Jim "Mudcat" Grant for Sievers and Ramos. That did not fly either.[115]

These kinds of fishing expeditions were *de rigueur* for Griffith and big-league owners during the winter and spring months. If there was a chance to get another team's future star or current well-performing veteran for a reasonable price, then it was Katie bar the door. For Griffith, he usually wound up with more "even steven" trades than anything else. For the players, baseball's reserve clause made them little more than pawns to be sacrificed to the Kings of baseball. The players knew their only choice was sign or sit.

But this year, Cookie Lavagetto said it was going to be different. "I mean it. No player is sure of his job and I'm going to give the youngsters the biggest chance they ever had. They're here to play big league ball and they're going to get the chance."[116]

Lavagetto was talking about many young players who had been laboring in the Senators' minor league system for several years: Dan Dobbek, Dickie Harris, John Schaive, Bob Allison, and Harmon Killebrew.

The last two, Allison and Killebrew, turned out to be the best chances Lavagetto ever took. Both young men had been bouncing around the Nats' minors since 1955, putting up very respectable hitting and fielding numbers. Both of them showed up well during spring training and were chosen as starters, Allison in center field and Killebrew at third base.

But it was their bats that would do the talking for them. Allison and Killebrew teamed up with veterans Roy Sievers and Jim Lemon to become the Senators' first legitimate "Murderers' Row." They were dubbed "The Fearsome Foursome" and the new "S.A.L.K vaccine" after Dr. Jonas Salk, who invented the polio serum. SALK stood for Sievers, Allison, Lemon, and Killebrew. With all pun intended, the four mighty musclemen became the "shot in the arm" the Senators needed, tearing up American League pitching. Killebrew would tie the Indians' Rocky Colavito for the league lead with 42 homers, Lemon popped 33 over the fences, Allison contributed 30, and Sievers, in an injury-plagued season, hit 21 round-trippers. The Senators hit 163 dingers, second only to the Indians' 167.[117]

In Cuba, the revolution and its subsequent aftermath put the island in chaos for a while, but Joe Cambria still had free rein over his baseball domain. Cambria was known by Batista and Castro, who looked upon him as just an American baseball man. He was very apolitical and posed no threat to Castro per se.

Cambria was still able to supply Washington with players, more so for the minor league system then the parent club. One young player who did make the grade, though, was Zoilo Versalles.

Zoilo Versalles (ZOY-lo vair-SY-yez) began his baseball career as a green 16-year-old rookie playing with the Fortuna Sports Club of the Cuban Amateur Athletic Union League in 1955. He played sparingly with Cienfuegos and Marianao in the Cuban professional leagues between 1957 and 1959. Versalles was the antithesis of the stereotypical "good field, no hit" Cuban shortstop. He had a good bat and could hit for power besides being a fine middle infielder. Cambria signed him to a free agent contract in 1958, and he headed to the U.S. to find his fortune.[118]

The transition proved to be exceedingly difficult for the 19-year-old. Versalles struggled not only with the English language but also with severe bouts of depression and homesickness. He threatened repeatedly to leave America to be with his family and especially his teenage sweetheart, María Josefa Fransillo, whom he had met when playing with the Fortuna club. His anxieties were soothed over with the help of Cuban veterans Julio Becquer and Sandy Valdespino.

As was their wont, the American press had difficulty with the name "Zoilo" and began referring to him as "Zorro" after the popular Disney TV show of the same name. He made the team in 1959, sharing shortstop duties with Billy Consolo and Jose Valdivielso. His debut on August 1 was less than august. He struck out three times and flied out once. In 29 games, he managed only nine hits, one of which was a home run, and a paltry .153 batting average.

Versalles was sent down to the Fox City Foxes of the Three-I League, where he did very well, hitting a respectable .278 with nine homers: however, his league-leading 34 errors were disconcerting. Lavagetto did not give up on him though. He had another cup of coffee with the Senators in 1960, then made the transition to Minnesota in 1961.[119]

The Senators knew they would have to legitimately cross the color barrier and began taking steps to do so. Joe Black, the great Dodgers reliever, was signed in 1957, but he appeared only in relief, and it was obvious that he was at the end of his career. He was shelled mightily in the 22 innings he pitched and let go at the end of the season.

Len Tucker had the distinction, if one could call it that, of being the first Black player signed by the St. Louis Cardinals in 1953, although Tucker looked upon it as less than a distinction. "I never looked upon it as anything but a guy who was signing," said Tucker, who hit .385 with nine homers and 41 RBIs in 148 at-bats during his final season at Fresno State.

> They brought attention to me by saying I was Black. And I thought, "What are you trying to say, that a Black shouldn't be here or that it's a miracle?" If they were so concerned that I was Black, and [Cardinals president August] Busch got a lot of publicity from it the night I signed, then why didn't I ever go further with them? I didn't disgrace them out of college. And that was worth something. But after a while, they just let me go.[120]

"Lightning Len" Tucker hit a ton in the minors, but he was ultimately let go. So he tried his hand in the Mexican and Canadian Leagues, picking up the knowledge of first base along the way. In 1959, the Senators bought the Poza Rica franchise of the Mexican League and were extremely impressed with his hitting. He was signed by Lavagetto but spent most of spring training riding the bench. Shortly before the team broke camp to go north, Len Tucker got his shot in an exhibition game against Cincinnati. He hit a home run in his first at-bat. The next day, Lavagetto had him stay at camp while the team was on a road trip to work out at first base. Unfortunately, he was sent down to the Miami Marlins the next day. Tucker said:

> I stayed behind to work at first base and picked up everything but the earth. I looked good and now they sell me to the Marlins after one game. Lavagetto told me he didn't think I was better than anyone he already had. Roy Sievers was playing first at the time and they had a Cuban guy [Julio Becquer] backing him up.[121]

Len Tucker spent 1960 through 1963 in the Northwest and California Leagues and finally hung them up at the end of the 1963 season. With his degree from Fresno State, he taught social studies and physical education for 20 years in the Fresno school system. He passed away in July of 2011.

The Senators were sure that Tucker would be their first American Black position player to join the team. That distinction, however, would go to Lenny Green. Green was acquired by the Senators in a straight-up swap with the Baltimore Orioles for Albie Pearson. Pearson's Rookie of the Year .275 batting average looked huge against Green's .218 average; however, Green had only played in 88 games over a two-year period, so the comparison was a bit skewed.

When he was asked by the *Baltimore Afro-American* what he had planned for Green, Lavagetto responded, "At the moment, I'm not sure. I've watched the boy for quite a spell and I liked what I saw. But also at the moment, you have to realize I can't disturb my starting outfield. All three of my guys are hot at present. When one of 'em cools off, Lenny goes in."[122]

Lenny Green got into 88 games over the remainder of the season. In 192 at-bats, he got 46 hits, six doubles, two homers and scored 29 runs for a .242 batting average. Green added a lot of bench strength to the team and made the starting lineup in 1960.

As always, change occurs.

Fleeing from their crumbling stadiums and falling fan bases, the New York Giants and the Brooklyn Dodgers, after decades of inhabiting New York City, infamously moved their franchises to California at the end of the 1957 season. New York was left with only one American League team, and this did not please William Shea.

Bill Shea (the namesake of Shea Stadium), prominent New York attorney and businessman, wanted desperately to get another Major League team back to New York and began almost immediately planning the move. In August of 1959, he formed a new, third major league, the Continental League, and named Branch Rickey as its president. The league was to begin play in April of 1961, and eight cities, New York, Houston, Minneapolis/St. Paul, Toronto, Denver and later, Atlanta, Buffalo and Dallas/Ft. Worth, all had owners willing to put up the concomitant fees to begin the new franchises and build new stadiums.

This did not sit well with Major League Baseball owners. Afraid of losing both the autonomy which they had in all baseball operations and, more importantly, their precious anti-trust exemption (which would, in turn, affect their reserve clause), the major league owners proposed to the new Continental League owners that they would agree to the expansion of the existing National and American Leagues to ten teams each and would definitely place one franchise in New York City. Against Rickey's advice and protestations, the Continental League owners agreed, as long as expansion would continue in the future to all of the cities who had agreed to the Continental League's original mandate. Of all the original Continental League cities, only Buffalo has remained without a major-league baseball franchise.[123]

Calvin Griffith clearly wanted to move the Senators out of Washington, his statements to the contrary notwithstanding. Griffith Stadium was old and dilapidated, there was no place to park, and many white fans were apprehensive about driving into "that part of town" to watch a night baseball game. He had been secretly courting offers from Los Angeles and Minneapolis, among other cities, to move the Senators franchise there.

Upon hearing the news that Griffith wanted indeed to move the Senators to Minnesota, the hue and cry in Washington, D.C., was immediate and loud. The District of Columbia had become the ritualistic home of baseball since William Howard Taft threw out the first ceremonial "first pitch" in 1910. Many Senators or Congressmen were privy to the perks of a free ticket in the Presidential box. Although they did not show up with any great alacrity, the D.C. metropolitan area fans loved their "lovable losers" and were hard-pressed to see them go.

Senator Estes Kefauver (D–Tennessee) began a Senate subcommittee on Anti-Trust and Monopoly in 1951, which continued until 1963. The Committee took on such major corporations as U.S. Steel, General Electric, General Motors, Ford, Chrysler, and the big oil companies in an effort to uphold the county's anti-trust laws against restraint of trade. They also wanted to question professional athletes about monopolies in boxing and baseball. In 1958, Casey Stengel testified for an hour in his famous brand of "Stengel-ese" double talk, which did nothing to mollify the Senators on that day's committee about the possibilities of baseball's involvement in anti-trust activities. It did, however, raise the specter that baseball was being scrutinized, and the talk about a new league was not going to help Calvin Griffith's chances of moving his team to Minnesota.[124]

Griffith used his influence, garnered by his late Uncle Clark's revered position in the baseball world, to soothe the savage breast of the Washington politicos. He convinced the other owners to put a replacement franchise in Washington if he were allowed to move to Minnesota, which was waiting with bated breath and a new stadium already built. They approved and, in the spring of 1961, the expansion Senators and the Los Angeles Angels became the two newest members of the American League. The following year, the New York Metropolitans and the Houston Colt .45s became the new National League teams.

Laboring like a one-armed wallpaper hanger, Joe Cambria used the news about this new third league to cajole and convince Major League Baseball to start (what else!) a Latin baseball league. Still writing for the *Times of Havana* in 1959, Cambria used his bully pulpit to expound upon the virtues of baseball played with an international flavor.

There's no question that today's World Series is just a plain, ordinary city series. Just imagine if Venezuela won and had to play at New York. Today's Yankee Stadium would not be big enough because of the large Latin population there. The same would happen in Venezuela or any of the other countries involved. New stadiums would have to be built to hold from 100,000 to 120,000 people in each country.[125]

Cambria was quick to point out the progress made by Puerto Rico, Mexico, Panama, the Dominican Republic, and of course, his own Cuba. And he went on to click off the names of the many Latins playing in the Big Time at that moment.

When asked where he would find the players to populate such a league, Cambria quickly said, "In this part of the world they have the climate and can play all year 'round and develop players. Just think of the pitchers our country has produced, like Camilo Pascual, Pedro Ramos, Dolf Luque, Connie Marrero, Juan Pizarro and Mike Fornieles, to name a few."[126]

Cambria suggested that in the first two or three years, an all-star team could be assembled from all of the Latin American countries to oppose the winners of the American "World" Series to make a real and true World Series. He further cited the goodwill benefits that would be wrought by the addition of a Latin league: "It would mean more business, more co-operation and more fellowship. They would soon all be speaking the same language, would understand each other more in a sportsmanlike way. Baseball is the word that can do it."[127]

As if on cue, newly installed Cuban prime minister Fidel Castro arrived in Washington in April to talk with politicians and the press and to participate in ceremonies around the city. Though his visit was officially informal, he was treated with the respect of any visiting dignitary and was greeted by Vice President Nixon. There was a huge fête in his honor at the Cuban Embassy, where he talked baseball for an hour with countrymen Pedro Ramos and Camilo Pascual. Cambria was also there and took the opportunity to invite Castro to pitch against Mickey Mantle at the Senators-Yankees game on April 22. Castro was on his way to Princeton, New Jersey, and then to New York City and had to graciously decline.[128]

The Fidel Myth

Being in Washington and with Cambria, the sportswriters continued to use column inches to promote the legend that Joe Cambria had scouted and could have signed Castro to a Senators contract in the 1940s. It is important at this juncture of the narrative to help dispel this myth.

Yale University Professor Roberto Gonzalez Echevarria (*The Pride of Havana*), noted SABR author Peter C. Bjarkman (*Fidel Castro and Baseball*), and University of Illinois Professor of History Adrian Burgos, Jr. (*Playing America's Game: Baseball, Latinos and the Color Line*) have written extensively on the Castro and baseball myth. And it is exactly that, a myth, mostly propagated by Cambria himself. He always stated to whoever would listen that he "scouted" Castro when he was pitching for the University of Havana in the 1940s. Camilo Pascual and Jose Valdivielso both supported the idea that the story was a myth. Pascual said he was there, there was baseball everywhere, and that everyone knew who was playing where and with whom. Castro never pitched for any organized team in any league, amateur or professional, in Cuba. Gonzalez Echevarria scoured the Havana newspapers of the time and found only one mention of an F. Castro pitching and losing, 5–4, in an intramural game between the University of Havana Law and the Business School.[129]

A mediocre pitcher in college, Fidel Castro still loved the game of baseball as much as any 12-year-old Cuban boy. Here, Castro is lecturing to members of the Almendares Cuban baseball team (private collection of Sean Grogan).

Cambria had, of course, been on the island since bringing Roberto Estalella to America in 1934 and was well aware of what was going on in Havana. Pascual did support my premise that it was entirely possible that Cambria could have seen Castro pitch in some amateur capacity when he was on the island; however, Cambria never filled out a report card or sheet on Castro. Cambria repeatedly told reporters that "Castro had a good curve, but he lacked major league stuff. I looked him over. He would have been a B league pitcher, maybe A, so I didn't sign him."[130]

The myth was further compounded by Don Hoak, with the help of journalist Myron Cope, in a *Sport* magazine article in June of 1964. Hoak claimed that in his off-season of 1950–1951, anti–Batista rebels took over a baseball field where his Cienfuegos ball club was playing Marianao. During the fifth inning, forces streamed onto the field and their leader, Castro, confidently strode to the mound, threw a few warmup pitches, then motioned Hoak to dig in. Hoak supposedly fouled off a few "wild but hard" fastballs, until the umpires grew tired of the whole affair and ordered government forces to get rid of the rebels.

The above story is in brief, but inaccurate nonetheless. (Peter Bjarkman's account is impeccable and is readily available on the Internet.) Research has shown that Hoak was never on the island in 1950–1951 and never played for Cienfuegos until 1953–1954, Batista was not in power until 1952, and Castro was imprisoned in 1953. Misspelling and misrepresentations abound in the full story, but it survives to this day. The story has been told and retold and has even been mentioned on telecasts by unwitting announcers.[131]

After the 1959 revolution, Castro did start a baseball team, for which he pitched. It was laughingly called "*Los Barbudos*" or the "Bearded Ones" in English. He and Che Guevara and several more of his hirsute followers donned official-looking uniforms and played a series of exhibition games in Havana. It was, by no means, an official baseball team of any sort.

As the old saying goes, "when you have to choose between history and legend, print the legend." Cambria seemed to enjoy the story and continued to tell it until his passing. It is perhaps one of the greatest "what if" stories of the ages, and it only helped to further mythologize Cambria in the retelling. In essence, it was good for business.

In Cuba, the kids were losing interest in baseball to television and soccer. Dozens of major league scouts were crowding Cambria out and beating him to the punch with the kids who were available. Cambria had time on his hands. But not for long. This year, he decided to make some money with his old friend Satchel Paige.

Cambria assembled a group of Cuban youngsters, dubbed them the Havana Cuban Stars, and set about to showcase them in barnstorming and exhibition games throughout the United States. The big drawing card was, of course, Satchel Paige, still throwing his "giddy-up" and "hesitation ball" to the delight of audiences everywhere.

On August 20, Cambria arranged for a game at Griffith Stadium with his Stars and the Kansas City Monarchs. The Monarchs, once one of the greatest of the Negro Leagues teams, now made their living by barnstorming primarily. Both teams were an aggregate of rookies (average age of 17 by Cambria's estimation) with a sprinkling of former players thrown in. "It is a very good arrangement," said Cambria. "Satch brings [in] the customers and the kids are learning to play. Also they are seeing the country like you and nobody else ever saw."[132]

That statement was, of course, a gross understatement. The kids literally lived on the bus, traveling hundreds of miles between cities, and never stopped in the same place twice. Rooms were not always readily available, and showers were usually taken in the clubhouses if they were lucky enough to play in stadiums that had them!

On this night, however, 'Ol Satch did what he always did. He made Cambria and Monarchs manager Modesto Perez sweat it out in the clubhouse. Satch arrived when Satch arrived. He was never one for great alacrity. By the second inning, he showed up and immediately went to the box office to collect his cut of the gate receipts. (Dozens of years of barnstorming had proved the old adage, "always get paid up front.") Satchel Paige finally took the mound, wearing a White Sox uniform, twirled a few innings, the crowd went wild, and everyone went home happy. Everyone made a little money, and the kids climbed back on the bus and headed for Poughkeepsie.[133]

The 1959 Senators

Remember the quote about insanity? Here it is again. The Senators had sole possession of last place, and the rest of the teams in the American League were happy to let them have it. One of the few good things that could be said about the team was they finished at least a bit better than 1958, posting a 63–91.

Of all of Cambria's Cubans, Julio Becquer did the best among the position players.

Becquer got into 108 games, joining with Norm Zauchin at first base to spell Roy Sievers. Becquer had 59 hits, scored 20 runs, and posted a .268 batting average. Zoilo Versalles, Jose Valdivielso and Billy Consolo were all part of Lavagetto's "shortstop by committee" brigade. Consolo, with the most at-bats (202) had 43 hits, and scored 25 runs, but posted an anemic .213 average. Valdivielso was statistically better, with a .286 average for 15 plate appearances and four hits. Versalles played more games than Valdivielso but posted a horrible .153 average, with nine hits and runs. Most of the position players posted batting averages below the .250 mark.[134]

The pitching bright spot went to Camilo Pascual, who posted a wonderful 17–10 record in 32 games, had an impressive 2.64 ERA, and led the mound staff with 185 strikeouts. Unfortunately, the low spot was Pedro Ramos, who went 13–19, led the league in losses for the second year, threw 95 strikeouts but posted a lousy 4.16 ERA. Russ Kemmerer and Bill Fischer had losing records, and Tex Clevenger's 3.91 was the lowest ERA of the three. The pitching staff actually did a little bit better this year than last. They had the fifth-lowest ERA (4.01) and were only third in hits allowed (1,358), third in runs allowed (701), and sixth in homers allowed (123). The Tigers gave up a whopping 177 long balls.

The big story of the year was, of course, the Fearsome Foursome. Killebrew, Allison, Lemon and Sievers combined to hit 126 of the team's 163 home runs for second place in the league, beating out those damn Yankees. However, there was a two-fold problem: aside from the big four, nobody else was hitting, and even with all their homers, the big guns did not drive in many runs. Of their 126 home runs, 72 were solo shots. A lot of noise, yet unproductive.

Yet there was hope on the horizon. Right fielder Faye Throneberry contributed 10 big homers and 82 hits to the overall team average, Camilo Pascual led the league with six shutouts and Bob Allison had a career year and won the American League Rookie of the Year Award, following Albie Pearson, who won it in 1958. It was the first time a last place team won back-to-back ROY Awards.

CHAPTER 9

1960 and Beyond:
A Career at Its Close

In the Washington, D.C., metro area of the 1980s, there was a television commercial that would stick in the mind like termites eating through a log. Aired almost hourly on WDCA Channel 20, "Nobody Bothers Me," written in 1978 by legendary guitarist and D.C. native Nils Lofgren, was the commercial used to promote the Taekwondo studios of Grandmaster Jhoon Rhee. Rhee, a student of the great Bruce Lee, utilized that commercial to open 11 martial arts studios throughout Maryland, Virginia, and the District. The commercial ended with Rhee's five-year-old daughter smiling at the camera and saying, "Nobody bothers me!" and then cut to Rhee's nine-year-old son winking at the camera and saying, "Nobody bothers me either!"[1]

This was Joe Cambria's basic response when the *Charlotte News* reporters asked him if he was concerned that things were getting a little hot in Cuba in 1960. "No, no trouble at all," said Cambria. "They got a little something going—among themselves. I go and come as I please. Sure, they have a little Fourth of July from time to time. It's their way. Otherwise, everything's okay."[2]

This was, in essence, the truth of the matter. Cambria had been established on the island for such a long time that, by now, he had freedom to come and go. He stayed away from the troubles and went about his business of finding young ballplayers to fill the Senators' ever-wanting rosters. The people of Havana knew him and took care to look after him. In a phone interview, Julio Becquer said, "Everybody knew Joe. He was a nice man, and everyone protected him."[3]

The real truth of the matter, however, was that there was a major paradigm shift occurring in Cuba, and changes were coming about rapidly. To the press, Cambria was uncharacteristically pessimistic, for the first time in a long time. "I'm an American," he said, "but they don't bother me in Cuba. I mind my own business and I don't talk politics. Since we lost International League ball, there's nothing left in baseball except club leagues or sandlot ball. But people have more on their minds than baseball in Cuba. It's sad all over."[4]

What Joe Cambria was alluding to was Castro's embargo on baseball. In June of 1960, Castro nationalized all U.S. owned business in Cuba. On July 8, baseball Commissioner Ford Frick, fearing for the safety of the American players and under pressure from the State Department, announced that the Miami Sugar Kings would move to Jersey City, New Jersey, and become the Jersey City Jerseys. The International League, consisting of eight teams, six from the U.S., one from Canada, and one from Cuba, was the closest thing to major league ball that the Cubans would see. Sugar Kings owner Bobby

Maduro vehemently opposed the move, citing financial bankruptcy if it occurred, and several Cuban members of the team refused to go with the move in a show of solidarity with Castro. The team lasted until the end of the 1961 season, folding due to poor attendance.[5]

The loss of the International League teams was not the only thing bothering Cambria. He was now beginning to feel the heat from the other scouts on the island. Said Cambria to *The Sporting News*, "It used to be that I had that territory all to myself, but I stumble all over scouts in Cuba now. Why do so many big-league teams want Cubans? It's easy. You can get them cheaper than the American kids and they try harder. A Cuban kid at 15 or 16 already is a polished fielder. He works at the game all the time. He's still 'hungry.' The American kid is lazy and has too many distractions."[6]

Yet, despite all that he had done for the Senators and to promote baseball in Cuba, Cambria was now beginning to become the butt of jokes, especially around the press box. Bob Maisel of the *Baltimore Sun* reported on a spring training incident at Al Lang Field in St. Petersburg:

> The Yanks and the Senators were locked in a tight pitching duel and during at least a part of the game, Griffith and George Weiss, New York, general manager, were seated together in a box not too far below the press box. It was a known fact that the Yanks were anxious to pry either Camilo Pascual or Pedro Ramos from Washington, and everyone was expecting a deal to break out. Just as they appeared to put their heads a little closer together than ever before the boats [in the bay behind the stadium] sailed beautifully in behind the fence. At this point a Washington newsman leaned out of the press box, and in a voice loud enough to be heard throughout the little park, yelled "Don't make that deal now Calvin. Here comes Joe Cambria with another load!" Apparently, everybody in the park knew Joe's name, because the remark laid them out in the aisles.[7]

I am sure Cambria would have just shrugged off the joke and then tried to get even by bringing in a young, hungry Cuban who would eventually grow into a superstar. But the story just goes to explain the disdain many had for the Senators and their last-place ways, and he suffered guilt by association. Things were tough in Cuba and pickings were becoming slim. Joe Cambria would have to work harder, and Calvin Griffith had to trade harder.

As 1960 spring training began, Griffith had his eyes and ears out for whatever trade he could swing that would help his ball club and, more precisely, put more butts in his seats. His three consecutive last-place finishes were destroying both his bottom line and his (unfounded and unannounced) move to Minnesota. Big hitters Bob Allison and Harmon Killebrew seemed immune from the trading block, but Camilo Pascual, Pedro Ramos, Clint Courtney, and Roy Sievers had all become chum for the trade waters.

Sievers, in particular, was dangled in front of the maw of almost every American League club. Calvin Griffith talked deals with Cleveland, Detroit, and New York, all of which fell through. But a deal with the White Sox did not.

Griffith was not a "what have you done for me lately?" guy; he was a "what can you do for me *now*?" kind of guy. Sievers had been injured several times during the 1959 season. He was hit by a pitch in the elbow during the spring, which sat him down for a week. Calf strains and back muscle pulls ate away at his playing time. An unintentional spiking incident by Detroit's Jerry Lumpe at first base nearly severed his Achilles tendon and kept him out of the lineup for nearly two weeks. These injuries took their toll on his home run production. He hit only 21 homers in 1959 as opposed to Killebrew's league-leading 42. This may have caused Griffith to look upon Sievers as damaged goods.

In a trade that defied logic and showed off Calvin Griffith's ineptitude, Bill Veeck, now owner of the pennant-winning Chicago White Sox, pried Sievers away from Griffith for catcher Earl Battey, rookie Don Mincher, and $150,000 in cash. What made this so implausible was that Griffith could have had so much more, and from Veeck, no less!

In June of 1959, Veeck wanted more long-ball insurance as the White Sox were making a run for the AL pennant. Veeck offered Griffith outfielders Al Smith and Jim Rivera, pitcher Ray Moore, one of two catchers (Johnny Romano or Earl Battey), one of two infielders (Billy Goodman or Earl Torgeson), *plus* $250,000 in cash for Sievers, catcher J.W. Porter, and a pitcher to be named later. The total deal would have been worth around $400,000.[8]

Griffith turned it down.

To make room for Battey, Griffith traded catcher Clint Courtney and infielder Ron Samford to the Orioles for "good field-no hit" second baseman Billy Gardner, which solved Lavagetto's continual second base problem. Killebrew was moved from third base to first base, Reno Bertoia moved to third, and Lenny Green took over center field. Don Mincher and Julio Becquer were platooned at first base with Killebrew and used for pinch-hitting duties.

Cambria may have been slowing down, but he was not out yet. He dug down a little deeper, went a few extra miles out of his way, and still found a few more players to add to the Senators' rosters. Clark Griffith may have died, but Joe Cambria's love for the Washington Senators had not.

Reyes Figueroa, who sounds more like a boulevard in Los Angeles than a ballplayer, was found by Cambria playing for Ponce in the Puerto Rican winter league. He did well in some inter-squad games but did not make the parent club. He was sent down to Charlotte and remained in the Nats' farm system until 1961.[9]

Dagoberto "Bert" Cueto was signed by Cambria out of the Cuban winter leagues in 1956. He bounced around in the Senators' low minors until he made a good showing in Charlotte, going 6–5 with a 2.45 ERA in 1959. This got him a call-up to training camp in 1960, where he did well but not well enough. He finally made his debut with the 1961 Twins. He pitched in seven games, and in 21⅓ innings, he went 1–3, with a 7.17 ERA. He gave up 27 hits, 24 runs, seven homers, five strikeouts and 10 walks. Not the stuff of legend, Cueto was sent down to Vancouver and remained in the Twins' system until he hung up his cleats in 1964.[10]

Hector Maestri was another of Cambria's kids he found in the Cuban sandlots. Cambria signed him to the Elmira Pioneers in 1956. He got a call-up for the 1960 training camp, where he pitched well, but was ultimately sent back down to Charlotte. There, he had a spectacular time. In one 20-inning stretch, he gave up only one unearned run and threw 10 innings of perfect ball. This got him a September call-up to the parent club. He pitched two scoreless innings in relief against the Orioles in September, giving up one hit, one walk and one strikeout. Sent down again in 1961, he bounced around on three teams until he got another call from the expansion Senators. Starting against the Athletics on September 17, Maestri pitched six innings, gave up three runs, and took a 3–2 loss. He was sent back down again and remained in the Twins' system until 1966.[11]

Oscar Chinque, signed by Cambria in 1956, spent seven seasons in the Senators/ Twins' minor league system, earning call-ups to spring camp in 1960 and 1961. Chinque never saw enough to warrant him staying with the parent clubs and he never made it out of the minors.

Minnie Mendoza was a portrait in determination. He was signed out of the Cuban amateur leagues by the Cincinnati Reds. He started his career with the Miami Beach Flamingos of the Florida International League in 1954. He knocked around the Reds' farm system and the Mexican Leagues from 1954 through 1957. Cambria signed him to the Missoula Timberjacks as a free agent in 1958, where he shared the stage with Bert Cueto, Sandy Valdespino, and future Hall of Famer Jim Kaat. After a look-see at the 1960 spring camp, Mendoza was sent to Charlotte. For the next 10 years, he tore up Sally and Southern League pitching, posting averages in the .280s to .300s each year. Mendoza finally got his day in the sun in 1970. Used primarily at third base and shortstop, he played 16 games for the Twins. In 16 at-bats, he had two runs, three hits, two RBI, and a .188 average. His "Moonlight Graham" moment now over, Mendoza was sent back down to the minors and finished his career with Monterrey of the Mexican League in 1973. After his playing days were over, he became a coach in the minor leagues and with the Orioles organization.[12]

Rudolph Albert "Rudy" Hernandez, first signed by Giants Hall of Famer Carl Hubbell in 1950, spent three years in the Giants' minor league system before being let go in 1958. Cambria signed him to a Washington contract after seeing him pitch in the Dominican winter leagues. Hernandez had winning records with Chattanooga in 1959 and with Charleston in 1960. He got his call-up, debuting on July 3, 1960, against the Indians in relief. On that day, he became only the fourth Dominican to play in the majors and the first pitcher. He preceded Juan Marichal by 16 days. Hernandez went 4–1 with a 4.41 ERA in 21 games in 1960.

In 1961, he was picked up by the expansion Senators, becoming one of only three players (with Hal Woodeshick and Hector Maestri) to play in consecutive seasons for the original and expansion Senators. Hernandez went 0–1 with a 3.00 ERA in only seven games for the new Nats. He was sent down to Syracuse in 1962 and remained in the minors until 1964.[13]

The biggest headache that plagued Lavagetto throughout spring camp was actually Cambria's fault. Zoilo "Zorro" Versalles was a genuine Hoover vacuum cleaner with his glove and a legitimate thief on the basepaths. His biggest liability, however, was his mouth.

"Zorro will be shortstop. I theenk I best," said Versalles to the *New York Times* in the oft-misquoted language of the day. Things like that do not endear oneself to a manager. With a more than able command of the English language, Versalles was cocky and overly self-confident. He also had a problem with team protocols, which got him in his deepest trouble. He went to Cookie Lavagetto and said he only had one suit and he could not continue in this fashion. He asked for and received some advance money and permission to buy suits. Unbeknownst to Lavagetto, Versalles' suits were in a pawn shop in Havana. He left for a week and returned with his clothes and his girlfriend. He got his suits and the bench.

"He needs discipline!" growled Lavagetto. Evidently, Napoleon Rayes, manager of the 1959–1960 Marianao *Tigres*, felt the same way. Versalles, the better hitter, was relegated as a backup to Jose Valdivielso, inferior in talent but superior in coachability. Consequently, Versalles spent much of the 1960 season as he did in Cuba, on the bench, backing up Jose Valdivielso at shortstop.[14]

By the time they broke camp to head north, Cambria had a hand in placing six Latins on the roster: Rudy Hernandez, Hector Maestri, Camilo Pascual, Pedro Ramos, Jose Valdivielso and Zoilo Versalles. Cambria bragged that Ramos, Pascual, Valdivielso and Becquer cost him only $750 total. (Phone interviews with the aforementioned attest to the veracity of that statement.) But there was no animosity amongst them, as Pedro Ramos told Bob Addie:

> Cambria has been like a father to us. He's given hundreds of Cubans a chance to play ball. All of us didn't make the big leagues, but at least we had our chance. Take my case. I was work-ing for $22 a week in a cigar factory when Cambria offered me $200 and then a salary of $200 a month. Maybe that's why there are so many Cubans in baseball. They can afford to take the hard knocks and get what Americans consider a small salary. It's worthwhile if you make it to the Majors.[15]

Cambria continued to scout throughout the islands of the Caribbean, bring-ing to Washington anyone who had a least a chance of making either one of the minor league teams or a shot at the Senators themselves. In an effort to educate many a young Cuban, Cambria did what he did the previous year. He assembled a team of young, hun-gry Cuban boys dying for the experience of American baseball. Calling his team the Caribbean Kings, he enlisted (hired!) the aid of Detroit Tigers pitching star Virgil "Fire" Trucks and, as always, the indefatigable Satchel Paige.

"My squad is made up of young, fast, sharp, aggressive talent who always provide colorful baseball," said carnival barker Cambria. He had Mike Perez as his manager, who once coached the Cienfuegos *Elefantes* to a Latin Winter League championship in Panama. As before, the team barnstormed from the West to the East Coast between May, June, and July, playing sandlot, semi-pro and a few minor league teams along the way.[16]

The 1960 Senators

The 1960 Senators surprised everyone, including themselves. They should have known that it would be a good year when ace Camilo Pascual struck out 15 batters and won the Nats' Opening Day game, 10–1. Playing competent baseball, the Nats coasted into fifth place in the American League with a 73–81 record. Even without Roy Sievers' big bat, the team managed to place third in the league in home runs with 147. Big Jim Lemon led the barrage with 38 dingers, besting Harmon Killebrew's 31 bombs. Earl Bat-tey and Bob Allison contributed 15 taters apiece. Everyone in the lineup had respectable batting averages, but the sleeper was Lenny Green. He only had five long balls, but his timely hitting accounted for his .294 average, highest on the team. The combined team average, however, was only good enough for seventh place in the league. They placed seventh in hits (1,283) and fourth in runs scored (672).

The biggest surprise was the pitching staff. For the first time in a long time, several starters had a winning record. Pedro Ramos, logging a staggering 274 innings pitched, trailed Frank Lary of the Tigers as the workhorse of the league by one out. He posted an 11–18 record and a 3.45 ERA, with 24 homers allowed, 99 walks and 160 strikeouts. Camilo Pascual was coming into his own by now. In 151⅔ innings, "Little Potato" posted a 12–8 record and a 3.03 ERA with only 11 homers allowed, 53 walks and 143 strike-outs. Jack Kralick, a minor league sensation for the White Sox, posted a respectable

8–6 record in 151 innings pitched. He gave up only 12 homers and 45 walks and posted 71 strikeouts. The real sleeper of the staff was former Tigers moundsman Don Lee. He also carried a heavy load, pitching 165 innings with an 8–7 record, 3.44 ERA, 16 homers allowed, 64 walks and 88 strikeouts. Chuck Stobbs posted a handsome 12–7 record in 119 innings, giving up only 13 homers to go along with 38 walks and 72 strikeouts. Team averages were much better than before. They were fifth in league ERA (3.77), third in hits allowed (1,392), third in runs allowed (696), and fourth in homers allowed (130).[17]

Lavagetto, who received a $5,000 reward for his outstanding efforts that year, summed it up nicely when he told Shirley Povich, "Our major accomplishment this past season was convincing our kids they could win the American League. Now that they've tasted that experience, they're going to be a lot tougher in '61."[18]

Fun fact: On July 23, 1960, Whitey Herzog, playing with the Kansas City Athletics, hit into the first all–Cuban triple play in MLB. With two men on base, he hit a line drive straight back to Senators pitcher Pedro Ramos, who threw to first baseman Julio Becquer for the second out, and he threw to shortstop Jose Valdivielso covering second to double off the other runner.

The season may have ended, but the fireworks were just about to begin.

The political climate in Cuba was becoming more and more untenable as the year progressed. Castro's rhetoric against "Capitalist aggression," aimed primarily at the United States, became more and more strident. His policy changes came swiftly and without warning.

After taking power, Castro abolished legal discrimination, brought electricity to the countryside, provided for full employment, and advanced the causes of education and health care, in part by building new schools and medical facilities. But he also closed down opposition newspapers, jailed thousands of political opponents, and made no move toward elections. Moreover, he limited the amount of land a person could own, abolished private business, and presided over housing and consumer goods shortages. With political and economic options so limited, hundreds of thousands of Cubans, including vast numbers of professionals and technicians, left Cuba, often for the United States.[19]

This, in particular, affected the Senators' first baseman, Julio Becquer. Becquer's wife was a licensed pharmacist. Castro had placed a ban on professionals, like doctors and engineers, from leaving the country. Julio recalled how Cambria used his diplomatic wiles to get his wife and young son out of Cuba before Castro completely shut down the island in 1961.[20]

Castro's anti–American sentiments were becoming more bellicose as the year progressed. His famous four-and-a-half-hour speech at the United Nations General Assembly that September, one of the longest in the history of the U.N., was a tirade against American Colonialism and Neo-Colonialism, and his threat to purge American-owned businesses in Cuba.

In September, acting out of an abundance of caution, Commissioner Ford Frick ordered all American ballplayers to stay out of Cuba. He sent a letter to all the minor league officials stating the same. Eventually, he added Venezuela and Nicaragua to that list. He did not, however, bar the native Cubans like Pascual, Ramos, Minoso and Mike Fornieles from participating in winter league ball if they so desired. Quoted in *The Sporting News* in September, Frick said, "American players are free to contract with clubs in Puerto Rico, Panama and Venezuela. However, the situation in Cuba has reached a point at which I no longer want to be responsible for the lives and welfare, and financial return, of American players there. The order barring Americans from Cuban clubs is self-explanatory."[21]

Cuban Winter League play lasted from September to March. Commissioner Frick and the club owners were also afraid that Castro might try to prevent the Cuban players from returning to the United States to begin their spring training in February. This would have deeply impacted the Senators, who were relying on Pascual, Ramos, Becquer, Valdivielso and Versalles to be front-line players. It would have also affected teams throughout both leagues.

In a phone interview, Camilo Pascual recounted those times.

AUTHOR: In 1960–'61, you almost didn't get out of Cuba because Castro threatened (not to release the ballplayers.)
PASCUAL: "That's true, we came back through Mexico to the U.S."
AUTHOR: Did Joe Cambria help you guys get out of Cuba?
PASCUAL: "Yes. At that time, we already belong to the Senators and Cambria was still working with the Senators in Cuba and he had about five players and he send those five players through Mexico to Orlando in spring training."
AUTHOR: So he helped get you out of Cuba?
PASCUAL: "Yes, he was very helping."
AUTHOR: So that must have been a scary time then?
PASCUAL: "No it wasn't that difficult. We not have any problem really."[22]

It may be just Pascual's Cuban *machismo* to downplay the events, but the threats were real, as was Castro's truculence towards the United States.

"Griffith Moves Nats to Minneapolis; D.C. Gets New Club in 1961 Season," screamed the headline in the *Washington Post* of October 27, 1960. Calvin Griffith, who vowed in 1956 that the Washington Senators would "stay here next year, the year after that, forever," in a move that would have surely broken his Uncle Clark's heart, broke the hearts of thousands of loyal Senators fans and officially moved the original franchise to Minnesota.[23] Griffith had been receiving offers from San Francisco, Los Angeles, Louisville and

A true ace, Camilo Pascual was the younger brother of Senators reliever Carlos. Mentored by the great Adolfo Luque, Camilo became the ace of the Senators' and the Minnesota Twins' pitching staffs, earning an American League pennant with the Twins in 1965 (National Baseball Hall of Fame Library, Cooperstown, New York).

Minneapolis–St. Paul, and he had approached the other owners three times in the past four years about moving the team, but had been rejected each time.

One of the biggest aspects of the move revolved around the stadium deal. Griffith did not like the proposed D.C. Armory Stadium deal concerning the ownership, parking, rent and concessions.[24] He got a much better deal from the good burghers in Minneapolis, a deal that had been years in the making and contained many moving parts: a new stadium, over which he would have more control and more parking, a 750,000 per year attendance guarantee, and a $430,000 media contract, among other perks.[25] As mentioned before, the other part of this deal was that, in allowing Griffith to move his franchise, the other American League owners agreed to expand the league in 1961 to ten teams and replace the old Senators with a new franchise.

Although Joe Cambria was sad to see the Senators move out of the District, it turned out to be a good deal for him personally. He would be able to pitch his boys to two clubs now, instead of just one.

1961 and Beyond

The Senators may have had a new state, a new city, and a new name, but the same old problems haunted them.

Tired of Castro's belligerent tirades against American colonialism and his threats to close down the American embassy in Havana, President Eisenhower severed all diplomatic relations with the Castro government on January 3, 1961. On January 4, hundreds of American and Cuban nationals crowded docks and runways in an attempt to flee the country. Castro promised "absolute guarantees" of the rights of all Americans who wished to leave. TWA airlines added dozens of extra flights to and from the island. However, many chose to stay, including almost all of the American print correspondents and one old baseball scout.[26]

"Everybody in Cuba knows Cambria," said Calvin Griffith. "They all love him and call him 'Papa Joe.' I haven't talked to Cambria in about a week but he assured me, the last time I talked to him, that we'd have no trouble getting our boys back. I'd hate to think of what we'd be without them."[27]

Calvin Griffith was alluding to the greater problem Major League Baseball would have: would Castro let the Cuban ballplayers leave the island to play in the next season in the U.S.?

Rumors abounded for days. Castro made assurances. Club owners put on a brave face. By week's end, it was finally announced. A high-ranking official in the Cuban foreign ministry said the government would not interfere with ballplayers leaving for the U.S. "We will do everything possible to solve your problems," the government official told the players. "The Revolutionary Government will not interfere with your departure. This is a special case and we are going to work it out with acting foreign minister Carlos Olivars."[28]

The major league clubs with Cuban players had to submit the names of the players to the U.S. State Department, which, in turn, would notify the Swiss Ambassador.

Cuban players then would need only exit permits from the Cuban police. The Foreign Ministry promised that it would be "no problem."

But not all diplomatic activity was confined to U.S. shores. On Monday, January 9, Cambria and Nats pitcher Camilo Pascual paid a courtesy call to the Swiss Ambassador in Cuba, who had promised to look after American interests there. Minnie Minoso, White Sox outfielder and president of the Cuban Baseball Association, paid a similar visit to Captain Felipe Guerre Matos, Cuban sports director, to further explain the players' situation.[29]

That may have assuaged the anxieties of the baseball owners, but it did little to temper the feelings of some fiery Latins. Angered by the fact that Castro had confiscated his and his parents' little cigar factory in San Luis, Pinar Del Rio, volatile pitcher Pedro Ramos made statements to the press that he would join the rebels and fight Castro "if they call me. I would fight," said Ramos. "Sometimes you have to fight for what you think is right." Told by friends he might get hurt, Ramos responded, "You can't live forever."[30]

Both Joe Cambria and Cookie Lavagetto took him aside and asked him to stop discussing politics. "Concentrate on baseball," Cambria told Ramos. In the end, Ramos told the press he was "just kidding" about leaving to fight, but his teammates begged to differ. Ultimately, Ramos saw the light and remained in Minneapolis.[31]

By June, Cambria had another fire to stomp out. He had been traveling with the club throughout some of the season, trying to be a calming influence on his mercurial Latins. Pedro Ramos had been serving up so many gopher balls (18 homers in 18 games) that he was beginning to lose his cool on the mound, plunking batters and throwing "chin music." Cambria did his best to calm him down.

His bigger problem was Zoilo Versalles. Still only 20 years old, Versalles, who had become increasingly moody, frequently changed his mind about playing. When Versalles, who had been scouted and signed by Cambria, failed to show up for a game against the Los Angeles Angels on July 5, he was fined $500 and suspended indefinitely. He immediately told the

"The Cuban Cowboy," Pedro "Pete" Ramos, honed his English language skills by watching television Western programs and emulating "Hopalong" Cassidy. He had a great curve ball, but also a penchant for throwing the long ball (National Baseball Hall of Fame Library, Cooperstown, New York).

club he was returning to Cuba "as soon as I can." Versalles said he was physically tired from playing too much baseball (he had played summer and winter ball in Cuba the year before), and he was upset because Twins management did not arrange to get his 17-year-old bride out of Cuba on time. He was also in financial trouble for too much installment spending and, furthermore, miffed that he was not picked to play on the American League All-Star team that had been chosen the week before.[32]

All of this weighed heavily on the youngster's mind. Cambria called Versalles from Miami on July 7, telling him to meet the team in Washington, and said he would try to have his wife there to meet him. Versalles said no, he was going home, even though his wife said it was foolish. "I am going to call her and tell her to stay in Cuba and finish school," Versalles told Cambria.[33]

A wealthy Minnesota couple and new Twins fans, Mr. and Mrs. Farrell C. Stiehm, who had just met Versalles, agreed to take him and his wife into their home to help him with his troubles and to get him out of his hotel room. "We invited him to come out and make himself at home," Mrs. Stiehm said. "He can rest or do whatever he wants to do."[34]

Mrs. Stiehm's mothering may have helped. Cambria's intervention may have helped. Versalles's wife certainly did help.

Versalles was able to talk with his wife for an hour and a half on July 7, and she and Cambria were able to talk him off the ledge. He agreed to rejoin the team, and Griffith agreed to lift the suspension when he returned from the July 11 All-Star Game.[35]

All of this became too much for the youngster. Complaining of stomach distress, Versalles was examined and tested for ulcers. Luckily, no ulcers were found. Doctors diagnosed his condition as caused by parasitic worms, for which he was treated. Cambria, who had flown in from Miami to smooth out the situation, met Calvin Griffith to explain it all. Versalles would return to the team as soon as his wife arrived.[36]

It would be safe to assume that the tensions with the Cuban players could have caused the poor performance of the Twins that first season. The original threat of not releasing the Cuban players in January was just the tip of the political iceberg. Matters were made even worse when the Cuban players learned that, due to the strained relations between the two countries, they might not be allowed to re-enter the United States for the next season. Griffith confirmed that the situation "was a mess and we are right now trying to do something about it."[37]

To stay in the country, the Twins' Cubans would have to file immigration papers as a step towards U.S. citizenship. This would effectively thwart their return to the island. A Minnesota executive told the media that their temporary work visas, given to them preferentially by Castro at the beginning of the year, would expire in October, and that the arrangement was out for next year.[38] The players were not sure they wanted to renounce their Cuban citizenship. They all had families there and were concerned about what would happen to them if they decided to remain in the U.S. Said one of the Cuban players, "they told us we would not get special treatment like this year. We must wait our turn to leave [the island] because so many want to leave the country. It is all very mixed up and sad. We are baseball players, not fighters, not politicians. How come it is got to be like this?"[39]

With six Cubans on the Twins, this political miasma would have the greatest impact on the Twins in particular and on all of organized baseball in general. There were, all told, 29 Cubans in the major leagues and about 150 in the minors. All of them were expressing the same concerns as the Minnesota players.

All of this became a little too much for Cambria as well. By now, he had lost most of his influence with the Castro regime, and he decided to move back to the States. He had, of course, scouted and signed a majority of the island's best players, and "Papa Joe" acted as a personal advisor for many of his signees. His loss would be greatly felt on the island.[40]

The international tension put the Twins into a death spiral. After 59 games and a 23–36 record, Calvin Griffith once again fired his manager in mid-season. Lavagetto was replaced by veteran coach Sam Mele, who did only slightly better for the remainder of the season with a 47–54 record. The Twins placed seventh in their inaugural season, 70–90. The bats kept blasting, though. Harmon Killebrew hit a massive 46 homers but was dwarfed by Roger Maris' record-setting 61 homers. Bob Allison hit 29, Jim Lemon hit 14, and Earl Battey hit 17 and led the team with a .302 average. Pedro Ramos (11–20, 174 strikeouts), Camilo Pascual (15–16, 221 strikeouts), and young Jim Kaat (9–17, 122 strikeouts), all pitched hard but had losing records. Lefty Jack Kralick (13–11, 137 strikeouts) had the only winning record among the starters.[41]

Cambria still shuttled back and forth between the U.S. and Cuba because of the many connections he had on the island. The embargo against the taking of Cuban players would go into effect soon, but Cambria was able to get one youngster out in the nick of time.

Pedro Oliva II (his birth name) grew up in the baseball talent-rich village of Pinar del Rio, where he learned the game of baseball from his father. Pinar del Rio was also the hometown of Pedro Ramos. Oliva was a young slugger playing for the Los Palacios village ball club that competed in a strong provincial league in western Cuba. Playing alongside him was a journeyman and another Pino del Rio native, Roberto Fernandez Tapanes. Tapanes, who had been scouted and signed by Cambria to Big Springs in 1948, called Cambria and alerted him to this hot young lad who could hit the cover off the ball.[42]

Joe Cambria signed Oliva to a contract in the Twins' farm system in February of 1961. A bit late in the season, it did not leave Oliva adequate time to get his affairs together in order to leave the island. He was just 20 years old and did not have a passport, and it was a little over a week before he had to report for spring training. His brother Antonio, however, did have a passport he was not using. Consequently, a switch was made, and Pedro was able to escape the island before the shutdown took place, using his brother's name. Unfortunately, Pedro was registered as Tony and, despite legally changing his name back to Pedro later on, he would be forever linked as Tony Oliva.[43]

It did not really matter what his name was. Tony Oliva became a star for the Minnesota Twins, spending his entire 15-year career in the Twin Cities. After just a year in minor league ball, Oliva became an instant sensation in Minneapolis. He became the first Latin player to win a batting championship in his rookie year, the first player to win a batting title in his first two years of play, and the first Cuban to win the Rookie of the Year Award in 1964.

Oliva went on to win another batting crown in 1971 and was an eight-time All Star. Painful knee injuries plagued him constantly and shortened his major league career; however, Oliva's tremendous baseball output finally garnered him a place in the Baseball Hall of Fame in Cooperstown in 2022.[44]

Cambria found another solid player on a trip to Mexico City. Playing for the University of Mexico baseball team, Orlando "Marty" Martinez's good glove and quick bat

In a truly one-of-a-kind photograph, Tony Oliva, Frank Ryan, Joe Cambria, and Charlotte Hornets general manager Phil Howser are shown here in Joe Cambria's hospital room in Charlotte, North Carolina, in 1962. Ryan, a representative of the Louisville Slugger bat company, presented Oliva with a special bat in honor of his MVP season with the Hornets. Howser was the general manager of the Hornets from 1935 to 1970. Oliva enjoyed 15 great years with the Minnesota Twins, earning a berth in the Baseball Hall of Fame in 2022 (private collection of Tony Oliva).

impressed Cambria enough to sign him to a contract with the Senators' Class-D Erie Sailors in 1960. His good work there got him a promotion to the Wilson Tobs of the Class-B Carolina League. His .265 average at Wilson was enough to convince the Twins to bring him up to the parent club in 1962. Despite a good year as a utility man, Martinez was sent down. He spent three years in the Twins' system and was recalled to Minnesota in 1966. He spent seven years in the majors and 13 years in the minors. After his major league playing career was over, Martinez played, coached, and managed in the Rangers' minor-league system for four years before becoming player-manager of the Double-A Tulsa Drillers in 1977. He managed the Drillers for two years and won a first-half championship in 1977. Afterward, he became a scout and coach for the Seattle Mariners and was named interim manager of the team for one day in 1986.[45]

Although Cambria thought about leaving Cuba, *The Sporting News* reported that he returned to Cuba after spending 17 days in Mercy Hospital in Baltimore for a check-up. In an interview with Bill Tanton of the *Baltimore Sun*, Cambria once again told the old saw about how he viewed Castro as a pitching prospect. "Castro had a good curve ball, but not much of a fastball" is how he always described the Cuban leader. "I think now I should have signed him!" he said.[46]

Joe Cambria's fantasies about Castro aside, he was definitely slowing down. His 17-day "check-up" at Mercy Hospital was just a precursor of things to come.

But slowing down did not mean he was played out. Cambria still had the eyes for good talent and as always, some made it and some did not. He seemed to be scouting more on the mainland these days, especially in Florida. He signed two Tampa high school stars, Dayton Ward and Pete Busciglio, out of the Tampa Intersocial League in late 1961. His prognosis of the two went like this: "Ward has a lot of power but he needs to establish himself at the plate. He's got the tools. And Busciglio has a great arm. They impressed me with their size and desire to play. They're green and will need instruction. It all depends on them. I think if these boys pay attention to their instructors, they'll have a good chance because they're good-sized boys."[47]

The boys played in the Intersocial League and worked out with the Minnesota farmhands in Fernandina Beach the following spring. Unfortunately, there is no record of the two boys ever playing a day in any organized system.

The following year, Cambria found another youngster, Bob Brandon, playing for Brandon High School in Brandon, Florida. (His great-grandfather was the founder of the city of Brandon, and the high school was named after him). The sure-handed short-stop, pitcher and center fielder was scouted by Cambria and signed to a contract to play with the Class-D Wytheville Twins in the Appalachian League right out of high school. In 146 at-bats with the Twins, Brandon scored 31 runs with 36 hits, one homer, 21 RBI, and a modest .247 batting average in 1962. That got him a ticket to A ball, playing for the Erie Sailors of the New York-Penn league in 1963. His stats seem to imply he found the going a little tougher in the higher level. With 98 at-bats, he scored 11 runs on 29 hits, with no homers, seven RBI and a .204 average. According to Baseball-reference.com, those were his only two years in organized baseball.[48]

Tampa seemed to be a hotbed of talent for our man Cambria, and this time he got a little cute. In the spring of 1962, he signed Gary and Cary Overstreet, twin boys, from the University of Tampa baseball team. Cary enthusiastically stated, "I think this is a great opportunity," and Gary said, "I think this is a terrific chance. I've always wanted to play baseball so I'm going to go!"[49]

"Twins Sign Twins," beamed the Florida papers, of course having a field day with it. The boys worked out with the Class-A Charlotte Hornets and were reassigned to respective minor league teams in the lower levels. Second baseman Gary played only one year, 1963, with the Rock Hill Wrens in the Class-A Western Carolina league. He played in only 20 games, with 60 at-bats and only 11 hits for a paltry .183 average, and did not return the next year. Third baseman Cary did much better than his twin. Also at Rock Hill in 1963, Cary played in 95 games and compiled a wonderful .332 average. He spent 1964 first with the Statesville Cats (70 games, .338 average), then with the Durham Bulls (33 games, .315 average). Cary also retired after that season.[50]

These were the last two boys ever signed by Joe Cambria.

Old Father Time was doing some scouting himself and it was time for him to pick Papa Joe. In May of 1962, Joe Cambria underwent surgery at Mercy Hospital in Charlotte, North Carolina, for a heart ailment. In a *Minneapolis Star* article, he said, "I can't raise my right arm above my head."[51] The 72-year-old Cambria convalesced in Minneapolis, but as it sometimes goes with the elderly, an invasive operation can be an undoing.

"I don't believe in bonuses," Papa Joe Cambria always said. "I open the door to opportunity for ballplayers. But they have to have ambition to make it to the majors.

Bonuses make them too satisfied. The ball is round, the bat is round, but sometimes the head is flat."[52]

Joe Cambria, "The Baltimore Laundryman," "The Wash Tub Thumper," *El Lavandero*, who found his American dream in baseball, passed away peacefully at St. Barnabas Hospital in Minneapolis on September 24, 1962. His childless marriage to his wife Charlotte was offset by the dozens of kids he helped squire into their American dream, starting new lives, making their own opportunities.

Camilo Pascual, Pedro Ramos, Julio Becquer, Jose Valdivielso, and Tony Oliva, all interviewed for this book, echoed Cambria's sentiments. All of them attested to the fact that Cambria was the only one, at that time, who was willing to take chances on Cuban boys who had not experienced American baseball but burned with the desire to try. As Camilo Pascual stated, "O my goodness, he was very good to me. He give me the opportunity. At that time, you know if Cambria sign somebody, you know some young kid he's doing nothing in Havana, he's got no future, he give you the opportunity to be a baseball player, what else do you want more?"[53]

Joe Cambria spent nearly 50 years in the baseball life. At one time, he owned or managed ball clubs in every classification in organized baseball. He reportedly signed between 400 and 500 players to major and minor league contracts. He was asked to pick two teams of players he had signed.

Americans	Position	Cubans
Mickey Livingston	catcher	Fermin Guerra
Mickey Vernon	1st base	Julio Becquer
George Myers	2nd base	Gilberto Torres
Russ Peters	shortstop	Zoilo Versalles
Ed Yost	3rd base	Jose Valdivielso
Taft Wright	left field	Roberto Ortiz
George Case	center field	Roberto Estallella
Babe Phelps	right field	Rene Monteagudo
Early Wynn	pitcher	Camilo Pascual
Dutch Leonard	pitcher	Pedro Ramos

Joe Cambria also added Willie Miranda (ss) and pitchers Connie Marrero, Mike Fornieles, and Sandy Consuegra, all Cubans.

Plaudits of course came streaming in from players and executives alike.

The day after Cambria's passing, the usually acerbic Bob Addie, one of the Deans of Washington baseball scribes, wrote a heartfelt retrospective of "Papa Joe" as he was known.

> In the excitement of the imminent clinching of the pennant by the Yankees and a heavyweight title fight in Chicago, little attention was paid up here to the passing of Joe Cambria, probably the best baseball scout that ever lived. Even without these major distractions, it's unlikely the New York papers would have devoted much space to "Papa Joe," as hundreds of Cubans called Cambria when he scouted on the small economy plan for the ever-poor Washington baseball club.
>
> There was one story Castro himself had issued an order that Popa Joe was not to be molested. "I'm not in politics," Cambria said simply. "Besides most of those young fellows carrying guns around played for me at one time or the others. They won't bother me."
>
> About a month ago in Baltimore, I was sitting with Papa Joe, now a shadow of the vigorous

man who had been so energetic. Age had blurred his features and the light in his eyes were dim. I teased him about switching allegiances from Washington to the Twin Cities.

"You remember," he said, "I once told you I wanted to be buried in a Washington uniform?" I tried to change the macabre subject because now it was just too close, but Papa Joe insisted. He looked around him cautiously and lowered his voice. "I'll tell you I haven't changed my mind. I still want to go out in a Washington uniform. Washington was Mr. Griffith's club."

I hope Papa Joe got his wish.[54]

Calvin Griffith paid tribute to the little Italian scout, calling Cambria "one of the most fabulous men I've ever met. I can understand why the ballplayers called him Papa Joe. He was like a father to them. Once he signed them, he never forgot they were his boys."[55]

Later on, Griffith went further:

Cambria was more than a scout. He owned more clubs and players than my uncle did. When the Senators needed help, my uncle would get ahold of Cambria, and he would supply us with the players. When he heard about a boy, he took a look at him no matter where he had to go. He went to places no other scout ever thought of going. Actually, Joe was our unofficial farm system![56]

Herman Helms, writing in the *Charlotte Observer*, would put the coda on Cambria's composition, using Clark Griffith's own words.

The 72-year-old [Cambria was] an original among mortals. Clark Griffith, who gave him his start in baseball and remained a close friend until death separated them, used to say, "when the Lord made Joe, He was either so pleased or so disgusted with his creation that he vowed never to try and copy it."[57]

But the saga does not end there. Joe Cambria's overriding wish was to bring enough players to Mr. Griffith to make a championship team. At a previously mentioned luncheon hosted by the Washington Baseball Historical Society in 2003, Julio Becquer brought up that fact: that the 1965 Minnesota Twins, with Cambria signees Camilo Pascual, Zoilo Versalles, Tony Oliva and Hilario "Sandy" Valdispino, along with Jim Kaat, would have been the Washington, D.C., championship team.[58]

Joe Cambria had been Clark Griffith's "angel." He made the old man proud.

Cambria's impact on American baseball did not die with his passing. He was remembered and applauded for many years after his death. One op-ed piece in the *New York Times* was especially telling. Pedro Galana, former Baseball Commissioner in Cuba from 1939 through 1957, set the record straight about Castro's government taking credit for the development of baseball on the island.

To the Editor:

In the December 13 *Times* I read a story from Havana in which the present Communist Government of Cuba took credit for the island's development in baseball. I was Baseball Commissioner in Cuba from 1939 to 1957 and I can assure you the present Communist Government has nothing to do with the sports development of my country. They are reaping the harvest of the seeds we all planted as members of the Sports Commission down there from 1939 to 1958.

Everything they brag about was already there when they came into power in 1959. And if credit has to be given to anyone, I think it should go to a very dear friend Cuba had in the United States, the late Joe Cambria, scout of the Washington Senators of the American League. For it was Joe, based in Havana, who suggested to me in 1939, that as baseball Commissioner in the island I should promote baseball championships among the juveniles.

Cambria promised me that he would sign the best players of the crop and that was incentive enough to start working.

Following Mr. Cambria's recommendations, we held baseball championships for the juveniles every year, throughout the island, plus a short championship for semi-pro players.

During the war years of 1942, 1943 and 1944, we sent, through Mr. Cambria, more than 15 players to Organized Baseball to help keep the game going while the American boys were saving democracy for the world.

Señor Galana went on to point out that the Cuban government was going to start teaching baseball to other Communist countries, using it as a guise not to promote player development but to prepare other Communist countries for the Olympic Games in Mexico in 1968, to beat the Americans at their own game.[59]

Preston Gomez, who had a fine career managing in the major leagues from 1969 to 1980, started his playing career as one of Cambria's proteges. Cambria found him playing in the semi-pro leagues in Oriente Province and working in a sugar mill for $30 dollars a month. He signed him to a contract and placed a "to whom it may concern" letter in his pocket, explaining to whoever read it to deliver the non–English-speaking Gomez to Chattanooga, Tennessee. His fondness for Papa Joe Cambria rose to great heights, as he explained; "Someday the Cuban players ought to build a monument to Joe Cambria in Cuba. He was our saint. He was tough but a lot of us got to eat because of him. If it weren't for him, I might still be working in a sugar mill."[60]

In 1967, San Lacy of the *Baltimore Afro-American* pointed out that the "National Pastime" had undergone a significant change, with Blacks and Latins now dominating a formerly almost all-white landscape, with a special nod to Joe Cambria. The following chart reflects the top five for each year.[61]

1965

Batting Average	Home Runs	Runs Batted In
Roberto Clemente	Willie Mays	Deron Johnson
Tony Oliva	Willie McCovey	Frank Robinson
Hank Aaron	Billy Williams	Willie Mays
Willie Mays	Frank Robinson	Rocky Colavito
Billy Williams	Ron Santo	Billy Williams

American League MVP—Zoilo Versalles—National League MVP—Willie Mays

1966

Batting Average	Home Runs	Runs Batted In
Matty Alou	Frank Robinson	Hank Aaron
Manny Mota	Hank Aaron	Frank Robinson
Felipe Alou	Dick Allen	Roberto Clemente
Rico Carty	Harmon Killebrew	Dick Allen
Dick Allen	Willie Mays	Harmon Killebrew

American League MVP—Frank Robinson—National League MVP—Roberto Clemente

1967

Batting Average	Home Runs	Runs Batted In
Roberto Clemente	Carl Yastrzemski	Carl Yastrzemski
Bob Johnson	Harmon Killebrew	Harmon Killebrew

Batting Average	Home Runs	Runs Batted In
Tony Gonzalez	Hank Aaron	Orlando Cepeda
Matty Alou	Jim Wynn	Roberto Clemente
Curt Flood	Frank Howard	Hank Aaron

American League MVP—Carl Yastrzemski—National League MVP—Orlando Cepeda

Joe Cambria saw only one color: green. Clark Griffith would have seen more green had he not been so afraid of the Black color line he refused to cross until too late. Cambria did as much as he could to democratize baseball at a time when American democracy was in total flux. Yes, he made a buck or two from his low-budget sales practices. Had he been a greedy man, he would have lived in a mansion. Instead, he lived in a room in a Havana hotel, where young men would line up daily, seeking their dream of an American life. Joe Cambria's legacy will always be one of opportunity and inclusion.

What could be more democratic?

CHAPTER 10

Griffith, Cambria, the Cubans and Race

There can be no satisfactory discussion of Joe Cambria's life and career without addressing the obvious question: Were Joe Cambria and Clark Griffith racists?

In light of the ongoing racial tensions of the day, this is not a matter for light conversation. It is also most difficult since there are precious few people, if any, who are still alive who would know the inner feelings of both Cambria and Griffith. It is a topic that can be reviewed through research and tempered through the fires of other writers. It is a complex intersection between the two of them, with Griffith as the progenitor. To know Griffith and his attitudes on race, it is important to know a little bit about baseball's racial beginnings and how Griffith may have come to these identities.

Baseball in America was segregated before it was ever professional. During the 1860s, whites and blacks sometimes played against each other. But in December of 1867, the Pythians of Philadelphia, a Black team, applied for membership in the National Association of Base Ball Players, the first governing body of the game. They were denied. Not only were they denied, but the NABBP recommended "against the admission of any club which may be composed of one or more persons of color." The stated goal was to "keep out of the convention ... any subject having a political bearing." The NABBP and later the major leagues maintained segregation in the game, officially or, more often, unofficially, for the next 80 years.[1]

Griffith

Clark Griffith was born November 20, 1869, just a few years after the end of the American Civil War. He literally grew up in baseball, starting as a batboy for a local Stringtown, Missouri, team. He was not a good student because he could never concentrate on his studies when baseball season came around. It was virtually all he knew.

Griffith came to his societal attitudes at an early age. Growing up in a log cabin in Clear Creek, Missouri, he saw the effects of the Reconstruction era firsthand:

> Missouri was sort of half and half during the war. Some of the boys went to service for the North and some for the South. And some didn't go for either side. Bushwhackers, they were called. They stayed home and robbed and pillaged and abused women. When the veterans

came home and heard [what these fellows had done], they founded a Vigilante Committee and made a list of about 40 bushwhackers they were gonna hang as fast as they caught them.[2]

Griffith learned a crude form of base ball from the soldiers returning from the Civil War, and quickly fell in love with the game. When the family moved to Illinois, he learned of a more nuanced game than that proffered by the soldiers. He played the game throughout his youth and high school days. By 1888 he was playing professionally as a pitcher, and he developed into one of the craftiest moundsmen of the Deadball Era.[3] In his 20 seasons, he compiled a 237–146 record and a 3.31 ERA.[4]

It was in 1894, during his days with the National League Chicago Colts (later the Cubs), where he may have picked up first on the racial inequalities of the game from his manager, Cap Anson. Anson, a notorious bigot, refused several times to play games against teams with Black players, most prominently George Stovey and Moses Fleetwood Walker, the first two African American players in organized baseball. According to author Brad Snyder in *Beyond the Shadow of the Senators,* Anson did not singlehandedly institute the color line but was surely instrumental in the development of the "gentlemen's agreement" which forbade African Americans from playing baseball.[5]

In 1887, another incident occurred where the St. Louis Browns were scheduled to play a game against the New York Cuban Giants. In the late 19th and early 20th centuries, many Black baseball teams called themselves "Cuban" and spoke a sort of gibberish language on the bases, in hopes of "passing" as a Cuban team, thereby getting better treatment from white audiences. Most of the Browns' players sent a letter to club owner Chris Von der Ahe stating that they "do not agree to play against [B]lacks tomorrow but they would cheerfully play against whites at any time."[6]

In 1901, Griffith, Charles Comiskey and Western League president Ban Johnson formed the new American League. It was here that he saw firsthand how the "gentlemen's agreement" worked and to what lengths the owners would go to enforce it.

John McGraw, manager of the American League Baltimore Orioles, happened to spy a young Black player shagging ground balls at an adjacent ball field during the Orioles' 1901 spring training in Hot Springs, Arkansas. The gentleman was Charlie Grant, second baseman for the Columbus Giants of the Black Chicago club. Grant was also playing that summer for the hotel team at which he was employed. So taken was he by Grant's fielding proclivities, that McGraw recruited him and tried to pass off the light-skinned Grant as a "full-blooded Cherokee" named Charlie "Chief" Tokahoma; however, many saw through this ruse.

Before Tokahoma ever played a game at second base for the 1901 Orioles, Comiskey exposed McGraw. Griffith's boss bellowed: "If McGraw really keeps this 'Indian' I will put a Chinaman on third base! This Cherokee is really Grant fixed up with war paint and feathers. His father is a well-known Negro in Cincinnati where he trains horses."[7]

Both incidents must have resonated with the young Griffith when he jumped into the fire of hiring racially mixed players. After his pitching days were over, Griffith found a job managing the Cincinnati Reds from 1909 to 1911. In early 1911, Reds secretary and business manager Frank Bancroft came back from a trip to Cuba extolling the virtues of a speedy outfielder, Rafael Almeida, and his interpreter, Armando Marsans, and suggesting Griffith sign them. Griffith was less impressed with Almeida than he was with Marsans, who would go on to have an eight-year career in the majors.

The issue of their race was handled thusly: "Griffith informed Reds president Gary

Herrmann, 'we will not pay Hans Wagner prices for a pair of dark-skinned islanders.' [Consequently] the Reds received documentation from Cuban officials that the two light-skinned players were of 'Castilian and not Negro heritage.' The Cincinnati press described Almeida and Marsans as 'two of the purest bars of Castilian soap ever floated on these shores.'"[8]

By then, Griffith would surely be aware of the racial attitudes within the United States in general and in Cincinnati in particular. The experiment worked for the Reds. Almeida and Marsans became gate attractions, and the press' explanation of their ethnicity was obviously enough to assuage the racial tension of major league baseball.

Marsans and Almeida were quickly followed by the most outstanding Cuban player of the pre–War era, Adolfo "Dolf" Luque. Luque spent 21 years in the majors (1914–1934) and 34 years in Cuban baseball, compiled a 193–179 record and a very respectable 3.24 ERA. Luque, a proud man of Spanish heritage, was known for his temperamental behavior which, unfortunately, only helped to fuel the stereotype of the "hot-blooded Latin." A most often misquoted story goes thusly:

> On a midsummer's day in 1923, Luque and the Reds were playing to a packed house at old Redland Field against John McGraw's New York Giants. McGraw was basically the cheerleader for a whole squad of race baiters. With the dugouts so close together on the field, it was easy for Luque to hear the never-ending torrent of racial epithets loosed by the Giants' bench. By the middle innings, the riding had become unbearable. The words "Cuban nigger" came from the mouth of one of the more vociferous bigots, outfielder Bill Cunningham, not Casey Stengel as is so often reported. Having had enough, Luque gently put the ball and his mitt on the mound and rushed the Giants' dugout. He swung viciously at Cunningham, missed, and hit Stengel square on the jaw. Obviously, the resulting bench-clearing brawl resulted in Luque's ejection from the game, but not before he returned to the field, brandishing his Louisville Slugger and calling out Cunningham.[9]

Griffith liked what he saw in the Cuban players: they worked cheap and, armed with "Castilian identity," he knew they were "good gate." In 1912, he left the Reds when the Washington Senators made him the offer to be field manager and, after mortgaging his family ranch in Montana to come up with the $27,500 fee, become the largest shareholder of the team. One of the first things he tried to do was to purchase Almeida and Marsans, who were having issues with the Reds. After the Reds resolved their issues, he recruited Pedro "Merito" Acosto from the Habana Cubans and Jacinto Calvo from the Almendares clubs in Cuba. Between 1920 and 1928, Griffith recruited Jose Acosta, Ricardo Torres and Emilio Palmero. All of them would go on to have brief careers with Washington, but long careers in the American minors. With the coming of Joe Cambria and Roberto Estalella in 1934, Cuban players became a fixture in Washington, D.C.

The Castilian Identity

As mentioned previously, Griffith found that by utilizing the notion of Castilian identity for his two Cuban players, he could "whiten" them enough so they would be acceptable to white baseball audiences. This construct is eloquently explained by University of Illinois history professor Adrian Burgos in his seminal book, *Playing America's Game: Baseball, Latinos, and the Color Line:*

Castilian identity was inserted into the parlance of ethnoracial identification within organized baseball to alleviate concerns about possible indigenous or African ancestry that came with being labeled a Mexican American or Mexican National [as well as Cuban]. Constructed as the negation of indigenous or African roots, Castilian identity became a powerful label that validated inclusion of a limited number of players from Spanish-speaking America. Just as significant, the label reiterated the main principal of the color line—the elevation of whiteness associated with European ancestry and the denigration of blackness. Equally important, disassociation with indigenous or *mestizo* roots meant that "Castilian" would be located at a different point on the color line than Native Americans.[10]

Mestizo and *Mulatto* are Hispanic terms used to describe any person of mixed race or blood coming from any predominantly Latin country. Any combination of two cultures (Hispanic-Black, Hispanic-Indigenous Indian, Hispanic-Chinese, White European-Black etc.) qualifies as *mestizo*.

This ability to "whiten" players by the major league team owners helped the careers of all the Latin-American players during the 1930s and beyond, in particular Vernon "Lefty" Gomez, whose colorful mound antics earned him the nickname the "Crazy Castilian," as well as Melo Almada, Roberto Estalella, Jose "Chile" Gomez, and of course, Ted Williams. Born to a Hispanic mother, Williams vigorously downplayed his Hispanic heritage. All these players were from Latin-American heritage, spent their childhoods growing up on the West Coast, and were all bilingual, save for Williams. Future White Sox manager Al Lopez was of Cuban extraction, was born and raised in Florida, yet constantly was referred to as "Señor Lopez" or just "Senor" by the press of the day.

Griffith was always a sentimental child. He was also sentimental in his adult disposition towards baseball. He was slow to adapt to any sort of changes; again, a 19th-century mind in a 20th-century game. Usually, he would complain about it or try to utilize theories to disprove them until eventually coming around to accepting them. In 1940, Bob Considine and Shirley Povich postulated, in a momentous article for the *Saturday Evening Post*, about Griffith's mercurial nature: "His befuddling changes of heart must spring principally from the fact that he is only living owner who came up the hard way—from batboy, to semi-pro, to minor leaguer, to big leaguer, to manager, to magnate."[11]

In Brian McKenna's *Clark Griffith: Baseball's Statesman*, he ticks off a list of just a few of Clark Griffith's pet peeves: "As such, he was among the biggest initial opponents of nighttime baseball, the All-Star game, the minor league system, football in the District of Columbia and negros in baseball; however, he became among the loudest supporters of each after a complete analysis of the subject."[12]

His aversion to night baseball was most famously quoted to Shirley Povich in the *Washington Post*: "This game wasn't meant to be played at night," said Griffith. "It was meant to be played in the Lord's broad daylight just as it always has been played for more than 100 years. There's more to a ball game than just a ball game. There's fresh air and sunshine and everything that goes to make up a fine afternoon."[13]

In most of Griffith's reversals, money became the deciding factor. The Senators were taking a beating at the ticket booth during World War II, and Griffith had to concede to playing night games in order to accommodate the day workers in the defense industry surrounding the D.C. area. Installing lights in 1941, he asked Commissioner Landis for more night games but was denied. He went to his old friend, Franklin Roosevelt; consequently, he got all the night games he wanted.

Griffith and the Black Community

Perhaps the greatest conundrum of this narrative is Griffith's relationship with the Washington Black community. Although opposed to racial integration in baseball, he was still a tremendous supporter of the community in general, particularly with his availability of Griffith Stadium. African Americans of the city, in turn, embraced him for the opportunities he provided … to a point.

Built in 1911, burned down that same year, and rebuilt in 1912, National Park was renamed Griffith Stadium in 1923, oftentimes referred to as Griffith Park. The stadium became a mainstay for entertainment in the Black community of the Shaw district. It was located between Georgia Avenue and 7th Street and Georgia and W Street. It was razed in 1965 when the expansion Senators moved to Robert F. Kennedy Stadium, and it eventually became the site of Howard University Hospital.

Griffith regularly allowed the local community to use the stadium for dozens of purposes, almost always free of charge. The Georgetown Hoyas football team played there regularly between 1921 and 1950, as did the George Washington Colonials (1930–1960) and the Maryland Terrapins (1948). Howard University and Lincoln University of Pennsylvania held their annual Thanksgiving "Turkey Bowl" game years before the District of Columbia Interscholastic Athletic Association started their annual High School holiday contest.[14] Both contests attracted crowds numbered in the thousands.

From the end of World War I and well into the 1970s, one of the biggest forms of youth community involvement was the drum and bugle corps. These corps were sponsored by dozens of fraternal and community organizations like the Veterans of Foreign Wars, American Legion, Boy Scouts of America, Catholic Youth Organization, Police Athletic Leagues, municipal Volunteer Fire Departments, and many high schools throughout the United States. All these groups consisted of a combination of drum lines, bugle players, flag color guards, rifle teams, baton majorettes, and sword carriers. Competitions were held at Griffith Stadium, almost always free of charge, with trophies and in some instances cash awards given to the winners.

Griffith allowed the District's high schools to hold their annual Drum and Bugle Corps and Cadet Drill Team competitions, as well as fraternal organizations like the Elks, Moose and Masons, to hold charity baseball games at the stadium. The All-American Girls Professional Baseball League played many games at the stadium during their existence as well.[15] The stadium was also home to hundreds of amateur and professional boxing matches, most famously the heavyweight title fight between Joe Louis and Buddy Baer in 1941.[16]

One particularly notorious event occurred the night of July 23, 1942. It was the height of the Big Band era, and a "Battle of the Bands" was scheduled between saxophonist Charlie Barnett and trumpet legend Louis Armstrong. Barnett was riding high on the fame of his two big hit dance arrangements of "Cherokee" and "Skyliner," and Armstrong was of course, the Babe Ruth of jazz to the Black community. Twenty thousand people came out to see a music battle but instead saw a battle-royal. Barnett played to polite applause; however, when Armstrong started, thousands of fans rushed the stage, which was located at second base, to get a better look at Armstrong and dance to his jazz. Auxiliary police and many servicemen attempted to form a ring around the bandstand, much to the chagrin of the paying customers in the seats, who were unable to see the show. Bottles and other things were thrown at the mob, who promptly picked up the bottles and threw them back; consequently, a dangerous game of "bottle catch" ensued. Order was not restored, and the show ended at 11:00 despite the bands' good intentions.[17]

Perhaps the greatest thing that Griffith did to endear himself to the Black community was allowing them the use of the stadium for religious services. By the early 1900s, Washington, due to its status as a "free" city and because of the job opportunities in the federal government, had the largest percentage of Blacks of any city in the nation.[18] They brought with them their deep Southern Baptist and A.M.E. religious traditions. The late-19th and early–20th century gave rise to both the Fundamentalist and Evangelical movements. Preachers like Aimee Semple McPherson in Los Angeles and the Reverend Lacy K. Williams of Chicago preached to thousands of parishioners each week.

One of the most prominent and charismatic of these Evangelical preachers was the Elder Solomon Lightfoot Michaux. Ordained a minister in the Church of Christ (Holiness) in 1918, Michaux (me-SHAW) started in a small church in Hampton, Virginia. In 1929, after he established his own independent Church of God, his wife convinced him to move to Washington and develop his ministry there. Michaux was one of the very first church leaders to utilize radio as a method for proselytization. Broadcasting first out of WJSV in Virginia and later, on CBS radio, Michaux developed a throng of millions of avid listeners.[19]

Between 1934 and into the 1960s, Michaux held tremendous mass baptisms, marriages, and prayer rallies at Griffith Stadium, usually three or four a year, as well as Friday night services. Starting with just a handful of parishioners and sponsors, Michaux grew his audience into the thousands. In September of 1934, 15,000 watched as Elder Michaux married 100 couples free of charge.[20] In 1940, 20,000 filled Griffith Stadium to watch him preach and baptize over 100 people.[21] Michaux continued these ministries until his death in 1968.

In July of 1939, 15,000 people crowded into Griffith Stadium to hear the prestigious "Wings Over Jordan" choir perform gospel and spiritual songs, to the delight of the audience. The choir was founded in 1935 by the Rev. Glenn T. Settle, pastor of Gethsemane Baptist Church in Cleveland, Ohio. The Reverend Settle believed in using Negro spirituals to spread Christianity. Like Michaux, he established a radio program to address the Negro community and introduce the non–Negro to the Negro experience. In 1937, the ensemble performed weekly on the "Negro Hour" over radio station WGAR, a CBS affiliate.[22]

All this community outreach went a long way in establishing Griffith's credibility within the Washington Black community, again up to a point. He hired Blacks as ushers, ticket sellers, concession stands workers and groundskeepers, all jobs held traditionally by whites. Upon Griffith's passing in 1955, Al Sweeney, writing for the *Baltimore African American,* lauded Griffith for his efforts in community outreach, citing how he would regularly give free use of the stadium to civic groups like the Junior Police and Citizens Corps and the National Negro Opera Company:

> There were many residents in the area of the stadium who would find gifts coming their way thanks to Griff's kindness. I used to visit his office every spring in the interest of persuading him to hire colored players. I found him gracious. He talked with me for hours. There was doubt where he stood on the subject. Which was more than I could say for some of the self-proclaimed liberals around town. They masqueraded as great friends, but you can never catch them or get a straight answer on a particular subject involving race. I just think it's unfortunate that he held out [on] the color line for so long.[23]

However, in keeping with traditions, he still enforced segregated seating, allowing Blacks to sit only in the right field bleachers.

To say that Clark Griffith was "just a traditionalist" would be like calling the Pope "just a Catholic." In his 19th century mind, baseball was "a walk in the park on a sunny day," and he wished it could be forever so. Many of his decisions might be traced back to his moralist upbringing on the Kansas-Nebraska prairie. However, more often than not, they were predicated simply on his need for money to run his ball club. Cases in point: Many stadiums allowed for the sale of beer at games; Griffith, a teetotaler, did not, not even 3.2 percent alcohol "near-beer." Griffith did not relent on that decision until the 1950s.

The Senators started broadcasting their games on CBS radio in 1934, featuring the avuncular Arch McDonald as announcer; however, Griffith only allowed away games to be broadcast, saying listening to games on the radio kept the fans away. (The St. Louis Cardinals had been broadcasting games on the mighty KMOX since 1926.) He did not relent on that decision until 1938, when he was again desperate for the money generated by advertising sales.

Probably the most puzzling of his financial and moral decisions came with his association with the Redskins football team and Negro League baseball.

Anxious for the revenues he perceived would come from professional football, Griffith struck a deal with the new Boston Redskins owner, George Preston Marshall, for the use of the stadium starting in 1937. Marshall was somewhat of a local hero. Like Joe Cambria, he made his fortune in the laundry business, although he inherited a string of laundry stores from his father rather than building it up on his own like Cambria. Enamored at first by the attention brought by the Redskins, he became increasingly truculent with the Washington press:

> In August of 1938, Griffith expressed some frustration that the local sports reporters were taking a great deal of interest in the Redskins during their training camp, taking press away from the Senators. Unreasonably, Griffith threatened to lock the football team out of Griffith Stadium if the local papers did not stop covering football during the baseball season. He brought in a competitor. The Senators were now the worst major professional team in D.C., behind the [champion] Redskins and the Homestead Grays.[24]

Griffith, though, bought himself a world of trouble with both Arch McDonald and George Preston Marshall. McDonald, a real "good 'ol boy" from Chattanooga, Tennessee, was known to allow his racial prejudices to slip every once in a while during his broadcasts. It was Marshall, however, who resisted integrating his football team. Even when he had the opportunity of number one draft picks, he was famously quoted as saying, "We'll start signing Negroes when the Harlem Globetrotters start signing Whites."[25] Marshall was forced to sign a Black player in 1964 after Secretary of the Interior Stewart Udall and Attorney General Robert F. Kennedy threatened to revoke his government-controlled lease on the new District of Columbia (now RFK) Stadium.

Griffith's greatest conundrum was undoubtedly his adherence to the "gentlemen's agreement" of not breaking the color barrier. Although vehemently denied by Commissioner Landis in 1940, Griffith still believed in separate but equal leagues for Blacks and Whites. As early as 1932, Griffith praised their playing but insisted that the Negro Leagues should become better organized and put a better product on the field: "Negros are no longer willing to pay to see just any kind of ball. And least of all, here in this section of the country, and where they can see Babe Ruth and Lou Gehrig and other stars on regular big league teams instead. You must give them a comparative brand of ball."[26]

Throughout the War years and into the late 1940s, Griffith would not budge from his position on the Negro leagues:

> It is my opinion the colored people should lend all of their efforts to developing their own national following and if properly organized, could eventually take their place in the annals of baseball. It is my belief we should have white baseball leagues and colored baseball leagues. I have spent much time and lent my aid and the use of the ballpark here to the advancement to the National League in colored baseball.
>
> Should you ask any of my colored friends who have been instrumental in the development of colored baseball in Washington, I feel sure that they would say that I have been most co-operative and I know that a lot of other baseball parks have acted likewise.
>
> It is my opinion that organized baseball should lend their assistance to the colored man in helping him build an organization in which the people would have confidence and which would eventually put colored baseball on a solid foundation.[27]

Griffith also believed, and rightly so, that taking away the likes of Satchel Paige, Buck Leonard and Cool Papa Bell from the Negro Leagues would be exploitative and destroy the leagues. Griffith further believed that, with proper organization, there could be a Black versus White World Series to determine the best of both leagues.

The problem with this rhetoric was that Griffith was being situationally disingenuous, and the Black press called him out on it, much to their credit. Although polite and thankful for Griffith's free use of the stadium for their religious and civic activities, Louis Lautier and Sam Lacy of the *African American* took him to task for "fattening up" on the black community, who were in fact his most loyal supporters of the team. For all the Negro League games, Griffith took 20 percent of the gross receipts after taxes, a percentage of concession sales, and made the teams pay the stadium employees. The Homestead Grays were the powerhouse of the Negro Leagues throughout the 1930s and outdrew the Senators three to one at the box office. With that kind of profit, Griffith had no incentive to break the color line.

Sam Lacy became increasingly irked by the exclusion of Black ballplayers. He pointed out that major league baseball had used players from every known white ethnic group from Jews to Chinese to Cubans, the St. Louis Browns used a one-armed man to play the outfield, and the Senators used a one-legged man as a pitcher, and *still* they refused to admit Blacks into baseball, even while the war raged, and the white players went off to fight. Lacy went so far as to promote a "lily-white baseball day" where Blacks would boycott attendance, cab drivers would alter their routes, and park vendors would call in sick. In 1948, Lacy could not help but stick his finger in the eyes of the "lily-white Chicago White Sox and the Washington Senators" by pointing out that on a particular Wednesday game in Chicago, the White Sox and Senators drew fewer than 4,000 fans, while the Indians (with Larry Doby) drew 23,843 and the Dodgers (with Jackie Robinson) drew 19,491 fans.[28]

It would not be until 1949 that Griffith, like Branch Rickey, announced that he would start looking for "the right kind of boy for the team," and not until 1954 that he signed his first Black player. And here again, it was a Black Cuban, Carlos Paula, not an African American player. His first true Black player was former Brooklyn Dodgers great Joe Black, signed as a reliver in 1957. Joe Black did, however, go on to become his first African American scout.

No, Clark Griffith was not a man motivated by racial prejudice. Besides being an arch-traditionalist, he was a struggling businessman, trying to run a baseball team on a shoestring budget and without the benefit of a beer or candy fortune. His decisions seemed to be predicated purely on profit. By integrating major league baseball and weakening the Negro Leagues, he would have effectively cut his business profits by at least a third, placing him in more danger of failure. The Negro Leagues were saving his major league franchise. Why kill the cash cow?

He was damned if he did and damned if he didn't.

Cambria

If one makes a cursory internet search for the meanings of life, one finds hundreds of possibilities. For the purpose of this narrative, I would like to go with the concept that life is a series of events which build character. I believe there were several important events in Joe Cambria's life which helped shape his dealings with people in the baseball business in general and with the players he signed in particular.

As far as his racial attitudes were concerned, Joe Cambria was a bit more transparent than Clark Griffith; however, to elucidate them, one must become a quasi-"armchair psychologist."

The first and perhaps the greatest event in young Joe Cambria's life was his coming to America. The Cambria family came to the United States in the middle of the greatest immigrant wave in history. At the turn of the 20th century, people flocked to this country, emboldened by the great American dream that hard work equals success. Unfortunately, there were those who believed that their successes were more important than those of others. Stories by my Italian grandfather, who emigrated to this country in the early 1900s, told of the mistreatment he received from both ethnic and non-ethnic Americans, particularly the Irish. My grandfather told me the story of how he was beaten up by the Irish foreman at his job at a wood chipping plant because he asked for a drink of water.

There can be no question that Joe Cambria would have experienced similar racial profiling growing up in and around the greater Boston area most of his early life. Experiencing these effects would most surely have had a profound effect on his social attitudes. The Irish had a large conclave in and around Boston and were particularly hostile to the Italian community. "Guinea," "dago," "grease ball," and "wop" were some of the nicer epithets he would have surely heard, terms often used to describe even the great Joe DiMaggio.

Dr. Shawn Alfonso Wells, professor of cultural anthropology at Carnegie Mellon University, wrote in her dissertation: "The concept of race is perceived to be biologically real and is so ingrained in American society and thought that it has taken on a life and language of its own. The very infrastructure of American society was forged on designating and exploiting differences amongst human beings."[29]

As Kris Kristofferson wrote in his award-winning 1972 album *Jesus Was a Capricorn*, "Everybody's gotta have somebody to look down on."[30]

But in all research to date, there is no published evidence of Cambria using a slur to describe anyone. There were times when he would describe a player as "the big Swede" or "the big Pole" but never to their detriment. Being racially stereotyped at an early age must have played an important role in his treatment of his Cuban players; however, there is some ambiguity there that will be discussed later.

Cambria breaking his leg in a sliding accident in 1912 would surely have influenced him. Like the fabled Moonlight Graham saga in the movie *Field of Dreams*, Cambria must have thought he was equally cheated out of his destiny. He may have felt it was his duty to give a break (no pun intended) to young players so they could realize theirs. In the beginning of his baseball scouting career, he sought out young men to sign and develop, started numerous training camps for them, encouraged them and their families to see the benefits of the great game of baseball, and in general tried to give them all the opportunities that he felt he may have missed. Joe Cambria was not above big risk for big reward; he knew there were many diamonds in the rough on the numerous sandlots of America who, with polish, could net him a good financial reward.

The consequence of his childless marriage to Charlotte was another event that would shape his attitudes towards his young charges. Cambria treated all his young prospects as if they were his own. He may have thought this way instinctively, but once he heard the Cuban players call him "Papa Joe," he was hooked. He became very paternal with his young sandlotters. There was always another Bob Feller or Walker Cooper walking around out there, and he was sure to find him. He seemed to go out of his way in convincing Clark Griffith of their value, more often than not overstating it!

Cambria's attitude towards his Cuban signees was, however, a bit more complex. The sobriquet "Papa Joe," I am sure, made him feel very patrimonial towards them, and all the Cuban players interviewed for this book attested vigorously to his care and concern for their well-being: extra money when needed, constant words of encouragement, taking them to dine in Spanish restaurants, possibly a letter from home and, in some cases, getting their favorite rhumba records from Cuba. With the Cubans, he did what he could to make them feel comfortable in a foreign and in some cases a hostile land.

At the same time, he was a patronizing Neocolonialist as well.

Neocolonialism had been established in Cuba in the late-19th and into the early–20th centuries and became the dominant pattern that defined the United States' relationship with Latin America throughout the first half of the 20th century. The introduction of the Platt amendment (1902–1934) and the Truman Doctrine in 1950 all but solidified Cuba as an American "neocolony." By the 1930s, American companies controlled 56 percent of all Cuban production.[31] The introduction and maintenance of puppet governments by the United States only helped to solidify American dominance throughout the Latin American basin, all in the name of thwarting the rise of Communism in the region.

Joe Cambria, however, was not the first one to recognize and utilize Cuban and white ballplayers for his gain. No, that honor would go to none other than Branch Rickey. Lauded as the great humanitarian who broke the major league color barrier with the signing of Jackie Robinson for the Brooklyn Dodgers, Rickey is characterized by writer Kevin Kerrane as a "manipulative" operator: "Rickey introduced the use of non-binding agreements, which he called 'desk contracts.' Rickey taught his scouts the art of signing thousands of amateurs on a purely tentative basis. Utilizing this *quality out of quantity* principle, players, upon being signed, were sent to various outposts where they were scouted at a greater leisure, and perhaps ... released a few weeks later without money for transportation home."[32]

Joe Cambria was quick to learn the new ploy of the desk contract and utilized it frequently enough with his minor league players. But they cried foul so loudly that Commissioner Landis nearly tossed him out of baseball for his signing shenanigans.

Cambria had been involved with semi-pro baseball and scouting since the late 1920s. He realized quickly that American ballplayers were too savvy. Many of them demanded and got bonus money and learned how to play one scout against another to get better deals for themselves. Although he was successful in getting several excellent players like George Case, Jr., Mickey Vernon, Walt Masterson, and Hall of Famer Early Wynn, those signings were few and far between.

Knowing of the abilities of the Cuban players from his sandlot and minor league days, Cambria decided that Cuba was the place to be. With the predominant American "manifest destiny" attitude, he invaded Cuba like the fabled "Great White Hunter" portrayed in many American feature films (hence his nickname "the ivory hunter"). With his signing of Roberto Estalella, Rene Monteagudo, Thomas de la Cruz, Fermin Guerra, and many more during the late 1930s, word got around throughout the island that this *loco Americano* was throwing money around, signing up ballplayers left and right. He became inundated quickly with young men desperate and anxious for the dream of American baseball.

Cambria knew this and exploited it to his advantage. With the extreme working-class poverty on the island, playing baseball in America for a few thousand dollars for a few months' worth of work was indeed a dream come true. However, at the beginning of his Cuban scouting escapades, Cambria never gave out bonuses. One of his most famous quotes was he never paid a nickel of bonus money to any of his players. He did not want to make them instant stars or put that kind of pressure on them before they knew the rigors of the game. In the beginning of his scouting career, this was true for the most part. A bonus could have been travel money. But by the 1950s, the Cuban players smartened up. They realized the power of "no," and players like Camilo Pascual, Pedro Ramos and others did receive some bonus money to sign with the Senators.

Yet despite this manipulation, the Cubans welcomed his presence. By the 1950s, Joe Cambria had become *El Patron,* the big shot. He had a suite in the Hotel American in Vedado, one of the wealthiest parts of Havana. He owned a bar, a restaurant, and a boarding house, and he had a limousine driver and "female assistants." He wore the guayabera shirts commonplace with the island's men of influence, sported a white straw hat, had a small flask of Cuban rum in his breast pocket, and had a cigar called "The Papa Joe" named after him. Cuban sports writers like Jess Losada and others decried Cambria's presence on the island, calling him the "Christopher Columbus of baseball" for robbing the island of its talent. Losada further asserted that with his property holdings and his profligate spending, he was just another "mob-like" influence in Cuba. Speculations abounded that Cambria may have really been "mobbed up" or possibly even a snitch for Batista in the 1950s. Cambria reveled in the attention, his role as the big American fish in a little pond.

Joe Cambria's "American" attitude extended to everyone at all levels. In Albany, he signed a Canadian-Lithuanian pitcher Joe Krakaukas (kra-Kow-cus). He could not pronounce his name, so he jokingly called him "park your carcass." He signed Alex Kvasnak (kVash-nik) a journeyman outfielder who played five games for the Senators in 1942. He could not pronounce his name either and took to calling him "squash neck." He signed Venezuelan pitcher Alejandro Carrasquel, could not pronounce his name, and tried to convince the Washington press to call him "Al Alexander." Pitcher Rene Monteagudo also became "whitened" to Ray Montgomery. One might argue that Willie Mays also could not remember people's names, and "Say Hey" became his go-to sobriquet. Cambria did not try very hard to remember difficult names and did not seem to mind calling anyone what he felt like calling them.

As far as the Spanish language is concerned, Joe Cambria, at the beginning, did not try to learn the language. A few words and an expletive here and there, but he felt he was an American; they all should speak English. He may have been condescending at first; however, Tony Oliva said that by the time of Cambria's death, he spoke the language pretty well.

There is no question that Cambria exploited the Cuban players and their extreme poverty for his and his boss Clark Griffith's own gain; however, the Cuban ballplayers did not mind. The Cuban journalists minded, but not the players! Every Cuban player interviewed for this book attested to the fact they were grateful for the opportunities Cambria gave to the young ballplayers, opportunities they would not have had from anyone else. Even as they were being subjected to insults, bench-jockeying, discrimination, and problems with the language, they accepted it as the price to pay for their one possible chance at the American dream.

I believe Joe Cambria's heart was in the right place. His methods of going about it were a bit sketchy. Did he want his players to succeed? Sure! It was good for baseball, good for the Senators and good for his bottom line. After all, once a businessman....

The Cubans

The concepts of race and racialization for the Cubans in general and for the ballplayers in particular were exponentially more complex than for most Americans, albeit much less violent than the decades of lynchings in the Southern states. As noted Cuban historian and cultural anthropologist Jesús Guanch Pérez observed:

> The Cuban ethnos-nation is the historical-cultural and demographic result of multi-ethnic conglomerates (mainly Hispanic, African, Chinese and Antillean) that fused in a complex and dissimilar way beginning with the sixteenth century, creating a new identity based on the formation of an endogenous population, with its own reproductive capacity, independent of the migratory currents that gave rise to its historical unfolding, with its own set of characteristics.[33]

To all of us who are not cultural anthropologists, this means that basically, Cuba is and always has been a cultural melting pot of nationalities. Starting with the three indigenous Indian tribes (Taino, Guanahatabey and Ciboney), followed by the Spanish, British, African slaves, Chinese slaves, and peoples from the rest of the islands in the Caribbean, Cubans intermarried to create their own unique racial paradigm. Cuba did, within a span of a few centuries, what it took most countries several millennia to accomplish: developed its own cultural identity within its own form of racialization.

Cuban racial identity, however, has always been somewhat opaque. Cuban skin color could fall along a long spectrum of racial combinations dating back to the 16th century. In her doctoral dissertation, Professor Shawn Alfonso Wells identified no fewer than 31 different classifications of Cuban color identities. By way of example:

Blanco: white but not necessarily white by descent.
Capirro: red skinned or red headed white
Jabao: Mulatto with reddish skin tone and hair color
Jabao Capirro: mulatto with reddish skin tone who appears white but has slightly kinky hair.[34]

These color classifications were developed to place Cubans in three distinct racial categories, *blanco* (white), *mulatto/mestizo* and *negro*. *Mulatto* categorizes those who are mixed-raced leaning towards black, whereas *mestizo* categorizes those of mixed race who lean towards white.[35]

The one overarching concept with all the delineations and classifications of Cuban racialization was: "how white are you?"

For centuries, Cuba wanted to be perceived as a "White" nation. With their tremendous wealth of sugar cane and tobacco, they hoped to become players on the world stage. America and Europe were indeed entitled "White" nations, and this "whiteness" had social power. Since it was almost impossible to be completely "white" White in Cuba, being the right shade of dark became all-important.

The phenomenon of "whitening" was well known to the Cuban people for centuries. They even coined a term for it: *adelantar la raza* or advancing the race through whiteness. Dr. Esteban Morales Dominguez, one of Cuba's most prominent Afro-Cuban intellectuals and a member of the Cuban Academy of Sciences, published *Race in Cuba: Essays on the Revolution and Racial Inequality,* considered to be a seminal work on racial identity in Cuba. He explained the practice thusly: "The whitening practice began in Cuba because to be black was a stigma, a disadvantage at all levels of social life based on the institution of slavery. Capitalism, which needed the mass of ex-slaves as workers, applied what can be considered the phenomenon of the 'ratification of the working class.'"

Although class discrimination and racial discrimination are not equivalent, the working class is also the object of a discriminatory process, a workforce that must be preserved under that condition and be reproduced by means of the family. Racism and racial discrimination transcend the limits of classist structure, becoming a more general phenomenon that does not disappear with the elimination of capitalism.

Thus, the phenomenon of whitening in Cuba was not only a problem derived from policy, but the policy itself was generated and nourished by the economy and culture of Cuban society, surviving from the colonies to capitalism until the end of the 1950s. "[I]t is still common in Cuba today to meet people who do not take themselves as blacks or *mestizo*, but as whites, when in fact they are not white."[36]

Although the discrimination against people of color in Cuba was nowhere near as bad as it was in the Jim Crow South, it still existed on the island. Professor Adrian Burgos stated, "some within baseball circles perceived the Cubans as occupying an in-between space along the color line as neither black nor white."[37] Most of the Cuban players I interviewed said they perceived themselves as "White." Being treated as "Black" when they came to the States to play seemed incongruous to them. They were ill-prepared for the level of animosity they received once they began playing regularly in the United States. The racial epithets were disconcerting but nothing they had not heard before. The physical abuse, however, was new.

When he first came up to the big leagues, Roberto Estalella was routinely given healthy servings of beanballs, chin music, and brushbacks. In fairness to the pitchers of the time, Estalella notoriously crowded the plate. His being brushed back could have been a simple case of pitchers asserting their dominance of the inside corner of the plate. However, when he slid into a bag on a steal attempt, the tag was applied with vigor, usually to his face. Despite his "Castilian identity" with the Washington press, Estalella had his ethnicity questioned constantly: "Ossie Bluege [teammate and future manager] remembered that opponents expressed animosity despite Estalella's friendly demeanor, one teammate telling Estalella, 'You might be Cuban, but you're still a nigger sonuvabitch to me.'"[38]

In later interviews, Estalella denied vehemently that he was Black.

Another pivotal incident occurred in St. Louis in 1944. The St. Louis Browns, who had a history of refusing to play against Black players, had been mercilessly riding the Washington Senators all season, claiming that the 10 Cuban Senators on the roster (all signed by Cambria) were black, not Latin. Fed up with the season-long insults, six-foot, three-inch Roberto *"El Gigante"* Ortiz, one of the most popular players in all of Cuba throughout the 1940s and 1950s, planted himself squarely in front of the Browns' dugout during batting practice and called out the instigator of all the insults, Tom Turner. Benches cleared and fisticuffs ensued. Ortiz missed a few weeks of playing time because he fractured his thumb during the melee, but he won the respect of and support of his teammates from then on.[39]

As Adrian Burgos points out, the significance of the fight was not the fight itself; it was what it *could* have been. St. Louis was planted firmly in the Jim Crow South. During that time, if a Black man attacked a White, a riot could have occurred. That it did not points out the position that the Latin players occupied. They were not considered "White" by the Browns, but neither were they "Black" per se. It pointed out the "twilight" position that the Latin players occupied.[40]

These are, of course, just a few of the multitudinous incidences that occurred in the major leagues, and there were far more in the minor leagues.

In his book, *Beyond the Shadow of the Senators,* Brad Snyder states that Joe Cambria and the Senators cared little for the challenges faced by their Latino players, "subjecting them to the racially hostile environments in the South."[41]

I question that notion. Cambria started bringing Cuban players to the States in 1934, when he owned the Albany (New York) Senators, and there is where he placed them, quite far from the Jim Crow South. For a decade from 1934, Cambria owned teams predominantly in the north, such as Salisbury (MD), Harrisburg (PA), Trenton (NJ), Youngstown (OH), and Williamsport (PA.) It was not until 1945, when Cambria brought the Havana Cubans to Orlando to play in the Florida International League, that he himself placed his players in a Southern town. And in that instance, Florida had a burgeoning Latin population in the state. The Latin players were isolated in the northern cities more so than in Florida. Also, in 1940, Commissioner Landis issued an order that scouts could no longer own ball clubs, so Cambria had to send his boys wherever he was told.

Griffith, on the other hand, chose Florida as the Senators' winter camp after the war, and there was nothing one could do about the Florida Jim Crow laws of the time.

The Latin players ate and slept in segregated sections of the town but had little trouble once they broke camp and headed north. It was Griffith who owned teams in Tennessee, North and South Carolina, and later, teams in the Texas League, and there was no escaping the racial norms of the time in those cities.

It was Jackie Robinson who unfortunately felt the full weight of systemic American racism when he debuted in 1947. The Latin players continued to be jockeyed by the opposition but with much less vitriol than Jackie Robinson encountered. By the early 1950s, the Latin players were considered commonplace. In a phone interview, 95-year-old Brooklyn Dodgers pitching legend Carl Erskine explained that Cuban left fielder Sandy Amoros was never denied the use of the hotel dining rooms in St. Louis, but the Black players ate in their rooms.[42]

The challenges the Latin players faced from both the opposition and their own players were only half the problem. Even though they played for little money, which pleased Griffith, it frustrated the team's managers. Bucky Harris, who managed the Senators on three separate occasions (1924–1928, 1935–1942, 1950–1954) and Ossie Bluege (1943–1947) both found working with the Cuban players extremely frustrating. Bob Ruark, writing for the *Washington Daily News,* reported that "Harris nursed a deep-seated grudge against the chattering monkeys from General Batista's game preserve." In 1940, Harris' ire reached a boiling point when he exploded to a newspaper reporter's question, saying: "They're trash! They're doing no good and they ain't in place here. They don't fit! They've all got to show me something and show me quick or I'm cleaning out the joint. If I have to put up with incompetents, they better at least speak English!"[43]

Obviously, Harris' frustration and prejudice came from the language barrier. One Cuban, Rene Monteagudo, was able to get into his good graces: "Monteagudo is the only one of the Cubans who gets along with the club. He is a cheerful little cherub with a fair command of English and a willingness that is almost pitiful. He forever smiles and never sulks. His teammates even speak to him on the street!"[44]

To their credit, they at least made an attempt to ameliorate the situation. In the late 1930s, Cambria brought up Roberto Ortiz, ostensibly to be a pitcher. At the time, there were no other Cubans on the roster. Harris asked permission from the Boston Braves to use the services of their catcher, Al Lopez, as an interpreter. Similar circumstance occurred when Harris returned to the Senators in the 1950s. He was insistent on re-signing backup catcher Fermin "Mike" Guerra, a Cuban fluent in both languages. Harris told *Washington Post* reporter Dan Daniel, "I simply have to get this Guerra to run my Spanish-speaking pitching staff. I have no Spanish beyond 'si, si' and there is no English among [then Senators pitchers] Sandalio Consuegra, Conrado Marrero, Julio Moreno and the rest of my Cuban-Castilian cast."[45]

Guerra performed admirably, acting as translator and interpreter for Harris and handling the catching chores when the Cubans pitched. By the 1950s, the Cubans performed very well on the field. They became more friendly with their teammates and vice versa. By the mid–1950s, all of the Cubans Cambria brought up to the club spoke English somewhat, and many became stars in Washington and in Minnesota, once the team moved in 1960.

The problem with the language may also have been exacerbated by the players. Bill Keefe, writing for the *New Orleans Times-Picayune,* penned a story concerning a Puerto Rican player, Chico Salgado, playing for the New Orleans Pelicans of the old Southern Association. The article, entitled "Good hear-No Talk," explained,

Chico Salgado's release from the Pels [Pelicans' nickname] brings to mind stories that are told of many Cubans who, in recent years, have adhered to the "no-talky-English" policy while they are playing baseball during the summer months in this country. It could be that Old Joe Cambria, who was the first scout to beat the canebrakes of Cuba in quest of baseball material, learned that the boys would get along better if they never expressed their opinions or uttered complaints or let on that they knew what was going on when the manager bawled them out.[46]

This concept would not be out of the realm of possibility. Feigning to understand English along with the smiling and joking that the Latin players enjoyed would go a long way to defuse potentially angry and embarrassing situations brought about by not being able to understand fully the English language. Articles in the *Washington Post* alluded to the fact that the Senators did attempt to hold English language classes during spring training during the war years.

During the war years, with many of the front-line players enlisting in the service, Cambria brought dozens of Cubans up to the majors because of their draft-exempt status. When Cambria moved his Springfield franchise to Williamsport, Pennsylvania, in 1944, he populated the team almost exclusively with Cuban players, preparing them for the majors, whose owners he was sure would be looking for good, low-cost players to shore up war-depleted rosters. He did encourage his young players to learn rudimentary English language skills. But there, too, they were subjected to enormous race hatred.

I can remember to this day an incident that occurred when I was a high school junior in 1966. I had befriended a young, painfully shy Korean exchange student who, at age 16, was a remarkable pianist. One day in the hallway, I spied her talking with her younger sister in their native language. As I passed by to say hello and compliment her musical expertise, they both turned bright red, fell deathly silent, and stared at their shoes, fearful to even acknowledge my kind solicitation.

This was, after all, the United States of manifest destiny that had flexed its muscles and defeated world-wide socialism. Americans felt the whole world should speak English. If you lived or worked in the U.S., you spoke English or were asked to leave. Perish the thought that you should be caught speaking your mother tongue in public!

As one can imagine, the national press reflected widespread insensitivity during the mid–20th century. They thought nothing of deriding the Cuban players and Joe Cambria as well. Case in point comes from the *Salisbury Daily Times* of 1938. The unknown writer of the article is describing the obstinacy of Ismael Morales, Joe Cambria's very first signee. At the time, Morales was playing for the Dayton Ducks of the Mid–Atlantic League. In a close game with the Wheeling club, with two men on, Morales was told to attempt a sacrifice bunt. Morales ignored the order and swung away, missing a homer by inches. Manager Ducky Holmes, coaching at first base, furiously charged down to the plate and told him to bunt. Again, he ignored it, swung away, and again missed a homer by a few feet. Holmes again charged Morales at the plate and threatened to fine him $50 for ignoring the order. As reported by the paper, Morales said: "Ducky Holmes, you clazy. Me no sacrifly. Me all time hita da runs in. Me wanna hit ball 500 miles over fence. Easy for me. Win game." Holmes shouted, "You'll go 500 miles away from here when the ball game is over—back to Papa Yoe!!" Morales stepped back into the batter's box, didn't move a muscle, watched the third strike go by, and was consequently shipped back to Cambria.[47]

Articles abounded in national as well as regional papers, where the Latin players were quoted in "pidgin" or "Spanglish" and made to look like fools. Whitney Martin, writing for the New York *Wide World of Sport,* was adept enough to insult both Cambria and two of his Latin players in one article:

> Joe Cambria is still on the job. For a time we thought something might have happened to him. We visioned him wandering about lost in some clammy cave to which he had tracked some elusive ball player, or hanging helplessly with his breeches caught on a cornstalk in some deserted outfield where he hoped to ambush an innocent lad.
>
> Just how Sanchez and Mario Perez, the other Puerto Ricans, evade Cambria is a mystery, as the swarthy, stocky [Italian] has an ear for Spanish and can spot a prospect hanging in the trees or knifing his way through the cane fields.[48]

Cambria was almost always referred to as swarthy, pudgy, stocky, mysterious, elusive or some other adjective made to make him out as a seamy character with a checkered career. He was simultaneously further described as a "laundryman" or a "wash tub thumper" or some such term meant to cast aspersions on his scouting abilities. He was constantly depicted as chasing Cuban players "through the canebrakes" or looking in caves for them. The insinuation was always that the Cubans were ignorant, aboriginal-like tribesmen and Joe Cambria the "great white hunter" bringing back his trophies to mount above the fireplace. It was probably meant to sell newspapers, but it just aided and abetted the stereotypification of the Latin player as a savage, made to be tamed by good ol' American baseball, which further led to his derision by white American audiences.

An incident that occurred in 1941 with pitcher Alejandro Carrasquel highlights the tremendous inequities and racial attitudes of the U.S. Government towards aliens at the time.

As told by *Orlando Reporter-Star* sports editor Wilson McGee, when it came time for Carrasquel to report to Senators' spring training, he was nowhere to be found. He had missed the last boat out of Caracas. Clark Griffith became concerned and started calling consulates and local police. Once located, Alex Carrasquel was at a loss: no boat and no money. Griffith wired him $200 for travel.

Now the trouble began. When Carrasquel cashed the check, he wound up with only $128.00. Venezuela was still on the gold system, and the exchange rate was what it was at the time. He arrived in Miami with an empty wallet and an empty stomach, only to be confronted by agents yelling and haranguing him for his "head tax."

In brief: The United States began implementation of a Head Tax, sometimes known as a Poll Tax, as far back as the first Immigration Acts of the 1870s. In 1917, all the previous Acts were consolidated into one, and an $8 Head Tax was imposed upon all aliens wanting to come to America. That, along with many other exclusions, in particular against the Chinese, Japanese and a majority of the Persian countries, was a blatant and jingoistic attempt at keeping America white. Curiously, Canada, Newfoundland, Cuba, and Mexico were exempt from the tax. Alex Carrasquel was, alas, Venezuelan.

Back in Miami, the white-coated immigration officials were screaming, "YOU PAY HEAD TAX OR YOU NO GET INTO COUNTRY!" thinking that by yelling at him he would understand. Carrasquel had a far better command of his pitching skills than he did of his English language skills."

With a bit of understanding, Carrasquel said, "Me pay tax? Me no pay! Papa Griff, he pay. If he no pay, Papa Yo pay!" He was referring, of course, to Clark Griffith and Joe Cambria.

The agent, having no idea of the relevance of those parties, threw Carrasquel into jail for the night. Word finally reached the proper ears, taxes were paid, and Carrasquel was released and sent on his way to training camp.

Typical American bureaucracy, complete lack of empathy, or failure on the part of either Cambria or the Senators to educate the Latin players on the immigration rules, call it what you will. One would think that in Miami, hardly bereft of Spanish speakers, one person could have been found to help out the situation. As the war years went on, more of this confusion would come into play.[49]

Despite the half-hearted attempts of using Spanish-speaking players as interpreters, the Senators organization did little to accommodate the Latin players from the beginnings when Cambria brought them to the club in the 1930s. It was Cambria who bought minor league clubs predominantly in the North. The Senators tended to buy in the segregated South. No one in the organizational hierarchy spoke Spanish, and they hired no one to do so. Up until the time of Jackie Robinson's appearance, the club was focused more on "whitening" the Latin players so they would be accepted societally and within the ranks of baseball. Despite Cambria's minuscule attempts like Spanish dinners and rhumba records, the organization placed the onus squarely on the shoulders of the Latin players to acculturate, even when placed in the Jim Crow South.

All the players interviewed for this book played for the Senators in the mid– to late 1950s. They attested to the fact that they had no trouble playing or living in any of the places they were sent to, primarily because they all spoke English well enough to understand and be understood, and because, by that time, Latin players had become commonplace. Many of them, like Roberto Clemente, Camilo Pascual, Vic Power, Orestes Minoso, and others, outperformed their white counterparts and therefore received the grudging adulation of white American audiences.

They were undoubtedly strangers in a strange land.

The Essence of Racial Inequity

Perhaps one of the most scathing diatribes on the racial inequities of the times came from the pen on G.C. Miller. Writing for the *New York Age*, one of the leading Negro newspapers of the mid–1900s, Miller, logically and with measured verbiage, ostensibly attacked the Chicago Cubs but, at the same time, all of baseball and America. it is too important to be paraphrased, and I beg the reader's indulgence by printing the article in its entirety below.

Sports of the Age

From the Chicago Cubs "News," a periodical devoted to the activities of the team issued by the Chicago National League baseball club: "**This year baseball celebrates its 100th anniversary as America's favorite sport and entertainment…. Baseball knows no race, creed or color. It belongs to the people.**" The remarkable thing about this quoted statement is the fact that so many outright lies could be uttered in so few words.

Lie No. 1—Race. How about the Jim Crow restrictions imposed upon qualified members of a large part of the American people, the Negroes, which keep them from participating in our so-called national pastime? It is true that Negroes are allowed to play baseball, but only among themselves and for coffee and cake money while other players, so long as their skin is white, can command fabulous salaries.

Lie No. 2—Color. It is true that the doors of organized baseball are open to Indians, Cubans, Porto [*sic*] Ricans, Hawaiians, etc., but only if their skin, hair and features will pass muster as evidence of membership in the White race. This writer defies any member of the above-mentioned national groups to obtain entrance into the major leagues with a black skin, or even mahogany colored, lest he be hailed as a "nigger" as was Adolfo Luque, swarthy Cuban pitcher of the New York Giants, by the "sportsman" when he made his first appearance on the mound in St. Louis.

Lie No. 3—Ownership. The notion that the game "belongs to the people" is of course, just as fantastic as saying Standard Oil belongs to the people. The continued discrimination against Negro players in the face of protests of Negro and White ball players, sports writers, and fans, proves that the game most emphatically does not belong to the people, but rather to the sixteen major league owners who do with it what they please.

There is a reason behind the appearance of this fairy tale in the "News." During the World Series last year, the proceedings were somewhat marred for the baseball magnates by the vision of picket lines in protest against Jake Powell, Yankee outfielder who had previously made an insulting remark about the Negro race in a radio interview. The pickets were representatives of various civic organizations. [In a radio interview on July 29, 1938, Powell, purportedly a deputy on the Dayton, Ohio, police force, infamously told WGN announcer Bob Elson that he stayed in shape during the off-season by "cracking niggers over the head with my night stick." He received a 10-day suspension from Commissioner Landis.]

In order to avoid any reoccurrence of this demonstration of militancy by Negros, it looks like the Cubs management is taking an early opportunity to "appease" the injured group. But they can come out from behind that mask of innocence. We know them for what they are. We refuse to believe in any talk about baseball being "America's National Pastime" until the barriers excluding Negro players from the major leagues have been lifted.[50]

As so eloquently stated above, anyone who could pass as being white enough to play in the big leagues was granted the honor. Not so the Negros. Indeed, every nationality *was* included in "America's Game," just not the Negro.

The African American press was unrelenting on the question of racial disparity in American baseball. Historic Black newspapers like the *Chicago Defender, Baltimore Afro-American* and *New York Amsterdam News* published articles daily on the subject. Dan Burley exposed Clark Griffith's soft underbelly in a scathing article in the July 19 edition of the *New York Amsterdam News*. He attested that Griffith Stadium, located in the heart of Negro Washington at Georgia Avenue and U Street, had been the gathering place for the black community, which had made Griffith and George Preston Marshall, president of the Washington Redskins football team, very wealthy men by way of their attendance at sporting events:

Griffith, to escape criticism and to avoid a rash of picket lines in front of his park as they have paraded in front of Mike Uline's Arena, long ago got together with representatives of Negro organized baseball, including the late Cum Posey of the Homestead grays, and worked out a proposition in which Griffith Stadium is listed as one of the regular places where they play Negro baseball. Along the line, Posey, with an eagle eye on the War-swollen population of the capital, swung his famous nine into Griffith Stadium and in his publicity, gave them the new surname of "Washington Homestead Grays." It worked out all right, as did most of Posey's operations in baseball, and now the Grays are part and parcel of Griffith Stadium when the Senators are on the road.[51]

However, this was all Griffith was prepared to do at that time. He famously went on to stress that the Negro Leagues should build themselves up into a money-making organization on their own and compete simultaneously with white baseball—separate but equal. Griffith would rather hire Cubans of "the right color" than have a Negro on his team, said Burley.

It was not until Griffith saw the money Brooklyn was making with Jackie Robinson in the lineup and later when Larry Doby broke in with the Indians, that he changed his mind and applauded the effort. Then he made the decision, as Branch Rickey had done, to find the "right boy" to integrate the Senators.

During the Mexican League drama, when he was not actively complaining about the lack of Negro talent in the major leagues, Sam Lacy of the *Baltimore Afro-American* was having a wonderful time just reporting the truth. Describing the Mexican League All-Star Game in 1946, Lacy gleefully reported the number of Negro Leagues players on the winning team, including Ray Dandridge (Newark Eagles), Bill Wright (Baltimore Elite Giants), and Theolic Smith (Cleveland Buckeyes), among others who outclassed the white major league stars, such as Danny Gardella, Sal Maglie (Giants), Mickey Owen (Dodgers) and others.

He further reported that the Vera Cruz Blues, with white stars like Max Lanier, Mickey Owens, Danny Gardella, Ace Adams, and Luis Olmo, were languishing in seventh place while the all-colored Tampico and Monterrey teams were battling it out for first place in the Mexican League. Lacy reported that the Negro League players were making only half as much as the white Major League stars, but still it was 100 percent more than what they would have made in the Negro Leagues at home.[52]

It seemed that inequality followed them wherever they went.

Were Clark Griffith and Joe Cambria racists?

No.

As stated by Charles Cambria, great-great nephew of Joe Cambria, "they were just creatures of their time."[53]

CHAPTER 11

The Good, the Bad, the Ugly

Joe Cambria, along with so many of those mentioned in this book, was a product of his times. Prevailing moral and racial attitudes, as well as world events, played a great part in the myriad decisions that were made daily. Some were bad and some were good. Cambria should be held accountable for both.

The Good

1. Cambria was aware of the racist attitudes in America and tried to hide his Cuban players on teams in the North, like Albany, Springfield, Trenton, Williamsport and later in Texas, in which there was a large Hispanic culture. In some instances, it worked, and in others it did not.

2. Cambria seemed to hold a paternal attitude toward the young men he signed to many of his teams throughout his career. He did take care of his players, especially his Cuban players. "Papa Joe" always had a little extra money available, when necessary, for sundries and entertainment. He provided them with their favorite Cuban recordings, helped them to learn rudimentary English skills, arranged for phone calls and travel to and from the island, and was a constant presence in their lives. The Cuban players respected him for his efforts on their behalf.

3. He was fiercely loyal to Clark Griffith and the Senators. Despite being wooed by other teams, he stayed loyal to Griffith, calling him the "greatest man in baseball." Griffith, in turn, allowed him an almost free hand with his Latin signings, provided monetary support, and came to his aid on numerous occasions when he got into trouble with Commissioner Landis. Cambria vowed that when he died, he wanted to be buried in a Senators uniform.

4. Despite statements to the contrary, Cambria provided the opportunity for hundreds of young Cuban men to play minor and major league organized baseball and start a new life in America, with all of the opportunities that implies. Many players to whom I spoke said that their association with Cambria was "life altering." Julio Becquer was able to rescue his whole family from the Castro regime.

The Bad

1. "Desk contracts." The signing of players to a blank contract was a prevailing convention of many scouts throughout the early part of the 20th century. Cambria may have just been going along with those conventions, but it was wrong. Desk

contracts allowed him to post-date player signings and reassignments, which further allowed him to alter their wages. This practice got him fined several times by Landis and eventually prompted Landis to outlaw them altogether.

2. Bad bookkeeping. In the beginning of Cambria's career as a minor league owner, he paid little attention to the myriad rules and details of baseball ownership. It was purported that, early on, he kept all his records in a little black book in his coat pocket. He once attended a minor league game to scout a player he had already signed. He once sent two whole squads of men to a spring training facility without providing their names to the coaches.

3. Quantity over quality. Just like Branch Rickey, Cambria thought he could solve a staffing problem by throwing more players at it, predominantly pitchers. There were so many young players eager to play American baseball that he had all he could have in the 1930s and 1940s. Because of the speed with which Cambria provided players to Griffith, he may have signed over 400 Latin players to major and minor league contracts. There were over 50 Latins who made it onto the official Senators rosters; only four signed by Cambria became legitimate stars: Pedro Ramos, Camilo Pascual, Zoilo Versalles, and Tony Oliva.

4. Loss of players' status. As mentioned above, young players clamored to get signed by Cambria and go play American baseball. This caused a major problem. Cuban players who played for two years at any organized level of American baseball and did not stick in the majors or the minors lost their amateur status in Cuban when they returned home. They could no longer play in the Cuban amateur leagues and were possibly not good enough to play in their professional leagues. Many of Cambria's signees made a good living playing in the mid–minor league classifications or simply went to leagues in Mexico.

5. Ignorance or bending of rules. In the beginning, a lot of Cambria's errors were mostly due to his ignorance of baseball rules, hence the intercession of Griffith into his early foibles. In his later years, he simply bent the rules to suit his pocket. He continued to play fast and loose with contracts and team business, especially when he became a founding member of the Florida International League.

6. Player strikes. Cambria had trouble with players from both his Salisbury and Albany teams who refused to play until they were paid what they were owed. Paychecks were obviously not paid out with great alacrity.

The Ugly

1. Colonialization. Cambria's raiding of the Latin countries in search of baseball talent was pure colonialization, which had been an American mindset since before the turn of the century. William Howard Taft, the first American Governor-General of the Philippines (1901–1904) and later the 27th President of the United States, coined the term "our little brown brothers" to describe the Filipino population during America's colonialization of the islands in the late 19th and early 20th centuries. It was not meant to be a derogatory term but was looked upon as a term of paternalistic racism. Joe Cambria had the same kind of paternalism about his dealings with the Cuban players. It some cases it was sincere; in other cases, it was disingenuous. He would use it to his advantage.

2. The American press. The press only exacerbated this situation described above by constantly referring to Cambria, as well as other baseball scouts, as "ivory hunters." The descriptions of Cambria tromping through the canebrakes, smoking ballplayers out of caves or climbing after them up palm trees was a prevailing racist description of the players as aboriginals who needed to be "tamed" by the Great White Hunter. That kind of reporting only heightened the racial tensions which the Cuban players had to face. It was, unfortunately, the prevailing American attitude of the early 20th century.

3. The backlash from the Cuban press. Cambria's "theft" of four players from under the noses of the Cincinnati Reds and the Cuban Baseball Commission earned him a major enemy: Jess Losada. Losada, the Dean of the Cuban sports reporters, was extremely vocal about Cambria's cheap signing practices and his robbing the island of its baseball talent. He went so far as to propose an official moratorium on Cambria to stop him from taking so many players out of Cuba. Losada and others of the Cuban Sports press became Cambria's most ardent critics.

4. Lack of acculturation with the Cuban players. In the early years of Cambria's scouting career, he did very little to help his young Cuban players navigate the waters of American culturalization. In 1934, he famously pinned a note to Roberto Estalella's jacket asking that he sent to Albany and gave him a card which simply stated "ham and eggs" so he could show it to a waitress and get food. He may have thought that he was being helpful. In realty, he was treating them as little more than a FedEx package. Cambria did this on more than one occasion, until such time as the Cuban players, through their own pipeline, taught their countrymen how to negotiate those situations. Cambria must have thought they would simply pick it up as they went along.

5. Cambria's own lack of assimilation. By the 1950s, he was living almost full-time in Cuba; however, he never became proficient in the language. He had interpreters with him always. He may have learned a phrase or two, but never enough to be conversant. Again, the American ideal of paternalistic racism: I speak English. Everyone else should.

6. Taking advantage of poverty. Joe Cambria most assuredly was well aware of the crushing poverty of the Cuban people. He knew he had the power to change young men's lives by signing them to professional contracts or getting them tryouts. He signed them for almost nothing, never paid any bonus money, paid only for transportation, sometimes lodging and walking money. The wealthy American *Padron* knew that the few thousand dollars a year he would pay his Cuban players was more money than they could make in a lifetime of toil on the island. He knew it and used it to his advantage.

7. Nepotism. When Joe Cambria was banned from team ownership in 1940, he sometimes sold his teams outright or turned his teams over to his brother John, who was not an experienced baseball man, and sort of ran them by proxy. This way, he would show no ownership but could still control the operations.

Joe Cambria was not an evil or bad man. He was just clever enough to learn the American way of doing business at the time and use it to his advantage. He did good things; he did bad things. Many people do.

Epilogue

A baseball team, for all its bravado and machismo, is a fragile thing. From the owner down to the batboy, a team must believe in itself, the players have to believe in each other, and they all have to believe in the manager in order to bring home the coveted prize of a championship flag. Team chemistry also becomes critically important. In my opinion, consistency of personnel becomes the single biggest factor in team success. The Yankees set the gold standard for consistency with players like Earle Combs, Bill Dickey, Babe Ruth, Lou Gehrig, Joe DiMaggio, Whitey Ford, Mickey Mantle and Yogi Berra spending their entire careers with the team. The Baltimore Orioles became a dominant franchise with the longevity of Brooks and Frank Robinson, Jim Palmer, Mark Belanger and Boog Powell. Stan Musial, Red Schoendienst, Pepper Martin and Terry Moore anchored the St. Louis Cardinals for many years. Constant turnover of personnel and reshuffling the lineup card can breed distrust, turmoil, and uncertainty.

The Washington Senators were a ballclub born out of turmoil, in a contentious fight between the National League and Byron Bancroft "Ban" Johnson and Charles Comiskey, progenitors of the new American League in 1900. Clark Griffith was instrumental in the recruitment of players from the National League to jump to this new upstart league, but not without a lot of backlash from other team owners. Washington, along with other powerful eastern cities like Philadelphia, Baltimore, and Boston, became one of the charter members of the new league and fought for new fans and new revenue.

The magnificently mediocre early Senators started their bottom-feeding life in the second division for their first 11 years until Clark Griffith and his brother quite literally "sold the farm" to put up the necessary monies to purchase control of the Nationals franchise. Here is where the team's turmoil began. Griffith did not have a beer, candy or publishing fortune, and the concomitant gobs of money with which to buy high-priced ballplayers. Griffith did not come from money and never had much. He started his ownership journey from scratch and continued that way throughout his tenure as the team's president.

It was luck that brought him Walter Johnson in 1907. One of the game's greatest baseball attractions, Johnson kept the turnstiles humming, and the team remained in the first division of the American League for 16 out of 22 seasons from 1912 through 1933. But it was Clark Griffith's baseball savvy and player knowledge (something his nephew Calvin did not possess) that brought him and the team its most success. Cobbling together some of the greatest trades in the game's history, Griffith assembled a team of winning veterans and put a fiery 27-year-old named Stanley "Bucky" Harris in charge of them, quickly dubbed "The Boy Wonder." They won pennants in 1924, 1925, and 1933 and became the darlings of the people and presidents.

The 1930s started with a bang for the Nats and ended with a whimper. From 1930 through 1933, they were a highly competitive team and remained in the first division, ultimately winning the American League pennant in 1933. But the Great Depression would hit with a vengeance in 1933. Griffith was forced to sell his superstar player/manager Joe Cronin to the hated Red Sox in 1934 in order to make his payroll and clear his debts. From that date on, the team remained almost exclusively in the second division with the exception of 1936, 1943 and 1945, when they would make it back into first division.

Here is where Joe Cambria became a willing participant in the team's turmoil and downward fortunes. Instead of trying to trade for superior talent, Griffith took a chance and heeded the advice of Cambria, who sold him on the idea of low-cost Cuban ballplayers. Cambria would deliver them to Griffith by the bus loads. Colorful, cheap, and expendable, the Cubans made for good gate but in the end, they did not pull their weight. The almost constant influx of tan faces along with the resultant racial strife only enhanced the turmoil. Yes, they were extremely helpful in keeping the team competitive during the War years, but throughout the 1930s and 1940s they did little to help the team's standings. Cambria, entrepreneur, businessman and inveterate lover of all things baseball, truly believed he was doing the right thing and helping his friend Griffith.

In the 1940s, the greatest change to occur was the Second World War. The stage was global, the antagonists were stronger, and the effects were longer-lasting. The war years did much to disrupt the psyche of baseball. Players were coming and going with great alacrity. In the major leagues, thankfully, only three players were lost to combat. The minor leagues did not fare as well, and many were lost. This kind of disruption hurt major league baseball in the fact that no one knew who would be next. It disrupted team chemistry, an aspect of vital importance in team culture. The Senators fared well in 1943 and 1945, but it was too little too late.

The 1950s saw a significant amount of peace, prosperity, and cultural change, in spite of the United States' "police action" in Korea. Jobs in the new tech industries, spawned by post–war experimentation, were booming, as were new home and car sales. For the first time in modern times, kids had disposable income and the freedom to choose what to spend it on.

The first big change to occur in the 1950s was the introduction of the transistor radio. The transistor radio was and is still considered to be the most popular electronic communication device and single greatest boon to the social psyche of the 1950s and 1960s. No longer glued to the huge Philco in the living room, kids were unconstrained by their parents' choices in entertainment. Now they had immediate access to news, music, sports, celebrity and, above all, rock 'n' roll. Parents, especially those in the big East Coast commuter cities, were also hungry for their own brand of news, weather and sports and quickly embraced this new technology. Radio personalities Murray the K, Dick Clark, and Wolfman Jack became just as popular as Red Barber and Bob Wolff. Small enough to fit in a pocket, the transistor radio let you listen to your ball games on the go. Car radios had been around since the 1930s but were expensive. By the mid–1950s, they became smaller, more readily affordable, and equipped with both AM and FM bands. Some kids were able to buy cars. Once that occurred, they and their friends were constantly on the move. The kids of the 1950s now had money, mobility, and endless possibilities. When they were stuck at home with their parents in the 1940s, baseball became of primary import. Now, it became secondary.

The second big change was also technological, the advent of mass television. A quick Google search of television history will show that the concept of viewing live pictures goes back to the mid–19th century. Television developed over the course of a century, and by the late 1940s, commercially broadcast television became available for mass consumption. Early television programs were basically recreations of already existing radio shows like *Amos and Andy, The Milton Berle Show, The Howdy Doody* Show, and news programs featuring John Cameron Swayze and Edward R. Murrow. Lagging in ratings, ABC began broadcasting *Baseball's Game of the Week* in 1953 to mixed success; however, when the other networks began their broadcasts in 1955 and 1957, the *Game of the Week's* popularity soared. The new revenue streams brought in much-needed cash to second-division teams.

The third change was what was described as "white flight." Whites of varying European cultures became uncomfortable with the influx of Blacks into the major cities and with school desegregation. In large numbers they migrated out of the cities and into the suburbs, where they would find solace among those of their kind. Consequently, travel back into the cities for ball games became less frequent. Many venerable inner-city ballparks like Ebbets Field, the Polo Grounds, and Griffith Stadium were becoming old, dilapidated, and devoid of safe parking for nighttime baseball. With the popularity and the proliferation of television, people found more comfort in their living rooms than at the stadiums. Also, the new-found television revenues became a boon to many struggling franchises; hence, the less popular second-division clubs began looking for greener pastures. The Boston Braves moved to Milwaukee in 1953, the St. Louis Browns moved to Baltimore in 1954, and the Philadelphia Athletics moved to Kansas City in 1955.

In 1955, upon taking control of the franchise after the passing of his uncle Clark, Calvin Griffith quietly began looking westward towards Los Angeles, all the while vehemently denying any ideas of a shift as "careless rumors." He went so far as to say to Shirley Povich of the *Washington Post* that he would never in his lifetime move the Senators out of Washington. Meetings with outside interests occurred still, however.

Roy Sievers's All-Star status, his prodigious home runs, and his ability to make the turnstiles turn, along with minority owner H. Gabriel Murphy's fierce protestations and threatened lawsuits by both himself and the National Brewing Company, forced the parsimonious Calvin Griffith to keep the team in Washington, D.C., even after being courted by a consortium of interests in Los Angeles, San Francisco, Louisville, and Minneapolis. The National Brewing Company held the radio and television rights to all the Senators games for three years, with another five-year option, and were loath to let the Senators opt out of that contract. Murphy was famously quoted as saying [about the team moving to another city] that they might move 60 percent of it, but his 40 percent was staying in Washington. Griffith's flimflamming with outside buyers was just more fuel for the feud that had erupted between himself and Murphy. Quoted by Dan Daniels of the *New York World Telegraph & Sun*, Murphy berated Griffith publicly at the 1956 All-Star Game, saying he was dissatisfied with the club's administration, which needed an "overhauling." Matters came to a head at the January 1957 stockholders meeting. Murphy, in a five-page statement, charged Griffith and his administration with being "loose and incompetent," and "without any real leadership." Murphy also hired private auditors to go over the Senators' books, which further incurred Griffith's wrath. Murphy quit his job as club treasurer and vowed to fight Griffith in every court in the land.

Perhaps Sievers's celebrity and the intersection of baseball and politics caused powerful Tennessee Senator Estes Kefauver to add major league baseball to his Senate antitrust proceedings after hearing of Griffith's intentions to move the team from the Federal City. The Kefauver committee proposed many sweeping changes to organized baseball, including an unrestricted minor league player draft, revenue sharing, and a taciturn acceptance of Branch Rickey's Continental League, which was seeking to lure major players into a third league to expand to underrepresented cities in the Midwest and the West Coast.

Roy Sievers also had the "ear" of Vice President Richard Nixon, a self-avowed "Sievers fan," who was a frequent guest at Griffith Stadium, and Sievers visited the vice president's mansion on several occasions. It was Nixon who gave Sievers the keys to his new Mercury station wagon when the Senators honored him with a special "night" to celebrate his winning the AL home run and RBI crown on September 23, 1957. Many a politico was entertained by Griffith during Sievers's tenure from 1954 to 1959, and they enjoyed free passes to the game or sat in the owner's box for free. That perk was not overlooked. All the while, minority owner H. Gabriel Murphy's running feud with Griffith over keeping the team in Washington escalated to the DC and Federal courts and, unsuccessfully, to the United States Supreme Court.

The Kefauver hearing became more show than substance, with venerable Casey Stengel putting on one of the greatest displays of "Stengel-ese" in the history of jurisprudence. Many witnesses declined to answer directly any of Kefauver's questions for fear of Major League Baseball being stripped of its beloved anti-trust status and the reserve clause. Ultimately, Major League Baseball agreed to expand both the American and National Leagues in 1960, on the condition that a new team would be installed in Washington. In so doing, it effectively quashed Branch Rickey's dream of a third league. Griffith ultimately won and moved the original franchise to Minnesota. In its place, a new, magnificently mediocre group of bottom-dwellers was installed.

All that was mentioned above brought with it significant change, turmoil, and disruption. Clark Griffith tried his best to deflect and defend his team, but in the end, it seriously affected the Washington Senators' team psyche. The constant reshuffling of personnel, along with the unwanted presence of the Cuban players, ultimately led to the Senators remaining mired in the low second division for most of their baseball existence. It would not be until the mid–1950s, with the advent of stars like Roy Sievers, Jim Lemon, Harmon Killebrew, Bob Allison, Pedro Ramos, and Camilo Pascual, that the Nats began to gel. They were not winners, but they began to coalesce as a team. It would not be until 1965 that they would win a pennant as the Minnesota Twins. By then, Joe Cambria had passed and Cuban had been shut down.

Things changed. New players emerged and life went on. The one constant in the whole story was baseball.

Appendix I: Selected Players Signed by Cambria

Alejandro Eloy *"El Patón"* Carrasquel Aparicio

Born July 24, 1912, in Caracas, Distrito Federal (Venezuela). Died August 19, 1969, in Caracas, Distrito Federal (Venezuela)

Washington Senators 1939–1945, Mexican Leagues 1946–1948, Chicago White Sox 1949

Career: WAR-6.1, W-50, L-39, ERA-3.73, G-258, GS-64, IP-861, SO-252

Although his career was not as storied and successful as Early Wynn, Alejandro Carrasquel was a man of many firsts. He was the first Venezuelan to play in the Major Leagues, throw a shutout, hit safely, and stroke a home run. He was famously signed by Joe Cambria while sitting on a park bench in Havana in 1938. Already a seasoned veteran of the Venezuelan and Cuban leagues, by age 27 he was ready for his debut on April 23, 1939, where he faced his first three batters: Joe DiMaggio, Lou Gehrig, and Bill Dickey. He retired them all. "Alex" compiled a winning record of 50–39 in his seven years with the Senators and was an integral part of the Nats' pitching rotation during the war years. After jumping to Jorge Pascal's outlaw Mexican League in 1946, he never regained his Major League form; however, he holds the distinction of being one of the first of Joe Cambria's successful Latin ballplayers.

(Source: SABR biography, baseball-reference.com)

George Washington Case, Jr.

Born November 11, 1915, in Trenton, NJ. Died January 23, 1989, in Trenton, NJ.

Washington Senators 1937–1945, Cleveland Indians 1946, Washington Senators 1947.

Career: WAR-18.1, AB-5016, H-1415, HR-21, BA-.282, R-785, RBI-377, SB-349, OBP-341

Three time All-Star, six-time stolen base leader, 76.2 success rate, Ranks 112 all-time.

Blessed with blazing speed as a high schooler, George Case caught the attention of the great Connie Mack, who gave him a tryout at Shibe Park. After seeing him hit and run, Mack suggested he try becoming an outfielder instead of a second baseman. Flush with too many outfielders at the time, Mack further suggested to his friend Clark Griffith that he take a look at young Case. Griffith liked what he saw. Case was signed by Joe Cambria to a contract with the Senators' affiliate York White Roses in 1935. He came to the Senators in 1937, where he was mentored by Clyde "Deerfoot" Milan, himself a prodigious base stealer with the Senators from 1907 to 1922. Early Wynn famously remarked, "it seemed like [Case] was always starting at full speed."

(Source: SABR biography, baseball-reference.com)

Conrado Eugenio *"El Curveador"* Marrero Ramos

Born April 25, 1911, in Sagua La Grande, Villa Clara (Cuba). Died April 23, 2014, in La Habana, La Habana (Cuba)

Washington Senators 1950–1954, one-time All-Star

Career: WAR-8.6, W-39, L-40, ERA-3.67, G-118, GS-94, IP-735⅓, SO-297

By the time 39-year-old "rookie" "Connie" Marrero debuted with the Senators in 1950, he had already pitched a lifetime. He had already pitched for 18 years with sandlot, amateur and American professional teams before coming to Washington. He had three consecutive 20-win seasons for Joe Cambria's Havana Cubans from 1947 to 1949. Once in Washington, he teamed up with fellow Cubans and Cambria signees Sandalio Consuegra and Julio Moreno to form the nucleus of the Senators' pitching rotation for the early 1950s. His huge, everpresent Cuban cigar, his broken English, and his joking about his questionable age endeared him to the press. His colorful wind-up motion, famously described as a cross between a windmill gone berserk and a duck flying backwards, made him a fan favorite. With his deceptively wicked curve ball and his utter control of the strike zone, Marrero baffled big-league hitters. After his baseball days were over, he continued to coach in his native Cuba well into his 80s. Marrero was enshrined in every Latin baseball Hall of Fame and died two days short of his 103rd birthday.

(Source: SABR biography, baseballreference.com)

Pedro "Tony" Oliva López Hernández Oliva

Born July 20, 1938, in Pinar del Rio, Pinar del Rio (Cuba)

Minnesota Twins 1962–1976

Career: WAR-43.0, AB-6301, H-1917, HR-220, BA-.304, R-870, RBI-947, SB-86, OBP-.353

Eight-time All-Star, five-time league leader in hits, four-time league leader in doubles, Gold Glove Award 1966, three-time batting champion, Rookie of the Year Award 1964, National Baseball Hall of Fame inductee 2022

Pedro "Tony" Oliva was the capstone to Joe Cambria's scouting career. Oliva was signed by Cambria in February of 1961, just months before Fidel Castro banned the importation of Cuban ballplayers to the American major and minor leagues. Anxious to get to spring training on time, Oliva did not have a passport, so he used his brother Antonio's. Upon arriving in America, he was labeled as "Tony" and, despite changing his name legally to Pedro Oliva, Jr., the name Tony stuck. He bounced up and down between the Minnesota Twins and the minors for four years before finally winning the starting right field job with the Twins in 1964. And what a year it was! He won just about every title he could earn that year. He led the league in runs, hits, doubles, and total bases. He won the first of his three batting championships with a stellar .323 batting average, and he won Rookie of the Year honors. Oliva would further have the distinction of being the first Cuban to win the Rookie of the Year Award, the first Latin to win a batting crown, and the first to win it twice in a row, 1964 and '1965. Overlooked and undervalued

Joe Cambria's last big signee, Hall of Famer Tony Oliva, had to use his brother's passport to escape Castro-controlled Cuba in 1960. Tony became the "patron saint" of the Twins, spending his entire career and his retired life with Minnesota (National Baseball Hall of Fame Library, Cooperstown, New York).

like so many of the Black and Latin players of the Golden Age, Oliva, an eight-time All-Star, finally earned a plaque in Cooperstown in 2022, celebrating his 15-year career, all played for his beloved Twins.

Camilo Alberto *"Patato Pequeño"* Pascual Lus

Born January 20, 1934, in La Habana, La Habana (Cuba)

Washington Senators 1954–1960, Minnesota Twins 1961–1966, Expansion Senators 1967–1969, Cincinnati Reds 1969, Los Angeles Dodgers 1970, Cleveland Indians 1971.

Six-time All Star, three-time league leader in complete games, three-time league leader in shutouts, three-time league leader in strikeouts

Career: WAR-40.9, W-174, L-170, ERA-3.63, G-529, GS-404, IP-2930⅔, SO-2167

Camilo Pascual was actually signed by Joe Cambria twice! He was first signed by the Chickasaw Chicks in the Class-D Sooner State league in the summer of 1951. After bouncing around with a couple of C class teams that summer, Pascual was not resigned. He went back home to pitch in the Cuban leagues and was given a second chance by Cambria, who resigned him as a free agent to the Senators in the spring of 1952. He was assigned to the Tampa Smokers and then to Cambria's Havana Cubans, where he posted stellar numbers for two years. Pascual began his big-league journey with the Senators on April 15, 1954. He struggled to have a winning season for five years, predominantly through a lack of run support from his Washington teammates. He hit his stride in 1959, posting a 17–10 record and leading the league with 17 complete games and six shutouts. Pascual went on to have nine winning seasons in his 18-year career, winning 20+ games in 1962 and 1963. After his career ended, Pascual spent several decades as a Caribbean scout for the Los Angeles Dodgers. Pascual was one of the 10 initial inductees into the new Cuban Baseball Hall of Fame in 2014.

(Source: SABR biography, baseball-reference.com)

Pedro *"The Cuban Cowboy"* Ramos Guerra

Born April 28, 1935, in Pinar del Rio, Pinar del Rio (Cuba)

Washington Senators 1955–1960, Minnesota Twins 1961, Cleveland Indians 1962–1964, New York Yankees 1964–1966, Philadelphia Phillies 1967, 1969, Pittsburgh Pirates and Cincinnati Reds-1969, Expansion Senators-1970

Career: WAR-21.9, W-117, L-160, ERA-4.08, G-582, GS-268, IP-2355⅔, SO-1305

One-time All-Star, two-time league leader in games started

Pedro Ramos and fellow Cuban Camilo Pascual were inexorably linked together. Both were signed by Joe Cambria as teenagers out of the Cuban amateur leagues. For seven years, they were the Senators' one-two punch in the rotation, although most opposing teams punched back harder. Ramos became the workhorse of the rotation, twice leading the league in starts and averaging 220 innings a year in seven seasons with the Twins. Ramos also holds the dubious honor of leading the league in losses in four straight seasons. He will be forever linked with Mickey Mantle, who smashed a home run that missed going completely out of old Yankee Stadium, hitting the white façade on the roof and bouncing back into the park. Ramos surrendered 316 long balls in his career, which is dwarfed by the likes of Jamie Moyer (511) and Warren Spahn (434). Both Ramos and Pascual were saddled with the same debt: both were rushed to the big leagues before they were ready, both pitched in the cavernous Griffith Stadium, and both were surrounded by weak-hitting and sloppy-fielding players early in their careers. When "Pistol Pete" came to the United States, he loved all things American, especially the television Westerns of the day. He patterned himself after Hopalong Cassidy, hero of a popular Western cowboy show that ran between 1952 and 1954, so much so that he bought Cassidy's signature black tasseled Western outfit complete with two silver pistols. Despite his penchant for delivering the long ball, Ramos was a durable pitcher for his 15-year career. He had the distinction of throwing the last game for Clark Griffith's original Senators in October of 1960 and being the first pitcher for the expansion Minnesota Twins in April of 1961.

(SOURCE: SABR biography, baseball-reference.com)

James Edward "Pete" Runnels

Born January 28, 1928, in Lufkin, TX. Died May 20, 1991, in Pasadena, TX.

Washington Senators 1951–1957, Boston Red Sox 1958–1962, Houston Colt .45s 1963–64.

Career: WAR-29.8, AB-6373, H-1857, HR-49, BA-.291, R-876, RBI-630, SB-37, OBP-.375

Three-time All-Star, two-time batting Champion 1960, 1962, Coach for the Red Sox 1965–1966.

After graduating high school, Pete Runnels did a stint in the Marine Corps, where he honed his baseball skills. After his discharge, he was invited by St. Louis manager Eddie Dyer to the Cardinals' spring training camp in 1949. At the end of camp, he was not offered a contract, so he returned home. He played for Chickasaw and Texarkana in the Sooner and Big State Leagues for two years. He was signed by Joe Cambria to the Chattanooga Lookouts in 1951 and was promoted to the Washington Senators in mid-season. He never returned to

Pete Runnels gives some fielding tips to movie star Dorothy Provine before a Senators game. Runnels would struggle with the 40-foot wall in Griffith Stadium, but he enjoyed the friendly confines of Fenway Park in Boston, becoming a two-time batting champ (National Baseball Hall of Fame Library, Cooperstown, New York).

the minors. Runnels played all over the infield for the Nats from 1951 through 1957. Traded to the Red Sox in 1958, he was mentored by the great Ted Williams, who taught the lefty Runnels how to wait on his pitches and smack the ball off Fenway Park's Green Monster in left field. Unencumbered by the 30-foot-high right field wall in Griffith Stadium, Runnels blossomed into a solid .300 hitter, winning batting titles in 1960 and 1962. After his playing days were over, he coached for the Red Sox in 1965 and 1966, serving as interim manager for 16 games at the end of the 1966 season.

(SOURCE: SABR biography, baseballreference.com)

James Barton "Mickey" Vernon

Born April 22, 1918, in Marcus Hook, PA. Died September 24, 2008, in Media, PA.

Washington Senators 1939–1943, 1946–1948, Cleveland Indians 1949–1950, Senators 1950–1955, Boston Red Sox 1956–1957, Cleveland 1958, Milwaukee Braves 1959, Pittsburgh Pirates 1960

Career: WAR-35.5, AB-8731, H-2495, HR-172, BA-.286, R-1196, RBI-1311, SB-137, OBP-.359

Seven-time All-Star, two-time batting champion, three-time league leader in doubles

Joe Cambria was actually beaten to the punch. He went to see Vernon play for his freshman Villanova college team and wanted to sign him. Unfortunately, he was already inked to a deal with the St. Louis Browns' Class-D affiliate Easton Browns of the Eastern Shore League.

Cambria saw a lot of Vernon, playing against his own Salisbury Indians of the ESL. Vernon hit .287 with 10 home runs for Easton in 1937, but the Browns did not pick up his option. Cambria found out about it and immediately scooped him up. It was one of Cambria's smartest baseball moves. Vernon had a stellar 20-year career, smacking a Hall of Fame–worthy 2,495 hits, beating out Ted Williams and Al Rosen for batting championships, and becoming President Eisenhower's favorite player. Vernon also became the expansion Senators' first manager from 1961 to 1963. From 1965 to 1988, he managed, coached, and scouted in the major and minor leagues. All told, he spent 52 years in baseball and was regarded as one of kindest and humblest men in baseball. He remained a fan favorite in Washington until his passing.

(Source: SABR biography, baseball-reference.com)

Early "Gus" Wynn

Born January 6, 1920, in Hartford, AL. Died April 4, 1999, in Venice, FL.

Washington Senators 1939, 1941–1948, Cleveland Indians 1949–1957, Chicago White Sox 1958–1962, Cleveland 1963

Career: WAR-61.1, W-300, L-244, ERA-3.54, G-691, GS-611, IP-4564, SO-2334

Nine-time All-Star, five-time 20-game winner, three-time league leader in innings pitched, two-time league leader in strikeouts, five-time league leader in games started, two-time league leader in wins, Cy Young Award winner 1959, elected to the Hall of Fame 1972

Seventeen-year-old Early Wynn wandered into a tryout camp in Sanford, Florida, in 1937 and so impressed manager Clyde Milan with his fastball that he signed him to a Senators contract on the spot. After a year with the Nats' Class D Sanford team, he was signed by Joe Cambria to the Charlotte Hornets. After a disastrous 0–2, three-game outing with the Senators in 1939, Wynn was sent back down for more seasoning. He came back to the parent club in 1941, and there he stayed. With little more than a fastball, Wynn struggled to earn wins. He was traded to the Indians in 1949. Once there, pitching coach Mel Harder helped him develop an impressive arsenal of pitches, teaching him how to throw a curve, slider, and knuckleball. With his new pitching repertoire, a disturbing scowl permanently etched on his face, and his commanding 200-pound mound presence, "Gus" Wynn became one of the most feared and intimidating pitchers in the American League. Any batter who tried to crowd the plate was subjected to a variety of "chin music" from the redoubtable Mr. Wynn. When he heard that Mickey Mantle and others said he would throw at his own mother, Wynn famously replied, "Only if she were diggin' in." After his playing days, Wynn became a pitching coach for the Indians and the Twins from

Asked if he would "brush back" his own mother in the batter's box, Early Wynn replied, "Only if she were diggin' in." A fierce competitor, Wynn struggled with the Senators from 1941 through 1948 but went on to a Hall of Fame career with the Indians and the White Sox, winning exactly 300 games and striking out over 2,300 batters (National Baseball Hall of Fame Library, Cooperstown, New York).

1964 through 1967 and briefly managed in the minor leagues. After his induction into the Hall of Fame in 1972, he became a broadcaster for the Blue Jays and the White Sox.

(SOURCE: SABR biography, baseball-reference.com)

Edward Fredrick "Eddie" Yost

Born October 13, 1926, in Brooklyn, NY. Died October 16, 2012, in Weston, MA.

Washington Senators 1944, 1946–1958, Detroit Tigers 1959–1960, Los Angeles Angels 1961–1962

Career: WAR-35.0, AB-7346, H-1863, HR-139, BA-.254, R-1215, RBI-682, SB-72, OBP-.394

One-time All-Star, six-time league leader in walks, three-time leader in games played and OBP

After impressing some scouts with his two-sport ability at New York University, 17-year-old college freshman Ed Yost got a week-long tryout with the Boston Red Sox in the spring of 1944. Manager Joe Cronin liked what he saw; general manager Eddie Collins did not. Joe Cambria got wind of the situation and signed him to a Senators contract for $500, a day before the Philadelphia Athletics offered him double. Yost made his Nats debut in August of 1944 and played only six games for the year. After service in the Navy in 1945, he returned to the Senators in 1946. With the help of manager Ossie Bluege, Yost learned and earned the third-base job for the Senators and stayed there for 13 years. With his tremendous knowledge of the strike zone, he earned the sobriquet "The Walking Man" because of his ability to draw a base on balls, 1,614 of them in fact. He ranks 11th in MLB history in walks. The durable Mr. Yost was also a three-time league leader in games played, a six-time leader in walks, and an All-Star once. After his playing days were over, he became invaluable as a third base coach for the expansion Senators from 1963 to 1966, with the Mets from 1967 to 1976, and with the Red Sox from 1977 to 1984.

(SOURCE: SABR biography, baseball-reference.com, https://www.nytimes.com/2012/10/18/sports/baseball/eddie-yost-baseballs-walking-man-dies-at-86.html)

Appendix II: Chronology of Cambria's Minor League Ownership

1924—Buys the Label Men's Oval and renames it Bugle Field after the name of his laundry business, The Bugle Apron & Coat Company. Upgrades the field and installs lights in 1930.

1928—Takes over the Baltimore Homesteads amateur league team and renames them The Bugle Coat and Apron Nine, usually shortened to the Buglers.

1929–30—Buys the Hagerstown Hubs, Class D, Blue Ridge League. Installs lights. Moves the team to Parkersburg, WV, and renames them the Parkers on 28 June 1931. Moves the team yet again to Youngstown, OH, on 12 July 1931, renames them the Tubers, and affiliates with the Mid–Atlantic League.

1932—Buys the Baltimore Black Sox in the Negro National League, disbands team in 1934 due to the Depression.

1933—Buys the Albany Indians, Class AA International League, and renames them the Senators. Sells team to the Giants in 1936 for huge profit.

1935—Buys the Harrisburg Senators, Class A New York-Penn League. Due to a flood, moves the team to York, PA, then to Trenton, NJ, in 1936. Renames then the Trenton Senators. In 1938, the NY-Penn League renamed the Eastern League. In 1939, moves team from Trenton to Springfield, MA, and renames them the Nationals.

1935—Takes over York, PA, team, Class D Keystone League.

1937–40—Buys the Salisbury Indians, Class D Eastern Shore League. Refurbishes old stadium and installs lights.

1938—Buys the Greenville Spinners, Class B South Atlantic League.

1938—Buys the St. Augustine Saints, Class D Florida State League. Builds new park and adds lights.

1938—He and Calvin Griffith buy the Shelby Nationals, Class D Tar Heel League.

1940—Ordered by Commissioner Landis to sell his minor league teams.

1944—Moves Springfield team to Williamsport, PA, and renames it the Greys. Hides many draft-exempt Cubans there.

1946—Becomes one of three investors in the Havana Cubans, Class C Florida International League.

1956—Becomes an investor and Director of Personnel for the Class AAA Louisville Colonels. Loses team due to debt.

1956—In mid-season, buys the Florida State League Orlando Sertomans, renames them the Colonels, and loses his shirt.

Appendix III:
The Latin Senators

Below is a listing of all the Cuban and other Latin players officially signed by the Washington Senators. The listing is compiled from *www.baseball-reference.com* from each year of the Senators' existence from 1902 through 1960. Unless otherwise noted, the majority of the players were from Cuba and were signed by Joe Cambria.

1913–1916, 1918	Pedro "Merito" Acosta	OF	
1913/1920	Jacinto "Jack" Calvo	OF	
1920–1921	Jose Acosta	P	
1920–1922	Ricardo Torres	C	
1926	Emilio Palmero	P	
1935, 1936, 1938, 1942	Roberto Estalella	OF, 3B	
1937/1944–1946	Fermin "Mike" Guerra	C	
1938/1940/1944	Rene Monteagudo	P, RF	
1938	Baldomero "Mel" Almada	CF	(Mexico)
1939–1945	Alejandro "Alex" Carrasquel	P	(Venezuela)
1940/1944–1946	Gilberto Torres	IF	
1941–1944/1949–1950	Roberto Ortiz	RF	
1942	Jose Luis "Chile" Gomez	IF	(Mexico)
1944	Preston Gomez	IF	
1944	Oliverio "Baby" Ortiz	P	
1944	Luiz Suarez	3B	
1944–1945	Santiago "Sandy" Ulrich	P	
1944	Roberto "Roy" Valdes	PH	
1945	Armando Roche	P	
1945	Jose Zardon	OF	
1946–1947	No Cubans on the team		
1948	Angel Fleitas	SS	
1949	Julio Gonzalez	P	
1950–1953	Sandalio "Sandy" Consuegra	P	
1950–1954	Conrado "Connie" Marrero	P	
1950	Rogelio Martinez	P	
1950–1953	Julio Moreno	P	
1950	Carlos Pasquel	P	
1951–1953	Francisco Campos	OF	

1951	Guillermo "Willie" Miranda	SS	
1952	Miguel "Mike" Fornieles	P	
1952	Raul Sanchez	P	
1953	Pompeyo "Yo-Yo" Davalillo	SS	(Venezuela)
1954–1960	Camilo Pascual	P	
1954–1956	Carlos Paula	OF	
1955/1957–1960	Julio Becquer	1B	
1955	Vibert "Webbo" Clark	P	(Panama)
1955	Juan Delis	3B	
1955–1960	Pedro Ramos	P	
1955	Vincente "Vince" Gomez	P	
1955–1956, 1959, 1961	Jose Valdivielso	IF	
1956–1957	Evelio Hernandez	P	
1958	Oswaldo "Ossie" Alvarez	SS, 2B	
1959, 1960	Zoilo Versalles	IF	
1960–1961	Rudolph "Rudy" Hernandez	P	(Dominican Republic)

Minnesota

1961	Dagoberto "Bert" Cueto	P	
1962	Ruben Gomez	P	(Puerto Rico)
1962	Orlando "Marty" Martinez	IF	
1962–1976	Pedro "Tony" Oliva	RF	

Chapter Notes

Chapter 1

1. Mark Choat, *Emigrant Nation: The Making of Italy Abroad* (Cambridge, MA: Harvard University Press, 2008).

2. All Cambria genealogy compiled by Ms. Virginia Cromwell Van Poole Atwell, a member of the Virginia Genealogical Society, with deepest thanks. All data culled from https://familysearch.org through name search.

Joe Cambria birth records: "Italia, Messina, Messina, Stato Civile (Comune), 1866–1910," database with images, FamilySearch (https://familysearch.org/ark:/61903/1:1:KCNQ-JJK: 4 December 2014), Santa Palella in entry for Carlo Giuseppe Cambria, 09 Jul 1889; Birth, citing Messina, Messina, Italy, certificate 861, Archivio di Stato di Messina (Messina State Archives, Messina); FHL microfilm 1,641,515.

1900 Census data: "United States Census, 1900," database with images, *FamilySearch* (https://familysearch.org/ark:/61903/1:1:M9Y9-4J1: accessed 2 May 2020), Joseph Cambria in household of John Cambria, Precinct 1 Boston city Ward 6, Suffolk, Massachusetts, United States; citing enumeration district (ED) 1219, sheet 10B, family 238, NARA microfilm publication T623 (Washington, D.C.: National Archives and Records Administration, 1972.); FHL microfilm 1,240,677.

"United States Census, 1910," database with images, *FamilySearch* (https://familysearch.org/ark:/61903/1:1:M2K1-RR4: accessed 2 May 2020), Joseph Cambria in household of Charles Cambria, Boston Ward 17, Suffolk, Massachusetts, United States; citing enumeration district (ED) ED 1514, sheet 11A, family 208, NARA microfilm publication T624 (Washington D.C.: National Archives and Records Administration, 1982), roll 620; FHL microfilm 1,374,633.

"Massachusetts, Naturalization Records, 1906–1917," database with images, *FamilySearch* (https://familysearch.org/ark:/61903/1:1:QLYR-6GK9: 16 March 2018), Joseph Carl Cambria, 1912.

"Massachusetts, Naturalization Records, 1906–1917," database with images, *FamilySearch* (https://familysearch.org/ark:/61903/1:1:QLY5-5TNP: 16 March 2018), Joseph Carl Cambria, 1915.

"Massachusetts State Vital Records, 1841–1920," database with images, *FamilySearch* (https://familysearch.org/ark:/61903/1:1:KBZR-8GC: 22 October 2019), Margaret F Fitzpatrick in entry for Joseph C Cambria and Lottie F Kane, 04 Jan 1916; citing Marriage, Boston, Suffolk, Massachusetts, United States, certificate number 45, page 4, State Archives, Boston.

"United States World War I Draft Registration Cards, 1917–1918", database with images, *Family Search* (https://familysearch.org/ark:/61903/1:1:-KZNM-RSF: 24 August 2019), Joseph Carl Cambria, 1917–1918.

"United States Census, 1920," database with images, *FamilySearch* (https://familysearch.org/ark:/61903/1:1:MFMC-7FK: accessed 2 May 2020), Guiseppe Cambria, Boston Ward 2, Suffolk, Massachusetts, United States; citing ED 39, sheet 36A, line 74, family, NARA microfilm publication T625 (Washington D.C.: National Archives and Records Administration, 1992), roll 728; FHL microfilm 1,820,728.

3. "Messina," Wikipedia, https://en.wikipedia.org/wiki/Messina, https://www.britannica.com/place/Messina, and Ohio.edu/Chastain/rz/risogim.htm.

4. Britannica.com/place/Italy/land-reform.

5. Genealogy Census records.

6. *Ibid.*

7. Brian McKenna, "Joe Cambria," SABR Biography Project, https://sabr.org/about/person/4e7d25a0; and Richard J. Conners, "Laundry Man Cambria Runs Club as a Hobby, But Knows How to 'Wring Out' Success," *Sporting News*, 14 December 1933, 5.

8. All information on Cambria's Canadian baseball years was compiled by Center for Canadian Baseball researcher Benno Rosinke. All data comes from uncredited articles from the *Berlin News Record* of 1911–1912 and from Rosinke's self-published book, *The Berlin Green Sox: A Day by Day Account of a Magic Season* (Kitchener, Ontario: Flatbush Press, 2013).

9. *Ibid.*

10. *Ibid.*

11. "Massachusetts State Vital Records, 1841–1920," database with images, *FamilySearch* (https://familysearch.org/ark:/61903/1:1:KBZR-8GC: 22 October 2019), Margaret F Fitzpatrick in entry for Joseph C Cambria and Lottie F Kane, 04 Jan 1916; citing Marriage, Boston, Suffolk, Massachusetts,

United States, certificate number 45, page 4, State Archives, Boston. Weather information from https://w2.weather.gov/climate/xmacis.php?wfo=box.

Chapter 2

1. All information on the Cambrias and the laundry business compiled by Ms. Amanda Hughes, chief archivist at the Enoch Pratt Free Library, Resource Center, Maryland Division, from Baltimore City directories from 1900 through 1950.

2. *Baltimore Sun*, 16 May 1922, 5.

3. *Baltimore Sun*, 18 October 1922, 24.

4. *Baltimore Sun,* Legal Notices, 15 February 1924, 16.

5. *Baltimore Sun,* Legal Notices, 13 December 1933, 23.

6. "Local Amateur Teams In League," *Baltimore Sun*, 21 May 1924, 12.

7. Povich quote.

8. Edward C. Lastner, "I Remember Bugle Field and The Label Men," *Baltimore Sun,* 29 March 1953, MG2; and Bill Johnson, "Bugle Field," in *Baltimore Baseball*, ed. Bill Nowlin (Phoenix: Society for American baseball Research, 2021), 65.

9. *Ibid.*

10. "Buglers Bow To Foresters," *Baltimore Sun*, 14 May 1928, 12.

11. "Bugle Ball Outfit Continues March," *Baltimore Sun*, 4 June 1928, 24.

12. "Lead Retained By Foresters," *Baltimore Sun*, 16 July 1928, 11.

13. "Buglers Will Oppose York Co. Leaguers Today," *Baltimore Sun*, 16 June 1929, 24.

14. "Late Attack Beats Bugles," *Baltimore Sun*, 9 September 1929, 12.

15. "Buglers Finish Series By Taking Twin Verdict from Bloomingdale Foe," *Baltimore Sun*, 29 October 1929, 20.

16. https://www.theguardian.com/sport/2016/sep/21/house-of-david-baseball-religious-sect.

17. "House of David Tossers Trim Buglers By 10–8," *Baltimore Sun*, 8 July 1929, 10.

18. "Bloomer Girls Put Up A Battle," *Baltimore Sun*, 15 July 1929, 13.

19. "Chief Bender Twirls Bugles to Victory Over North Philly," *Baltimore Sun*, 5 August 1929, 13.

20. https://sabr.org/gamesproj/game/september-7-1929-havanas-luis-e-tiant-knocked-out-baltimore-exhibition-game.

21. *Ibid.*

22. "Buglers No Match for Sox Tossers," *Baltimore Sun*, 21 September 1929, 14.

23. https://sabr.org/gamesproj/game/september-7-1929-havanas-luis-e-tiant-knocked-out-baltimore-exhibition-game.

Chapter 3

1. "It's All in the Viewpoint," Paul Menton, editor, *Baltimore Sun*, 15 May 1930, 32.

2. "Hubs May Go to Joe Cambria," *Baltimore Sun*, 23 December 1929, 10.

3. "Terse Tips on Sport," *The News* (Frederick, MD), 26 December 1929, 6.

4. https://www.baseball-reference.com/bullpen/Poke_Whalen.

5. "'Pop' Reitz Now With Hubs," *Morning Herald* (Hagerstown, MD), 3 February 1930, 10; https://loyolagreyhounds.com/honors/hall-of-fame/emil-reitz/105.

6. "Salary Limit and Player Limit Remain the Same," *Morning Herald* (Hagerstown, MD), 24 January 1930, 14.

7. "Hagerstown Club Signs Two More Men," *Baltimore Sun*, 11 January 1930, 10; "Hubs Land Pair of Men," *Morning Herald* (Hagerstown, MD), 10 January 1930, 12.

8. "66 men are Signed by Hagerstown Club," *Baltimore Sun*, 12 March 1930, 13.

9. "Meola Returns Signed Contracts to New Boss," *Morning Herald* (Hagerstown, MD), 19 March 1930, 8.

10. Frank Colley, "Joe Cambria Makes Choice After Watching a Workout," *Morning Herald* (Hagerstown, MD), 27 March 1930, 10.

11. All promotional information taken from *Morning Herald* (Hagerstown, MD), 21 May, 19 June, 27 June, 30 June, 1 August, 8 August 1930.

12. "Games for Every Night in Week Plan of Officials," *Morning Herald* (Hagerstown, MD), 8 August, 1930, 19.

13. Lloyd Johnson and Miles Wolff, eds., *The Encyclopedia of Minor League Baseball* (Durham, NC: Baseball America, 1993), 177.

14. "Hagen Picked to Face Yanks Here Tonight," *Daily Mail* (Hagerstown, MD), 25 August 1930, 10; https://sabr.org/bioproj/person/832d87fc.

15. Frank Colley, "The Colley-See-Um of Sport," *Daily Mail* (Hagerstown, MD), 2 August 1930, 10.

16. "Bugled Swamp Philly Rivals," *Baltimore Sun*, 23 April 1930, 12; "Bugles Annex Two from House of David" 21 June 1930, 14.

17. "Buglers Trim Havana Team," *Baltimore Sun*, 26 May 1930, 10.

18. "Bugles Lay Claim to Semi-Pro Title," *Baltimore Sun*, 1 September 1930, 22.

19. "One Killed in 3-Car Accident," *Daily Mail* (Hagerstown, MD), 2 August 1930, 2.

20. "Judge Inquiring," *Baltimore Evening Sun*, 18 June 1930, 26.

21. "Tony Citrano to Ask Landis for Forgiveness," *Courier-Post* (Camden, NJ) 28 August 1925, 21.

22. "Bugle Nine Signs Four Vet Players," *Baltimore Evening Sun*, 13 February 1930, 33.

23. "Three Hub Players Sold to the Washington Team," *Morning Herald* (Hagerstown, MD), 10 September 1930, 11.

24. "Deal Pending for Sale of Three Hub Players," *Morning Herald* (Hagerstown, MD), 20 December 1930, 10.

25. "Hass and Cochrane, 'A' Stars, in Court

Joust Here Feb.9," *Baltimore Evening Sun*, 29 January 1931, 28.

26. "Wheltle Cautions Baltimore Basketers on Amateur Status," *Baltimore Evening Sun*, 2 February 1931, 21.

27. "May Lift Ban on Basketers," *Baltimore Sun*, 25 February 1931, 16.

28. "Bugles are Primed for House of David Basketball Joust," *Baltimore Evening Sun*, 9 February 1931, 20.

29. "Blue Ridge, the Oldest Class D Loop, Disbands," *The Sporting News*, 19 February 1931, 2. The Blue Ridge League, founded in 1914, was one of the oldest leagues in organized baseball and had sent many great players to the majors, including Lefty Grove, Hack Wilson, Jimmy Dykes, and Clyde Barnhart.

30. Frank Colley, "The Colley-See-Um on Sports," *Daily Mail* (Hagerstown, MD), 16 February 1931, 8.

31. "Says Baltimore is 'Hick Town,'" *Baltimore Sun*, 15 January 1931, 28.

32. "Sunday Ball Only Hope of a Local Club," *Daily Mail* (Hagerstown, MD), 28 March 1931, 12.

33. Frank H. Young, "Farm System Hardship on Poor Clubs," *Washington Post*, 3 July 1932, M11.

34. "Washington to Help Hubs," *Morning Herald* (Hagerstown, MD), 7 March 1931, 18.

35. David Pietrusza, *Judge and Jury: The Life and Times of Judge Kenesaw Mountain Landis* (South Bend, IN: Diamond Communications, 1998), 368.

36. *Ibid.*, 361.

37. *Ibid.*, 348.

38. "Carlin's Park: 'Baltimore's Million Dollar Playground.'" https://www.mdhs.org/underbelly/2018/08/02/carlins-park-baltimores-million-dollar-playground/.

39. *Ibid.*

40. "Ice Moguls to Meet Tonight and Adopt Rules for Circuit," *Baltimore Evening Sun*, 9 December 1931, 30.

41. "Protest Turned Down; Walbrook Team Dines," *Baltimore Sun*, 27 March 1932, S2.

42. "Baseball, Hockey Leagues Favor Liberal Sunday Law," *Baltimore Sun*, 25 April 1932, 20.

43. "Sports, Shows Set for Next Sunday; Clark Claims Victory on Popular Vote," *Baltimore Sun*, 3 May 1932, 1.

44. "Asks to Withdraw," *Baltimore Sun*, 5 December 1931, 25.

45. "Landis, Here, Hears 4 Players' Appeals," *Washington Post* 29 January 1932, 13. Research could not find any resolution to this incident.

46. "Boswell Awarded Pay Claim against Cambria," and "Cambria Still Hopes for a Break."

47. *The Sporting News*, 14 November 1932, 2; *The Sporting News*, 8 December 1932, 7.

48. "Joe Sephus's Cullings," *Cumberland Sunday Times*, 6 March 1932, 6.

49. Brian Mckenna, "Joe Cambria," Society for American Baseball Research website, sabr.org/bioproj/person/4e7d25a0.

50. Bill Gibson, "Here Me Talkin' To Ya," *Baltimore Afro-American*, 4 June 1932, 14.

51. *Ibid.*

52. Bernard McKenna, *Baltimore Black Sox* (Jefferson, NC: McFarland, 2019).

53. *Ibid.*

54. *Ibid.*

55. "Quite a Few Surprises," *Baltimore Sun*, 21 May 1932, 8.

56. Bernard McKenna, *Baltimore Black Sox.*

57. E-W League Features," *New York Amsterdam News*, June 8, 1932, 12.

58. "East-West League Moguls Abandon Hope of Survival," *Baltimore Afro-American*, 2 July 1932, 15.

59. "East West League Introduces Drastic Changes," *Baltimore Afro-American*, 11 June 1932, 15.

60. *Ibid.*

61. "League Heads Make Changes; Sox in Front," *Baltimore Afro-American*, 25 June 1932, 14.

62. "House of David Nine Defeat Black Sox," *Baltimore Sun*, 7 July 1932, 11.

63. C.M. Gibbs, "Frenzy of Face Fringes," *Baltimore Sun*, 22 April 1932, 16.

64. "Black Sox will battle New York Black Yankees tonight," *Baltimore Sun*, September 11, 1932, S5.

65. Bill Gibson, "Hear Me Talkin' To Ya," *Baltimore Afro-American*, 25 June 1932, 14, 16.

66. *Ibid.*

67. "Adopt Price Scale for All-Star Ball Clashes with Sox," *Baltimore Evening Sun*, September 22, 1932, 29.

68. Bill Gibson, "Hear me Talkin' to Ya," *Baltimore Afro-American*, 22 October 1932, 16.

69. All scores and accounts taken from *Baltimore Evening Sun*, 26 September through 30 October 1932.

70. Bill Gibson, "Hear me Talkin' to Ya," *Baltimore Afro-American*, 22 October 1932, 16.

71. Bill Gibson, "Hear me Talkin' to Ya," *Baltimore Afro-American*, 9 July 1932, 15.

72. "In the Wake of the Game," *Washington Post* 17 August 1932, 9.

73. C.M. Gibbs, "Gibberish," *Baltimore Sun*, 7 February 1933, 10.

74. "Albany To Have Two Camps," *The Sporting News*, 9 March 1933, 8.

75. *Ibid.*

76. "Albany Contracts Come Hard," *The Sporting News*, 2 March 1933, 2.

77. "The History of Baltimore," http://www.baltimorecity.gov/sites/default/files/5_History.pdf.

78. Jesse Linthicum, 'Ring and Rasslin' Racket," *Baltimore Sun*, 12 March 1933, S5.

79. Paul Merton, "Johnny Simply Lacked His Stuff," *Baltimore Evening Sun*, 13 April 1933, 28.

80. "Working Out with the Minors," *The Sporting News,* 13 April 1933, 2.

81. Lloyd Johnson and Miles Wolff, *The Encyclopedia of Minor League Baseball*, (Durham, NC: Baseball America, 1993), 182.

82. "New Baseball Association formed in Mid-West," *Baltimore Afro-American*, 21 January 1933, 16.

83. "Black Sox Not To Disband," *Baltimore Afro-American*, 18 February 1933, 17.

84. Rollo Wilson, "Sports Shots," *Pittsburgh Courier*, 11 March 1933, 14.

85. "Black Sox Have New Berth in League," *Baltimore Afro-American*, 13 May 1933, 16.

86. "Black Sox to be Strong Club," *Pittsburgh Courier*, 3 June 1933, 14.

87. "Seeks to Bar Nine's Use of 'Black Sox' Name," *Baltimore Sun*, 24 May 1933, 15.

88. Bill Gibson, "Hear me Talkin' to Ya," *Baltimore Afro-American*, 17 June 1933, 17.

89. "Cum Posey's Pointed Paragraphs," *Pittsburgh Courier*, 12 August 1933, 15.

90. "Wagner and Jimmy Foxx to Lead Major Leaguers in Games Here Today," *Baltimore Sun*, 8 October 1933, 27.

91. *Ibid.*

92. All information on the 1933 All-Star series taken from *Baltimore Sun* and *Evening Sun*, 17 September through 18 October 1933.

93. Richard Conners, "Laundryman Cambria Runs Club as Hobby, But He Knows How to 'Wring Out' Success," *The Sporting News*, 14 December 1933, 5.

94. *Ibid.*

95. "Sale of Albany Falls Through," *The Sporting News*, 9 November 1933, 9.

96. "Baltimore Joins Eastern Ball Loop; Grays Fail to Get Berth," *Chicago Defender*, 3 March 1934, 11.

97. "Baltimore Owner Must Talk to 'Chief'," *Pittsburgh Courier*, 24 March 1934, 14.

98. "N.Y., Baltimore Out of N.N. Loop; Schedule Fixed," *Pittsburgh Courier*, 21 April 1934, 14.

99. "Black Sox Bow to Harrisburg," *Baltimore Afro-American*, 5 May 1934, 18.

100. "Cambria, Who Started Organized Baseball Career Here, Making a Name For Self In International," *Hagerstown Daily Mail*, 15 February 1934, 11.

101. "Griffith Might Sign Cambria," *Brooklyn Daily Eagle*, 2 March 1934, 21.

102. *Ibid.*, note 99.

103. "Part of Albany Squad Trains in Martinsville," *Washington Post*, 24 February 1934, 16.

104. David Pietrusza's Capital Region Baseball Timeline Part III: 1931–1950 http://www.davidpietrusza.com/capital-reg-baseball-3.html.

105. Bill Dooly, "Scribbled by Scribes," *The Sporting News*, 12 April 1934, 4.

106. All biographical information for Mark Filley taken from: John B. Keller, "Albany Recruit Bought by Nats," *Washington Evening Star*, 13 April 1934, 43; Rory Costello, SABR bio project https://sabr.org/bioproj/person/mark-filley.

107. "Whiskers of New Nat Pitchers Stir Furor in Nation's Capital," *The Sporting News*, 23 August 1934, 1.

108. *Ibid.*

109. Frank Young, "Bearded Hurler to Face Sox Today," *Washington Post*, 19 August 1934, m13.

110. *Ibid.*

111. "Allen Benson, 'The Human Mulberry Bush,'" Diamonds in the Dusk, accessed February 1, 2022, http://www.diamondsinthedusk.com/uploads/articles/354-BENSON_Allen.pdf.

112. Francis Stan, "Diggs May Share M'Coll's Burden," *Washington Evening Star*, 7 September 1934, 39.

113. https://www.baseball-reference.com/players/d/diggsre01.shtml.

114. John Kieran, "Sports of the Times: Minor Matters," *New York Times*, 23 August 1934, 23.

115. "Scribbled by Scribes," *The Sporting News*, 19 July 1934, 4.

116. "Cambria May Not Accept Major Offers," *Brooklyn Daily Eagle*, 23 September 1934, 10.

117. "Antics of Altrock to Add Gayety to All-Star Fray," *Washington Evening Star*, 6 October 1934, 8.

118. "Bankroll of Deans take a $14,000 Jump Since World Series," *Washington Evening Star*, 15 October 1934, 21.

119. John B. Keller, "Rebuilding Plan Snubs Veterans," *Washington Evening Star*, 16 August 1934, 40.

120. John B. Keller, "Powell is Final of Seven Bought," *Washington Evening Star*, 8 September 1934, 12.

121. Denman Thompson, "Best Team Won World Series; Unbiased View of Washington; Finest Box Work in Years," *The Sporting News*, 12 October 1933, 1.

122. "Ruth Definitely Out as Senators' Pilot; Harris Confers with Griffith About Post," *New York Times*, 28 October 1934, S1.

123. Harry Grayson, "Sports Tips," *Fredrick News*, 6 March 1935, 7.

124. "Albany To Have Young Team, Assert Cambria," *Baltimore Sun*, 13 January 1935, S8.

125. Bill Lamb, "Al Mamaux," SABR Biography Project https://sabr.org/bioproj/person/al-mamaux/.

126. "Evers May Get Post With Albany Senators," *Baltimore Sun*, 1 February 1935, 13.

127. Thomas E. Schott, SABR Biography Project, https://www.baseball-reference.com/players/w/wilsoha01.shtml.

128. *Ibid.*

129. All data on Edwin Pitts taken from http://baseballhistorian.blogspot.com/2012/03/rise-and-fall-of-legendary-alabama.html and from Josh Davin and Hank Utley, SABR Biography Project: https://sabr.org/bioproj/person/alabama-pitts/.

130. Andy Clark, "Roundup," *Tampa Bay Times*, 18 December 1935, 14.

131. *Ibid.*; SABR biography.

Chapter 4

1. "Albany Ends Chiefs Seven-Game Streak," *Rochester Democrat and Chronicle*, 4 June 1935, 18.

2. "Griffith to Add Two Farms to Chain," *Washington Post*, 8 March 1935, 21.

3. "Young Pitcher Reappears, Ends Hunt," *Washington Post*, 13 July 1935, 19; "Missing H.S. Ball Star Returns with Contract," *Pottsville Republican*, 12 July 1935, 1.

4. Roberto Gonzalez Echevarria, *The Pride of Havana: A History of Cuban Baseball* (New York: Oxford University Press, 1999), 264.

5. Joanne Hulbert, SABR bioproject https://sabr.org/bioproj/person/bobby-estalella-2/.

6. https://www.baseball-reference.com/teams/WSH/1935.shtml.

7. https://www.baseball-reference.com/players/e/estalbo01.shtml.

8. Hulbert biography.

9. *Ibid.*

10. All biographical information on the Cuban signees from www.baseball-reference.com.

11. "Dickey to Play Former Stars," *Baltimore Sun*, 4 August 1935, S2.

12. Francis Stan, "Joe Cambria, Griffith's Ally, is Master Showman of Baseball," *Washington Evening Star*, 21 September 1935, 12.

13. Jesse A. Linthicum, "Sunlight on Sports," *Baltimore Sun*, 26 February 1936, 17.

14. https://www.baseball-reference.com/register/player.fcgi?id=jolley001sme.

15. Jack McDonald, "New Look at Legend Smead Jolley," *The Sporting News*, 25 January 1964, 7.

16. Bill Nowlin, SABR Bioproject, https://sabr.org/bioproj/person/smead-jolley/.

17. *Ibid.*

18. "He'll Never Forget Shanty Hogan," *Nashville Banner*, 30 March 1960, 27.

19. *Ibid.*

20. https://www.baseball-reference.com/register/player.fcgi?id=hogan-001jam.

21. "Linton is to Catch for St. Paul Team," *Courier-Journal*, 4 February 1936, 12.

22. *The Sporting News*, 20 February 1936, 4.

23. "Seven Cubans to Bolster Albany in Flag Scramble," *Orlando Sentinel*, 12 March 1936, 9.

24. William H. Shank, *Great Floods of Pennsylvania: A Two Century History* (York, PA: American Canal and Transportation Center Publishing, 1993).

25. "Above 30-Foot Stage, 3 M," *Harrisburg Evening News*, 19 March 1936, 1.

26. All information on the York/Trenton situation taken from the following articles, all published by *Harrisburg Evening News*: "Senators NY-P Franchise May Be Given York," 26 March 1936; "Transfer of Baseball Club Not Permanent," 27 March 1936; "The Talk," 28 March 1936; "Move York Club to Trenton for NY-P Last Half," 2 July 1936.

27. Ed Johnson, *The Story of the 1936–1938 Trenton Senators* published at the D.C. Baseball History blog site; https://dcbaseballhistory.com/2018/03/the-story-of-the-1936-38-trenton-senators/.

28. George Case III, personal phone interview with author, November 2019.

29. *Ibid.*; https://www.baseball-reference.com/players/c/casege01.shtml.

30. https://www.hockeydb.com/ihdb/stats/leagues/72.html.

31. Robert Garricon, "Hockey Palace Get Another Setback," *Washington Post*, 23 October 1936, X23.

32. "Cambria Charges Efforts to Freeze Him Out of International," *The Sporting News*, 3 September 1936, 1.

33. "Shorter Series for International Advocated by Cambria," *The Sporting News*, 22 October 1936, 3.

34. "Ruth is Offered Post as Albany Pilot," *Washington Post*, 25 November 1936, X19.

35. "Albany Berth Fails to Interest Babe Ruth," *Baltimore Sun*, 25 November 1936, 18.

36. "Ruth Considering Albany's Offer," *New York Times*, 29 November 1936, S7.

37. "International Loop Eager For Ruth," *Washington Post*, 1 December 1936, X18.

38. "Report Ruth to Manage Albany," *Harrisburg Evening News*, 3 December 1936, 21.

39. Jack Cuddy, "Old Fox: Does He Seek Ruth to Manage Nationals after Albany Job?" *Washington Post*, 2 December 1936, X18.

40. "Babe Ruth Declines Offer to Head Club in Minor Circuit," *Pensacola News Journal*, 9 December 1936, 5.

41. "Giant Seeking Albany," *New York Times*, 16 December 1936, 38.

42. "Stoneham is Negotiating for Purchase of Albany," *Trenton Evening News*, 18 December 1936, 35; "Cambria to Delay Albany Club Sale," *Washington Post*, 22 December 1936, X23; C. M. Gibbs, "Gibberish," *Baltimore Sun*, 30 December 1936, 13.

43. "Albany Loses No Time Seeking New Franchise," *The Sporting News*, 7 January 1937, 1.

44. "Shaughnessy Wins His Spurs Early," *The Sporting News*, 7 January 1937, 4.

45. Charles Young, "Albany Side of Controversy in Int," *The Sporting News*, 14 January 1937, 4.

46. "Albany Pays Through the Nose," *The Sporting News*, 14 January 1937, 4.

47. History of the Toronto Maple Leafs; https://en.wikipedia.org/wiki/Toronto_Maple_Leafs_(International_League).

48. *Encyclopedia of Minor League Baseball*, 190–193.

49. "Major and Minor Leaguers Here to Revive Shore Loop," *Salisbury Times*, 14 January 1937, 1; "Eastern Shore Baseball Loop Assured," *Washington Post*, 15 January 1937, 20.

50. "Six Clubs Apply for Ball Berths," *Salisbury Times*, 1 February 1937, 1.

51. The story of the Salisbury Indians' amazing comeback of 1937 is documented in many publications and was the top story in newspapers around the country. The story contained herein is taken from the following sources: Bill James, *Bill James Historical Baseball Abstract* (New York: Simon & Schuster, 2001, 162–165; Lloyd Johnson and Miles Wolff, *The Encyclopedia of Minor League Baseball* (Durham, NC: Baseball America, 1993), 191.

52. "Eligibility Dispute Rises in Shore Loop," *Cumberland Evening Times*, 17 June 1937, 16.

53. "Salisbury to Plead Before Judge Landis," *Baltimore Sun*, 30 July 1937, 17.

54. Jesse A. Linthicum, "Sunlight on Sports," *Baltimore Sun*, 17 June 1937, 16; 19 June 1937, 11.

55. *Ibid.*; Bill James Abstract, 163.

56. *Ibid.*

57. "Club Will Appeal to Directors," *Salisbury Times*, 21 June 1937, 1.

58. "Judge Landis Denies Intervention in Loss of Salisbury's Games," *Salisbury Times*, 3 August 1937, 8; Mason Brunson, "Cambria Renews Fight to Retain Lost Games," *Salisbury Times*, 4 August 1937, 9.

59. *Ibid.*; Bill James Abstract, 163.

60. "Salisbury Sells Stars to Griffmen," *Washington Post*, 31 August 1937, 17.

61. "Joe Kohlman is Selected 'Most Valuable Player'," *Salisbury Times*, 7 September 1937, 7.

62. "Kohlman Pitches Second No-Hitter," *Washington Evening Star*, 10 September 1937, B6.

63. Edgar G. Brands, "Barrow, McKechnie, Allen, LaMotte, Flowers and Keller Win '37 Accolade," *The Sporting News*, 30 December 1937, 1–2.

64. "Indians Take Tight Contest Form the A's," *Salisbury Times*, 21 September 1937, 7.

65. "Indians Defeat House of David 7–4," *Salisbury Times*, 21 September 1937, 7; "Indians Drop Game to House of David," *Salisbury Times*, 22 September 1937, 7.

66. Jesse A. Linthicum, "Sunlight on Sports," *Baltimore Sun*, 17 September 1937, 18.

67. *Ibid.*

68. "Joe Cambria Opens Business in City," *Salisbury Times*, 4 November 1937, 12.

69. "Cambria Promises Salisbury Rookies," *Hagerstown Daily Mail*, 31 December 1937, 4.

70. Baltimore City directories and business holdings archives in various volumes. Information courtesy of Amanda Hughes, Enoch Pratt Free Library, State Library Resource Center, Maryland Department.

71. "Scoopin' 'Em Up with Carter (Scoop) Latimer: Joe Cambria, Baseball Santa," *Greenville News*, 20 December 1937, 6.

72. https://en.wikipedia.org/wiki/Greenville_Spinners.

73. Scoop Latimer, "Grandstand, Bleachers at Meadowbrook Seat 5,000; Club to Train in Florida," *Greenville News* 7 January 1938, 17.

74. Scoop Latimer, "April 4–18 Open to Lads Seeking Posts," *Greenville News,* 13 January 1938, 11.

75. Harvey Lopez, "New Park, With Lights, Under Way at St. Augustine," *The Sporting News,* 6 January 1938, 9.

76. Mark Hornbaker, "Washington DC Baseball History-Spring Training," https://dcbaseballhistory.com/2019/02/washington-d-c-baseball-history-spring-training/.

77. "Clark Griffith Wants Franchise of Orlando Team," *Washington Post,* 8 March 1938, X17.

78. "Trenton Gets Krakauskas," *Washington Post,* 10 May 1938, X14.

79. Rich Westcott, *Mickey Vernon: The Gentleman First Baseman* (Philadelphia: Camino Books, 2005), 47–49.

80. *Ibid.*, 49.

81. "Guerra Deserts the Tribe, Other Players Are Sought," *Salisbury Times*, 2 June 1938, 1.

82. "Flowers Not Signed by Indians," *Salisbury Times,* 8 March 1938, 1.

83. "Club to Place near the Top Say Officials," *Salisbury Times,* 28 March 1938, 7.

84. "Indians Take Shore League Pennant Again," *Salisbury Times,* 17 September 1938, 1; Linthicum, Jess A., "Pennant Won by Salisbury," *Baltimore Sun,* 17 September 1938, 13.

85. Chris J. Holaday, *Professional Baseball in North Carolina: An Illustrated City-by-City History, 1901–1996* (Jefferson, NC, McFarland), 158–160.

86. "City of Homes Prepares House-Warming for O.B.," *The Sporting News* 22 December 1938, 1; *Encyclopedia of Minor League Baseball*, 196.

87. Francis Stan, "46 to be Tested in Big Effort to Rebuild," *Washington Evening Star,* 1 January 1939, 11.

88. *Ibid.*

89. Rob Nelson, *Baseball's Greatest Sacrifice*, http://www.baseballsgreatestsacrifice.com/biographies/brewer_lefty.html.

90. Francis Stan, "Win, Lose, or Draw," *Washington Evening Star,* 1 January 1939, 11.

91. *Baseball's Greatest Sacrifice.*

92. *Ibid.*

93. Shirley Povich, "Nats' Man of Moods Moves to White Sox," *The Sporting News*, January 31, 1946, 2.

94. Lou Hernandez, Alex Carrasquel SABR Biography Project, https://sabr.org/bioproj/person/alex-carrasquel/#sdendnote2sym.

95. Alex Carrasquel https://www.baseball-reference.com/register/player.fcgi?id=carras002ale.

96. Roberto Gonzalez Echevarria, *The Pride of Havana: A History of Cuban Baseball* (New York: Oxford University Press, 1999), 282–283.

97. "Sports of Sorts," *Hagerstown Daily Mail,* 24 February 1939, 8.

98. Shirley Povich, "Nationals' New Hurler Arrives Today," *Washington Post,* 23 February 1939, 21.

99. Shirley Povich, "Buddy Myer, Ferrell May Be Lone Vets," *Washington Post,* 18 December 1938, X5.

100. "Joe's Cubans At Washington," *Baltimore Evening Sun,* 8 April 1939, 8.

101. Francis Stan, "Long Grind Leaves Griffs Still Short," *The Sporting News,* 12 April 1939, 3.

102. "Three No-Hit Games in Four Starts, Hurler's Record," *Baltimore Evening Sun,* 31 May 1939, 28.

103. "Hollidayoke Strikes Out 23," *Baltimore Evening Sun,* 24 April 1939, 12.

104. "Sandlotter Signed By Washington Team," *Salisbury Daily Times,* 12 June 1939, 8; 13 June 1939, 10.

105. *Salisbury Times* box score, 7 July 1939, 9.

106. *Salisbury Times* box score, 13 July 1939, 9.

107. "Landis Lifts Crackdown on Joe Cambria," *Salisbury Daily Times,* 26 August 1939, 1.

108. *Salisbury Times* box score, 29 June 1940, 7; 18 July 1940, 13.

109. George H. Steuart, "The Shame of It! Marines Top Tars!" *Baltimore Evening Sun,* 27 December 1940, 28.

110. William Hollidayoke: https://www.baseball-reference.com/register/player.fcgi?id=hollid001wil.

111. "Pofahl's Purchase Brings Trade Talk with Travis to Go," *The Sporting News,* 24 August 1939, 1; "Sports Sparks," *Wilkes-Barre Record,* 26 August 1939, 14.

112. Pofahl, 2.

113. "Landis Lifts Crackdown on Joe Cambria," *Salisbury Daily Times,* 26 August 1939, 1.

114. *Ibid.*

115. Bob Hayes, "Top O' the Morn," *Orlando Morning Sentinel,* 21 September 1939, 6.

116. "Seven Indian Players Made Free Agents," *Salisbury Times,* 27 November 1939, 7.

117. "Landis Edict Costs Joe Cambria $1,000" *The Sporting News,* 12 December 1939, p.11.

Chapter 5

1. "Cuban Government Becomes Scout for Reds Baseball Team," *Wilmington News-Journal,* 14 June 1939, 1; "Cuban Ball Players to Try Out with Reds," *Tampa Tribune,* 23 October 1939, 9.

2. Herman Canal, "Young Cuban Officer Spreads Game on Wide Scale in Island," *The Sporting News,* 29 February 1940, 3.

3. *Ibid.*

4. George Kirksey, "Reds Offer Cuban Players Chance to Make Big Show but Griffs Grab Two Best," *Miami News,* 16 March 1940, 11.

5. Jess Losada, *Carteles* Magazine, Year 21, Number 32, 11 August 1940, La Habana, Cuba, 54–55.

6. Kirksey.

7. "Ire of Reds, Cubans Stirred by Cambria's Latest 'Steal,'" *Trenton Evening Times,* 15 March 1940, 26.

8. Kenesaw Mountain Landis file, National Baseball Hall of Fame Library; Commissioner's Bulletin, "In re: Farm Systems and Working Agreements," 15 January 1940, and "Landis Edict Costs Joe Cambria $1,000," *The Sporting News,* 14 December 1939, 11.

9. Leo Durocher, *Nice Guys Finish Last* (New York: Simon & Schuster, 1975), 70–71, 76.

10. K. M. Landis, 1940 Commissioner's Bulletin, "In re; Farm Systems and Working Agreements," 15 January 1940.

11. George Kirksey, "Sees System as Ruination of Baseball," *Pittsburgh Press,* 6 December 1929, 60.

12. "Landis Lays Down Law for Farms, Working Agreements; Detroit Loses Title to 91 players, must pay 15 Others," *The Sporting News,* 18 January 1940, 1.

13. Tom Noonan, "MacPhail Blasts Landis Over 'Chain Store' Ruling," *Pittsburgh Press,* 2 February 1940, 39.

14. The majority of the player information comes from a near-daily series of articles from the *Washington Post,* "Nats' Rookie Parade at Orlando Camp," from 19 February through 15 March 1940. Statistics taken from individual players' Baseball-Reference.com page.

15. Mellendeck information compiled from personal interview with his nephew, William G. Mellendick, and Joe Mellendick reference page, https://www.baseball-reference.com/register/player.fcgi?id=mellen001jos.

16. "School for Young Baseball Players Started in Orlando by Joe Stripp," *Orlando Sentinel,* 13 March 1936, 10.

17. *Ibid.*

18. Shirley Povich, "This Morning with Shirley Povich," *Washington Post,* 11 March 1936, 19.

19. "Washington Scout Finds a 'Prospect,'" *Palm Beach Post,* 24 January 1940, 10.

20. "Five Stripp Players Sold to Pro Clubs," *Orlando Sentinel,* 12 February 1941, 8.

21. "Caught on the Fly," *The Sporting News,* 11 April 1940, 10.

22. Denman Thompson, "Gee Gosh-Awful? Capital Mystified," *The Sporting News,* 8 August 1940, 5.

23. "Ball Team Strikes for Back Pay as Season's End Nears," *Hagerstown Daily Mail,* 6 September 1940, 10; "Another Baseball Team on Warpath," *Fort Lauderdale News,* 7 September 1940, 8.

24. *Encyclopedia of Minor League Baseball,* 201.

25. "Joe Cambria Scouts Again," *Baltimore Sun,* 28 October 1940, 13; https://www.baseball-reference.com/register/player.fcgi?id=feinbe001edw.

26. Warren Bornscheue, "Reuban Levin Takes Control of Salisbury from Joe Cambria," *The Sporting News,* 14 November 1940, 2; Chick Feldman, "Eastern League Sets Up $3,000 Reserve, Keeps 140-Game Chart," *The Sporting News* 21 November 1940, 10.

27. Shirley Povich, "This Morning with Shirley Povich," *Washington Post,* 13 October 1940, 17.

28. Shirley Povich, "This Morning with Shirley Povich," *Washington Post,* 22 February 1941, S1.

29. *Ibid.*

30. Whitney Martin, "Nats are 'Claiming' Champs of American," *Tampa Tribune,* 19 March 1941, 13.

31. *Ibid.*

32. "Cambria's Report to Griffith Reads Like a Blitzkrieg," *Washington Post,* 18 June 1941, 21.

33. "Bar Files Charges Against W.R. Jones," *Baltimore Sun,* 27 March 1941, 13.

34. "Willis R. Jones Denies Charges," *Baltimore Sun,* 4 April 1941, 12.

35. "Excessive Fees Charged to Jones," *Baltimore Sun,* 22 April 1941, 14; "Jones Found Innocent of Bar's Charges," *Baltimore Sun,* 29 April 1941, 26.

36. https://en.wikipedia.org/wiki/History_of_professional_baseball_in_Milwaukee.

37. "Nats May Buy Milwaukee Club 'If Price is Right,'" *Washington Post,* 21 June 1941, 16.

38. Paul Dickson, *Bill Veeck: Baseball's Greatest Maverick* (New York City: Walker, 2012).

39. Fredrick J. Frommer, *The Washington Nationals 1859 to Today* Lanham, MD: Rowman & Littlefield, 2006), 99.

40. Red Canup, *Anderson Independent,* as quoted in "Scoopin' 'Em Up with Carted (Scoop) Latimer," *Greenville News,* 14 January 1942, 8.

41. Ted Leavengood, *Clark Griffith: The Old Fox of Washington Baseball* (Jefferson, NC: McFarland, 2001), 114.

42. "Baseball Heads Give $25,000 for Army Sport," *Washington Post,* 18 December 1941, 26.

43. Richard Moraski, "The Washington Senators in Wartime," in *Who's on First: Replacement Players in World War II,* ed. Marc Z. Aaron and Bill Nowlin (Phoenix: Society for American Baseball Research, 2015), 338.

44. *Ibid.*

45. *Ibid.,* 339.

46. "Nats Relinquish Greenville Farm-at Cost of $28,000," *Washington Post,* 27 February 1942, 25.

47. https://www.baseballinwartime.com/baseball_in_wwii/baseball_in_wwii.htm.

48. Lloyd Johnson and Miles Wolff, editors, *The Encyclopedia of Minor League Baseball* Durham, NC: Baseball America, 1993).

49. Fredrick Williams, "Baseball Welcome Cuban 'Entertainers,'" *Miami Daily News,* 31 May 1942, 36.

50. Fredrick Williams, "Scout Cambria Top Good Will Agent to Cuba," *Greenville News,* 3 June 1942, 12.

51. Richard Goldstein, *Spartan Seasons: How Baseball Survived the Second World War* (New York: Macmillan, 1980), 162–165.

52. Gerry Moore, "Eddie Lyons, Just Out of High, May Be Season's Find," *Boston Globe,* 28 March 1942, 4; Baseball-Reference.com; https://en.wikipedia.org/wiki/Ed_Lyons.

53. *Spartan Seasons,* 167–169.

54. "Ossie Bluege, 41, To Try Comeback," *Greenville News,* 19 January 1942, 7.

55. Fredrick Frommer, "The Misfits of Summer," *Washingtonian Magazine,* May edition, published 30 April 2017.

56. Arthur Daley, "Sports of the Times," *New York Times,* 29 December 1944, 19.

57. Jeff Obermyer, "The Business of Baseball During World War II," in *Who's on First: Replacement Players in World War II,* ed. Marc Z. Aaron and Bill Nowlin (Phoenix: Society for American Baseball Research, 2015), 7.

58. https://sabr.org/bioproj/person/ed-butka.

59. https://sabr.org/bioproj/person/jug-the senga.

60. Personal interview with son, George Case III, via Facebook, 2/14/2021.

61. Shirley Povich, "Tales of Scout Cambria in Mexico," *Washington Post,* 30 March 1942, 21.

62. https://www.baseball-reference.com/players/k/kvasnal01.shtml.

63. Fredrick Frommer, "The Misfits of Summer," *Washingtonian Magazine,* May edition, published 30 April 2017.

64. "Immunity to Draft for Latin Americans," *New York Times,* 16 April 1944, S3.

65. "15 More Cubans for Senators," *New York Times,* 18 March 1944, 16.

66. Guy Butler, "Topics of the Tropics," *Miami News,* 30 April 1942, 10.

67. Sam Lacy, "Griff Says Organize Colored," *Baltimore Afro-American,* 25 July 1942, 22; Ralph Matthews, "Clark Griffith Won't Budge on Use of Colored Players," 18 December 1943, 23.

68. "Sport Hears Emergency Measures," *Washington Post,* 6 January 1943, 10.

69. https://sabr.org/bioproj/person/ossie-bluege/#sdendnote12sym.

70. *Ibid.*

71. Jesse Linthicum, "Sunlight on Sports," *Baltimore Sun,* 3 February 1943, 15.

72. All information on the 1943 rookies compiled from "Youth Latest of Cambria's Mound Finds," *Washington Post,* 17 March 1943, 16, and from each player's individual page at Retrosheet.org.

73. Hugh Fullerton, Jr., "Looking Them Over," *Tampa Times,* 27 March 1943, 9.

74. Information of Carrasquel and Ortiz taken from their individual baseball-reference.com pages.

75. "Veteran Hurler Finds Youth in Nats Bullpen," *Fort Lauderdale News,* 10 July 1942, 8.

76. Sandy Stiles, "Sport Styles," *Tampa Bay Times,* 23 March 1943, 9.

77. Dillon Graham, "Cuban Baseball Players +++Successful in Major League Ball," *Fort Lauderdale News,* 7 June 1943, 8.

78. Merrell W. Whittlesey, "War Bond Game Glitters Before $2,000,000 Gate," *The Sporting News,* 3 June 1942, 5.

79. Jesse A. Linthicum, "Sunlight on Sports," *Baltimore Sun,* 3 September 1943, 14.

80. "Major League Notes," *The Sporting News,* 14 October 1943, 16.

81. Compiled from: "Elites, All-Stars Divide," *Baltimore Afro-American,* 9 October 1943, 19; "Elites Lose to All-Stars," *Baltimore Afro-American,* 16 October 1943, 18; "Major Leaguers Play at Bugle Field Today," *Baltimore Sun,* 10 October 1943, 28.

82. Richard Moraski, "The Washington Senators in Wartime," in *Who's on First: Replacement Players in World War II,* ed. Marc Z. Aaron and Bill Nowlin (Phoenix: Society for American Baseball Research, 2015), 341.

83. Shirley Povich, "This Morning," *Washington Post,* 27 December 1943, 8.

84. Timeline taken from https://en.wikipedia.org/wiki/Timeline_of_World_War_II_(1944), and

wartime service decorations taken from https://www.baseballinwartime.com.

85. "One Minute Sports Page," *Tallahassee Democrat,* 10 December 1943, 7; "Cubans May Keep Minor League Baseball Alive," *Palm Beach Post,* 10 January 1944, 8.

86. Title taken from James Quigel, Jr., "Little Havana on the Susquehanna: Cuban Seasons and Wartime Baseball in Williamsport," *Pennsylvania Heritage Magazine,* summer 2004 issue.

87. James Quigel, Jr., "Constructing the Cuban Pipeline: Papa Joe Cambria Brings the Cubans to Williamsport, Pennsylvania, 1944 to 1945," *Cooperstown Symposium on Baseball and American Culture, 2003–2004,* William M. Simons, editor.

88. Morris A Bealle, *The Washington Senators: An 87-Year History of the World's Oldest Baseball Club and Most Incurable Fandom* (Washington D.C.; Columbia Publishing, 1947, 163.

89. "Offers City Inside Track to F.L. Club," *Williamsport Sun-Gazette,* 5 January 1944, 2.

90. Shirley Povich, "Four Players Remain on Unsigned List," *Washington Post,* 5 March 1944, M7.

91. 90 Congressional Record, 78 Congress, 2nd Session, 1944, 31–34; Quigel, "Constructing the Cuban Pipeline," footnote 12, 119.

92. "Immunity to Draft for Latin Americans," *New York Times,* 16 April 1944, S3.

93. "Nats' Hopes Receive Blow," *Baltimore Sun,* 11 April 1944, 14.

94. Quigel, "Cuban Pipeline" footnote 27, 120.

95. *Ibid.,* 112.

96. *Ibid.*

97. *Ibid.,* 111.

98. Robert Considine, "Ivory from Cuba," *Collier's,* 3 August 1940, 19.

99. Quigel, "Cuban Pipeline" 115–116.

100. *Ibid.,* 116.

101. "Club Owners Look to South," *Tallahassee Democrat,* 3 April 1944, 5.

102. "Sports Shorts," *Tallahassee Democrat,* 22 March 1944, 5.

103. Jess Losada, 'Julio Moreno is a "Tropical Bob Feller," *Carteles Magazine,* Ano 25, numero 14, 2 April 1944, 34–35.

104. Dan Daniels, "Ban on Recruiting by Majors Sought by Cuban Sports Chief," *The Sporting News,* 7 December 1944, 4.

105. Sam Lacy, "Looking 'Em Over," *Baltimore Afro-American,* 4 March 1944, 14.

106. Sam Lacy, "Looking 'Em Over," *Baltimore Afro-American,* 8 April 1944, 14.

107. Fred Young, "Young's Yarns: Griff's Scout Finds Travel Real Problem," *Pantagraph* (Bloomington, IL), 4 August 1944, 14.

108. Edgar G. Brands, "'Men of Year' Named in Majors and Minors," 28 December 1944, 1.

109. Jake Wade, "Papa Joe Cambria: Talent Scout," *Esquire,* October 1944, 68, 174–176.

110. *Ibid.,* 176.

111. Frank O'Neill, "Cambria Covered-Wagon Man of Game," *The Sporting News,* 18 January 1945, 3.

112. Ted Meier, "Future Vague for Baseball, Pro Football," *Washington Post,* 25 December 1944, 6.

113. *Ibid.,* 7.

114. *Ibid.*

115. https://sabr.org/bioproj/person/eddie-yost/.

116. Bus Ham, "Washington Is Depending On 12 Aliens," *Washington Post,* 19 January 1945, 10.

117. *Ibid.*

118. "Cambria Receives Gifts From Players and Scribes," *The Sporting News,* 18 January 1945, 3.

119. https://en.wikipedia.org/wiki/Jorge_Pasquel, https://remezcla.com/features/sports/the-secret-history-of-how-mexico-pushed-baseball-toward-racial-integration; John Virtue, *South of the Color Barrier: How Jorge Pasquel and the Mexican League Pushed Baseball Toward Racial Integration* (Jefferson, NC: McFarland, 2008).

120. Shirley Povich, "Senators Playing in Cuba Face Crack-Down Edict," *Washington Post,* 22 November 1945, 18.

121. Ray J. Gillespie, "'O.B. Getting Dose of Own Medicine—Pasquel,'" *The Sporting News,* 28 February 1946, 2.

122. Rory Costello and Lou Hernandez, "Tony Zardon," In *Who's on First: Replacement Players in World War II,* edited by Marc Z. Aaron and Bill Nowlin (Phoenix: Society for American Baseball Research, 2015), 337–342.

123. *Ibid.,* 352.

124. *Ibid.,* 353.

125. Frank (Buck) O'Neill, "Nats' Latin Quarter Spins Into Register," *The Sporting News,* 20 April 1944, 5.

126. James Quigel Jr., *Gateway to the Majors; Williamsport and Minor League Baseball* (University Park, PA: Keystone Books, 2001), 117.

127. Guy Butler, "Florida International Loop Born," *Miami News,* 24 September 1945, 10; https://en.wikipedia.org/wiki/Florida_International_League.

128. Jesse A. Linthicum, "Baseball to Carry Goodwill to Cuba," *Baltimore Sun,* 25 November 1945, 23.

129. Richard Moraski, "The Washington Senators in Wartime," in *Who's on First: Replacement Players in World War II,* ed. Marc Z. Aaron and Bill Nowlin (Phoenix: Society for American Baseball Research, 2015), 341–342.

130. https://sabr.org/bioproj/person/bert-shepard/.

Chapter 6

1. "Griffith Honored in Havana for his Aid to Cuban Game," *The Sporting News,* 14 March 1946, 2.

2. *Ibid.*

3. Bus Ham, "U.S.-Mexican Baseball Row Menaces 'Neighbor' Policy," *Washington Post,* 12 April 1946, 10.

4. Theodore A. Ediger, "'O.B. Like Slave Market,'

Mexican Paper Charges," *The Sporting News,* 7 March 1946, 2.

5. "DeWhitt's Methods Lauded by Mexicans, Mexican Side of Story Given," *The Sporting News,* 28 February 1946, 2–4.

6. "Ferrara's Raiding Story Denied by Joe Cambria," *The Sporting News,* 14 March 1946, 5.

7. Denman Thompson, "Griffith Blind to Mexican's Good-Wil Gesture," *Sunday Star Sports,* 17 March 1946, A-16.

8. John Virtue, *South of the Color Barrier: How Jorge Pasquel and the Mexican League Pushed Baseball Toward Racial Integration* (Jefferson, NC, McFarland, 2008), 183.

9. *Ibid.,* 188–192.

10. Fredrick Turner, *When the Boys Came Back: Baseball and 1946* (New York: Henry Holt, 1996), 56.

11. All information on the Players Guild narrative taken from Turner above, 137, 191–193; Virtue, 158–160; https://sabr.org/journal/article/the-owner-player-conflict; and from personal interviews with Roy Sievers, 2015–2018.

12. "Cambria on Committee to Pick Sandlot Ace," *Evening Star* 13 February 1946, 12.

13. Fausto La Villa, "Former Senators and Minor Leaguers Make Havana Entry Strong Combine," *Miami News,* 12 April 1946, 22.

14. "20,000 Shares of Havana Nine Bought by Griff," *Washington Post,* 19 July 1946, 14.

15. Shirley Povich, "Nats Ending Cuban Era, Call Off Canebrake Scout," *Washington Post,* 8 January 1947, 11.

16. "Cambria Still Scouts Cuba," *The Sporting News,* 29 January 1947, 19.

17. Roscoe McGowen, "Rickey on Trail of New Cuban Star," *New York Times,* 25 February 1947, 35.

18. "Across the Nation: Babe Will Take Miami Fishing Trip," *Washington Post,* 5 April 1947, 6.

19. Information on the Cambria case taken from: "Allen Opens Investigation of Cuban Club" *Tampa Bay Times,* 4 August 1947, 9; John McMullan, "Acosta Cleared, Havana's Cambria Must Explain $9,000 Spent for 'Scouting,'" *Miami News,* 4 August 1947, 17; John McMullan, "Griffith Man to Check Into Havana Case," *Miami News,* 5 August 1947, 19; "Allen Delays Cuban Probe," *Miami Herald,* 6 August 1947, 20; and John McMullan, "'Whole Club Guilty,' Havana Fined Record $500 for Salary Violations," *Miami News,* 17 August 1947, 23.

20. McMullan, "Whole Club Guilty."

21. Al Costello, "Yost, Kept Off Farm by GI Bill of Rights Reaps Bumper Harvest at Nats' Hot Corner," *The Sporting News,* 20 August 1947, 9.

22. Morris Siegal, "Carolina Has 3 Sellouts in Openers," *Washington Post,* 21 September 1947, C4.

23. https://www.baseball-reference.com/register/player.fcgi?id=dozier002wil.

24. Shirley Povich, "This Morning with Shirley Povich," *Washington Post,* 15 June 1947, C1.

25. Shirley Povich, "This Morning with Shirley Povich," *Washington Post,* 8 October 1947, 21.

26. Chuck Hosch, "Cambria Predicts Majors Will Seek Berth at Havana," *Tampa Times,* 5 December 1947, 16.

27. Travis M. Larsen, *Ahead of the Curve: A History of the National Baseball Congress Tournament in Wichita, Kansas, 1935–2005,* unpublished master's degree theses for the degree of Master of Arts, Fort Hays State University, Hays, Kansas, found at https://scholars.fhsu.edu/cgi/viewcontent.cgi?article=3207&context=theses.

28. "Cambria Named Commissioner," *Tampa Tribune,* 20 January 1948, 13.

29. www.baseballreference.com/joekuhl.

30. "Rossiter Added as Senators Scout," *Pensacola News Journal,* 2 March 1948, 2.

31. "Caught on the Fly," *The Sporting News,* 10 March 1948, 27; 14 April 1948, 27.

32. "Washington Player Hurls Race Epithet," *Baltimore Afro-American,* 11 September 1948, 7.

33. *Ibid.*

34. "Caught on the Fly," *The Sporting News,* 3 November 1948, 26.

35. *Encyclopedia of Minor League Baseball,* 223, 240, 248.

36. Bobby Hicks, "Acosta Hopes FIL Owners Will End Petty Wrangles," *Tampa Tribune,* 1 September 1948, 17.

37. "Cubans to Retain Oscar Rodriguez as Manager," *Tampa Times,* 30 December 1948, 12.

38. "Havana is Ready to Take Place of Newark in Int," *The Sporting News,* 8 December 1948, 32.

39. Guy Butler, "Acosta to Yield Reins of Cubans," *Miami News,* 6 February 1949, 41.

40. Bobby Hicks, "Acosta Urges 'Better Deal' for Havana," *Tampa Tribune,* 22 February 1949, 13.

41. Morris McLemore, "Morris McLemore Says—The Real Trouble," *Miami News,* 5 May 1949, 23.

42. John McMullan, "Cuban Crowds up 3,880 Over 1948, 'Being Forced out of FIL' Havana Attacks Gate Set-Up," *The Miami News,* 15 May 1949, 39.

43. *Ibid.*

44. *Ibid.*

45. *Ibid.*

46. Jimmy Burns, "Havana Chief Charges 'Gouging' to FI Clubs," *Miami Herald,* 4 May 1949, 39.

47. Individual stats on all players are from www.baseball-reference.com.

48. Griffith quote taken from: Sam Lacy, "Clark Griffith Sees the Light," *Baltimore Afro-American,* 2 April 1949, 1.

49. "Cambria's Cubans Bob Up Again, This Time in Texas," *Washington Post,* 22 April 1949, B3.

50. Whitey Kelley, "Solis, Lopez Pay Dividends with 32 Victories for Miami," *Miami Herald,* 7 August 1949, 26.

51. "Zardon Fined for Desertion," *Miami Herald,* 14 September 1949, 35.

52. Guy Butler, "Topic of the Tropics: Cubans Sell Four Hurling Stars," *Miami Herald*, 27 September 1949, 4.

53. Jimmy Burns, "Vote on Gate Receipts Delayed Until December," *Miami Herald*, 31 October 1949, 23.

54. All statistics from www. Baseball-reference. com.

55. "Nats in Market for New Manager," *Hagerstown Daily Mail,* 4 October 1949, 10.

Chapter 7

1. "Battle Opens Over Control of Cubans," *Tampa Tribune*, 18 March 1950, 10.

2. Barney Waters, "Court Tangled Cubans Drilling Under Cambria," *Miami Herald*, 21 March 1950, 25.

3. Morris Siegel, "Bluege Puts Down 'Insurrection' in Cuba," *Washington Post*, 23 March 1950, 19.

4. "Trautman O.K.'s Griff as Owner of Havana Team," *Washington Post*, 24 March 1950, B5.

5. "F-I Prexy Probes Havana Squabble," *Miami News*, 29 March 1950, 11; "Cubans to Field Team on Monday," *Palm Beach Post*, 30 March 1950, 15.

6. Guy Butler, "Acosta Ruled Head of Havana F-I Club, Rodriguez Goes as Manager," *Miami News,* 3 August 1950, 18.

7. Jimmy Burns, "Griff to Fight Cuban Court Ruling Restoring Acosta as Havana Boss," *The Sporting News*, 16 August 1950, 17.

8. Guy Butler, "We Still Run Havana Club—Cambria," *Miami News*, 13 August 1950, 36.

9. *Ibid.*

10. *Ibid.*

11. Guy Butler, "Topics of the Tropics," *Miami Daily News,* 8 September 1950, 2-B.

12. John McMullan, "Last year for Havana in F-I?" *Miami News*, 12 June 1950, 5.

13. *Ibid.*

14. "Senators Buy Farm Club in Big State Loop," *Tampa Tribune*, 26 September 1950, 13.

15. All Havana Cubans stats taken from: Lloyd Johnson and Miles Wolff, editors, *Encyclopedia of Minor League Baseball* (Durham, NC: Baseball America, 1993). Information on Roberto Maduro from https://sabr.org/bioproj/person/bobby-maduro.

16. All statistics come from each individual's Baseball-reference.com page.

17. Joe Reichler, "Senators Skipper Plans to Rebuild Club with Rookies from Coast Loop," *Hagerstown Daily Mail*, 27 January 1950, 13.

18. All statistics come from each individual's Baseball-reference.com page and from https://www.statscrew.com/minorbaseball/roster/.

19. https://sabr.org/bioproj/person/conniemarrero/.

20. *Ibid.*

21. "Harris Picks Cuban," *Baltimore Evening Sun,* 8 March 1950, 51.

22. *Encyclopedia of Minor League Baseball*, 224–240.

23. https://sabr.org/bioproj/person/conniemarrero/.

24. Shirley Povich, "This Morning with Shirley Povich," *Washington Post*, 25 July 1950, 13.

25. https://www.britannica.com/event/Point-Four-Program.

26. Shirley Povich, "Griffith Makes Pitch for Catcher Guerra," *Washington Post*, 8 November 1950, 18.

27. Shirley Povich, "This Morning with Shirley Povich," *Washington Post*, 21 February 1951, 17.

28. Shirley Povich, "Griff's Rumba Boys Still Out of Step," *Washington Post*, 4 March 1951, C1.

29. *Ibid.*

30. Shirley Povich, "Bucky Eyes Cuban for Garden, Too," *The Sporting News*, 21 February 1951, 9.

31. William Portuondo, "Negro Players Barred from Florida League," *Pittsburgh Courier*, 5 May 1951, 15.

32. "Dodgers Say Griff Can Have Tan Player," *Baltimore Afro-American*, 21 April 1951, 17.

33. Hector Rodriguez reference page: https://www.baseball-reference.com/register/player.fcgi?id=rodrig001hec.

34. "Nats Eye 'Crazy Top' Rodriguez, New Cuban Pitching Sensation, Expert on El Strikeout," *Washington Post*, 10 June 1951, C1.

35. *Ibid.*

36. https://www.baseball-reference.com/register/player.fcgi?id=rodrig004fer.

37. "Cuban's Success with Nats Bring Protests in Havana," *The Sporting News*, 18 July 1951, 33.

38. Ben F. Meyer, "Cambria Says Havana Fans Want Higher Type of Ball," *Tampa Tribune,* 3 September 1951, 11.

39. Shirley Povich, "Way Paved for Negroes on Senators," *The Sporting News*, 28 November 1951, 16.

40. *Ibid.*

41. Shirley Povich, "Nats Have Two Negro Players on Havana Team," *Washington Post*, 25 November 1951, C2.

42. Callum Hughson, "Silvio Garcia; Branch Rickey's Pick to Break the Color Barrier," http://mopupduty.com/silvio-garcia-branch-rickeys-pick-to-break-the-colour-barrier/.

43. Shirley Povich, "Griff to Swing Big Broom on Senators," *The Sporting News*, 26 September 1951, 8.

44. Shirley Povich, *The Washington Senators* (New York: Putnam, 1954), 234.

45. Dr. Layton Revel and Luis Munoz, Forgotten Heroes: Silvio Garcia, Center for Negro League Baseball Research 2014.

46. Shirley Povich, "This Morning with Shirley Povich," *Washington Post*, 7 March 1952, B7.

47. Morris McLemore, "F-I Directors Go Too Far," *Miami News*, 27 April 1952, 10.

48. Bill Beck, "Time for Sports"—"How about Pascual? Cuban Prexy Cambria Doesn't Know, Either," *Tampa Bay Times* 25 May 1952, 29.

49. *Ibid.*

50. *Ibid.*

51. https://www.baseball-reference.com/register/player.fcgi?id=mott--001eli.

52. Wilbur Kinley, "Cubans Refuse to Accept Bitsy Mott. Paper, Radio 'Boycott' Tampa Player. He may hook on with Tampa Smokers," *Tampa Times*, 7 May 1952, 13.

53. https://en.wikipedia.org/wiki/Bitsy_Mott.

54. Oscar Ruhl, "From the Ruhl Book—Tribe Sluggers in Middle—Between Pair of Sluggers," *The Sporting News*, 9 April 1952, 14.

55. Ben, F. Meyer, "Cuban Boss Expects Guerra To Do Great Things with Havana in FIL This Season," *Tampa Times*, 5 April 1952, 13.

56. Shirley Povich, "Harris Admits Porterfield is His Only Solid Pitcher," *Washington Post*, 7 March 1952, B7.

57. *Ibid.*

58. Shirley Povich, "This Morning with Shirley Povich," *Washington Post*, 4 September 1952, 16.

59. *Ibid.*

60. https://www.baseball-reference.com/players/f/fornimi01.shtml.

61. Shirley Povich, "Cuban Doctors Rate Campos Their No.1 Sew-Up Boy," *Washington Post,* 9 March 1952, C3. Statistics fromhttps://en.wikipedia.org/wiki/Frank_Campos and Retrosheet.org.

62. Statistics from https://en.wikipedia.org/wiki/Frank_Campos and Retrosheet.org.

63. Shirley Povich, "This Morning with Shirley Povich," *Washington Post*, 28 December 1952, C1.

64. Statute 66, Public Law 414, Chapter 477, H.R. 5678, Section 101-(H).

65. Bill Beck, "Among Other Hazards Faced by F-I League, There is McCarran Act," *St. Petersburg Times*, 22 June 1952, 14.

66. *Ibid.*

67. "Joe Cambria's Brother Dies in Cincinnati," *Palm Beach Post*, 11 December 1952, 16.

68. Shirley Povich, "This Morning with Shirley Povich," *Washington Post*, 11 March 1953, 20.

69. *Ibid.*

70. Shirley Povich, "Two Negros Join Nats at Orlando Base Today," *Washington Post*, 22 February 1953, C1.

71. *Ibid.*

72. Herb Heft, "Pint-Size Pompeyo Newest Pet in Capital," *The Sporting News*, 19 August 1953, 3.

73. Burton Hawkins, "Consuegra, Davalillo Cleared, but Others Face Indefinite Wait," *Washington Evening Star*, 3 March 1953, 13.

74. *Ibid.*

75. Shirley Povich, "Chattanooga Manager Ermer Tells Bucky Sima, Dixon, Pearce, Stewart Are Ready to Go," *Washington Post*, 4 March 1953, 16; statistics from Baseball-reference.com.

76. Shirley Povich, "Venezuelan to Join Nats' Latin Colony," *The Sporting News*, 31 December 1952, 9.

77. All statistics taken from Retrosheet.org.

78. https://www.nytimes.com/2021/02/03/sports/baseball/wayne-terwilliger-dead.html.

79. Jimmy Burns, "Havana's F-I Cubans Shift to Key West," *The Sporting News*, 15 April 1953, 33.

80. "The Morning After by 'Holly'"—"Havana May Lose Cubans," *Tampa Tribune*, 9 April 1953, 21.

81. "Cambria Happy Over Key West As 'Home' Site," *Tampa Bay Times,* 7 April 1953, 14.

82. "Havana Cubans Seek Home Games," *Miami News*, 13 April 1953, 28.

83. "Diagnosing Some Of Baseball's Ills," *Palm Beach Post*, 6 September 1953, 13.

84. Shirley Povich, "Busby Crowds Mickey Bob as Nat MVP," *The Sporting News*, 2 September 1953, 13.

85. Shirley Povich, "FBI Probes Reported Ban on Nats' 7 Cuban Negroes," *Washington Post*, 19 March 1954, 35.

86. "Protection Promised by City Officials," *Baltimore Afro-American*, 27 March 1954, 14.

87. "Nats' Negro Farmhands are Shifted," *Washington Post*, 23 March 1954, 29.

88. Bob Addie, "Winter Garden Denies Ban, But Nats' 7 Negroes Leave," *The Sporting News*, 31 March 1954, 17.

89. *Ibid.*

90. Shirley Povich, "This Morning with Shirley Povich," *Washington Post*, 12 March 1954, 29.

91. Personal interview with author at Sievers' home in St. Louis, Spring 2015.

92. Sievers history taken from Paul Scimonelli, *Roy Sievers: The Sweetest Right-Handed Swing in 1950's Baseball* (Jefferson, NC: McFarland, 2018); statistics taken from https://www.baseball-reference.com/players/s/sievero01.shtml.

93. Personal interview with the author by phone, March 2018; "New Bright Cuban Hurler Discovered," *Shreveport Journal*, 11 March 1953, 23.

94. https://sabr.org/bioproj/person/cholly-naranjo.

95. Nick Diunte, "The President's Senator for a Day," La Vida Baseball, 24 August 2018, https://www.lavidabaseball.com/.

96. Three letters displayed as part of the "Chasing Dreams" Exhibit hosted by The National Museum of American Jewish History, from the private collection of LTC (retired) Dane Grob, used by permission.

97. https://www.startribune.com/ossie-bluege-important-but-forgotten-figure-in-twins-history/484338361/?refresh=true.

98. "Pitcher Goes, Added Help Is Expected," *Vernon Daily Record*, 27 May 1952, 5.

99. Sports Review interview with Bob Wolff on WWDC Radio 1954, undated. Library of Congress radio archives collection, public domain.

100. Shirley Povich, "This Morning with Shirley Povich," *Washington Post*, 3 March 1954, 12.

101. *Ibid.*

102. *Ibid.*

103. Shirley Povich, "Harris May Have Another Prize Rookie in Julio Becquer," *Washington Post*, 13 March 1954, 13.

104. Shirley Povich, "This Morning with Shirley Povich," *Washington Post*, 4 February 1954, 19.

105. Burton Hawkins, "Harris to Keep Scull to Defend in Late Innings," *Washington Evening Star*, 24 March 1954, 58.

106. "Nats Launch Spring Work," *Orlando Sentinel*, 21 February 1954, 13.

107. Larry Brunt, "Carlos Paula, the Man who Integrated the Washington Senators," https://baseballhall.org/discover-more/stories/going-deep/carlos-paula-integrated-washington-senators.

108. Ralph Warner, "Miami to Move to Better League, Scout Predicts," *Miami News*, 30 April 1954, 9.

109. Stephen Smith, "The Long Forgotten Florida International League," *The National Pastime: Baseball in the Sunshine State* (Miami, 2016), https://sabr.org/journal/article/the-long-forgotten-florida-international-league/.

110. Bobby Hicks, "FIL May Not Get State Loop Team," *Tampa Tribune*, 8 January 1954, 17.

111. Camilo Pascual, interview with author by phone, September 2019.

Chapter 8

1. Shirley Povich, "Nats Refuse to Nibble at Big League Bait," *The Sporting News*, 15 December 1954, 21.

2. Kevin Hennessy, SABR biography of Calvin Griffith, https://sabr.org/bioproj/person/calvin-griffith.

3. *Ibid.*, footnote 12.

4. *Ibid.*

5. Pedro Ramos, interview with author by phone, June 2019.

6. Jose Valdivielso, interview with author by phone, August 2019.

7. Julio Becquer, interview with author by phone, April 2019; https://twinstrivia.com/interview-archives/julio-becquer-interview.

8. Sam Lacy, "Alex Crespo finally lured to States, age, long bus rides, not 'big money'," *Baltimore Afro-American*, 16 April 1955, 17.

9. Miguel Calzadilla, "News from the Mexican League," *The Sporting News*, 13 July 1955, 46.

10. "Reds in Black $68,065 for '54 After Four Seasons of Losses," *The Sporting News*, 22 December 1954, 4.

11. Joseph Wancho, SABR biography, https://sabr.org/bioproj/person/harmon-killebrew.

12. Cuco Conde, "Cambria, Figura discutide en el Baseball Cubano," *Carteles* Magazine, Ano 3, Numero 44, 30 October 1955, 91.

13. Brian McKenna, "*Clark Griffith, Baseball's Statesman*," 2010, self-published, 313–318.

14. *Ibid.* p. 322–325.

15. Shirley Povich, "Need of Young Talent Spurred Nats' Action," *The Sporting News*, 16 November 1955, 3.

16. *Ibid.*

17. *Ibid.*

18. *Ibid.*

19. Shirley Povich, "Own Farms Barren, Griffith Seeks Talent from Rivals' Chain," *The Sporting News*, 21 December 1955, 12.

20. *Ibid.*

21. *Ibid.*

22. Shirley Povich, "This Morning with Shirley Povich," *Washington Post*, 6 February 1956, 13.

23. Shirley Povich, "Nats Hear Pleasing News About Newcomer Plews," *The Sporting News*, 22 February 1956, 14.

24. Shirley Povich, "Wiesler-Berberet Battery Long Coveted by Senators," *The Sporting News*, 15 February 1956, 19.

25. *Ibid.*; Povich, *Sporting News*, 22 February 1956.

26. Shirley Povich, "This Morning with Shirley Povich," *Washington Post*, 6 February 1956, 13.

27. All statistics from retrosheet.org.

28. Shirley Povich, "This Morning with Shirley Povich," *Washington Post*, 19 February 1956, C1.

29. "Bleacher Beer Gardens Opens Tonight for Griffith Stadium's Thirsty Ones," *Washington Post*, 10 August 1956, 1.

30. Shirley Povich, "Senators' Farm Buildup Braced with Louisville as Triple-A Post"; Tommy Fitzgerald, "Cuban Owners at Louisville Drop Color Line," *The Sporting News*, 18 January 1956, 17.

31. *Ibid.*

32. Tommy Fitzgerald, "Horse-Riding, Gun-Shooting Menocal 'Grateful' to Buy Cols," *Louisville Courier-Journal*, 27 January 1956, 28.

33. "Louisville Group Comes Here Today," *Washington Post*, 7 January 1956, 13.

34. Francis Stann, "Win, Lose or Draw," *Washington Evening Star*, 8 May 1956, 48.

35. "Colonels' Pilot Just Another Rookie to Cuban Newcomer," *The Sporting News*, 16 May 1956, 28.

36. "Colonels' Cuban Newcomer Went to Wrong Charleston," *The Sporting News*, 18 July 1956, 31.

37. Billy Thompson, "Pressbox Pickups," *Lexington Herald*, 13 September 1956, 14.

38. *Ibid.*

39. "Tampa Man to Buy Louisville Club," *Lexington Leader*, 23 September 1956, 14.

40. "Colonels Solid Now, But No Player Help Due," *Orlando Evening Star*, 2 August 1956, 38.

41. Norris Anderson, "Sports Today," *Miami News*, 8 September 1956, 6.

42. "New Orlando Club Owners Eye Class B League in Florida," *Orlando Sentinel*, 22 July 1956, 11.

43. Bob Howard, "Top O' The Morn," *Orlando Sentinel*, 31 August 1956, 12.

44. "Tampa May Get Colonels if Club Leaves Louisville," *Tampa Tribune*, 27 October 1956, 19.

45. "Joe Cambria Barred From State League," *Miami News*, 29 October 1956, 17.

46. *Ibid.*

47. "Joe Cambria Mapping Fight on FSL Ban," *Miami News*, 31 October 1956, 15.

48. *Ibid.*
49. "Cambria to Fight State Loop Action," *Tampa Tribune*, 30 October 1956, 19.
50. "Nats to Back Cambria in '57," *Orlando Sentinel*, 16 November 1956, 3.
51. "Stockholders Hit Free Franchise," *Baltimore Sun*, 24 November 1956, 17.
52. "Louisville Baseball Looks Up," *Orlando Star*, 24 November 1956, 7.
53. "Cambria Challenges AA Move," *Orlando Sentinel*, 27 October 1956, 5.
54. "Cuban Interests Fight to Keep Louisville Club," *Tampa Tribune*, 4 December 1956, 20.
55. Johnny Carrico, "Court May Accept Bid for Cols Today," *Louisville Courier-Journal*, 13 December 1956, 39.
56. "Seven FSL Clubs Post Entry Fees," *Tampa Tribune*, 17 December 1956, 21.
57. Bob Howard, "Loop Prexy Sanctions Transaction," *Orlando Sentinel*, 23 December 1956, 11.
58. Bob Howard, "Top O' The Morn," *Orlando Sentinel*, 14 April 1957, 4.
59. "Cuba's Independence Day Celebrated at Nats' Game," *The Sporting News*, 23 May 1956, 24.
60. Shirley Povich, "Griffith Quick to Say Club Will Stay Right Here, Faces No Crisis," *Washington Post*, 23 May 1956, 51.
61. *Ibid.*
62. Camilo Pascual, personal interview with author by phone, 9/13/2019.
63. Shirley Povich, "Pete Runnels Rounding Out Infield Cycle," *The Sporting News*, 9 January 1957, 10.
64. https://en.wikipedia.org/wiki/Louisville_Colonels_(minor_league_baseball).
65. Morris Siegal, "Unsweet Memories," quoted in the *Louisville Courier-Journal,* 14 March 1957, 31.
66. Norm King, SABR biography, https://sabr.org/bioproj/person/jimmie-hall.
67. Gregory H. Wolf, SABR biography, https://sabr.org/bioproj/person/bob-allison.
68. https://en.wikipedia.org/wiki/Dan_Dobbek.
69. Baseball Reference.
70. *Ibid.*
71. Sam Gazdziak, "R.I. P. Baseball," Dick Hyde obituary, https://ripbaseball.com/2020/04/23/obituary-dick-hyde-1928-2020.
72. Oscar Ruhl, "From the Ruhl Book," *The Sporting News*, 22 May 1957, 31.
73. https://www.baseball-reference.com/bullpen/L%C3%A1zaro_Rivero.
74. Sam Lacy, "'I came to make the team,' Sam Hill, Senators' hope says," *Baltimore Afro-American*, 9 March 1957, 12.
75. *Ibid.*
76. Burton Hawkins, "The Baseball Beat," *Washington Evening Star*, 19 March 1957, 45; https://www.baseball-reference.com/register/player.fcgi?id=harris003ric.
77. Peter Dreier, SABR biography, https://sabr.org/bioproj/person/joe-black.
78. Shirley Povich, "Spink Foresees Another All-N.Y. Series," *The Sporting News*, 17 April 1957, 2.
79. Bill Fuchs, "Two Eisenhower Pitches Divided by Griffs, Orioles," *Washington Evening Star*, 15 April 1957, 1.
80. Paul Scimonelli, *Roy Sievers: The Sweetest Right-Handed Swing in 1950's Baseball* (Jefferson, NC: McFarland, 2018), 78.
81. Roy Sievers, personal interview with author, 5 April 2015.
82. Scimonelli, footnote 191.
83. Bob Addie, "Bob Addie's Column," *Washington Post*, 5 September 1957, C2.
84. Baseball Reference.
85. Bob Addie, "Bob Addie's Column," *Washington Post*, 5 September 1957, C2.
86. Joe Cambria, "Don't Die on Third," *Times of Havana*, 29 April 1957, 14.
87. *Times of Havana*, 24 April 1957, 14.
88. *Times of Havana*, 8 April 1957, 14.
89. Originally the makers of typewriters, The Remington Rand Corporation, by the early 1950s, had become the biggest makers of main frame computers, called the UNIVAC. By 1957, they merged with the Sperry Corporation and devoted most of their time to computer engineering.
90. Norris Anderson, "Sports Today," *Miami News*, 21 March 1958, 51.
91. Roy Sievers interview.
92. Bob Howard, "Top O' the Morn," *Orlando Sentinel*, 12 January 1958, 29.
93. Dick Pierce, "Saban's Winter League Work Worth Senator Look-See?" *Charlotte Observer*, 10 January 1958, 13.
94. Bob Addie, "Nats Start Spring Drills Wednesday," *Washington Post*, 16 February 1958, C1.
95. Baseball reference.com.
96. "Nats Sign Rookie, 'Shortstop of Future,'" *Washington Post*, 7 February 1958, D1.
97. Jose Valdivielso, phone interview with author, 14 August 2019.
98. Bob Addie, "Pascual Fit, Ready, Says Joe Cambria," *Washington Post*, 19 January 1958, C2.
99. *Ibid.*
100. Bob Addie, "Bob Addie's Column," *Washington Post*, 5 March 1958, D2.
101. *Ibid.*
102. "Cuban Giants to Bid for Pioneer Spot," *Great Falls Tribune*, 13 July 1958, 16.
103. "Mrs. Joe Cambria Dies; Wife of Baseball Scout," *Baltimore Evening Sun*, 19 September 1958, 4.
104. All stats from baseball-reference.com.
105. Shirley Povich, "This Morning with Shirley Povich," *Washington Post*, 9 December 1958, B8.
106. Bob Addie, "Nats Increase Scouting Staff to 29, Second Only to Orioles," *Washington Post*, 21 December 1958, C1; https://en.wikipedia.org/wiki/1958_Washington_Senators_season.
107. Bob Considine, "Griffiths Nice People but Lack Clark's Savvy," *Washington Post*, 31 August 1958, C2.

108. https://www.britannica.com/event/Cuban-Revolution/The-rise-of-Castro-and-the-outbreak-of-revolution.

109. Bob Addie, "Nats Not Planning to Withdraw Players from Cuban League," *Washington Post*, 3 January 1959, A8.

110. *Ibid.*

111. Camilo Pascual, interview with author by phone.

112. Bob Addie, "Lavagetto Will Shake Up Nats and Give Big Chance to Youngsters," *Washington Post*, 18 February 1959, C1.

113. *Ibid.*

114. Bob Addie, "Nats Reject Deal for Sievers," *Washington Post*, 3 December 1958, C4.

115. Bob Addie, "Indians Offer Nats Minoso, Grant, Held for Sievers and Ramos," *Washington Post*, 15 February December 1959, C1.

116. *Ibid.*

117. Paul Scimonelli, *Roy Sievers: The Sweetest Right-Handed Swing in 1950's Baseball* (Jefferson, NC, McFarland, 2018), 125.

118. Peter Bjarkman, Zoilo Versalles SABR biography, https://sabr.org/bioproj/person/zoilo-versalles.

119. *Ibid.*

120. Kevin T. Czerwinski, "Big League shot eluded 'Lightning Len'," https://www.milb.com/news/gcs-344050, 29 February 2008.

121. *Ibid.*

122. Sam Lacy, "Senators Get Green in Trade," *Baltimore Afro-American*, 6 June 1959, 14.

123. Chris Blake, "Rickey shaped Baseball's Future Via Continental League," https://baseballhall.org/discover/inside-pitch/rickey-reshaped-baseballs-future-via-continental-league and https://en.wikipedia.org/wiki/Branch_Rickey.

124. https://en.wikipedia.org/wiki/Estes_Kefauver; Daniel Scroop, "A Faded Passion? Estes Kefauver and the Senate Subcommittee on Antitrust and Monopoly," https://thebhc.org/sites/default/files/scroopdf.

125. J. G. Taylor Spink, "Cambria Urges Latin Big League," *The Sporting News*, 4 March 1959, 1; Joe Cambria, "Don't Die on Third," *Times of Havana*, 9 February 1959, 12.

126. *Ibid.*

127. *Ibid.*

128. "Castro Invited to Pitch in D.C.," *Baltimore Sun*, 21 April 1959, 11; "Fidel Castro Talks Baseball with Ramos," *Washington Post*, 17 April 1959, D3.

129. Roberto Gonzalez Echevarria, *The Pride of Havana: A History of Cuban Baseball* (New York: Oxford University Press, 1999), 6.

130. Bob Addie, "Addie's Atoms," *The Sporting News*, 18 March 1959, 22.

131. Peter C. Bjarkman, https://sabr.org/bioproj/topic/fidel-castro-and-baseball.

132. Francis Stan, "Win, Lose or Draw," *Washington Evening Star*, 21 August 1959, 49.

133. *Ibid.*

134. All statistics from Baseball-reference.com.

Chapter 9

1. Harrison Smith, "Jhoon Rhee, who helped popularize Taekwondo in the United States, Dies at 86," https://www.washingtonpost.com/local/obituaries/jhoon-rhee-who-helped-popularize-taekwondo-in-the-united-states-dies-at-86/2018/05/01/db60f3da-4d45-11e8-af46-b1d6dc0d9bfe_story.html.

2. "All's Well in Cuba with Papa Joe," *Charlotte News*, 20 April 1960, 22.

3. Julio Becquer, telephone interview with author, 26 April 2019.

4. Bob Addie, "Bob Addie's Column," *Washington Post*, 20 August 1960, A13.

5. https://en.wikipedia.org/wiki/Havana_Sugar_Kings.

6. "Quotes," *The Sporting News*, 23 March 1960, 14, attributed to Bob Addie's column, taken from *Washington Post*.

7. Bob Maisel, "The Morning After," *Baltimore Sun*, 5 April 1960, S23.

8. Edgar Munzel, "Veeck's 400 G Package Bid for Sievers Refused," *The Sporting News*, 24 June 1954, 4.

9. Bob Addie, "Senators Young Pitchers Sharp," *Washington Post*, 7 March 1960, 14; baseball-reference.com/Reyes Figueroa.

10. https://en.wikipedia.org/wiki/Bert_Cueto.

11. Pat Smith, "Maestri has Pitched the 'Perfect' Game—Strung Out over 10-Day Period," *Charlotte News*, 12 August 1960, 16.

12. Minnie Mendoza. https://www.baseball-reference.com/register/player.fcgi?id=mendoz002cri.

13. Rudy Hernandez, https://en.wikipedia.org/wiki/Rudy_Hern%C3%A1ndez.

14. Arthur Daley, "Sports of the Times: The Mark of Zorro," *New York Times*, 17 March 1960, 42.

15. Bob Addie, "Cubans Hurdle Barriers to Crash Big Time," *The Sporting News*, 20 April 1960, 5, 14.

16. "Kings Loaded with Young Latin Players," *Oroville Mercury*, 6 June 1960, 7.

17. All statistics from baseball-reference.com.

18. Shirley Povich, "Nats Reward Cookie with 5-Gee Pay Hike," *The Sporting News*, 12 October 1960, 25.

19. https://www.history.com/topics/cold-war/fidel-castro.

20. Becquer recounted this story personally at a Saturday morning brunch at the Bethesda Holiday, Bethesda, Maryland, hosted by the Washington Baseball Historical Society, March 22, 2003.

21. Dan Daniels, "Frick Declares Cuba Off Limits to U.S. Players," *The Sporting News*, 7 September 1960, 1.

22. Camilo Pascual, phone interview with author, 13 September 2019.

23. Shirley Povich, "Griffith Moves Nats to Minneapolis; D.C. Gets New Club in 1961 Season," *Washington Post*, 27 October 1960, A1.

24. Calvin Griffith, "Griffith not Happy with Armory Stadium Site," *Washington Post*, 15 January 1958, A18.

25. Kevin Hennessy, "Calvin Griffith: The Ups and Downs of the Last Family-Owned Business," SABR biography, https://sabr.org/journal/article/calvin-griffith-the-ups-and-downs-of-the-last-family-owned-baseball-team-2.

26. "Americans Open Trek From Cuba," *Fort Lauderdale News*, 4 January 1961, 1.

27. Bob Addie, "Cubans Expected to Play," *Washington Post*, 5 January 1961, D1–4.

28. "Officials Promise to Assist Ball Players' Exit," *Minneapolis Star*, 6 January 1961, 33.

29. "Cuban Baseball Players Told They Can Join Teams in U.S.," *New York Times*, 7 January 1961, 14.

30. "Ramos May Quit to Fight in Cuba," *Star Tribune*, 8 April 1961, 24.

31. *Ibid.*

32. Charles Johnson, "Zoilo Determined to Leave for Cuba," *Minneapolis Star*, 6 July 1961, 33.

33. News Dispatches, "Versalles Now Going Back to Cuba," *Washington Post*, 8 July 1961, A14.

34. *Ibid.*

35. Sid Hartman, "Hartman's Roundup," *Star Tribune*, 9 July 1961, 33; "Geraghty Eyes Pilot's Role in 1962," *Star Tribune*, 10 July 1961, 28.

36. "Diagnosis on Versalles: It's Not a Stomach Ulcer," *Minneapolis Star*, 13 July 1961, 37.

37. Morris Siegal, "Cubans Face dim Chance for Return to U.S. in '62," *The Sporting News*, 19 July 1961, 7.

38. *Ibid.*

39. *Ibid.*

40. Bob Bassine, "Top O' The Morn,'" *Orlando Sentinel*, 21 July 1961, 21.

41. All stats from Basebal-lreference.com.

42. Peter C. Bjarkman, Tony Oliva SABR biography, https://sabr.org/bioproj/person/tony-oliva.

43. *Ibid.*

44. *Ibid.*

45. Joseph Gerade, Marty Martinez SABR biography, https://sabr.org/bioproj/person/marty-martinez.

46. "Cambria Returns to Cuba," *The Sporting News*, 13 December 1961, 28; "Papa Joe Cambria Almost Signed Castro," *Orlando Evening Star*, 26 October 1961, 41.

47. Jim Selman, "Minnesota signs Two More Tampans," *Tampa Tribune*, 1 November 1961, 32.

48. Bill Purvis, "Brandon Inks Twins Pact," *Tampa Tribune*, 19 June 1962, 10.

49. "Twins Sign Twins for FSL Season," *Orlando Evening Star*, 17 April 1963, 16.

50. All stats from Baseball-reference.com.

51. "No Bonuses for Cambria," *Minneapolis Star*, 18 September 1962, 26; "Master Sleuth," *The Sporting News*, 23 May 1962, 30.

52. "No Bonuses."

53. Camilo Pascual, phone interview with author.

54. Bob Addie, "Bob Addie's Column," *Washington Post*, 26 September 1962, B3.

55. Dwayne Netland, "Calvin Pays Tribute to Scout 'Papa Joe,'" *Minneapolis Star Tribune*, 25 September 1962, 24.

56. Bob Martel, "Griffith Knew Poverty before Success Arrived," *Jersey Journal*, 28 September 1965, 3.

57. Herman Helms, "Garlic and Ice Cream Cones Pappa Joe's Recruiting Tools," *Charlotte Observer*, 30 November 1960, 22.

58. See footnote 20.

59. Pedro Galana, "Sports Editor's Mailbox," *New York Times*, 27 December 1964, 126.

60. Jack Murphy, "Gomez Seeks to Visit Cuba for Talent Hunt," *Miami Herald*, 31 May 1969, 26; "Padres' Pilot Preston Gomez Misses Cuban Baseball Talent," *Miami Herald*, 6 May 1969, 29.

61. Sam Lacy, "Baseball's Our 'National Pastime?'" *Baltimore Afro-American*, 16 September 1967, 9.

Chapter 10

1. Stephen R. Keeney, *Blurring the Color Line: How Cuban Baseball Players Led to the Racial Integration of Major League Baseball*, SABR Publications: The National Pastime: Baseball in the Sunshine State (Miami, 2016).

2. Ed Fitzgerald, "Clark Griffith: The Old Fox," *Sport Magazine* May 1954, 45, 77.

3. Mike Grehek, SABR Biography Project, Clark Griffith; https://sabr.org/bioproj/person/clark-griffith.

4. https://www.baseball-reference.com/players/g/griffcl01.html.

5. Brad Snyder, *Beyond the Shadow of the Senators* (New York: McGraw Hill, 2003), 65, footnote 35, "Anson, according to early baseball historian Sol White, kept both Walker and Stovey from being signed by the New York Giants or any other National League team." White, *Sol White's Colored Base Ball*, 76.

6. *Ibid.*, Keeny, footnote "A Color Line in Baseball," *New York Times*, 12 September 1887.

7. *Ibid.* Snyder 65, footnote 37.

8. *Ibid.*, Snyder, 66, footnote 39.

9. Peter Bjarkman, SABR Biography Project, https://sabr.org/bioproj/person/dolf-luque.

10. Adrian Burgos, *Playing America's Game: Baseball, Latinos, and the Color Line* Berkeley: University of California press, 2007), 147.

11. Bob Considine and Shirley Povich, "Old Fox: Baseball's Red-Eyed Radical and Archconservative, Clark Griffith," *Saturday Evening Post*, 13 April 1940, 14.

12. Brian McKenna, *Clark Griffith, Baseball's Statesman*, self-published at www.Lulu.com, 2010.

13. Shirley Povich, "This Morning" *Washington Post*, 18 May 1939, 19.

14. https://en.wikipedia.org/wiki/Griffith_Stadium.

15. *Ibid.*

16. Ted Leavengood, *Clark Griffith: The Old Fox of Washington Baseball* (Jefferson, NC, McFarland, 2011, 142.

17. "Stadium Battle of Music Turns to Battle Royal," *Washington Post* 23 July 1942; https://en.wikipedia.org/wiki/Charlie_Barnet.

18. https://www.culturaltourismdc.org/portal/a-brief-history-of-african-americans-in-washington-dc.

19. https://www.blackpast.org/african-american-history/michaux-elder-solomon-lightfoot-c-1885-1968.

20. "Elder Michaux to Marry 100 Couples Free, Sunday," *Baltimore Afro-American*, 8 September 1934, 11.

21. Margaret Lewis, "20,000 Watch as Elder Michaux Baptizes 100," *Baltimore Afro-American*, 12 October 1940, 10.

22. https://singers.com/group/Wings-Over-Jordan.

23. Al Sweeney, "There was Another Side to Griffith," *Baltimore African American*, 19 November 1955, 20.

24. Brian McKenna, *Clark Griffith, Baseball's Statesman*, 239.

25. Thomas G. Smith (March 5, 2002). "Civil Rights on the Gridiron," *ESPN*.

26. T. W. Anderson, "Properly Organized Baseball Will Pay, says Clark Griffith," *Baltimore African American*, 10 September 1932, 16.

27. Ralph Matthews, "Clark Griffith Won't Budge on Use of Colored Players," *Baltimore African American*, 18 December 1943, 23.

28. Sam Lacy, "Looking 'em Over," *Baltimore African American*, 20 January 1945, 18; "From A to Z with Sam Lacy," *Baltimore African American*, 7 August 1948, 7.

29. Shawn Alfonso Wells, *Cuban Color Classification and Identity Negotiation: Old Terms in a New World*, unpublished Doctoral Dissertation, University of Pittsburgh, 2003.

30. Kris Kristofferson, *Jesus was a Capricorn*, Sony/ATV Music Publishing.

31. Samuel O. Regalado, "Latin Players on the Cheap": Professional Baseball Recruitment and the Neocolonialist Tradition," *Indiana Journal of Global Legal Studies* 8 (2000).

32. Kevin Kerrane, *Dollar Sign on the Muscle: The World of Baseball Scouting,*1989, Prospectus Entertainment Ventures LLC.

33. Jesus Guanche, *Componentes etnicoss de la nacion cubana,* Havana, Fundacion Fernando Ortiz, 1996.

34. Shawn Alfonso Wells, unpublished Doctoral Dissertation, 17.

35. *Ibid.*, Chapter 2.

36. Estaban Morales Dominguez, *Race in Cuba: Essays on the Revolution and Racial Inequality* (New York: Monthly Review Press, 2013), 51–52.

37. Adrian Burgos, *Playing America's Game: Baseball, Latinos, and the Color Line* Berkeley: University of California press, 2007), 147.

38. Robert Heuer, "The Cuban Slide; Who Really Broke Baseball's Color Barrier?" *Chicago Reader,* 26 September 1997, 12.

39. Burgos, 158, also footnote 43.

40. *Ibid.*, 158.

41. Snyder, 70–73.

42. Carl Erskine phone interview with author August 15, 2020.

43. "Cuban Ball Players on Washington Senators Snubbed by Own Teammates," *Pittsburgh Courier,* 8 June 1940, 16, excerpted from *Washington Daily News,* Bob Ruark reporting.

44. *Ibid.*

45. Burgos, 160.

46. Bill Keefe, "Viewing the News," *New Orleans Times-Picayune,* 4 April 1953, 14.

47. "Fiery Cuban Morales Ends Scouting to Bolster Outfield for Salisbury Indians," *Salisbury Daily Times,* 29 June 1938, 7.

48. Whitney Martin, "Joe Cambria Still on Job," *Baltimore Sun,* 8 April 1942, 15.

49. Wilson Mcgee, "Sporting Around," *Orlando Evening Star,* 21 March 1941, 8; Library of Congress law Library, Immigration Act of 1917.

50. G. C. Miller," Sports of the Age," *New York Age,* 25 February 1939, 8.

51. Dan Burley, "Confidentially Yours," *New York Amsterdam News,* 19 July 1947, 10.

52. Sam Lacy, "10 Sepia Stars in Mexican Classic," *Baltimore Afro-American,* 20 July 1946, 16; "Major Leaguers Outclassed in Mexican Baseball," 20 July 1946, 16.

53. Charles Cambria phone interview with author, September 2020.

Bibliography

Books

Bealle, Morris A. *The Washington Senators: An 87-Year History of the World's Oldest Baseball Club and Most Incurable Fandom*. Washington, D.C.: Columbia, 1947.

Bready, James H. *Baseball in Baltimore: The First 100 Years*. Baltimore: Johns Hopkins University Press, 1998.

Brioso, César. *Last Seasons in Havana: The Castro Revolution and the End of Professional Baseball in Cuba*. Lincoln: University of Nebraska Press, 2019.

Frommer, Fredrick. *The Washington Nationals, 1859 to Today: The Story of Baseball in the Nation's Capital*. Lanham, MD: Taylor Trade, 2006.

_____. *You Gotta Have Heart: A History of Washington Baseball from 1859 to the 2012 National League East Champions*. Lanham, MD: Taylor Trade, 2013.

Goldstein, Richard. *Spartan Seasons: How Baseball Survived the Second World War*. New York: Macmillan, 1980.

González Echevarría, Roberto. *The Pride of Havana: A History of Cuban Baseball*. New York: Oxford University Press, 1999.

Hernández, Lou. *Bobby Maduro and the Cuban Sugar Kings*. Jefferson, NC: McFarland, 2019.

James, Bill. *The New Bill James Historical Baseball Abstract*. New York: Free Press, 2001.

Johnson, Lloyd, and Miles Wolff, eds. *The Encyclopedia of Minor League Baseball*. Durham, NC: Baseball America, 1993.

Kerrane, Kevin. *Dollar Sign on the Muscle: The World of Baseball Scouting*. Online. Prospectus Entertainment Ventures, 2013.

Leavengood, Ted. *Clark Griffith: The Old Fox of Washington Baseball*. Jefferson, NC: McFarland, 2011.

Merriman, John, ed. *For Want of a Horse: Choice and Chance in History*. Lexington, MS: Stephen Green Press, 1985.

Moffi, Larry, and Jonathan Kronstadt. *Crossing the Line: Black Major Leaguers 1947–1959*. Jefferson, NC: McFarland, 1994.

Morales Domínguez, Esteban. *Race in Cuba: Essays on the Revolution and Racial Inequality*. New York: Monthly Review Press, 2013.

Povich, Shirley. *The Washington Senators*. New York: Putnam, 1954.

Price, S.L. *Pitching Around Fidel: A Journey into the Heart of Cuban Sports*. New York: HarperCollins, 2002.

Quigel, James P., and Louis E. Hunsinger, Jr. *Gateway to the Majors: Williamsport and Minor League Baseball*. University Park: Penn State University Press, 2001.

Riess, Steven A., ed. *Encyclopedia of Major League Baseball Clubs: Volume II, The American League*. Westport, CT: Greenwood, 2006.

Roberts, James C. *The Nationals Pastime: The History and New Beginnings of Baseball in Washington, D.C.* Chicago: Triumph, 2001.

Snyder, Brad. *Beyond the Shadow of the Senators: The Untold Story of the Homestead Grays and the Integration of Baseball*. New York: McGraw-Hill, 2003.

Stang, Mark, and Phil Wood. *The Nationals on Parade: 70 Years of Washington Nationals Photos*. Wilmington, OH: Orange Frazier, 2005.

Thomas, Henry W. *Walter Johnson: Baseball's Big Train*. Washington, D.C.: Phenom Press, 1995.

Turner, Fredrick. *When the Boys Came Back: Baseball and 1946*. New York: Henry Holt, 1996.

Virtue, John, *South of the Color Barrier: How Jorge Pasquel and the Mexican League Pushed Baseball Towards Racial Integration*. Jefferson. NC.: McFarland, 2007.

Westcott, Rich. *Mickey Vernon: The Gentleman First Baseman*. Philadelphia: Camino Books, 2005.

Newspapers

Asheville (NC) Citizen-Times
Baltimore Afro-American
Baltimore Sun
Charlotte Observer
Daily Mail (Hagerstown, MD)
Daily Times (Salisbury, MD)
Greenville (SC) News
Jersey Journal (Jersey City, NJ)
Miami Daily News
Morning Herald (Hagerstown, MD)
New York Times
Newark (NJ) Star-Ledger
Orlando Evening Star

Orlando Sentinel
Palm Beach Post
Pantagraph (Bloomington, IL)
Post-Standard (Syracuse, NY)
Sporting News
Tampa Bay Times
Tampa Tribune
Times of Havana
Trenton (NJ) Evening Times
Washington Evening Star
Washington Post

Magazines

Collier's Weekly, 3 August 1940
Esquire, October 1944, Vol. 22, No. 4
Life, 24 July 1939
Newsweek, 1 August 1949
Sport, May 1954

Articles and Dissertations

González, César. "The Secret History of How Mexico Pushed Baseball Towards Racial Integration." www.remezcla.com/features/sports.

Martínez-Echazábal, Lourdes. "Mestizaje and the Discourse of National/Cultural Identity in Latin America, 1845–1959." *Latin American Perspectives* 25.3 (May 1998): 21–42. Accessed November 27, 2020. http://www.jstor.org/stable/2634165.

Regalado, Samuel O. "'Latin Players on the Cheap': Professional Baseball Recruitment in Latin America and the Neocolonialist Tradition." *Indiana Journal of Global Legal Studies* 8. 1, Article 2. Available at: http//www.repository.law.indiana.edu/ijgls/vol8/iss1/2.

Vaughn, Gerald F., "Jorge Pasquel and the Evolution of the Mexican League". *National Pastime*, No. 12, 1992.

Waldron, Travis. "Havana's Forgotten Baseball Team Played A Key Role In U.S.-Cuba Relations." *Huffington Post*, March 19, 2016. Available at: https://www.huffpost.com/entry/havana-sugar-kings-obama-cuba-baseball_n_56ed806ee4b084c672206b17.

Wells, Shawn Alfonso. "Cuban Color Classification and Identity Negotiation: Old Terms in a New World, Pittsburgh." Unpublished doctoral dissertation, University of Pittsburgh. Available at: https://core.ac.uk/reader/12207560.

Index

Numbers in **bold italics** indicate pages with illustrations

299